DICKENS AND THE POPULAR RADICAL IMAGINATION

The relationship between the work of Charles Dickens and popular literature has often been noted, but the extent to which his fiction and journalism were rooted in, and continued to respond to, the popular radical culture of his time has so far been unexplored. Sally Ledger traces the influence of Regency radicals, such as William Hone and William Cobbett, and mid-century radical writers, such as Douglas Jerrold and the Chartists Ernest Jones and G. W. M. Reynolds. She offers substantial new readings of works from *Pickwick* to *Little Dorrit*, arguing that Dickens's populism bridged eighteenth- and nineteenth-century conceptions of the 'popular', the first identified with the political idea of 'the People', the second identified with a mass-market 'populace' that emerged during Dickens's career. Richly illustrated, this study also uncovers the resonance between Dickens's writings and popular graphic art by George Cruikshank, Robert Seymour, C. J. Grant and others.

SALLY LEDGER is Professor of Nineteenth-Century Literature at Birkbeck, University of London. She is the author of *The New Woman: Fiction and Feminism at the Fin de Siècle* (1997), *Ibsen* (1999), *Cultural Politics at the Fin de Siècle* (with Scott McCracken, 1995) and *The Fin de Siècle: A Reader in Cultural History* (with Roger Luckhurst, 2000).

CAMBRIDGE STUDIES IN NINETEENTH-CENTURY
LITERATURE AND CULTURE

General editor
Gillian Beer, *University of Cambridge*

Editorial board
Isobel Armstrong, *Birkbeck, University of London*
Kate Flint, *Rutgers University*
Catherine Gallagher, *University of California, Berkeley*
D. A. Miller, *Columbia University*
J. Hillis Miller, *University of California, Irvine*
Daniel Pick, *Birkbeck, University of London*
Mary Poovey, *New York University*
Sally Shuttleworth, *University of Oxford*
Herbert Tucker, *University of Virginia*

Nineteenth-century British literature and culture have been rich fields for inter-disciplinary studies. Since the turn of the twentieth century, scholars and critics have tracked the intersections and tensions between Victorian literature and the visual arts, polities, social organization, economic life, technical innovations, scientific thought – in short, culture in its broadest sense. In recent years, theoretical challenges and historiographical shifts have unsettled the assumptions of previous scholarly synthesis and called into question the terms of older debates. Whereas the tendency in much past literary critical interpretation was to use the metaphor of culture as 'background', feminist, Foucauldian, and other analyses have employed more dynamic models that raise questions of power and of circulation. Such developments have reanimated the field. This series aims to accommodate and promote the most interesting work being undertaken on the frontiers of the field of nineteenth-century literary studies: work which intersects fruitfully with other fields of study such as history, or literary theory, or the history of science. Comparative as well as interdisciplinary approaches are welcomed.

A complete list of titles published will be found at the end of the book.

DICKENS AND THE POPULAR RADICAL IMAGINATION

SALLY LEDGER

CAMBRIDGE UNIVERSITY PRESS

Cambridge, New York, Melbourne, Madrid, Cape Town, Singapore, São Paulo

Cambridge University Press
The Edinburgh Building, Cambridge CB2 2RU, UK

Published in the United States of America by Cambridge University Press, New York

www.cambridge.org
Information on this title: www.cambridge.org/9780521845779

First published 2007

Printed in the United Kingdom at the University Press, Cambridge

A catalogue record for this publication is available from the British Library

ISBN 978-0-521-84577-9 hardback

For Michael Slater

Contents

Illustrations

Acknowledgements

This book has been brewing for many years, and a very large number of people have contributed to it in diverse ways. I owe a huge debt of gratitude to Michael Slater for introducing me to the serious study of Dickens by inviting me to edit *The Christmas Books* for his Everyman Edition, by inviting me along to that great Birkbeck institution, Dickens Day, and by his extraordinary generosity in sharing his unrivalled knowledge of Dickens's work with me. In the early years of the book's formation I gained an immense amount from the series of seminars on Nineteenth-Century Radicalism hosted by the London Nineteenth-Century Studies seminar: Isobel Armstrong, Ian Haywood, Louis James, Anne Janowitz, Jo McDonagh, Rohan McWilliam and Michael Sanders in particular pointed me in a number of useful directions. The book has also been influenced by other Dickens scholarship, John Bowen's and Juliet John's work in particular illuminating Dickens's representational radicalism for me. Joss Marsh's work on William Hone has likewise been very influential. Early inspiration came from Chris Reid when I was an undergraduate at Queen Mary, University of London, and from Terry Eagleton when I was a postgraduate student in Oxford. Thereafter my whole scholarly career has been massively supported by Regenia Gagnier, who has always believed in this project and has influenced it in more ways than it is possible to describe.

My colleagues and students at Birkbeck have been a mainstay in the writing of the book, particularly during my period as Head of School. Hilary Fraser, Tom Healy and Sue Wiseman were the best of colleagues and friends, always 'there' and always supportive. Colleagues in Birkbeck's Centre for Nineteenth-Century Studies have been a constant source of intellectual stimulation, and I have had the good fortune to have been surrounded by an extraordinarily talented body of postgraduate students at Birkbeck during the composition of this book: Beth Carney, Ella Dzelzainis (now my colleague), Holly Furneaux, Anne Schwan and Ben Winyard in particular have really helped me to develop my thinking on the relationship between Dickens and popular radicalism. Ben Winyard saved my sanity in the project's final stages by working on the footnotes and bibliography – any remaining errors are my own, not his. Anne Humpherys's encouragement and support both during and after her period as Visiting Leverhulme Professor at Birkbeck have also been greatly appreciated, as have the long-term friendships of Roger Luckhurst, Scott McCracken and Jo McDonagh. Holly Furneaux and Ella Dzelzainis read the whole manuscript, and their sharp critical insights and generous sharing of their knowledge have been a godsend. Anne Holloway was a wonderful research assistant in the earlier phases of the project, probably spending more time in the Colindale Newspaper Library than ever in her life she imagined she would.

I am fortunate to have been provided with a good deal of funding to support the researching and writing of the book. The School of English and Humanities at Birkbeck has put its hand in its pocket more times than I care to remember to fund research expenses and research leave. I have also received generous financial support from the British Academy and the Arts and Humanities Research Council.

I'd like to thank the following librarians and archivists for their help in locating all the research materials for the project: Stephen Crook at the Berg Collection, New York Public Library; Julie-Anne Lambert at the John Johnson Collection, Bodleian Library; Ken Mackley at Birkbeck Library; the staff at the Butler Library, Columbia University; at the British Library; and at the Goldsmith's Library, Senate House, University of London.

Some of the material from the Introduction and from chapters 2, 3 and 7 has previously been published in an earlier form in *Victorian Literature and Culture* (© 2004 Cambridge University Press. Reprinted from *Victorian Literature and Culture*, 32:2, by permission of Cambridge University Press). Some parts of chapter 5 were published in an earlier form in *Nineteenth-Century Literature* (© 2002 by the Regents of the University of California. Reprinted from *Nineteenth-Century Literature*, 57:1, by permission of the University of California Press).

Many thanks for the support throughout of Linda Bree and her colleagues at Cambridge University Press; and thanks also to Laura Marcus, who gave me the title for the book. Most of all I would like to thank Jim Porteous, not only for giving the manuscript a sharply attentive final reading, but also for all the Dickens conversations over the last few years, for the footie matches at Stamford Bridge, and for the accompaniment of Neil Young; and Richard Porteous, whose brilliant guitar playing and outlandish antics on a skateboard have made the last few years a lot of fun.

Note on editions and abbreviations used

For ease of reference, where possible I have used the new Penguin paperback edition of Dickens's prose works. For *Sketches By Boz*, The Christmas Books, and *American Notes* I have used other available editions. I have referred throughout to the Clarendon Press twelve-volume Pilgrim edition of *The Letters of Charles Dickens*, abbreviated in the text to 'Pilgrim Letters'. Where possible I have used Michael Slater's four-volume Dent Uniform Edition of *Dickens' Journalism*, abbreviated thus throughout. Individual items not in Slater I have cited separately. Full references to the relevant volumes of the Pilgrim Letters and to Slater's edition of the journalism are given in the bibliography.

Introduction: Dickens and the popular radical imagination

On an autumn day in 1842, William Hone lay dying. He was by now an obscure figure, but through the services of an old friend, George Cruikshank, he sent a request to Charles Dickens that he might shake his hand before he died. The famous novelist agreed to the request, and for a brief moment Dickens, Cruikshank and William Hone came together in the latter's shabby London home. The meeting apparently meant little to Dickens, who, subsequently attending Hone's funeral, recounted with a sharply comic tongue Cruikshank's histrionics as his old friend was laid to rest. Writing to an American friend, Cornelius Felton, Dickens described how Cruikshank, feeling that the Reverend conducting the service had been disrespectful towards the dead man, had allowed his feelings to overflow: 'I was really penetrated with sorrow for the family, but when George (upon his knees, and sobbing for the loss of an old friend) whispered me "that if that wasn't a clergyman, and it wasn't a funeral, he'd have punched his head", I felt as if nothing but convulsions could possibly relieve me.'[1] The scene 'has choked me at dinner-time ever since', Dickens remarked.[2]

The encounter between Dickens, Cruikshank and Hone in 1842 is a little-known but with hindsight a significant convergence. For despite Dickens's seeming display of comic disrespect at the funeral of the ailing and rather threadbare old bookseller, the deathbed tableau crystallises an important and much-overlooked connection between Dickens's writings and an earlier popular radical tradition.[3]

Who was this man whose death Dickens exploited as good comic matter? And what was the exact nature of his relationship to Dickens and his work? Born in 1780, in the early nineteenth century William Hone, a radical pamphleteer and bookseller, had – in collaboration with George Cruikshank – for a brief spell wreaked political havoc with a series of satirical attacks on George IV, his government, the clerisy and the corrupt legislature that he saw all around him in Regency England. Hone's satires form an important part of a tradition of popular radical culture in the nineteenth century, to which Dickens's novels and journalism owe a more considerable debt than has yet been recognised.[4] From the nineteenth through to the twenty-first century much has been made of Dickens's debt to Smollett and Fielding, his boyhood heroes. The *London and Westminster Review*'s reflection in 1837 that 'The renown of Fielding and of Smollett is that to which [Dickens] should aspire, and labour to emulate, and, if possible, to surpass' has been echoed by a succession of critics in the last 150 years, with Lyn Pykett early in the twenty-first century once more identifying Smollett and Fielding as perhaps Dickens's most important antecedents.[5] Nods have even been made towards Juvenal and the Augustans in creating a satirical genealogy for Dickens's writings, with Sylvia Manning claiming that 'there is good evidence for Dickens's knowledge of Juvenal'.[6] Dickens's middle-class and, to a lesser extent, his classical satirical antecedents have been well documented, and doubtless he would have approved of this. Far too little, by contrast, has been made of the relationship between Dickens and the popular radical culture of the early nineteenth century. One of the aims of this book is to begin to reveal the extent of this hitherto more or less occluded relationship.

That Dickens was a radical political writer on the side of the poor and the dispossessed was blazingly clear to his contemporaries and to many critics in the first half of the twentieth century.[7] Most subsequent critics, though, have followed Humphry House's 1941 evaluation of Dickens as an essentially middle-class writer committed to middle-class values.[8] Even John Lucas, one of the few recent critics to have considered the contemporary political status of Dickens's fiction and journalism, places him firmly within a *middle-class* tradition of radical writers and publishers, positioning W. J. Fox, William Howitt and Percy Bysshe Shelley as Dickens's radical antecedents.[9] Whilst I would acknowledge the importance of Radicals such as W. J. Fox to the political cast of Dickens's novels and journalism, I want simultaneously to propose an altogether less respectable, more truly disruptive, more *popular* radical genealogy.

Dickens, like Hone and Cruikshank before him, was able to negotiate and frequently to transcend the boundaries between popular and radical culture in a way that virtually no other mid-nineteenth century writer was able to do; it is to his less acclaimed popular radical forbears that he owes this achievement. As an inheritor of the popular radical cultural networks of the early nineteenth century Dickens acted as a cultural bridge between, on the one hand, an older, eighteenth-century political conception of 'the People' and, on the other hand, a distinctly mid-nineteenth-century, modern conception of a mass-market 'populace' that had been created by the rise of the commercial newspaper press during Dickens's formative years as a journalist and a novelist. Moving between these twin conceptions of 'the People' (a political entity) and the (mass-market) 'populace' (a commercial entity), the extent of Dickens's attempt to politicise the latter was unrivalled in the second half of the nineteenth century. In the first part of the nineteenth century the boundaries between popular and radical culture had been highly permeable, with 'popular' as an epithet embracing both the political entity of 'the People' *and* the idea of a popular marketplace. But the 'popular' and the 'radical' (or, the 'popular' and 'the People') became increasingly distinct categories as the second half of the century approached, as a direct result of the rise of the mass-market commercial newspaper press in the 1840s. I will turn my attention to the bifurcation of the 'popular' and the 'radical' in the 1840s and 1850s, and to the negotiation of this process by Dickens, Douglas Jerrold and the Chartist writers G. W. M. Reynolds and Ernest Jones, in the central chapters of this book.

Dickens's ability to negotiate and even to disregard the gradually encroaching boundaries that were being erected between the popular and the radical in the Victorian period was quite remarkable. He was able to build on and promote popular radical cultural traditions at the same time as commercially exploiting them and becoming a rich man: by the end of 1837 part sales of *The Pickwick Papers* had reached 40,000 and *Oliver Twist*, too, was a huge commercial success.[10]

Dickens was also able, like William Hone before him, to transcend the boundaries between high and low culture. In the Regency years the demarcation between high and low culture had not yet been set in stone, with satire and parody in particular equally the tools of both. Dickens's cultural positioning in Victorian England was rather more difficult, with the literary classes of the period generally rather suspicious of what some regarded as his vulgar embrace of the popular: whilst Anthony Trollope rather sniffily characterised him as 'Mr Popular Sentiment' in *The Warden*, an anonymous reviewer for the *Saturday Review* derided Dickens's determined engagement with contemporary social and political concerns, remarking that 'Mr Dickens's writings are the apotheosis of what has been called newspaper English.'[11] Others, though, valorised his cross-class appeal, lauding him as a truly popular writer. Walter Bagehot, who deplored the political tenor of Dickens's novels, none the less admired the fact that 'There is no other contemporary English writer, whose works are read so generally through the whole house, who can give pleasure to the servants as well as to the mistress, to the children as well as to the master.'[12] The young Queen Victoria read and enjoyed *Oliver Twist*[13] and the poorest of the poor read *Dombey and Son*. Richard Altick has written of 'the old charwoman who never missed a subscription tea ... at a snuff shop over which she lodged when the landlord read the newest numbers of *Dombey and Son* to his assembled guests'.[14]

To be a popular writer is not merely to achieve high levels of circulation, although this is part of its meaning. As Arnold Kettle has put it, truly popular writing involves 'an attitude to art in which the audience is seen neither purely as consumer (the commercial relationship) nor as a superior group of like-minded spirits (the highbrow relationship) but in some sense as collaborator'.[15] To put it another way, the popular author needs to establish a sense of 'us' between himself and his readership, and this is something that both Dickens and William Hone before him achieved on a large scale. Dickens's 'us' is a conception of 'the People' that embraces the lower and middle classes of society, and in this sense it is very much of the eighteenth century. I follow Arnold Kettle in closely allying 'popular' literature to a political concept of 'the People': 'Dickens, then, sees the People not as a vague or all-inclusive term – an indiscriminate 'everybody' – but as a specific force in contradistinction to those who rule ... A popular tradition in literature implies, then, a literature which looks at life from the point of view of the People.'[16]

The persistence of 'the People' as a social and political category in nineteenth-century culture has been importantly debated by social historians and is key to understanding Dickens's work. Patrick Joyce has argued that the social vision promoted by popular radicalism in the nineteenth century was not primarily based on class, its vocabulary circling rather around key terms such as 'democracy' and 'freedom' rather than class conflict.[17] Whilst he never used those terms, this is the tradition of popular radicalism to which Dickens's work belongs. Where he does employ the language of class conflict, it is most often directed against the aristocracy, once again allying him with an eighteenth-century conception of 'the People'.[18] Where this study has used 'class' tags to identify social groups – the working class, the middle class and so on – I am again following historians such as Patrick Joyce and Gareth Stedman Jones in regarding class as a category of discursive and social formation through which identity may be constituted rather than as an economic category determined by one's relationship to the means of production.

Ian Haywood's important and generally sure-footed study of popular literature has argued that Dickens 'was not truly popular in the sense that he was available directly to working-class readers'.[19] Contrary to Haywood's view, reviews in the Chartist press suggest that Dickens did indeed have a literate non-elite readership. My quarrel with Haywood's brief account of Dickens, though, is that whether Dickens's fiction reached a lower-class readership directly is not, I would suggest, the litmus test of his popularity. Popular plagiarisms and theatrical adaptations of Dickens's work; communal family, landlord-lodger, coffee-house, and master-servant readings of his fiction; and, not least, Dickens's own public readings, meant that his popular 'reach' was quite staggering.

Dickens's project as a writer needs to be understood as the culminating point of a network of popular and radical cultural traditions that stretched from the late eighteenth century through to the last throes of Chartism in 1858. His fiction draws on a tradition of radical satire that began with Thomas Spence and John Wilkes in the late eighteenth century and which flourished in the 1810s in the popular radical pamphlets produced and circulated by William Hone and George Cruikshank. The Prince Regent's perceived marital outrages against Queen Caroline once he was crowned King, and the massacre of peacefully demonstrating men, women and children in Manchester's St Peter's Field were the two main political flashpoints of the Regency years, giving rise to what E. P. Thompson has described as the 'heroic age of popular radicalism'.[20] The radical satirical inheritance resonates not only in the work of Charles Dickens in the early and mid-Victorian period, but also in the fiction and journalism of Douglas Jerrold, his close friend and theatrical cohort, some of whose satirical writings will also feature in this study.

The significance of the term 'radical' in the nineteenth century was by no means stable.[21] Byron, writing in 1820, commented that the term was entirely new to him. Writing to John Hobhouse from Ravenna he commented that 'Upon reform you have long known my opinion – but *radical* is a new word since my time – it was not in the political vocabulary in 1816 – when I left England – and I don't know what it means – is it uprooting?'[22] Byron's etymological understanding of the term is spot on, and in an abstract way tells us all we need to know about the political force of nineteenth-century radicalism. More localised, and nicely in tune with the atmosphere surrounding the political and cultural uprising against Lord Liverpool's repressive administration in Regency England, is the satirical journalist Thomas Wooler's sharp-witted account of radicalism in his trial parody, *TRIAL EXTRAORDINARY: MR CANNING VERSUS THE RADICAL REFORMERS*:

JUDGE. What complaint have you to make, Mr Canning, against the men, whom I see there, behind you, looking so thin and pale, clothed in rags, and having pad-locks on their mouths and thumb-screws on their hands?
MR CANNING. Oh! Don't you know them? I thought all the world knew them! They are the Radicals.
JUDGE. The Radicals, Sir! What does that name mean?
MR CANNING. Mean! (What a fool the man must be – *aside*) Mean! Why, it means everything that is bad.[23]

Dickens's 'Young Barnacle', in *Little Dorrit*, thinks the mild-mannered, middle-aged Arthur Clennam a 'most ferocious Radical'[24] for daring to make some enquiries of his government department. Clearly in the 1850s Dickens was alert to the visceral response of some elements within the upper classes to anyone who seemed to challenge them, and the 'Radical' tag is humorously used to indicate this in his mature political novel. In the political culture of mid-Victorian England the title of 'Radical' tended to be attached to those politicians who wanted root-and-branch reform of Parliament, and in this particular sense Dickens was of their number. As Peter Ackroyd has put it: 'There was another central stance from which he never moved, his hatred of Parliament, and his disgust at a 'rotten' system of representative government … the self-interest and even bribery which Dickens always associated with the House of Commons. In that sense he was and remained a "Radical".'[25]

My own use of the phrase 'popular radicalism' refers quite specifically to the politics and culture of popular writers of the Regency period such as William Hone, Thomas Wooler and William Cobbett. This book traces the influence of these writers in the work of Dickens and other writers of the Victorian period whose work bears the hallmarks of the popular radical inheritance. The dominant rhetorical strategy of Regency popular radicalism was satirical, and this study will trace that radical satirical inheritance through Dickens's rewriting of radical trial parodies, through his harnessing of radical satire against the Poor Laws in *Oliver Twist*, through Douglas Jerrold's satirical journalism in *Punch* and *Douglas Jerrold's Shilling Magazine*, through Dickens's own satirical contributions to the *Examiner* and to *Household Words*, and will conclude with the extended satires on government and its institutions in *Bleak House* and *Little Dorrit*.

Alongside satire, the radical pamphleteers, essayists and writers of ballads in the Regency period also deployed a melodramatic mode of writing in their attacks on King and government, as the first chapter of this study will demonstrate. Melodrama had long been established as an aesthetic of protest when Dickens, Douglas Jerrold, G. W. M. Reynolds and Ernest Jones (amongst others) began to negotiate its conventions in the Victorian period.[26] Forged as a dramatic form during the French Revolution, the first melodrama (although it didn't name itself as such) is generally agreed to have been Boutet de Monvel's *Les Victimes cloîtrées*, written and performed in 1791.[27] Characteristic of French Revolutionary melodrama is Sylvain Maréchal's *Le Jugement dernier des rois*, first performed, to great acclaim, in Paris in October 1793, two days after the execution of Marie Antoinette. The play's melodramatic denouement involves the swallowing up of a whole crowd of European monarchs by a volcano, which 'consumes their very bodies'.[28]

Melodrama, with its roots in the theatrical semiotics of gesture, is a bodily aesthetic, prioritising non-verbal languages over dialogue. It is also, in Peter Brooks's words an 'intense emotional and ethical' genre, 'based on the Manichaeistic struggle of good and evil'. The purpose of melodrama is to 'recognize and confront evil, to combat and expel it, to purge the social order'.[29] As domestic melodrama developed across the first half of the nineteenth century as a popular form, it acquired a number of readily identifiable additional characteristics: the suffering of mothers and their children, trial scenes and last minute reprieves, sudden reversals of fortune, secret Wills, inheritances, and so on. In this study I will track the development of the melodramatic mode in popular radical fiction and culture across the period 1819–57. Beginning, again, with the popular radical responses to 'Peterloo' and the 'Queen Caroline Affair' in 1819 and 1820, thereafter the book will consider Dickens's negotiation of melodrama in *Oliver Twist*, the Christmas Books, and *Barnaby Rudge*; it will examine the Chartist encounter with melodrama in Ernest Jones's works of fiction; and will close with Dickens's simultaneous embrace and interrogation of melodrama in his great social novels from the 1850s.

Dickens's absorption into his writings of the melodramatic and satirical aesthetics of popular radicalism was powerfully combined with a consciousness that he could try to bring about positive social and political change, and to this extent he was a thoroughly instrumental writer. He stated his purpose as a novelist clearly in 1854:

To interest and affect the general mind in behalf of anything that is clearly wrong – to stimulate and rouse the public soul to a compassionate or indignant feeling that it *must not be* – without obtruding any pet theory of cause or cure, and so throwing off allies as they spring up – I believe to be one of Fiction's highest uses. And this is the use to which I try to turn it.[30]

Like William Hone, Dickens never allied himself to any particular party but preferred to attack individual social and political abuses. In this he was a political novelist in the broadest sense and should be distinguished from writers of more ideologically programmatic works of fiction such as Harriet Martineau and Benjamin Disraeli.[31]

Dickens none the less desired to influence government policy as well as public opinion through his writing of fiction and journalism, and in this he resembles another of his popular radical forebears, William Cobbett. Cobbett, whose anti-Malthusianism and anti-clerical satire would echo down the years in Dickens's works, had a similarly instrumental view of his work as a writer. He differed from Dickens, though, in his belief that he could achieve more as a parliamentarian than as a scribe. In his address 'To the Reformers of Leeds, Preston, and Botley', in which he berates over-expenditure on the Church's dependants, he comments that 'With my pen, I shall do what I can; but I cannot do with that pen a ten thousandth part of what I could do if I were in the House of Commons.'[32] Cobbett's desire to become an MP would be fulfilled in 1832, the year of the great Reform Act, when he would be returned as a Radical MP for Oldham. Dickens, although equally desiring to make a social and political impact, took a different course. Asked on three occasions to stand for Parliament between 1841 and 1851, he repeatedly declined, having a greater faith in the power of his pen to effect change than in any parliamentary role he may have taken on. This is hardly surprising from a man who would later tell his friend and biographer John Forster that it was his hope 'to have made every man in England feel something of the contempt for the House of Commons that I have'.[33] Dickens didn't need to be a Member of Parliament to influence the country: as the middle of the nineteenth century approached the population increasingly got its political opinions from journals and from novels, and it is in this way that he became an influential political figure.

Despite the different trajectory of their careers, Cobbett was as conscious as Dickens of the political role that his writing could play, and of the need to ensure a healthy circulation amongst as wide a readership as possible. As he projected the launch of *Cobbett's Evening Post* in January 1820, a newly 'stamped' publication, Cobbett sought to overcome the 4d per copy stamp duty by urging his readers to form 'themselves into little *reading partnerships* of twenty or thirty, and by getting one of their number to write to a news-man in London, sending him the money before-hand for a quarter of a year' so as to receive the paper 'regularly *by post*'.[34] Cobbett's vision of communal literary consumption looks forward to the shared reading of the shilling parts of Dickens's novels in the 1830s and beyond. In both cases the limits of literacy could be overcome with the more literate readers reading aloud to those unable to read. The links between Dickens and the popular radical culture of the early nineteenth century are, then, material as well as aesthetic, as I shall demonstrate in the first chapter of this book.

Popular radical culture in Regency England: Peterloo and the Queen Caroline Affair

PETERLOO, 1819

On 16 August 1819, a peaceful assembly of 60,000 men, women and children demonstrated in St Peter's Field, Manchester. The demonstration was the culminating moment of a series of popular protests in the years following the Battle of Waterloo. Excessively high levels of taxation, near-starvation amongst the poor, 'Borough-Mongering' in particular and the unrepresentativeness of the British Parliament in general all contributed to levels of popular unrest never to be exceeded in the nineteenth century. The meeting in St Peter's Field, as at Spa Fields in London three years earlier, demanded lower taxes, universal male suffrage, a secret ballot and annual parliaments.[1] Both meetings were led by the hugely popular radical leader Henry 'Orator' Hunt. As he took to the hustings to address them, the protestors in St Peter's Field were attacked by the Manchester Yeomanry, backed up by the Fifteenth Regiment of the British Hussars, many of whom were veterans of the Battle of Waterloo.[2] An unconfirmed number of protestors were killed, and between 300 and 400 were injured. An already ebullient popular radical press became positively mutinous.[3]

The 'Massacre at Peterloo' became an over-determined cultural moment in what Asa Briggs has described as 'one of the most troubled years of the nineteenth century'.[4] 1819 was also, though, the high water mark of the age of popular radicalism, the events at Peterloo provoking a veritable outpouring of radical satirical pamphlets, broadsides, ballads, songs and cartoons from across the cultural spectrum. Radicalism was 'popular' at this period in that it was a cross-class movement based on an eighteenth-century conception of 'the People' against 'Old Corruption'.[5] This harnessing of radicalism to a broadly defined popular culture greatly strengthened and emboldened radical writers in Regency England; the coalescence of popular and radical culture in the period was rarely repeated later in the century, but notably was achieved in a considerable body of writing by Charles Dickens.

The dominant aesthetic modes deployed by popular radical writers of the Regency period were satire and melodrama, both of which had a well-established radical genealogy. The foundations for radical Regency satire had been laid by John Wilkes and Thomas Spence in the late eighteenth century, whilst melodrama was a literary outgrowth of the French Revolutionary years. The satirical and melodramatic aesthetic vocabularies of Regency England, developed so memorably by William Hone, George Cruikshank and Thomas Wooler, persisted into the early and mid-Victorian years, when they would be adopted and adapted by Charles Dickens. The cultural inheritance of the popular radical writers of the second decade of the nineteenth century in Dickens's early and middle writings cannot be overstated, nor can the extent to which this inheritance contributed to his popular appeal.

Characteristic of the popular radical outcry against the massacre in St Peter's Field is a cartoon by George Cruikshank called 'Massacre at St Peter's, or "BRITONS STRIKE <u>HOME</u>"!!!' (See Figure 1). Hurriedly produced in the aftermath of the atrocity, the underlining of the word 'Home' punningly draws attention to the fact that soldiers from the Fifteenth Regiment of the British Hussars, who had been heroes on the battlefield of Waterloo four years earlier, were now killing their own people on home soil. Peterloo itself is representative of the turn in British politics at this period from militarism overseas to an enforced preoccupation with domestic affairs. The well-fed men on horses in the cartoon are the yeomanry, who are depicted urging their men: 'Down with 'em! Chop 'em down my brave boys! Give them no quarter, they want to take our Beef and Pudding from us – and remember the more you kill the less poor rates you'll have to pay so go it Lads show your courage and your Loyalty.'[6] Cruikshank's savage satire on the greedy and heartless yeomanry, whose 'courage' consists of attacking unarmed civilians, many of them women and children, is clear. Part of the affront of Peterloo was that the involvement of the yeomanry betrayed the very conception of 'the People' as a popular front against old corruption on which late eighteenth- and early nineteenth-century popular radical politics were predicated. The New Poor Law of 1834 would provoke exactly this sense of affront – and for comparable reasons – fifteen years later.

Published shortly after Cruikshank's illustration of Peterloo, Thomas Wooler's account of the 'Manchester Tragedy – A Horrible Farce' is equally trenchant in its satire. Wooler attacks the bullying cowardice of the yeomanry, using a harshly ironic vocabulary very close to that deployed by Cruikshank:

Had there been half a dozen pikes at the Manchester meeting, in the hands of the reformers, the Yeomanry Cavalry would have run to the regulars for protection, or

Figure 1 Robert, or possibly George Cruikshank, 'Massacre at St Peter's or "BRITONS STRIKE HOME"!!!' in Dorothy George, *Catalogue of Political and Personal Satires: Preserved in the Department of Prints and Drawings in the British Museum.*

dropped on their knees, and begged pardon of the people, for having attempted to *look like soldiers*. But the opportunity of putting to flight a peaceable assembly of unarmed men, women, and children, was not to be lost – it might never again return – and the *worthy* magistrates, who knew the metal of the hounds they were hunting with, slipped them upon the only scent such wolfish curs would follow. 'There is *no danger*, my lads! *charge away*! Cut away! Down with that child there! – see, the Jacobin is blowing a penny whistle! Some five or six of ye, gallop after that woman there, with the flag – cut her down! – cut her down! – bravo, lads! Bravo, there's *no danger*! Cut away!'[7]

Wooler and Cruikshank's repeated emphasis on the presence of women and children in the crowd, the sense that plebeian culture is itself under attack (the penny whistle, the closest thing to a weapon that the demonstrators are armed with), and the outraged sense of the yeomanry's cowardice in crushing such a defenceless 'enemy', are all typical of the protests against Peterloo.

The dominant satirical vocabularies of much of the radical protest against 'Peterloo' were complemented by a melodramatic mode of representation that can also be identified in Cruikshank's cartoon. Rooted as it was in the theatrical semiotics of gesture, melodrama readily adapted itself to visual modes of representation. In Cruikshank's cartoon, the representation of bodily violence and physical suffering draws on a developing melodramatic vocabulary that was to inform a huge body of radical writing across the nineteenth century. Also characteristic of the melodramatic mode is the implied narrative of working-class domestic distress in Cruikshank's illustration: the mother in the foreground, who is about to be sabred, determinedly but helplessly clutches her nursing infant to her breast; an infant whom, the picture implies, will soon be an orphan.

William Hone, bookseller and publisher, is, by common consent, one of the two most influential radical journalists of the post-war era of popular radicalism in Regency England, the other being William Cobbett;[8] James Epstein has nominated Hone as 'the greatest radical satirist of the Regency era'.[9] It was a long sequence of republican, anti-government and anti-clerical satires co-authored by William Hone and the young George Cruikshank that were the most widely circulated and influential radical pamphlets of the period 1815–21.[10] Best known of these is their twenty-four-page illustrated pamphlet *The Political House That Jack Built*, published in the latter part of 1819, when the memory of Peterloo was still raw in the popular radical imagination. William Hone had been particularly shocked by the fact that some of the amassed protestors in the crowd at Peterloo had themselves been veterans of Waterloo, and were now being attacked by a military they had but recently served. One such veteran was John Lees, whose wounds resulted in an agonising death. Hone's publishing of a 700-page account of the inquest into Lees's death was a more documentary, but much less popularly available and accessible radical response to Peterloo.[11] In *The Political House That Jack Built*, a determinedly populist enterprise, Hone characteristically mimics and subverts the popular form of the nursery rhyme in a three-pronged attack on what he saw as an oppressive legislature intent on curtailing freedom of expression, on a worldly and corrupt clerisy, and on a debauched, decadent monarchy.

George Cruikshank, at only nineteen years of age, provided Hone with thirteen woodcuts to accompany the text of the mock-nursery rhyme. Many of Cruikshank's illustrations are caricatures of government ministers and officials, of the Duke of Wellington and, most provoking of all, of the Prince Regent; his visual attacks on the Establishment greatly increased the popular appeal of Hone's pamphlet. Within months *The Political House That Jack Built* had sold over 100,000 copies, rapidly running to fifty-four editions.[12] Hone's pamphlet became one of the most influential satires to appear in the first three decades of the nineteenth century, and his publishing partnership with George Cruikshank was the most important and productive piece of teamwork in the popular radical cultural landscape of Regency England.[13]

The enormous success of the *Political House* can partly be accounted for by the way that it built on an existing tradition of nursery rhyme parodies. As Robert Patten has noted, 'The House That Jack Built' had been adapted for political satire many times before Hone's pamphlet appeared: Rowlandson and Williams, Isaac and George Cruikshank had all used the verses during the Old Price Riots of 1809.[14] The much greater popularity of Hone and Cruikshank's pamphlet derived from the extraordinary, insouciant energy of Hone's verse, its sheer cleverness, as well as the dazzling satirical effect of Cruikshank's woodcuts.

Appropriating and adapting the form – as well as some of the key phrases – of the popular nursery rhyme, the 'House' of the title of Hone's pamphlet is described as containing the long-established rights of the British people: the Magna Carta, the Bill of Rights and habeas corpus are all lodged there. Jack's 'House' is, though, 'Plundered' by key Government ministers and supporters, Cruikshank's caricatures immediately recognisable to a contemporary audience as depicting, variously, Sidmouth, Canning, Castlereagh, Gifford, Nadin and Wellington.[15] Hone characteristically gives the objects of his attack satirical nicknames, the simple, energetic nursery-rhyme lilts robbing these august Members of all dignity:

This is THE DOCTOR
Of *Circular* fame,
A Driv'ller, a Bigot, a Knave
Without shame:
And *that's* DERRY DOWN TRIANGLE
By name,
From the Land of mis-rule,
and half-banging, and flame:
And *that* is the SPOUTER OF FROTH
BY THE HOUR,
The worthless colleague
of their infamous power;
Who dubb'd *him* 'the Doctor'
whom he now calls 'brother',
And to get at his Place,
took a shot at the other.[16]

Cruikshank's caricature of the Home Secretary, Lord Sidmouth, is particularly harsh, the government minister having a look of witless old age about him.

The nicknaming, Hone's penchant for which would be shared by Dickens a generation later, is here quite sophisticated.[17] 'Derry-Down Triangle' refers to Castlereagh's Irish background and, gibingly, to the rumours that abounded concerning his condoning of torture during his time as Foreign Minister. 'The Doctor' was a nickname first given to Sidmouth by Canning, a slighting reference to Sidmouth's relatively humble background as the son of a country doctor. Although the satire here is quite complex, it is offset by the simplicity of the nursery-rhyme lilt, the repetitions of which here and elsewhere mean that the satire can readily be committed to memory.

The combining of sophisticated satire with the form of the nursery rhyme, and the simple visual impact of Cruikshank's caricatures, meant that *The Political House That Jack Built* could and did appeal to a very wide readership, to the semi-literate as well as to more educated readers. Even the illiterate had access to *The Political House* in as much as that it could be chanted or sung, and thereby circulated within a plebeian culture that did not depend on the written word. Songs and ballads were among the oldest forms of political expression amongst the poor, and Hone greatly enhanced the role of the mock-nursery rhyme in the inventory of radical cultural forms. Iain McCalman has remarked that Hone's earlier satirical *Political Litany* had been chanted in Spencean Tavern Debating Clubs in 1817, and had advertised itself to be 'said or sung'.[18] It seems likely, then, that *The Political House* would also have been 'said or sung' and circulated in a comparable manner. In this way it was able to transcend the boundaries – which were in any case highly permeable during the Regency period – between 'high' and 'low' culture, a feat that would but rarely be achieved in the Victorian period other than in the writings of Charles Dickens. Satire in particular was an aesthetic that was deployed in both 'high' and 'low' cultural publications and illustrations in Regency England, and Dickens would make ample use of this literary device, too, in his early and middle novels.

The pamphlet form also assisted Hone in his attempt to reach as wide a readership as possible. Newspapers were relatively expensive in the 1810s, due to stamp duty (it was not until the 1840s, with the rise of the mass-market newspaper press, that the cost of newsprint came down), and the pamphlet form, like the broadside, offered popular and radical writers an alternative means of commenting on 'news'. Although at one shilling *The Political House That Jack Built* was too expensive for most working people to buy,[19] James Catnach, an opportunistic producer of broadsides, ballads, 'last dying speeches' and so on, brought out cheap, bowdlerized editions of all of Hone's most successful pamphlets, which made them more widely accessible.[20] This publishing practice would be repeated twenty years later in imitations and bowdlerisations of Dickens's first two novels, *The Pickwick Papers* and *Oliver Twist* and, despite the great author's frustration with it, the plagiarism industry had the same popular-ising effect on his work as it had had on Hone's.

One of the best-known, and most influential, of Cruikshank's memorable woodcuts for *The Political House That Jack Built* is his caricature of the Prince Regent (see Figure 2), accompanied by Hone's daringly jeering text:

> This is THE MAN – all shav'n and shorn,
> All covered with Orders – and all forlorn;
> THE DANDY OF SIXTY,
> who bows with a grace,
> And has *taste* in wigs, collars,
> cuirasses and lace;
> Who, to tricksters, and fools,
> leaves the State and its treasure,
> And, when Britain's in tears,
> sails about at his pleasure[21]

Reusing a phrase ('all shav'n and shorn') from the original nursery rhyme, under attack here is the Prince Regent's notorious vanity, his sporting of huge sideburns, false curls and perukes.[22] Cruikshank's caricature empha-sises the Prince's pomposity and vulgarity: the traditional Fleur-de-Lys worn by the Prince Regent is displaced by three Peacock feathers, indicat-ing his misplaced pride in his now elderly, obese figure. He is covered in

Figure 2 George Cruikshank, 'THE MAN – all shaven and shorn', in William Hone, *The Political House That Jack Built.*

(unearned) military medals and his frequent state of inebriation is gestured towards by Cruikshank's addition of a corkscrew amongst the Orders of Honour hanging from the Prince Regent's ample belly. The ageing Regent's sexual promiscuity is crudely indicated by the pointed coat-tails poking down between his legs, which are astride.

Cruikshank's caricature of the Prince was one of several produced by him, and it was much imitated.[23] This image of the 'Dandy of Sixty' 'all shav'n and shorn' made such an impact on the popular consciousness that Hone immediately had it enlarged and printed separately with extracts from his verses. Robert Patten has recorded that the caricature so damaged the Regent's image that on 23 May 1820 Carlton House paid Cruikshank seventy pounds 'for the Copyright of a caricature titled the Dandy at 60'.[24] Clearly it was an image of the Prince Regent with which Charles Dickens was still familiar in 1853, for although republican satire is rare in Dickens's fiction, he nonetheless takes an effective side-swipe at the Regency in the figure of Old Turveydrop in *Bleak House*. Turveydrop, an elaborately dressed, vain, pompous (but poor) dancing master, christens his son 'Prince' as an act of homage to his hero, the Prince Regent, whom he adulates on account of his 'Deportment'. With his lampooning of George IV one is reminded of the cultural contiguity of Dickens's life and that of his Regency forbears.

Hone and Cruikshank's pamphlet, and its jeering attack on the heir to the throne, greatly annoyed the Prince Regent. G. J. Lawley's unpublished (and unfinished) monograph on the Hone–Cruikshank partnership quotes from a letter in which Hone comments both on the pamphlet's success and on the threat of prosecution:

I forgot to say that the House that Jack Built has a sale so far beyond expectation that I am obliged to apologise to my friends for not sending them according to their orders. The Town demand is excessive. There has been a Cabinet Council on it in consequence of 'The Man's' anger – he insisted on a Prosecution, the Attorney General dissented – 'Old Baggs' was sent for, and seconded the Solicitor General, so it was determined not – for fear of the consequences. Poor creatures.[25]

The feared 'consequences' were almost certainly further public ridicule. For although the government hadn't hesitated to prosecute Hone for seditious blasphemy on the publication of his *The Late John Wilkes's Catechism*, *The Political Litany* and *The Sinecurist's Creed* two years earlier (he had been acquitted), to try him now for publishing a nursery rhyme threatened to destroy what credibility was left to both the Regent and his government.[26]

The text accompanying Cruikshank's caricature of the Prince Regent gestures towards the present as a time 'when Britain's in tears', a reference that fleetingly but pointedly directs the reader to the trauma of Peterloo and to the starvation conditions endured by England's poor in 1819. This passing reference is amplified in the next woodcut in the series, in which Cruikshank shifts from a satirical to a melodramatic mode of representation (see figure 3). A recurrent melodramatic iconography of the suffering poor in St Peter's Field can be identified in this sixth plate, powerfully accompanied by Hone's text, which itself swiftly modulates from the

" Portentous, unexampled, unexplain'd !
——————— What man seeing this,
And having human feelings, does not blush,
And hang his head, to think himself a man ?
————————— I cannot rest
A silent witness of the headlong rage,
Or heedless folly, by which thousands die——
Bleed gold for Ministers to sport away."

Figure 3 George Cruikshank, 'THE PEOPLE all tatter'd and torn', in William Hone,
The Political House That Jack Built.

mocking satire directed against the Prince Regent in the previous accumu-
lation to a melodramatic, declamatory vein, and back again:

THESE ARE
THE PEOPLE
all tatter'd and torn,
Who curse the day
wherein they were born,
On account of Taxation
too great to be borne,
And pray for relief,
from night to morn;

Who in vain, Petition
in every form,
Who, peaceably Meeting
to ask for Reform,
Were sabred by Yeomanry Cavalry,
who,
Were thank'd by THE MAN,
all shaven and shorn,
All cover'd with Orders –
and all forlorn;
THE DANDY OF SIXTY,
who bows with a grace,
And has *taste* in wigs, cuirasses and lace.[27]

Again Hone reuses a phrase from the original nursery rhyme ('all tatter'd and torn') but now attaching it to the poor protestors in St Peter's Field.[28] Hone and other Radicals had been particularly outraged by the message of thanks that the Prince Regent had sent to the magistrates who ordered the attack on the protestors in St Peter's Field, doubtless regarding it as an extreme instance of insult being added to injury.[29]

The melodramatic tropes of physical violence and domestic anguish are interestingly played out in both the background and the foreground to Cruikshank's 'Peterloo' illustration for *The Political House*. The iconography of Peterloo in the background is very clear, with a mother lying in the mud, clutching her infant to her breast, at the mercy of a merciless, sabre-wielding Yeomanry on horseback. In the foreground we are presented with infants who have presumably been separated from their mothers in the melee, left with their grieving male relatives. A perceived attack on, and the breaking-up of, the working-class family, suggested in this early Cruikshank woodcut, would be much amplified and elaborated upon in the visual and literary culture of the anti-poor law movement fifteen years later. The melodramatic literature of the anti-poor law movement would, in turn, both influence, and be influenced by, Dickens's second novel, *Oliver Twist*, a two-way influence that I shall examine in chapter 3.

The 'motto' beneath the broken and abject subjects in figure 3 is taken by Hone from William Cowper's long poem from 1785, *The Task*. Hone held Cowper in high esteem, and had already published a long extract from Book 5 of *The Task* in his radical journal, *Hone's Political Register*, in 1817. Each of Cruikshank's woodcuts in *The Political House* is accompanied by a verse fragment or aphorism from Cowper's text, and again one can appreciate Hone's ability to cross the high-culture/low-culture divide. *The Task* is full of commentary on the sufferings of the poor and is replete with aphorisms on the corrupting influence of power, of wealth and so on. The incorporation of Cowper into Hone's pamphlet gives it a 'respectable' literary dimension at the same time as retaining a radical political commitment. Like the complex satire on government ministers, the inclusion of Cowper's poetry is directed at Hone's more educated, literate readership. In a comparable way Dickens would, a generation later, incorporate Shakespearean and classical allusions in novels whose popular appeal was primarily based on their melodramatic narratives, their comic humour and their use of popular narrative tropes from folktales.

The final section of *The Political House That Jack Built* comprises an attack on 'The Clerical Magistrate', whose twin commitments, to God on the one hand and to the legislature of England on the other, Hone and other radicals of the period deemed irreconcilable. The vehemence of Hone's anticlericalism is such that the final section of *A Political House* is really a separate poem or rhyme: for although the derisive lilt of the nursery rhyme is sustained, none of the earlier accumulations are incorporated into this section of the pamphlet, which is wholly dedicated to an unveiling of a hypocritical clerisy. Hone's Clerical Magistrate, accompanied by a Janus-facing caricature by Cruikshank, has, we are told, been called:

> By the holy spirit
> To teach men the Kingdom of Heaven
> to merit;
> That, to think of the World and the flesh
> he'd cease,
> And keep men in quietness,
> Love, and peace

Hone contemptuously gives an account of the way in which the clerical magistrate then allows himself to be:

> sworn in a Justice,
> and one of the Quorum;
> 'Gainst his spiritual Oath,
> puts his oath of the Bench,
> And instead of his Bible,
> Examines a wench[30]

Hone was not alone in sneering in disbelief at the professed unworldliness of men of the church: anti-clericalism was almost *de rigueur* amongst radicals in the Regency period and, as Joss Marsh has so eloquently demonstrated, blasphemy shaded into sedition in numerous radical texts from the period, not least in Hone's parodies on the Catechism, the Litany and the Creed.[31]

The context for radical anti-clericalism in the Regency period is well established. In the 1810s, parsons often doubled up as magistrates, and were openly political, and nearly all Tory.[32] All but one of the bishoprics in the 1810s were Tory appointees, and all but two opposed parliamentary reform. Bishops were paid £25,000 per annum at a time when an annual income of £300 made one a gentleman.[33] More generally, the Church of England in this period was regarded as (and often was in fact) politically corrupt, overpaid and overfed, shambolically disorganised and indifferent to the sufferings of the poor.

Hone's Janus-faced clerical magistrate is charged, in *The Political House*, with responsibility for the dead and maimed in St Peter's Field, thereby bringing his pamphlet, at the close, back to the politically driven massacre that inspired it. Hone's clerical magistrate:

> Would indict, for Rebellion,
>   those who petition;
> And all who look peaceable,
>   try for Sedition;
> If the People were legally Meeting,
>   in quiet,
> Would pronounce it, decidedly – *sec. Stat.* –
>   a Riot,
> And order the Soldiers
>   'to aid and assist',
> That is – kill the helpless.
>   Who cannot resist.[34]

The clerical magistrate is similarly charged in many other popular radical responses to Peterloo. *The Queen That Jack Found* includes a corpulent, over-dressed Bishop:

> This is
> THE BISHOP
> to whom is given,
> In room of St Peter,
> THE KEYS OF HEAVEN!
> Who thinks,
>   *if he pleases*,
> to shut people out,
> Who dare of his *Creed* or his *Tenets* to doubt,
> But who never thought it
> A CAPITAL SIN
> To strike from Religion the Name of his
> QUEEN[35]

Radical Regency anti-clericalism persisted into the debates about the 1832 Reform Act, which the bishoprics in the House of Lords had voted against and defeated in October 1831: this is the backdrop against which Dickens's anti-clerical satires a generation later need to be understood.[36] From about 1835 a process of reform was under way in the Church of England and this, combined with the rise of Evangelicalism, meant that anti-clerical satires were less prevalent in the Victorian period than during the reign of George IV. All the same, Dickens's clerical satires, whilst less numerous than Hone's, are no less hard-hitting: Stiggins, the venal and hypocritical nonconformist preacher in *Pickwick*, and Chadband, the overfed and pompous low-church preacher-man in *Bleak House*, are worthy successors to Hone's clerical magistrate. What has changed is the specificity of Hone's attack: the Regency man's head-on assault on contemporary malpractices meant he sailed much closer to the wind, politically, than Dickens did a generation later.[37] Dickens's satires are none the less savage, and owe much to cultural mediations of anti-clericalism in the early nineteenth century.

Apart from the countless imitations of Hone and Cruikshank's pamphlet that rapidly appeared, other nursery rhymes were also put to service in the radical cause. One of the more noteworthy of these is a twenty-three-page pamphlet from 1819 called *Who Killed Cock Robin? A Satirical Tragedy*.[38] One of a deluge of cheaply produced pamphlets inspired by *The Political House That Jack Built*, the anonymously authored *Who Killed Cock Robin?* similarly appropriates a well-known nursery rhyme in order to attack those deemed by Radicals to be responsible for the massacring of law-abiding citizens at St Peter's Field in 1819. Here, the repetitious formula of the nursery rhyme is structured around a series of questions and answers. In this way (and very possibly consciously), *Who Killed Cock Robin?* mimics, in the secular form of the nursery rhyme, the question-and-answer mode of Hone's *Late John Wilkes's Catechism* that had been chanted in Spencean Tavern Debating Clubs in 1817.

Without ever matching the skill, energy and sheer enjoyment of *The Political House*, *Who Killed Cock Robin?* clearly mimics Hone and Cruikshank's satirical *tour de force*. The pamphlet begins with an illustration that draws on Cruikshank's melodramatic iconography of Peterloo: figure 4, like figures 1 and 3, emphasises the presence of women and children – and whole families – amongst the protestors, and the vicious and inappropriate aggression of the attacking soldiers. And as in Cruikshank's two illustrations, this cartoon draws attention to the essential respectability of the protestors: they are poorly but decently clad.[39] Here they are described in the text allegorically, the opening lines of the poem

Figure 4 'The Manchester Sparrows', in [Anon.], *Who Killed Cock Robin? A Satirical Tragedy.*

representing them as 'Poor Robins' attacked by 'The Manchester Sparrows':

THESE ARE
THE MANCHESTER
SPARROWS,
Who kill'd POOR ROBINS,
With Bows and Arrows.

In reality slain by the soldiers' swords, here the protestors are represented as having been killed by 'Bows and Arrows' so as to mould the pamphlet to the original contours of the nursery rhyme wherever possible.[40]

Who Killed Cock Robin? also incorporates a Cruikshank-inspired cartoon of the Prince Regent (see figure 5), here represented according to the pamphlet's bird-allegory as a Peacock, extending the satirical analogy gestured towards in Cruikshank's original. As in Cruikshank's illustration, a corkscrew is added to the ostentatious collection of military honours that covers the Prince's ample frontage; there is also, following Cruikshank, a gesture towards his sexual promiscuity – a disproportionately long sword dangles down rather aimlessly beneath the peacock-prince's fat stomach.[41]

Figure 5 'The Prince of Birds', in [Anon.], *Who Killed Cock Robin? A Satirical Tragedy.*

The attack on clerical magistrates in *The Political House* is also echoed in *Who Killed Cock Robin?*. In the second of the two pamphlets they are depicted as 'Magistrate Ravens' who divest themselves of their robes in their assault on the poor:

> Our Church then in danger
> throw off the black gown,
> And *save* ROBINS souls –
> *by cutting them down.*[42]

Much of the satire of *Who Killed Cock Robin?* depends on the bird-allegory and especially on the cartoon illustrations of variously readily identifiable government 'fowl'. Now and again, though, the satirical mask is dropped, to great effect, in a series of 'prophecies' that are super-imposed onto the original 'Cook Robin' (sic.) nursery rhyme. Each 'prophecy' suggests that justice will, finally, be done, and retribution visited upon the heads of the aggressors and their supporters. The first of the sequence plainly threatens vengeance, although of a lawful kind, and is characteristic:

PROPHECY.
These vile SPARROWS,
Who kill ROBINS so callous,
Will, sooner or later,
Take their *swing* from a *Gallows!*[43]

The gallows imagery at the close of *Who Killed Cock Robin?* is replicated in another animal parody from the period, this one from 1820. *The Old Black Cock and his Dunghill Advisers in Jeopardy; or, The Palace That Jack Built* is evidently inspired by Hone and Cruikshank's pamphlet, but seems equally to imitate the bird parody of *Who Killed Cock Robin?*.[44] The anticlericalism of both pamphlets is amplified in the more crudely entitled *The Old Black Cock*: it includes a woodcut of a magistrate who closely resembles traditional representations of the devil. Like Hone's clerical magistrate, this priest is preoccupied with worldly rather than spiritual concerns:

This is the PRIEST all shaven and shorn
A hunter for profit, and sleeves of lawn,
Whose speeches and sermons are *cunningly* made
With an eye to increasing the profits of trade; etc.[45]

The final plate in the pamphlet, though, mimics the ending of *Who Killed Cock Robin?* by implying that individually identifiable government ministers, attorneys and priests who do nothing to mitigate the suffering and injustices of the poor will eventually hang for it: figure 6 offers a starkly threatening message to government. The Shakespeare motto that accompanies it ('We'll have you, as our rarer monsters are, painted upon a pole') lends a high-cultural gloss to what is otherwise an image clearly drawn from street literature: gallows broadsides – with accompanying illustrations such as this one – were an immensely popular cultural form in the first half of the nineteenth century.[46] Like Hone's, this pamphlet traverses the high/low culture boundary by drawing liberally on Shakespearean blank verse and prose to leaven its cruder popular verse forms.

The popular radical response to Peterloo extended well beyond 1819, with Hone and Cruikshank's own *A Slap at Slop and the Bridge Street Gang* (1821) brilliantly sustaining the satirical attack on those they deemed responsible for the massacre.[47] Peterloo was, though, temporarily eclipsed in the popular radical imagination by the Queen Caroline Affair of 1820.

We'll have you, as our rarer monsters are, painted upon a pole.

Shakspeare.

Figure 6 'Justice Triumphant', in [Anon.], *The Old Black Cock and his Dunghill Advisers in Jeopardy; or, The Palace That Jack Built.*

QUEEN CAROLINE, 1820

The Prince Regent's wife, then Caroline, Princess of Wales, had been sent into exile in 1814, having failed to provide the Prince with a male heir, and long having lost any place that she might ever have held in his affections (the

Prince was notorious for his numerous extra-marital affairs).[48] The Regent had long encouraged rumours that his wife had herself committed adultery, and as early as 1806 he had instigated a 'Delicate Investigation' that, however, refuted all such rumours. When George III died in 1820, Caroline returned to England to claim the title of Queen. George IV, determined that she should not succeed, demanded that Parliament give him a divorce. The case – which effectively put the Queen of England on trial (she was cross-examined in the House of Lords) – opened on 5 July 1820. Lord Liverpool introduced a Bill of Pains and Penalties that would rob Caroline of the title of Queen due to her alleged adultery with an Italian servant.[49] The popular radical front in England once more erupted, again taking the opportunity to attack an unpopular monarch and his much-despised government.

The attack consisted of a sometimes vehement, sometimes witty defence of Caroline in an ocean of pamphlets, broadsides, ballads, poems, stories and even plays. Caroline's return to England was itself a cultural event of some magnitude: she was accompanied by long processions and met by delegations, and large meetings were held on the subject of her trial; the mainstream press combined with the radical press in a single voice in support of the Queen. The press campaign presented the trial of Queen Caroline as setting 'the People' against 'Old Corruption' in defence not just of the Queen, but of national identity itself.

Once more, the dominant aesthetic modes of the assault on the monarch and his government were satire and melodrama. The melodramatic literature of the Queen Caroline Affair focused on the Queen's innocence and virtue, on her feminine vulnerability, on her enforced separation from her daughter, Princess Charlotte, and on her charity and kindness towards the poor. She was presented, in brief, as a pattern melodramatic heroine. Typical of the hundreds of broadsides and ballads produced in support of the Queen is an anonymously authored and published poem, *On the Return of Queen Caroline to England*.[50] The Queen is presented as a courageous and virtuous victim, determined to prove her innocence by crossing the channel alone to face her accusers in a show trial. The poem emphasises the brutal separation of mother and child:

> On British ground resolv'd to face her King
> And meet the charges that her foes would bring.
>
> . . .
>
> But there's another name, whose mention will
> Thy tender heart with keenest anguish thrill!
> Thy sainted *Daughter*! – she whose heart for you
> Once beat with filial love – affection true;

> Had *she* survi ed, thy foes had never dar'd
> Their coward h ads against thee to have rear'd:

A broadside by James Catnach presents Caroline similarly, but this time using the Queen herself as poet-narrator:

> O ne'er can I forget those days
> When Charlotte was my only care,
> My choicest pleasure was to gaze,
> On her whose smiles my life did cheer.
> Torn from my arms – to meet no more,
> No more to fold her to my breast,
> 'My child, my child,' (whilst tears down-pour'd)
> Was all my trembling tongue express'd.[51]

The trope of the virtuous mother forcibly separated from her child is repeated in a substantial, forty-three-page (and relatively expensive) pamphlet, *The Magic Lantern; or, Green Bag Plot Laid Open; A Poem*, purportedly by 'A Wild Irishwoman'.[52] Emphasising the Queen's loneliness and vulnerability, the pamphlet presents her as an innocent object of perjuring schemers in the pay of the King, whom she blames for Caroline's separation from her only child:

> She's deserted, forsaken, and abandon'd by those
> Should defend and protect her from all human foes.
>   . . .
> They [her enemies] exalt in the pangs a mother must feel;
> Depriv'd of her darling – then she'll pray and she'll kneel.[53]

The melodramatic trope of the separation of mother and child echoes the many visual depictions of infants being torn from their mothers at Peterloo the year before, and thereby establishes a cross-class sense of identity between poor mothers and their Queen. This same trope would be reused fifteen years later in the explosion of anti-Poor Law literature that criticised the separation of mothers from their children in workhouses. In 1820 it performed important political work in the adoption of the Queen as a radical heroine. The presentation of the Queen as a maternal figure is extended in many popular radical texts from 1820 that represent her as a protectress of the poor, her maternal qualities extending to her subjects. *The Magic Lantern* typically casts Caroline as a caring, charitable figure who has won the hearts of the people:

> If you look straight in front, you can't miss the sight,
> How our Princess was passing each day and each night
> In relieving the poor, in assisting the old,
> By gifts and donations that in Heaven are told;

Her reward here she finds, for her charities claim
The love of the people that echo her name.[54]

William Cobbett had been in North America at the time of the Peterloo Massacre in 1819, having fled almost certain imprisonment following the suspension of habeas corpus in 1817. He returned, though, in November 1819, and in the following year would become a leading figure in the defence of Queen Caroline.[55] Over half of volume 37 (July–December 1820) of *Cobbett's Weekly Political Register* – in total 1,700 pages – is dedicated to addresses to the Queen from numerous parts of the country, expressing support. Denied access to the formal mechanisms of the law, 'the People' were instead able to constitute themselves as an unofficial defence counsel, using Cobbett's *Register* as a mouthpiece and thereby able to wrench the legal process from the grasp of government, notwithstanding Lord Brougham's later claim that he single-handedly saved the Queen.

Cobbett sent Caroline a continual stream of written advice, and her August 1820 letter of remonstrance addressed to her estranged husband – 'Letter from the Queen to the King' – which he returned unopened, was entirely Cobbett's idea.[56] In the 'Letter', Caroline presents herself as an innocent, forsaken wife, cruelly expelled from her home. She demands of the King how he could reconcile himself to having driven 'a wife from beneath your roof with an infant in her arms'.[57] She then goes on to present herself both as an orphan and as a grieving mother, now torn from her child:

Bereft of parent, brother, and father-in-law, and having my husband as my deadliest foe ... To see my daughter; to fold her in my arms; to mingle my tears with hers; to receive her cheering caresses and to hear from her lips assurances of never-ceasing love; thus to be comforted, consoled, upheld, and blessed, was too much to be allowed me. Even on the slave mart the cries of 'Oh! my mother, my mother! Oh! my child, my child!' have prevented a separation of the victims of avarice. But your advisers, more inhuman than the slave-dealer, remorselessly tore the mother from the child.[58]

Typical of the melodramatic mode of a great deal of Queen Caroline literature, Caroline's/Cobbett's letter (the *New Times* suspected that Cobbett wrote it himself)[59] emphasises not only the mother–child bond that has been torn asunder, but also her identification with non-elite peoples. One of the dominant tropes of Queen Caroline literature was the 'Green Bag'. Green Bags were document cases that were customarily used for official government papers; they had taken on an over-determined significance, though, in 1817, when a number of Radicals were arrested after the Prince Regent's carriage had purportedly been attacked with potatoes. Sidmouth was reported to have placed papers relating to sedition and unrest in one such Green Bag, an object which rapidly became a byword for unreliable and often faked government 'evidence'. 'Evidence' of Caroline's adultery was similarly conveyed in Green Bags three years later, and these receptacles thereafter took on a literary life of their own in the literature of popular radicalism in the period.[60] Cobbett made explicit the resonance of the Green Bags used in the government's attempt to convict Radicals in 1817 and their Queen in 1820, once again deploying the melodramatic trope of the wrenching-apart of parents and children:

If there had existed any doubt in the public mind as to the innocence of her Majesty, and as to the falsehood of the charges against her, that doubt would have been removed at once, by the bare circumstance of those charges having been conveyed to the parliament in *Green Bags*. The people had not so soon forgotten the *Green Bags* of 1817. They had not so soon forgotten, that those Bags and their contents, formed the pretext for sending into dungeons a great number of men, who there for a long while enduring all the sufferings of imprisonment, separation from wives and children, loss of precious time while those wives and children were starving, loss of health, loss of reason in one instance producing suicide.[61]

The Green Bag trope, then, bound the Queen and radical activists together, united in their endurance of the slings and arrows of a corrupt government.

Writers who co-opted Queen Caroline to the popular radical cause deployed satire, as well as melodrama, as a political tool. Thomas Wooler entitles one of his keynote 'Letters of the Black Dwarf' 'A QUEEN TO BE DISPOSED OF – A WIFE TO BE GIVEN AWAY'. Exploiting one of the conventions of Enlightenment literature, in which narrators from foreign lands report on the culture of the writer's own country,[62] the Black Dwarf's letters to his countryman, the 'Yellow Bonze of Japan', perform the function of lead article in Wooler's radical weekly:

Oh, my yellow friend! we are in a most pitiful plight. We are sadly in want of a little *Eastern Law*, concerning the *disposal* of wives! . . . Here is a woman, who was thought to have been decently and quietly got rid of; – and lo! here she is again, to disturb a nation, and frighten her husband out of his well-merited repose![63]

Wooler's is an extended satire in the manner of Swift or Defoe; more light-hearted and high-spirited was the flood of ballads, songs and handbills that satirically attacked the King whilst defending the Queen. A comically entitled handbill, *Caroline and the Italian Ragamuffins!!*, directs attention to the hapless Italian servants who were bribed by the King and his representatives to offer evidence of his wife's adultery to the trial judge. Like Hone in *The Political House*, the author of this squib sets it to a well-known nursery rhyme tune, energetically adapting the original so as to render the political 'rhyme' easily memorable. And as if the use of a nursery rhyme were not sufficient to poke fun at the King, he is further ridiculed by having him used as the nursery rhyme's first-person narrator. The poem is set to the tune of 'Oh Dear, What Can the Matter Be?', the original nursery rhyme used as a refrain throughout:

> For, oh! dear, she does so perplex me,
> I fear while I reign, she'll torment and vex me,
> And what's worse she says on the throne she'll sit next me;
> Dear Derry-Down what shall I do?[64]

Another well-known song used in the campaign against the King was the national anthem itself, daringly retitled as 'God Save the Queen'. Numerous versions were disseminated in handbill and broadside format, and notable amongst them was Samuel Bamford's. Bamford, an important eyewitness to the massacre in St Peter's Field, was one of many Radicals imprisoned for having taken part in the demonstration. In his anthem against the King, defiantly penned in his prison cell, Bamford attacks a politicised, corrupt and immoral clerisy in the pay of the monarchy:

> Those whom the people pay,
> Daily to preach and pray;
> Faithless have been.
> 'None for *her* soul did care,'
> Not a lip moved in prayer,
> For the lone wanderer,
> God help the Queen![65]

Not only songs and rhymes, but also mock adverts were used by radical publishers in their satirical campaign against George IV. Typical of these is an 'advert' for a new game of chess: ***THE KING** the Avowed Enemy of **THE QUEEN. A New ROYAL GAME OF CHESS**.*[66] The 'advert' is in fact an eighteen-page pamphlet, comprising not only the advert itself but also an extensive set of satirical 'rules' of the game:

Chess Royal.
This game differs from the ancient game of Chess, where the Queen stands by the side of the King, and is protected by him: there, they are a mutual support, and never fight except against another King and Queen; whereas in this new-fashioned game the King is the avowed enemy of the Queen, and does all he can to destroy her.[67]

In their deployment of mock adverts such as this one, radical satirists were able, in one parodical move, deftly to harness commercial culture to radicalism.[68] It was a manoeuvre very familiar to William Hone, who naturally found himself at the heart of the popular radical front in support of Queen Caroline. Once more in partnership with George Cruikshank, Hone's pamphlet, *The Queen's Matrimonial Ladder*, which was sold with an accompanying toy ladder, was one of the most popular and best-selling pamphlets to be published at the height of the Queen Caroline Affair. According to Marcus Wood, *The Queen's Matrimonial Ladder*, an eighteen-page pamphlet, was produced in 'hundreds of thousands of copies' and was the most successful of Hone's pamphlet satires after *The Political House That Jack Built.*[69] Hone advertised *The Queen's Matrimonial Ladder* as 'A National Toy, WITH FOURTEEN STEP SCENES; AND ILLUSTRATIONS IN VERSE', and drew attention to the accompanying toy ladder: 'This Pamphlet and the toy together ONE SHILLING.'[70] Given that all of Hone's pamphlets sold for one shilling, the toy ladder was in effect a free gift – a marketing ploy as well as a satirical device.

Hone later claimed that the idea for the toy ladder – both as a textual apparatus and as a 'free gift' – was his own. But his partner, the young George Cruikshank, had actually already been involved with producing parodic versions of children's ladder toys whilst working for lottery contractors some time before his partnership with Hone flourished; so it seems likely that Cruikshank would have played a significant part in the conception as well as the design of the pamphlet.[71] Hone's failure adequately to credit Cruikshank for his contribution to *The Queen's Matrimonial Ladder* eerily anticipates the illustrator's bitterness concerning the evolution of one of Dickens's novels a generation later. Cruikshank, now older and more experienced than when he worked with Hone, would complain after Dickens's death that he had played a more central role in the conception of *Oliver Twist* than the famous author had admitted.[72]

The Queen's Matrimonial Ladder is characteristic of Hone and Cruikshank's collaboration in its apparently effortless traversing of cultural boundaries that were as yet fluid in the Regency period: it is a popular as well as a radical text, and it has high-cultural elements as well as appealing to a broad, popular readership. It also characteristically combines the two dominant aesthetic modes of early nineteenth-century popular radical culture: satire and melodrama.

Each of the fourteen 'steps' of Hone and Cruikshank's 'ladder' has a title that represents a stage in the unfolding drama that would eventually engulf and defeat the King, from his marriage proposal through to his eventual defeat and humiliation. The illustrated 'steps' are: 'Qualification', 'Declaration', 'Acceptation', 'Alteration', 'Imputation', 'Exculpation', 'Emigration', 'Remigration', 'Consternation', 'Accusation', 'Publication',

Give not thy strength unto women, nor thy ways to that which destroyeth kings.
Solomon.

Figure 7 George Cruikshank, 'Qualification', in William Hone, *The Queen's Matrimonial Ladder*.

'Indignation', 'Coronation' and 'Degradation'. Each is accompanied by an illustration, by a motto, and by Hone's main verse-text. The pamphlet's satirical content is concentrated in the cartoon illustrations and accompanying mottos: the pamphlet begins with a characteristic, and immediately recognisable, Cruikshankian caricature of the Prince Regent (see figure 7). Fat, half-dressed and evidently inebriated, the unwholesome-looking monarch is surrounded by the accoutrements of his vices: empty wine bottles, gaming dice and cards, an empty and broken glass, a leering

He smelt — O Lord! how he did smell!
Southey's Minor Poems, vol. iii. p. 103.

Figure 8 George Cruikshank, 'Consternation', in William Hone, *The Queen's Matrimonial Ladder.*

devil's mask. The caricature is accompanied by a quotation from the Old Testament's *Song of Solomon*, the satirical and subversive intent of which barely needs to be stated: 'Give not thy strength unto women, nor thy ways to that which destroyeth kings.'[73]

More light-hearted and high-spirited is the 'Consternation' 'step' later in the pamphlet, in which the Regent is shown swooning after having been told of Caroline's return and her intention to claim the title of Queen (see figure 8). The fainting Regent – again immediately recognisable with his balloon-belly and elaborate coiffeur – is being given smelling salts by an anxious Lord Sidmouth (Home Secretary), whose caricature is also easily recognised from the earlier versions in *The Political House*. Caroline is shown waiting patiently but determinedly outside, characteristically dressed in travelling clothes. The motto accompanying the caricature is from Southey's *Minor Poems* and reads: 'He smelt – O Lord! how he did smell!', the *double entendre* providing the comedy.[74]

The choice of Southey as provider of the motto for this particular cartoon is something of a sly 'in-joke'. For Southey, having passed through a radical phase, was by now a Loyalist and was one of the objects of attack in Hone's biblical parody from 1817, *The Sinecurists' Creed* (Southey was in receipt of a government pension). In this sense then the satire is, here, quite complex; but the *double entendre* of the joke is of course simplicity itself, Hone once again appealing simultaneously to a popular and to a more sophisticated readership. Whilst the main text of *The Queen's Matrimonial Ladder* is not as memorable as that of *The Political House* – it is not based on a nursery rhyme, for example – it is all the same readily accessible, based as it is on simple rhyming couplets. And as in *The Political House*, Hone combines simple diction in his main text with various quotations, in the mottos that accompany the cartoons, from Shakespeare, the Bible, Cowper, Byron and Sheridan, as well as Southey, all of which lend a literary respectability to a popular pamphlet.

Hone's and other early nineteenth-century Radicals' penchant for anti-clerical satire is again in evidence in his attack, in the main verse-text, on the Bishops' ready – and (it is implied) immoral – support of the Regent's denunciation of his wife:

CONSTERNATION
Ah, what was that groan!
'twas the Head of the Church,
When he found she was come –
for he dreaded a search
Into what *he'd* been doing:[75]

Satire cedes to melodrama at various points in the pamphlet, and most especially in the 'Emigration' 'step', when Caroline is forced into exile in 1814, and thereby separated from her only child, Princess Charlotte. The verse-text accompanies an illustration in which a crowd of fat, aristocratic, ageing and lewd-looking women (the Regent's various paramours) drive a decent-looking Caroline away from her home towards the ocean in the background (see figure 9).[76] In the foreground a beseeching Princess Charlotte leans from a window, imploring her mother to return, Caroline herself looking back towards her daughter in desperation. Once more, the melodramatic trope of the mother separated from her child is put to service in the popular radical cause:

———— A wanderer, far away,
Neglected and reviled—
Phillips's Lament.

Figure 9 George Cruikshank, 'Emigration', in William Hone, *The Queen's Matrimonial Ladder.*

Then spies gather round, and malignants appear;
And cajole, wait, watch, insult,
alarm and betray,
Till from home, and her daughter,
they force her away.[77]

Cruikshank's illustration reveals the fact that Princess Charlotte was actually a grown woman when she was separated from her mother in 1814. All the more significant, then, is it that the vast majority of popular radical texts that dwelt on the separation of Caroline from her child strongly implied that the child in question was an infant. The force of the melodramatic trope depended on this, and Cruikshank's illustration is unusual in its acknowledgement of Charlotte's adulthood.

Thomas Laqueur has argued that the political purpose of Regency radicalism was overwhelmed and badly undermined by what he regards as a diversionary populist romantic and sentimental aesthetic generated by the Queen Caroline Affair. Iain McCalman has countered Laqueur with his reflection that the populism that Laqueur complains of was thoroughly implicated with (and, I would add, inseparable from) the radicalism that Laqueur prefers. McCalman's position is that the 'Caroline affair and its literature touched sections of the London population that were ordinarily indifferent or hostile to the appeal of popular radicalism'.[78] Anna Clark has seconded this, remarking that this extraordinary cultural flashpoint enabled radicals to develop a populist political language that could mobilise a mass movement.[79]

Laqueur's negative political apprehension of the popular radical cultural explosion of 1820 arguably derives from an historiography that regards 1819 as the chronological high water mark of popular radical activity in the early nineteenth century.[80] According to such an historiography, the so-called 'Gagging Acts' that came onto the statute books at the end of December that year, the arrest of radical leaders such as Henry Hunt, Major Cartwright, Richard Carlile and so on, all led to an abrupt 'falling off' in radical activity in 1820. But viewed from a more determinedly literary and cultural historical perspective, the literature of the Queen Caroline Affair built on and developed the satirical and melodramatic modes of radical writing that were already well established in the year of Peterloo, and that would persist well into the middle of the nineteenth century, not least in the writings of Charles Dickens, Douglas Jerrold and writers of Chartist fiction. It is to the work of these writers that I shall now turn, for in their fiction, drama and journalism the hitherto occluded cultural inheritance of popular radical Regency culture which I have addressed in this chapter can be shown importantly to shape the literary and cultural landscape of early and mid-Victorian Britain.

CHAPTER 2

Dickens and nineteenth-century show trials

TRIALS, THEATRE AND THE LAW

On 26 July 1815, William Hone involuntarily found himself caught up in a crowd of tens of thousands of spectators gathered to witness the hanging of one Elizabeth Fenning, a maidservant who had been convicted of poisoning her employer and his family.[1] Hone was greatly upset by the spectacle:

I was going down Newgate Street on some business of my own, I got into an immense crowd that carried me along with them against my will; at length I found myself under the gallows where Eliza Fenning was to be hanged. I had the greatest horror of witnessing an execution, and of this in particular; a young girl of whose guilt I had grave doubts. But I could not help myself; I was closely wedged in; she was brought out. I saw nothing, but I heard all. I heard her protesting her innocence – I heard the prayer – I could hear no more. I stopped my ears, and knew nothing else till I found myself in the dispersing crowd, and far from the dreadful spot.[2]

Prior to the hanging of this unfortunate young woman, Hone had gathered signatures on a petition for mercy, but it had failed.[3] Like the crowd of which he was a part, Hone's dismay at the young girl's execution rapidly turned to anger. On the evening of the hanging several hundred protestors gathered outside the prosecutor's house in Chancery Lane, and cries of 'Pull it down!' pierced the air; the police broke up the demonstration, which none the less re-formed on subsequent evenings.[4] Hone characteristically took up his pen to voice his own protest, defending the maidservant who had probably not poisoned her employers at all: she too ate the arsenic-laced yeast dumplings that had laid them low (no one had died), and she herself had become violently sick.

A Radical in politics, Hone was also very much a struggling publisher and bookseller who had to make a living, and his account of the production of his pamphlet in defence of Fenning illustrates the way that he dextrously adapted his campaigning political work to the commercial market, a *modus operandi* that anticipates Dickens's working methods, in a different form, a generation later. Characteristically taking up arms against what he perceived to be an unjust legal process, Hone pondered how best simultaneously to defend the dead woman's reputation and expose the inequities of the law. At the same time, though, he was penniless to the extent that he could not even afford to give his wife any money for food. In the midst of his dilemma – both moral and pecuniary – Hone passed a theatre that was showing a popular play taken from the French, *The Maid and the Magpie* (*La Pie Voleuse*) and was inspired with an idea as to how he could protest Eliza Fenning's cause and at the same time make money:

I went home and said to my wife, 'Give me a pair of candles and snuffers upstairs, and call for George Cruikshank.' He came; I said, 'Make me a cut of a Magpie hung by the neck to the gallows' – and I put my head on one side, and looked as like a dying Magpie as I could.
   I walked to my printers, and by six o'clock in the morning *The Maid and the Magpie* was completed – and a thousand struck off. Cruikshank was ready with the frontispiece; and my wife sewed them. When the coaches drove up for the newspapers, we were ready with our pamphlets. 'Will you have this?' – 'How many?' – 'Half a hundred' – 'A Hundred.' So we effectually roused the public as to the case of Eliza Fenning, and I and my family lived for four months on *The Maid and the Magpie*.[5]

A generation later Dickens would, like Hone, consistently combine the raw material of popular culture with moral and political commitment in order to produce a commercially viable literature of protest; and in this respect the two writers had a great deal in common.[6] Similar, too, is a political temperament that drew both men to particular causes rather than to political parties or philosophies.

   The Eliza Fenning case became something of a *cause célèbre*, strategically adopted by Radicals and the commercial press alike. While Hone claimed that his play had 'roused the public' as to Eliza's case, public awareness was in fact already at a high pitch.[7] But Hone's popularising of the young woman's plight (as well as the play, he also published a highly melodramatic sequence of letters apparently composed by her in the condemned cell) was none the less a significant factor in producing the popular outcry that led to 10,000 people attending her funeral procession in Lamb Conduit's Street and her burial near the Foundling Hospital.[8] Other Radicals joined the fray, not least Leigh Hunt. Hunt, recently released from jail for libelling the Prince Regent, complained of the Fenning case that '[O]f direct evidence there was not an atom', and fellow Radicals agreed with him, seeing in her doubtful conviction further evidence of a general malaise in English law.[9]

Thirty years later, the trial and execution of Eliza Fenning were still vividly etched into the English cultural imagination. One of Dickens's contributors to *All The Year Round* wrote an essay, with characteristically firm editorial guidance, about Fenning's plight. In a letter to Walter Thornbury in 1866 Dickens expresses anew the grave sense of doubt that had haunted earlier commentators concerned about the legal procedures applied to her case:

My Dear Thornbury,
I have looked up that passage in the *Annual Register*, and I do not think it at all conclusive. That poor girl, under the terrors of an Evangelical holding forth, may have made a general confession of sinfulness, I do not doubt. That she confessed the crime, I do most decidedly doubt. The argument that the Government of the day hanged her, is stark imbecility. The Government of the day would have hanged anyone.[10]

In a subsequent letter to W. H. Wills Dickens confirms the fact that the case of Eliza Fenning was still ripe in the popular memory more than thirty years after her death:

My Dear Wills,
No doubt Eliza Fenning will come down to Gad's. I will return her by post to you. I did not mean to negative her. Merely raised my eyebrows at a subject so well known.[11]

The persistence of the Fenning case in the popular cultural memory throughout and beyond the first half of the nineteenth century is strongly suggestive of the importance of the courtroom as a locus for cultural and political debate in the period. Dickens's novels and journalism are peppered with trial scenes: highlights include the hilarity of the Breach of Promise suit in *The Pickwick Papers*, Oliver Twist's poignant appearance before a magistrate, Jack Dawkins's comic bravado as his sentence is passed, the bullying judgement passed on Barnaby Rudge by a 'gentleman' country magistrate, the extended satire on a Chancery suit in *Bleak House* and the high melodrama of the four trials of Charles Darnay in *A Tale of Two Cities*.

This chapter argues that in developing set-piece trial scenes in his novels, Dickens drew on both popular and radical cultural histories of the legal process from the late eighteenth and early nineteenth centuries. His borrowings from both popular and radical textual fields enabled a fierce and intellectually serious – as well as a highly populist – critique of nineteenth-century English law. And in his figuration of set-piece trial scenes in his fiction Dickens, like Hone and others earlier in the nineteenth century, borrowed from both 'official' and unofficial texts, and from both high- and low-cultural fields, thereby effectively reaching out to an extraordinarily wide readership.

What was it, though, that drew the nineteenth century's most successful novelist to the law in general and to the set-piece trial scene in particular? The answer is partially rooted in biography. In Ackroyd's words, Dickens 'carried hatred enough for all forms of the law itself', and one cannot argue with his reflection that '[t]here is only one good judge in the whole of Dickens's work, few good solicitors, and really nothing but loud-mouthed barristers'.[12] At the same time, though, the novelist had a professional connection with the English legal system that endured even beyond the publication of his most extended satire on the law, *Bleak House*. He became a lawyer's clerk in 1827 and then a shorthand reporter in Doctors' Commons near St Paul's in 1829 (where he reported trials).[13] In 1834 he wrote to the Steward of New Inn stating that he intended 'entering at the bar, as soon as circumstances will enable me to do so', and there even came a time when he applied (more than once) to become a magistrate.[14] At the end of 1839 he joined Middle Temple with the idea of one day being called to the Bar; it was only in 1855, two years after the publication of *Bleak House*, that he finally withdrew his application. So although he 'detested and pilloried the Law', he was also magnetically drawn to it.[15]

The repetition of the set-piece trial scene in Dickens's fiction can be attributed not only to his personal interest in law, but also – and simultaneously – to his lifelong passion for the theatre. In the late 1820s, by his own account, he went to the theatre every night for at least three years. Not much of a success as a playwright, he was an excellent actor, and arguably did not take to the stage as a professional only because he was ill on the day of his audition in front of Charles Kemble and a Mr Bartley, the latter the stage manager of Covent Garden. And even though Dickens appears to have rejected a stage career, he had a lifelong involvement in amateur dramatics, his troupe of actors performing even before the Queen.[16]

It is out of a coalescence of law and theatre, then, that Dickens's set-piece trial scenes emerge. The trial is the most theatrical arena of the law, full of melodramatic exaggeration and gesture, and admirably well adapted both to a staging of the legal process and to exposing its abuses.[17]

The preponderance of trial scenes in Dickens's fiction cannot, though, be attributed to biographical influences alone. Set-piece trials were a long-established staple of popular culture in the nineteenth century: theatrical melodramas such as *Black-Ey'd Susan* (1829), *Sweeney Todd* (1847), *The Colleen Bawn* (1860) and *The Bells* (1871) all thrived on the inherent dramatic conflict of the courtroom scene.[18] Middle-class culture, and the novel especially, readily absorbed the melodramatic trial set piece that had its roots in popular culture: Elizabeth Gaskell and George Eliot, for example, incorporated highly dramatic trial scenes into their novels.[19] It is in Dickens's novels alone, though, that set-piece trial scenes contribute to a radical critique of the legal process: in other mid-nineteenth century fictions trial scenes are used more simply as generic supports to melo-dramatic plotlines.

It was not only in the theatre and the middle-class novel that trial scenes gripped the cultural imagination of the nineteenth century: street litera-ture, the literature of non-elite peoples, was similarly in thrall to the trial set piece. The prolific broadside and ballad industry of the first half of the nineteenth century was fuelled by the trial, sentence, last dying words and execution of a string of infamous murderers such as William Corder, François Courvoisier and Maria Manning. Broadside and ballad accounts of their trials, as well as accounts that he read in the middle-class newspaper press, would have contributed significantly to the shaping of Dickens's representation and critique of the legal process in his novels. Maria Manning erupts melodramatically from the text of *Bleak House* in the form of the murderous French maid, Hortense. Manning also leaps out from the pages of *A Tale of Two Cities* in the shape of the pistol-wielding Madame Defarge: one of the moments of high drama in the novel is her semi-comic life-and-death struggle with the doughty and all-too-English Miss Pross. Gatrell has remarked that broadsides were not exclusively read by common people in the streets, but had a wider cultural purchase,[20] and it seems likely that these texts would also have partially shaped Dickens's own fictional engagement with law and justice. He had an intense interest in the trial and conviction of such criminals, writing about them in letters to *The Times* and to the *Morning Chronicle* as well as in *Household Words*.[21] In some instances he attended executions, most memorably that of William and Maria Manning, whose lifeless bodies grimly haunt him during a sleepless night recounted in a *Household Words* essay, 'Lying Awake'.[22]

Prison Calendars that detailed the crimes committed and sentences passed upon prisoners by provincial and metropolitan Assizes were also very popular in the late eighteenth and early nineteenth centuries. Dickens's familiarity with such Calendars is indicated in *Oliver Twist* in the scene in Fagin's den where Oliver reads, and begins to feel a certain fascinated horror towards, the *Newgate Calendar*. Calendars from Newcastle, Durham and Morpeth in the 1830s include in their lists the sentencing in 1833 of one Elizabeth Shanks, aged eleven, to fourteen years' transportation for having stolen a pair of flannel drawers and trousers; and of one Edward Curry, a boy, to one year hard labour in 1837 for stealing two pocket handkerchiefs from his grandmother. These and other such Calendars give us some insight into the sort of punishments that the Artful Dodger and his cohorts might have expected in the 1830s.[23]

Show trials and accounts of the sentencing and execution of convicted prisoners held, then, a central place in the popular cultural imagination of the first half of the nineteenth century, and Dickens's novels are both shaped by and contribute to the formation of this textual field. The trial scenes in Dickens's novels are also, though, shaped by a *radical* cultural inheritance. From the second half of the eighteenth century onwards, the courtroom trial was very often a political arena where Radicals accused of sedition or libel took to the courtroom stage to argue their case for freedom of speech, for the freedom of the press, for the freedom of association and so on. The legal trial thereby provided Radicals, who were denied a political arena outside the walls of the courtroom, with a public platform on which they could make political speeches.[24] The trials of radical Regency activists such as Henry Hunt and Samuel Bamford, and of radical Regency journalists such as William Cobbett, Thomas Wooler, William Hone and Leigh Hunt; the dramatic conviction and execution of the Cato Street Conspirators in 1820; and the Chartist Trials of 1839 and 1848: there was a long history of political trials in the first half of the nineteenth century, all recorded in Howell's *State Trials* and in the *Annual Register*, long runs of which Dickens owned and drew upon liberally in his fiction.[25] The trial as a scene of class injustice was a perfect vehicle for radical expression, and Dickens's own sense of the class injustices daily played out in mid-nineteenth century Britain gives us another insight into the appeal, for him, of the set-piece trial scene.

Those radical activists and journalists who were tried and sentenced for sedition and libel in the late eighteenth and nineteenth centuries did not passively allow the law to take its course, but engaged both passionately, and very often parodically, with its discourses, leaving a rich trail of legal satire that would massively influence Dickens's own satires on the law in the 1830s, '40s and '50s. Alongside the official transcripts of such trials there also grew up a tradition of mock trials, in which the official language of the law was parodied and undermined; this tradition, too, echoes down the years in Dickens's trial scenes.

The trial scenes in Dickens's novels emerge, then, from a number of social and cultural fields: from his own biography, from popular culture (theatrical melodramas, ballads and broadsides), from official and other reports of the trials of radical activists and journalists, and from radical satires on the legal process.

TRIALS, LAUGHTER, AND THE POLITICS
OF LEGAL EXPRESSION

Both popular and radical cultures in the nineteenth century drew on the generic modes of satire and melodrama in their production of show trials, the same generic modes that had dominated the popular outcry surrounding Peterloo and the Queen Caroline Affair in the Regency years. The twin literary modes of melodrama and satire, favoured by radicals in the late eighteenth and nineteenth centuries, are the aesthetic tools with which Dickens works, in his fiction generally, and in his set-piece trial scenes in particular, as I shall elaborate further on in the chapter.

Satire and melodrama were, respectively, the modal choices of both writers of nineteenth-century trial literature and of the performers and participants in actual trials, and nowhere more so than in the trials of the radical journalists Thomas Wooler and William Hone in 1817.

James Epstein has written of political show trials in the nineteenth century that: 'In quite a fundamental sense, such trials were about the power of and over language, about who could say what to whom and under what conditions.'[26] Two such battles over 'who could say what to whom and under what conditions' were played out in 1817, when, firstly Thomas Wooler, the editor of the radical satirical weekly the *Black Dwarf*, and, after him, William Hone, radical journalist and pamphleteer, were tried respectively for seditious libel and for blasphemy. Both used the occasion of their trials to attack and ridicule the government and its trumped-up charges and both were acquitted by the special juries that tried them. In the course of their self-defence, the publications for which they were being tried were quoted from at great length, thereby thwarting the attempt to silence them. Both Wooler and Hone were well aware that they were participating in the production of a well-established literary form: there was a long-standing tradition of publishing key state trials, a long run of which, as I have already noted, Dickens would later own. Trial texts were also 'a popular form of political literature, published in newspapers and radical journals'.[27] Hone and Wooler would likewise have been conscious of their self-positioning within a tradition of mock trials, a literary form that had been established since the seventeenth century and reached a high water mark in Regency England.[28]

Following the suspension of habeas corpus by Lord Liverpool's administration in March 1817, Thomas Wooler was tried in June of that year for seditious libel on account of an article published in his radical weekly, the *Black Dwarf*. The offending article, 'Right of Petition', claimed that the people of England had no *de facto* right to petition, since the Prince Regent refused to receive their petitions. The prosecution's case was that in comparing the political position of the English people with that of 'the barbarians of the Mogul' Wooler's article was 'calculated to excite disturbances' amongst the populace.[29] Wooler mounted his own defence, thereby becoming a major actor in his own show trial. As part of the proceedings, Wooler's libellous essay was read out in court, the clerk broadcasting the very text that the prosecution was trying to put down. As the offending essay was read aloud, the court was interrupted by laughter from the public gallery:

The libel was then read; but the progress of the Clerk was frequently interrupted by the risibility of the audience below the bar: at one time the disturbance was so great, that it called for the interference of Mr. Justice Abbot.

Mr Justice ABBOTT – If any person presume again to disturb the Court by such indecent conduct, the officer must bring him forward, and he shall be punished.

Mr. ATTORNEY GENERAL – The Court must be cleared if silence be not preserved. – Courts of Justice ought to be open; but if people do not conduct themselves properly, the Court must be cleared for the due administration of public justice.[30]

The disruption of official, authoritative discourse by the laughter of the lower orders has a long history in radical culture, a history that would echo down the years in several of Dickens's novels, not least *The Pickwick Papers*, *Oliver Twist* and *Bleak House*.[31] Mikhail Bakhtin's now very familiar conception of the carnivalesque is pertinent to such a history. In his study of Rabelais and the emergence of festive, folk laughter in the official literature of the Renaissance, Bakhtin writes of medieval folk humour that:

It was marked by exceptional radicalism, freedom, and ruthlessness. Having on the one hand forbidden laughter in every official sphere of life and ideology, the Middle Ages . . . bestowed exceptional privileges of license and lawlessness outside these spheres: in the marketplace, on feast days, in festive recreational literature.[32]

It is when such festive laughter erupts in the official sphere, breaking down strictly erected boundaries between official and unofficial discourse, that a radical effect is produced. Bakhtin identifies the mock elections of popes and kings by the lower orders in the middle ages as an example of revolutionary culture, and in the context of nineteenth-century Russia he footnotes the socialist Alexander Herzen on the history of laughter:

It would be extremely interesting to write the history of laughter. In church, in the palace, on parade, facing the department head, the police officer, the German administrator, nobody laughs. The serfs are deprived of the right to smile in the presence of the landowners. *Only equals may laugh.* If inferiors are permitted to laugh in front of their superiors, and if they cannot suppress their hilarity, this would mean the farewell to respect. To make men smile at the god Apis is to deprive him of his sacred rank and to transform him into a common bull.[33]

It was one of the great, radical achievements of journalists such as Wooler and Hone in the Regency period, and of a novelist such as Dickens in the early and mid-Victorian years, that they were able, through the power of laughter, to transform official discourse and its representatives 'into a common bull'.

Six months after Wooler had been acquitted, William Hone found himself in London's Guildhall, before the same Justice Abbott, on a charge of seditious blasphemy. Arrested on 3 May 1817, Hone, unable to afford the bail payment of £1,000, spent time in prison with Wooler, whom he befriended; it was the success of Wooler's decision to defend himself that persuaded Hone to do the same.[34] Radical friends rallied round to help him: Major Cartwright helped research 'the mountain of references' used in his defence; George Cruikshank got together a list of caricatures in which Gillray had earlier parodied religious subjects in the service of political satire.[35] According to Robert Patten, Hone even rehearsed his defence in Cruikshank's studio.[36]

Hone was tried in December 1817 at London's Guildhall for writing and publishing three popular parodies: *The Late John Wilkes's Catechism of a Ministerial Member*, *The Sinecurist's Creed or Belief* and *The Political Litany*.[37] The three parodies were tried in succession before England's greatest judges: Justice Abbott presided over the first trial, and Lord Ellenborough over the second and third. All three juries found Hone not guilty. The actual trials were even more popular than the original trial parodies had been, with 20,000 people attending, spilling over into the halls and streets.[38] At each of the three trials the Attorney General found it necessary, in presenting the evidence against Hone, to read out extracts from the biblical parodies, and the result was that the court repeatedly erupted with mirth. In the second of the trials the Attorney General turned solemnly to the jury and read out, firstly, an extract from the Litany and, secondly, an extract from Hone's parody of it:

It was not necessary to remind the Jury that the Litany was a most solemn prayer to the Almighty, to the Redeemer of the world, and to the Holy Ghost ... 'Son of God, we beseech thee to hear us! Oh Lamb of God, that takest away the sins of the World, have mercy upon us!' He would not proceed; it seemed too solemn even for the solemnity of a court of justice; yet (would the Jury believe it?) the defendant had turned it into ridicule by making an impious parody of it. It began, 'O Prince,

Ruler of the people, have mercy upon us, miserable subjects. House of Lords, hereditary Legislators, have mercy upon us, pension-paying subjects. O House of Commons, proceeding from corrupt borough-managers, have mercy upon us, miserable subjects.' It was too disgusting to read the whole.

(These parts of the parody produced an involuntary burst of laughter from the auditory . . .)

Lord Ellenborough [the judge] – Where are the Sheriffs? I desired their attendance and they shall attend.

The Under-Sheriff. – My Lord, I have sent for them; but they live a great distance from this, and they have not yet arrived.[39]

In all three of Hone's trials the judge has to threaten the public gallery with arrest for contempt in an attempt to hold back the tide of carnivalesque laughter that undermines the dignity and self-importance of the legal process. When the spectators were not laughing, they were instead loudly applauding the defendant, in rude opposition to the prosecution case. On Hone's third acquittal a huge crowd threatened to overrun London's Guildhall, one of the supreme loci of state authority:

It appeared, that towards the close of the evening a prodigious crowd of persons, amounting to the number of not less than 20,000, had assembled in the Hall, and in the avenues leading thereto. Many of these persons were desirous of forcing their way into the Court, but their efforts were resisted.[40]

Hone's defence was based on his claim that his parodies attacked the government, and not the original biblical texts; he merely used the form of the Prayer Book to make political points.[41] The purpose of the parodies, then, was not to revile religion but to rebuke an oppressive government regime.[42]

Liverpool's government's mistake, in the case of Hone, was to try to fudge the real political motivation for his arrest by trying him for blasphemy rather than for sedition *tout court*. Hone's judicial triumph prompted celebrations in the streets; he was, for the moment, something of a folk hero. The trials themselves, which Hone published in full, became the early nineteenth-century equivalent of a best-seller: the first trial ran through twenty editions, the second eighteen and the third sixteen.[43] Once again, Hone had effectively combined a political stance with a successful commercial operation.

Still reflecting on Hone's trials in 1850, Harriet Martineau regarded them as 'amongst the most remarkable in our constitutional history', and claimed that 'They produced a more distinct effect upon the temper of the country than any public proceedings of that time.'[44] Wooler's more trenchant assessment, delivered in the manner of Pope, confirms the political power of laughter, reflecting that the government 'would render laughter high treason if possible':

> There is nothing more dangerous to folly, than the ridicule which it merits. It cannot bear the laughter which it is sure to excite. While it struts in the robe of office, it is unconscious of the ridiculous appearance which it offers to the crowd. It would render laughter high treason if possible; but it would have gained something if it could have obtained the verdict of a jury to establish that, to *laugh at*, was to *libel* them.[45]

DICKENS AND HONE: CARNIVAL IN THE COURTROOM

The carnivalesque disruption of the court and the legal process that Hone's trials occasioned is replayed twenty years later in *The Pickwick Papers*, a novel in which the eponymous hero is, like Hone and Wooler before him, tried in London's Guildhall. Undoubtedly benefiting aesthetically from the seditious laughter of Regency Radicals, Dickens elaborates with comic delight the trial of Mr Pickwick for a Breach of Promise. The radical journalist William Hone and the fictional Mr Pickwick are very different creatures of course: Hone was an historical figure, and a political victim, whilst Pickwick is a fictional victim of legal greed. In both Dickens's and Hone's trial parodies, though, what is being contested is, in Epstein's words, 'the power of and over language . . . who could say what to whom and under what conditions',[46] and to that extent both trials are political. Although sometimes dealing with political prisoners, as in the case of Charles Darnay, Dickens more often focused his attention on civilian victims of the law. In each case, though, the novelist stages a contest over language and power in his fictional trial scenes. Interestingly in this respect, it is worthy of note that Hone and Wooler were able to defend themselves and to articulate and publicise those very political beliefs whose utterance had led to their arrest. Writing in the immediate aftermath of the Prisoners' Counsel Act of 1836, though, Dickens has his hero subjected to its provisions: Mr Pickwick is not permitted to testify on his own behalf. Left to the inadequacies of Serjeant Snubbin, his rather hapless counsel, he has little chance of overcoming the legal machinations of Dodson and Fogg, the prosecuting lawyers.[47]

It is Sam Weller's carnivalesque disruption of the legal process that is central to, and the most memorable part of, the Bardell v. Pickwick trial at the heart of *The Pickwick Papers*.[48] From the start of this central chapter, Dickens lampoons the main legal players in the trial: Justice Stareleigh is caricatured as 'a most particularly short man, and so fat, that he seemed all face and waistcoat.'[49] As the interrogation of Sam proceeds, his playful responses lead to disorderly laughter amongst the spectators:

'Do you recollect anything particular happening on the morning when you were first engaged by the defendant, eh, Mr Weller?' said Serjeant Buzfuz.
'Yes, I do, Sir,' replied Sam.
'Have the goodness to tell the jury what it was.'
'I had a reg'lar new fit out o' clothes that morning gen'l'men of the jury,' said Sam, 'and that was a wery partickler and uncommon circumstance vith me in those days.'
Hereupon there was a general laugh; and the little Judge, looking with an angry countenance over his desk, said, 'You had better be careful, Sir.'
'So Mr Pickwick said at the time, my lord,' replied Sam; 'and I was wery careful o' that 'ere suit o' clothes; wery careful indeed, my lord.'
The Judge looked sternly at Sam for full two minutes, but Sam's features were so perfectly calm and serene that he said nothing, and motioned Serjeant Buzfuz to proceed. (*Pickwick*, pp. 463–4)

Refusing to recognise the prosecuting counsel's demand for evidence pertaining to the Breach of Promise suit, Sam's literal, digressive answers, at odds with the legalese of Buzfuz, insist on domestic detail as a riposte to the legal interrogation he faces. His direct, and (over-)familiar mode of address to the jury further disturbs the tenor of legal discourse that Buzfuz would prefer to maintain.

Sam is unperturbed by Buzfuz's increasingly bullying rhetorical questions as he attempts to lead Pickwick's manservant into compromising disclosures. Buzfuz hectoringly demands of Sam why, whilst standing in the passage, he did not see what was going on between Mr Pickwick and Mrs Bardell. Sam's riposte comically mirrors and hurls back at Serjeant Buzfuz the barrister's insolent interrogations:

'Now attend . . . You were in the passage, and yet saw nothing of what was going forward. Have you a pair of eyes?'
'Yes, I have a pair of eyes,' replied Sam, 'and that's just it. If they wos a pair o' patent double million magnifyin' gas microscopes of extra power, p'raps I might be able to see through a flight o' stairs and a deal door', but bein' only eyes, you see, my wisions's limited.'
. . . the spectators tittered, the little judge smiled, and Serjeant Buzfuz looked particularly foolish. (p. 464)

Bakhtin's definition of 'the laughter of the carnival' as bringing together 'the sacred with the profane, the lofty with the low, the great with the insignificant, the wise with the stupid' is as apposite in relation to Sam's performance in London's Guildhall as it is to the trials of William Hone.[50]

Such is the sharpness of Sam's wit, though, that who is 'wise' and who is 'stupid' is radically called into question.

A similar eruption of illegitimate laughter breaks out earlier in the novel when Mr Pickwick and Mr Tupman are before one Magistrate Nupkins, on this occasion having been arrested on suspicion of planning to fight a duel. It is once again Sam Weller's interventions that have the effect of ridiculing the legal process:

> 'What's your name, fellow?' thundered Mr Nupkins.
> 'Veller,' replied Sam.
> 'A very good name for the Newgate Calendar,' said Mr Nupkins.
> This was a joke; so Jinks, Grummer, Dibbley, all the specials, and Muzzle, went into fits of laughter of five minutes' duration.
> 'Put down his name, Mr Jinks,' said the magistrate.
> 'Two L's, old feller,' said Sam.
> Here an unfortunate special laughed again, whereupon the magistrate threatened to commit him, instantly. It's a dangerous thing laughing at the wrong man, in these cases.
> 'Where do you live?' said the magistrate.
> 'Vare-ever I can,' said Sam.
> 'Put that down, Mr Jinks,' said the magistrate, who was fast rising into a rage.
> 'Score it under,' said Sam. (p. 330)

Dickens's understanding of the politics of laughter resonates quite remarkably with Alexander Herzen's: the special constables can laugh at the magistrate's joke, but they can't laugh at *him*. The class relationship is such that laughter in the court is legitimate only when controlled and authorised by the magistrate: and his joke is of course extraordinarily un-funny (the reader having to be instructed by the narrator that it is indeed a joke). The spontaneous belly-laughter provoked by Sam's quick wit and lack of respect has to be instantly quelled lest it lead to a disordering and breakdown of the hierarchical relationship on which the court depends for its authority.

Inscribed within the tradition of trial parody, both Hone's and Pickwick's trials made a considerable impact on the contemporary legal process: Hone's humiliation of government meant that Liverpool's repressive administration suspended political trials for the whole of 1818; whilst the Bardell and Pickwick case was – perhaps rather surprisingly given its basis in fiction – a major legal touchstone in subsequent Breach of Promise suits across the nineteenth century.[51]

Resonances between the trials of Pickwick and Hone do not end with the actual three trials of William Hone in 1817. For as well as being the central performer in his own trials, Hone was well known as a writer of popular trial parodies. Whilst it is undoubtedly true that Dickens was partly inspired in his treatment of Bardell and Pickwick by the farcical proceedings of the Caroline Norton and Lord Melbourne adultery case of 1836, which I shall discuss further on in the chapter, it seems likely, too, that the longer tradition of mock trials, of which Hone was a major exponent, also shapes the legal scenes in this Dickens's first novel. One of William Hone's most popular and successful trial parodies was, like the Bardell v. Pickwick case, concerned with the perfidies of the marriage relationship. Hone's massively popular *Non Mi Ricordo! or, Cross-Examination Extraordinary*, a trial parody that ran to at least twenty-six editions in its first year, was written at the height of the Queen Caroline Affair.[52] Queen Caroline's trial for adultery in the House of Lords in 1820 anticipated the trial of Lord Melbourne for the same marital 'crime' sixteen years later (both were acquitted).[53] In 1820 George IV had refused to appear in court, and the response of pamphleteers such as Hone was themselves to put the King in the dock. In Hone's *Non Mi Ricordo*, a sixpenny pamphlet from 1820, the notoriously unreliable Italian prosecution witness, Signor Majocchi, who claimed to have knowledge of Caroline's love affairs, merges with the here ludicrous figure of King George. The witness in the trial parody is shifty and evidently dishonest, and altogether a figure of fun. In Hone's mock trial, the witness, like the Italian witness in the actual court case against Queen Caroline, answers 'Non mi ricordo!' ('I don't recollect') to any question that he would prefer not to answer. The witness's frequent and increasingly blustering repetition of the phrase leads to a comic revelation of truths that the King had rather kept secret:

> How many wives does *your* Church allow you?
> Non mi ricordo.
> How many have you had since you separated from your own?
> Non mi ricordo.
> Are you a member of the Society for the Suppression of Vice? Yes.
> *(with great energy)*
> The Cross-examining Counsel said that the Interpreter had materially altered the sense of the last question; he had in fact asked, if the Witness was a Member of the Society for the suppression of *Wives (a loud laugh)* which Witness had eagerly answered in the affirmative.[54]

The semantic obfuscations and the occlusion of truth in a court of law that Hone's and other mock trials of the Regency period attack are vividly rewritten in *The Pickwick Papers*. Serjeant Buzfuz, for the prosecution, skilfully deploys legal jargon to manoeuvre the unpractised Winkle into implicating Mr Pickwick with the lovelorn Mrs Bardell. In recounting the scene where he had come across Mrs Bardell swooning in Mr Pickwick's arms, poor Winkle recounts that: 'I heard him call Mrs Bardell a good creature, and I heard him ask her to compose herself, for what a situation it was, if any body should come, or words to that effect' (*Pickwick*, p. 460). Serjeant Buzfuz legalistically rescripts Winkle's testimony:

'Now Mr Winkle . . . Will you undertake to swear that Mr Pickwick, the defendant, did not say on the occasion in question, "My dear Mrs Bardell, you're a good creature; compose yourself to this situation, for to this situation you must come," or words to that effect?'

'I – I didn't understand him so, certainly,' said Mr Winkle, astounded at this ingenious dove tailing of the few words he had heard. (p. 460)

Hone's *Non Mi Ricordo!* also prefigures Dickens's trial set piece in its use of nicknames, a literary device favoured by both writers: Dickens's Buzfuz, Phunky, Dodson and Fogg are anticipated in Hone's legal parody by Twister, Lord Bathos, Lord Ratstail, the hungry Lord Le Cuisinier and sleazy Marquis Boudoir.

If there are echoes of Regency trial parodies in Bardell *versus* Pickwick, it also has a more contemporary purchase: Dickens was probably influenced by J. B. Buckstone's play *Second Thoughts*, which was first performed in London in 1832.[55] He would also have had fresh in his mind the ludicrous proceedings of the Norton v. Melbourne case that he had reported for the *Morning Chronicle* in June 1836.[56] Dickens's report on the trial covers thirty-five broadsheet columns, and its function as a piece of parliamentary reportage means that there is barely a trace of Dickens's satirical pen. There was, though, little need of it, since the evidence put forward by the prosecution counsel was so absurd that it needed no satirical elaboration to provoke laughter. Evidence of adultery between Caroline Norton and Lord Melbourne was so scanty that the prosecution had to resort to inferring intimacy from three short notes that the supposed lovers had exchanged. The content of the notes was so utterly mundane that the effect of reading them out in court was (unwittingly) comic. In the prosecution counsel's own words:

[The three notes] which have been found relate only to the hours of his coming, saying that he will be there at such and such an hour. There is nothing more in their contents, but there is something in their style which, trivial as they are, seems, in my mind at least, to lead to something like suspicion. Here is one – 'I will call about half past four. – Yours.' They do not commence, 'My dear Mrs Norton', or with any form which is usual with a gentleman writing to a lady. Here is another – 'How are you?' [a laugh] Not beginning like any other letter, 'I shall not be able to call to-day but probably shall tomorrow.' Surely this is not the note that would be written by a gentleman, ordinarily acquainted with a lady – nor this – 'No House to-day. I will call after the levee, about four or half-past; if you wish it later, let me know. I will then explain about going to Vauxhall.' The style and form of address of these notes, Gentlemen, seem to import much more than the words they contain.[57]

Clearly unconvinced, the gentlemen of the jury unanimously acquitted Lord Melbourne. Pickwick is less fortunate, even though the evidence mounted against him repeats in exaggerated form that which the young Dickens had had to listen to in Norton v. Melbourne. As part of the prosecution evidence, Buzfuz the serjeant-at-law produces two scrawled notes from Pickwick to Mrs Bardell: ' "Dear Mrs. B. – Chops and Tomata sauce. Yours, Pickwick" ' and: ' "Dear Mrs. B., I shall not be home till tomorrow, Slow coach." And then followed this very remarkable expression – "Don't trouble yourself about the warming pan" ' (*Pickwick*, p. 454). Both notes are interpreted by Buzfuz as a ' "covert, sly, underhanded" species of "substitute for some endearing word or promise. And what does this allusion to the slow coach mean? For ought I know, it may be a reference to Pickwick himself, who has most unquestionably been a criminally slow coach during the whole of this transaction" ' (pp. 454–5).

Both the Caroline Norton case and the fictional Breach of Promise suit have the potential for melodrama: Charles Norton attempted to remove his children from their mother – the very stuff of melodrama, echoing as it does Queen Caroline's removal from Princess Charlotte – and in the *Pickwick Papers* Buzfuz presents Mrs Bardell as a melodramatically deserted widow stranded alone in the world with her lone child. By and large, though, melodrama is eschewed in favour of satire in Dickens's first extended work of fiction, and especially in the trial scenes.[58]

The bathetic effect of the references to 'Chops and Tomata sauce' in Buzfuz's case against Pickwick resonates interestingly with an earlier trial parody by Thomas Wooler, in which some 'treasonable potatoes' are put on trial for attacking the Prince Regent's carriage in January 1817. In his parody, Wooler mimics the prosecuting counsel's case against a number of Radicals who had been in the vicinity of the Prince's carriage when it was struck. The logic of the prosecution case, as in the case of Bardell v. Pickwick twenty years later, is, it is suggested, absurd: 'In the emphatic language . . . of Mr Magistrate Hicks, – the POTATOES *speak for them-selves*. It is not the practice to pave streets with potatoes. *Ergo*, the potatoes must have been there with some treasonable design. They could have no lawful business outside the kitchen or the market place.'[59]

The Bardell v. Pickwick suit is arguably Dickens's most memorable comic engagement with trial literature. Significant too, though, are less central trial set pieces in *Oliver Twist*, *Bleak House* and *Great Expectations*, which similarly produce a satirical critique of the legal process. Towards the end of *Oliver Twist*, which Dickens began to write while he was still working on *The Pickwick Papers*, Charley Bates, Dawkins's fellow pick-pocket, sobs in grief when his friend is arrested. He is consoled, though, when Fagin reminds him of the Artful Dodger's final line of defence – he can disrupt the legal process through the power of laughter: 'and we'll have a big-wig, Charley, – one that's got the greatest gift of the gab, – to carry on his defence, and he shall make a speech for himself, too, if he likes, and we'll read it all in the papers – "Artful Dodger – shrieks of laughter – here the court was convulsed" – eh, Charley, eh?'[60] Charley is comforted by the thought of his friend taking centre stage in a courtroom, and cheerfully imagines 'All the big-wigs trying to look solemn, and Jack Dawkins addressing of 'em as intimate and comfortable as if he was the judge's own son, making a speech arter dinner – ha! ha! ha!' (*Oliver Twist*, p. 364). And Dawkins doesn't disappoint: assuming an air of self-importance as he is led into the court room, he:

with a show of being very particular with a view to proceedings to be had there-after, desired the jailer to communicate 'the names of them two old files as was on the bench,' which so tickled the spectators that they laughed almost as heartily as Master Bates could have done if he had heard the request.

'Silence there!' cried the jailer

'What is this?' inquired one of the magistrates.

'A pick-pocketing case, your worship.'

'Has the boy ever been here before?'

'He ought to have been a many times,' replied the jailer. '*I* know him well, your worship.'

'Oh! you know me, do you?' cried the Artful, making a note of the statement.

'Wery good. That's a case of deformation of character, any way.'

Here there was another laugh, and another cry of silence.

(*Oliver Twist*, pp. 367–8)

The unruly laughter doesn't prevent Jack from being convicted, but it does allow a certain defiance of the legislature that Dickens clearly shows, in *Oliver Twist*, to have failed in duty of care towards the children of the streets.

Even in *Bleak House*, in many respects a most sombre novel in which the paralysing (and paralysed) power of official legislature is shown to have a stranglehold on mid-century England, Dickens allows for the power of laughter to puncture authority. In this, Dickens's most substantial critique of law, there is a perhaps rather surprising absence of a trial set piece. The cursory inquest into Captain Hawdon's death, Gridley's sporadic and abortive appearances in Chancery and George Rouncewell's arrest on suspicion of the murder of Tulkinghorn, do not engage with the theatricalities of stage melodrama in the way that the trial of Jem Wilson in *Mary Barton*, or of Hetty Sorrell in *Adam Bede*, or indeed of Charles Darnay in *A Tale of Two Cities*, do. This is because Jarndyce v. Jarndyce specifically, and *Bleak House* more generally, is an extended satire on the legal process, which itself becomes a metaphor for a wider government bureaucracy that neglects to attend to the plight of the lost souls in Tom-All-Alones.

This extended satire is, though, telescoped down into a set-piece trial parody in the re-enactment, in the Sol's Arms, of both the inquest into Captain Hawdon's death and of the Smallweeds' personal 'inquest' into Krook's belongings after the shopkeeper's death. In his account of the inquest – or 'inkwhich', as Jo calls it – into Nemo's death, Dickens emphasises the reactions of the audience: this is inquest as spectacle. As Jo's evidence is summarily rejected, Dickens mimics the court reporter's shorthand: 'Boy put aside; to the great edification of the audience; – especially of Little Swills, the Comic Vocalist'.[61] The unconscious absurdities of the official inquest will be restaged as an explicitly comic spectacle that same evening, and in the same location – the legal inquest has been held in the Sol's Arms. 'Little Swills', the comic vocalist, will melodramatically re-enact the coroner's rejection of Jo and his evidence, with comic songs thrown in to keep his lower-class audience entertained. The official, legal inquest, and its parody in the evening, are linked not only by their taking place in the same location, but also by their sharing of the same audience: some of the jurors stay behind for the evening's entertainment. Momentarily, in this comic lampoon, Dickens allows the lower orders not to be cowed by a legal process and its parent legislature that ordinarily both oppresses and neglects them; for one night they are permitted to ridicule it, to subject it to subversive laughter.

The parodic re-enactment of Captain Hawdon's inquest in the Sol's Arms demonstrates Dickens's quite remarkable familiarity with popular metropolitan culture, based as it is on the activities of London's 'Judge and Jury clubs', a form of popular entertainment which reached its high watermark in the mid-nineteenth century. Judge and Jury Clubs were generally held in public houses, and comprised a burlesque court of law, presided over by a 'Lord Chief Baron'. The roles of counsel and witnesses were usually played by professional entertainers, whereas the jury was generally made up of amateurs. J. Ewing Ritchie's contemporary account of the clubs emphasised their lewdness and the 'low' nature of their proceedings:

A jury was selected; the prosecutor opened his case, which, to suit the depraved taste of his patrons, was invariably one of seduction or crim. con. Witnesses were examined and cross-examined, the females being men dressed up in women's clothes, and everything was done that could be to pander to the lowest propensities of depraved humanity.[62]

Ritchie is as much concerned, though, by the disrespectful stance of Judge and Jury clubs towards the legal process. His chapter on the clubs begins and ends with a protest at their undermining of the dignity of Law:

This is the comic age in which we live. We are overdone with funny writers. The ghastliest attempts at liveliness surround us on every side … For instance, is not law one of the most wonderful achievements of civilization? I do not go so far as 'the judicious Hooker'. I do not say with him that her seat is the throne of God, her voice the harmony of the universe, but is it not wonderful to think of the complex arrangements of which the judge, seated in his robes on the bench, administering law, is the outward sign? … The idea is good, and true, yet the burlesque is permitted, and exists, aye, even to this day.

It is years since I was at a Judge and Jury Club, but I believe their character is in no degree changed … and it is sad to think that, when the merriment is the loudest, and the drink is most stimulating, and the fellowship most jovial, there is burlesque even there.[63]

It is, then, the subversive humour of the Judge and Jury clubs, and their heedlessness of authority, that troubles this contemporary commentator as much as their alcohol-fuelled lewdness. Dickens, with his acute sense of the potential for popular culture to take on a subversive edge, emphasises in *Bleak House* the anti-authoritarian cultural timbre, and the challenge to official discourse, posed by the Judge and Jury clubs.

Legal laughter is not confined, in *Bleak House*, to the Sol's Arms. Whereas the lower orders get to laugh at the legal process in the Judge and Jury club, in Chancery it is the innocent victims of English law who provoke laughter. Dickens is, though, careful to distinguish between the lampooning laughter of the lower orders and the cynical mirth of lawyers. The reader is repeatedly told that the barristers in Chancery regard much of their work as free entertainment: both Gridley's case and that of the wards in Jarndyce v. Jarndyce are objects of fun amongst the legal profession. 'You're half the fun of the fair, in the Court of Chancery,' Inspector Bucket tells Gridley as he tries to cajole him back into life (*Bleak House*, p. 405); and when Jarndyce v. Jarndyce collapses under the weight of its own costs, the frequenters of Chancery 'came streaming out … [and] were all exceedingly amused, and were more like people coming out from a Farce or a Juggler than from a court of Justice' (pp. 973–4). A farce it may be, but by the novel's close the reader is in no doubt as to its tragic complexion.

Dickens's sense of the political purchase of the conflict between official and unofficial discourse emerges once again in a short but pivotal scene in *Great Expectations*. In this scene, the lawyer, Jaggers, is as irked as J. Ewing Ritchie by what he regards as a show of legal disrespect by the lower orders. In Joe Gargery's local, the Three Jolly Bargemen, Mr Wopsle, the as-yet amateur actor, melodramatically re-enacts a murder inquest, with Pip and Joe delightedly joining in:

There was a group assembled round the fire at the Three Jolly Bargemen. A highly popular murder had been committed, and Mr Wopsle was imbrued in blood to the eyebrows. He gloated over every abhorrent adjective in the description, and identified himself with every witness at the Inquest. He faintly moaned, 'I am done for,' as the victim and he barbarously bellowed, 'I'll serve you out,' as the murderer. He gave the medical testimony, in pointed imitation of our local practitioner; and he piped and shook, as the aged turnpike-keeper who had heard blows, to an extent so very paralytic as to suggest a doubt regarding the mental competency of the witness. The coroner, in Mr Wopsle's hands became Timon of Athens; the beadle, Coriolanus. He enjoyed himself thoroughly, and we all enjoyed ourselves, and were delightfully comfortable. In this cozy state of mind we came to the verdict Wilful Murder.[64]

This 'amusement of the people', to use Dickens's own phrase, is, though, quelled by the lawyer Jaggers, who objects to the irregularity of Wopsle's unofficial re-enactment of the inquest. Jaggers undercuts the mock heroics of Wopsle's hyperbolic theatre with a more systematic, official legal rhetoric, in an attempt to discipline the undisciplined proceedings of the Three Jolly Bargemen:

'Well!' said the stranger to Mr Wopsle, when the reading was done, 'you have settled it all to your own satisfaction, I have no doubt?'

Everybody started and looked up, as if it were the murderer. He looked at everybody coldly and sarcastically.

'Guilty, of course?' said he. 'Out with it! Come!'

'Sir,' returned Mr Wopsle, 'without having the honour of your acquaintance, I do say Guilty.' Upon this, we all took courage to unite in a confirmatory murmur.

'I know you do,' said the stranger; 'I knew you would. I told you so. But now I'll ask you a question. Do you know, or do you not know that the law of England supposes every man to be innocent, until he is proved – proved – to be guilty?'

'Sir,' Mr Wopsle began to reply, 'as an Englishman myself, I – '

'Come!' said the stranger, biting his forefinger at him. 'Don't evade the question. Either you know it, or you don't know it. Which is it to be?'

(*Great Expectations*, p. 166)

Dickens was infuriated by the interrogative skills of defence counsels such as Jaggers, objecting violently to their misuse – as he saw it – in the defence of notorious criminals. Twenty years before the fictional Jaggers's defence of Molly, his murderess housekeeper and mother of Estella, Dickens had expressed outraged disgust at Charles Philipps's defence of the murderer Francois Courvoisier in 1840.[65] In *A Tale of Two Cities*, though, published just one year before *Great Expectations*, one senses a grudging admiration for the otherwise dislikeable Mr Stryver, whose mastery of legalese matches that displayed by Jaggers.

FROM THE OLD BAILEY TO REVOLUTIONARY FRANCE: THE TRIALS OF CHARLES DARNAY

As if in compensation for the lack of a central set-piece courtroom scene in *Bleak House*, six years later Dickens incorporated four dramatic show trials into his novel based on the French Revolution, *A Tale of Two Cities*. Darnay is tried once in the Old Bailey as a spy, and three times before the French Revolutionary Tribunal as an aristocrat; these trials exploit the melodramatic potential of the trial scene to the full in this, the most inherently theatrical of all Dickens's novels. *A Tale of Two Cities*, an apotheosis of Dickens's embroilment with both theatre and law, deploys the ingredients of popular and radical culture to play off the loquaciousness and legalese of London's Old Bailey justice against the more cursory justice of the French Revolutionary Tribunal.

Although the novel has been read as an affirmation of English culture and justice against its French counterpart, I read it as a critique of contemporary British culture and legislature.[66] In the very first chapter Dickens reflects on the extent to which the years before the French Revolution were 'so far like the present period'.[67] Written two years after *Little Dorrit*, *A Tale of Two Cities* has a very similar political structure of feeling.

In the first trial of Charles Darnay, at the Old Bailey, the viciousness of the mob of spectators is barely distinguishable from the mob attending his subsequent trials before the revolutionary tribunal in France. Baying for blood, fickle and incontinent, the spectators in each case are concerned with spectacle and sensation rather than with justice. The English mob of 1780 is, as is ever the case in Dickens's historical novels, very much a reflection on the volatility of contemporary British culture: Dickens never regarded the 1850s with the equanimity of subsequent historians. Following Carlyle, he explicitly posits the 'The Terror' in France to be a direct consequence of poverty and oppression; and, as with his other novels from the 1850s, his feeling is that British culture could produce its own Terror if the sufferings of the poor remained unaddressed.

Charles Darnay's trial at the Old Bailey on suspicion of being a spy in the pay of the French King is presented as a commercial theatrical event rather than as a process focused on the dispensation of justice: 'For people then paid to see the play at the old Bailey just as they paid to see the play in Bedlam – only the former entertainment was much dearer,' he tells us (*Two Cities*, p. 63). The ironic, alliterative juxtaposition of Bailey and Bedlam economically discloses to the reader the narrator's stance towards the former. Dickens reveals his knowledge of the spate of late eighteenth- and early nineteenth-century treason trials in an ironically phrased exchange between Mr Lorry's messenger, Jerry Cruncher, and one of the spectators at the trial. The latter reflects on the probable fate of Charles Darnay:

' . . . and then his head will be chopped off, and he'll be cut into quarters. That's the sentence.'

'If he's found Guilty, you mean to say?' Jerry added, by way of proviso. 'Oh, they'll find him Guilty,' said the other. 'Don't you be afraid of that.'

(*Two Cities*, p. 64)

As well as pre-figuring the death sentence that will later be meted out to Darnay by the French Revolutionary Tribunal, this brief exchange confirms the more likely fate of a Charles Darnay in the Old Bailey in the late eighteenth century: as Victor Gatrell has reflected, 'Old Bailey Trials [at this period] were usually conducted at breakneck pace . . . and prejudice against the prisoner usually ruled.'[68] Dickens's original for Darnay, one Francis De la Motte, a French baron resident in England, was found guilty of espionage in 1781, and was sentenced largely on the evidence of a spy. As Andrew Sanders has noted, Dickens would have read about this case in the *Annual Register* for 1781, in which it was reported; and the text of Dickens's novel certainly reads as a lampooning imitation of the De la Motte trial. De la Motte was hanged; but Dickens spares Charles Darnay the usual kind of Old Bailey justice in order to preserve him for the summary justice of the Terror, at the novel's close.

Dickens had extensive experience as a professional reporter of legal speeches, and this partly accounts for his extraordinary alertness, in all his novels, to the lexicon and grammatical trickery of legal rhetoric. In the Old Bailey trial scene, Dickens achieves a satirical effect through a startling deployment of the techniques of indirect speech.[69] The reported speech of the opening indictment's unabashed pre-judgment of Darnay is lent pace and drama through its compression of the opening charge:

Silence in the court! Charles Darnay had yesterday pleaded Not Guilty to an indictment denouncing him (with infinite jingle and jangle) for that he was a false traitor to our serene, illustrious, excellent, and so forth, prince, our Lord the King, by reason of his having, on divers occasions, and by divers means and ways, assisted Lewis, the French King, in his wars against our said serene, illustrious, excellent, and so forth . . . (*Two Cities*, p. 65)

The elliptical 'jingle and jangle', as suspect here as Mr Jingle's excess of speech in *The Pickwick Papers*, and the repetition of greasily hyperbolic patriotic sentiments, combine to deflate the prosecution's case even as the prosecution itself attempts to puff it up. The text of the novel deftly slips between reported speech and narratorial intervention as it moves from the economical 'jingle and jangle' of authorial condemnation to the 'serene, illustrious, excellent' overstatement of the prosecution counsel. Dickens's lampooning of the original transcript of the trial is a tour de force of satirical concision: the initial indictment statement in the transcript of the trial runs to approximately 6,000 words; Dickens makes do with 133.[70]

Darnay is saved from death in the Old Bailey by the terse interventions of Stryver, his defence counsel, whose rapidly paced interrogation of Roger Cly, the prosecution witness, is a masterpiece of satirical economy:

Never been in a debtors' prison? – Come, once again. Never? Yes. How many times? Two or three times. Not five or six? Perhaps. Of what profession? Gentleman. Ever been kicked? Might have been. Frequently? No. Ever been kicked downstairs? Decidedly not; once received a kick on the top of a staircase and fell down stairs of his own accord . . . Expect to get anything by this evidence? No. Not in regular government pay and employment, to lay traps? Oh dear no. Or to do anything? Oh dear no. Swear that? Over and over again . . .

The virtuous servant, Roger Cly, swore his way through the case at a great rate . . . He had never been suspected of stealing a silver teapot, he had been maligned respecting a mustard pot, but it turned out only to be a plated one. He had known the last eyewitness seven or eight years; that was merely a coincidence.

(*Two Cities*, pp. 70–1)

In the first paragraph, a form of free indirect discourse evolves as the narrative shifts between reported speech and narratorial intervention. Cly's monsyllabic negatives are interrupted by the narrator's satirically inflected declarations of the witness's virtue: the repeated phrase, 'Oh dear no' towards the end of the first paragraph moves the passage away from reported speech towards an ironically implied authorial condemnation of the spy. Likewise, in the phrase 'Over and over again' we have the narrator ironically commenting on the quality of the witness's evidence, once again in a shift away from the mode of reported speech which generally characterises the interrogation.

In the second paragraph, Roger Cly's admissions are brought into sharp focus by their 'seeming to be reported without the questions that led to them'.[71] That they almost seem like voluntary statements ('He had never been suspected of stealing a silver teapot') increases their satirical effect.

Satire cedes to unadorned melodrama in Darnay's trials before the French Revolutionary Tribunal. Brutally stripped of legal rhetoric, and summarily sentencing Darnay to death, French justice, instead of being burdened by a self-serving legal discourse, has no settled legal lexicon at all. Dickens is far from happy about this: he never had any problem with law *per se*, but, rather, with what he regarded as a cumbrous, and often dishonest English legal process. His admiration for the newly evolving police force as a mechanism of law enforcement is evident in his *Household Words* essay from 1850, 'A Detective Police Party'.[72] Well known too are the rather curious incidences when Dickens himself tried to enforce the law. On one occasion he was seen helping a policeman arrest a tramp in St James's Park; on another occasion he threatened to take legal action against a baker's man seen relieving himself outside the gates of Tavistock House.[73]

What concerns Dickens about French Revolutionary justice is partly its fickle arbitrariness: whilst initially Darnay is tried as a returning émigré (a new law is introduced to outlaw this even as he leaves England), in the second French trial he is tried as an aristocrat, and in the final French trial he is convicted on the basis of a denunciation by Dr Manette.[74] In the French trial scenes in *A Tale of Two Cities* there is no emotional or aesthetic space for the nuances of satire that we find in London's Old Bailey scene: good versus evil, right versus wrong – melodrama is itself here stripped bare. The reason for this is that whereas satire, with its desire to correct wrongs through ridicule, can be effective in a context of the rule of law, in the lawless realm of the Terror it is ineffective as a political aesthetic. Dickens has recourse instead to a melodramatic expression of horror at the summary justice of the Revolutionary Tribunal, and to the melo-dramatic device of the swapping of identities to effect Darnay's escape. The reported speech is curt, bald and uninflected:

Charles Évremonde, called Darnay. Released yesterday. Re-accused and re-taken yesterday. Indictment delivered to him last night. Suspected and denounced enemy of the Republic, Aristocrat, one of a family of tyrants, one of a race proscribed, for that they had used their abolished privileges to the infamous oppression of the people. (*Two Cities*, p. 328)

The legal lexicon here is as summary as the injustice that it metes out. Although the bloodthirsty spectators in the French trial have their counterparts in the Old Bailey, the French jury is an altogether more daunting prospect than its English equivalent – one of its members is described as a 'craving man' who 'rubbed his hands together' with glee as Darnay is denounced.

Dr Manette's written testimony concerning the events that led to his own imprisonment in the Bastille tells a melodramatic tale of a peasant girl raped by the evil lords of the manor. The melodrama is heightened as Manette's daughter faints away. Her physical collapse interestingly replicates the conduct of many convicted women prisoners, whose demeanour when their sentences were read out was a major preoccupation of nineteenth-century broadside literature. The transference of this device to a beautiful and innocent victim who is mourning the imminent death of her husband increases its melodramatic effect still further.

A Tale of Two Cities is full of melodramatic devices, and not least of these is Dr Manette's forced testimony against his son-in-law, a testimony that has been written in his own blood whilst incarcerated in the Bastille. Here Dickens seems to draw, consciously or unconsciously, on the political and aesthetic testimony of the Chartist Ernest Jones, whose claim that he wrote poetry using his own blood as ink while a political prisoner between 1848 and 1850 was widely circulated in the radical press of the early 1850s.[75] He is also very likely drawing on Alexander Dumas's novel from 1844–5, *Le Comte de Monte Cristo*, which he knew and had written about.[76] Jones too may have been borrowing from Dumas in his melodramatic self-presentation as a victimised political prisoner. Dickens was not an apologist for Ernest Jones, whom he associated with Physical Force Chartism, and dismissed in his 1854 essay 'On Strike'. Characteristically, though, the novelist was greatly concerned by the legal procedure used to sentence the Chartists in 1848, Jones amongst them. In an essay written for the *Examiner* in 1848 Dickens defended them against the lack of impartiality in various judges' directions to juries in Chartist trials.[77]

The close of the novel, with Carton's martyrdom, provides the denouement denied to the crowd at the Old Bailey. In the earlier trial scene, Dickens describes the frustration of the mob when they are denied the execution and last dying words that broadside culture as well as Old Bailey justice had led them to expect: 'the crowd came pouring out with a vehemence that nearly took [Jerry Cruncher] off his legs, and a loud buzz swept into the street as if the baffled blue-flies were dispersing in search of other carrion' (*Two Cities*, p. 82). The French Revolutionary mob are not so denied: not only do they get the blood that they crave, Dickens also gives an account of Carton's demeanour as he is led to the scaffold – another device taken from broadside culture. And he even writes Carton a last dying speech by proxy, in which the self-sacrificing hero is said to imagine a reconstitution of the domestic sanctuary that Revolutionary justice has threatened to destroy.

Never politically systematic in a thoroughgoing way, Dickens's critique of law is not politically aligned here or in any other of his novels. But drawing, in his critique, upon the aesthetic modes of both popular and radical culture – melodrama and satire – he was able to address 'the People' in the widest sense. Marc Baer has commented that satirical excess, on the one hand, and melodramatic theatrical hyperbole, on the other, were both politically very effective in the first half of the nineteenth century. This is because both satire and melodrama drew on an aesthetic grammar that was comprehensible both to elite and to non-elite classes.[78] Like William Hone before him, Dickens was able to cross the boundaries between 'high' and 'low' culture, one effect of which was to produce a truly democratic as well as a politically alert literature.

CHAPTER 3

Dickens, popular culture and popular politics in the 1830s: Oliver Twist

OLIVER TWIST'S POPULAR ANTECEDENTS

One year after the publication of *Oliver Twist* in 1839, William Makepeace Thackeray castigated Dickens for his presentation of its criminal elements. Thackeray's view was that Dickens's novel romanticised and popularised crime:

> The power of the writer is so amazing, that the reader at once becomes his captive, and must follow him whithersoever he leads; and to what are we led? Breathless to watch all the crimes of Fagin, tenderly to deplore the errors of Nancy, to have for Bill Sikes a kind of pity and admiration, and an absolute love for the society of the Dodger. All these heroes stepped from the novel onto the stage; and the whole London public, from peers to chimney-sweeps, were interested about a set of ruffians whose occupations are thievery, murder and prostitution. A most agreeable set of rascals, indeed, who have their virtues, too, but not good company for any man . . .
>
> And what came of *Oliver Twist*? The public wanted something more extravagant still, more sympathy for thieves, and so *Jack Sheppard* makes his appearance. Jack and his two wives, and his faithful Blueskin, and his gin-drinking mother, that sweet Magdalen![1]

Thackeray was quite right about the popular power of *Oliver Twist*: the novel was widely adapted for the stage in numerous versions from the 1830s onwards. The first such adaptation, by Gilbert À Beckett, got its one and only performance in the St James's Theatre on 27 March 1838, when the novel was only half-way through its two-year serialisation in *Bentley's Miscellany*.[2] Five further theatrical adaptations were staged before the novel was finished.[3] Highly successful cheap plagiarisms also began to appear before Dickens had finished work on the original, including the *Life and History of Oliver Twiss, Edited by 'Bos'* (Thomas Peckett Prest), and *Oliver Twiss, The Workhouse Boy, Edited by Poz* (Gilbert À Beckett).[4] In its own right the serialisation of *Oliver Twist* and its subsequent publication in volume form was a huge success, greatly enhancing the popularity of the

65

miscellany in which it appeared.[5] The plentiful adaptations and wide circulation meant that the novel reached all social groups in one form or another, and in that respect it was truly popular.

Thackeray was wrong, though, that *Oliver Twist* was responsible for the public's enthusiasm for crime and criminals in the literary field: there had long been a popular demand for crime narratives, as has been detailed in chapter 2, and in *Oliver Twist* Dickens was characteristically responding to, as well as magnificently reshaping, existing popular crime narratives. Juliet John has written importantly about *Oliver Twist*'s relationship to the so-called Newgate novel and to the *Newgate Calendar* (a popular collection of criminal biographies).[6] The novel has significant antecedents in the crime narratives of street literature, and its relationship to one particular such narrative is the focus of the first part of this chapter.

William Hone, the small-time publisher and pamphleteer whose radical journalism has so far been a focus of attention in this study, was by no means averse to producing unabashedly popular, 'catchpenny'-type publications as a means of staying afloat financially. One of the most memorable of these is his *The Power of Conscience Exemplified in the Genuine and Extraordinary Confession of Thomas Bedworth*, an eighteen-page sixpenny pamphlet from 1815 that sensationally describes the savage murder of one Elizabeth Beesmore at the hands of her tormented, jealous lover, Thomas Bedworth.[7] There is a striking resonance between the frenzied knife attack at the centre of Hone's 1815 pamphlet and Dickens's mesmerising account of Sikes's murder of Nancy in *Oliver Twist* more than two decades later. The two texts have a number of affinities, not least the sexualised nuances of the murders. Hone's Bedworth, suspecting his lover of sexual betrayal, stabs her to death in an uncontrolled alcoholic rage. He then, like Dickens's Sikes, takes flight, full of guilt and despair, fleeing to St Albans and then Coventry before returning to London to be hanged. In the account of Bedworth's capture and hanging, Hone characteristically (and like Dickens) emphasises the banal inefficacy of the forces of law and order.

It is not known whether Dickens was familiar with Hone's melodramatic *Confession of Thomas Bedworth*, but it is significant that by 1815 George Cruikshank – the artist who would work in partnership with Dickens on *Oliver Twist* – was already firm friends and close collaborator with William Hone. Cruikshank drew and etched a folding frontispiece for Hone's *Confession*, an illustration that, tellingly, details 'The Horrid Murder of Elizabeth Beesmore'.[8] It is well known that after Dickens's death Cruikshank would claim that the conception of *Oliver Twist* had originally been his own.[9] Blanchard Jerrold seems to support this claim in his *Life of Gustave Doré* when he describes how Cruikshank's family had subsequently recalled that:

Dickens, calling one day in Armwell Street, saw a series of illustrations which Cruikshank had prepared for a story he had in his mind of the life of a thief. Dickens was so struck with them, and with the artist's account of his plan, that he determined to make London the scene of Oliver Twist's adventures. Those drawings ... had been lying about the studio for 17 years; initially sketched in 1819, they had been shown to Egan in the mid twenties and then thrust aside. With *Pickwick* reviving the novel about life in London, and [Ainsworth's] *Rookwood* popularizing novels about criminals, the time seemed right to both George Cruikshank and Charles Dickens for a contemporary novel about London's thieves.[10]

Produced in 1819, the drawings that Jerrold refers to are nearly contemporaneous to the ones that Cruikshank etched for Hone's *Confession of Thomas Bedworth*, and it seems reasonable to speculate on the extent of the illustrator's influence not only on the evolution of *Oliver Twist* but on the murder of Nancy, too. Henry James, for one, saw Cruikshank's influence powerfully at work in the novel: '[*Oliver Twist*] perhaps even seemed to me more Cruikshank's than Dickens's; it was a thing of such vividly terrible images'.[11] An earlier reviewer had also detected the hand of George Cruikshank in Dickens's novel:

It is hardly fair to conclude an article, however brief and desultory, upon *Oliver Twist*, without making some allusion to the obligations under which author and reader are laid by the graphic running commentary of Mr Cruikshank's etchings. This, we suspect, may be as great an artist in his own way as Boz himself – and it is difficult to say, on laying down the book, how much of the powerful impression we are conscious of may be due, not to the pen, but to the pencil.[12]

Tantalisingly, of course, there is no illustration of the murder of Nancy, and one can only speculate as to the extent of the influence of Cruikshank's work with William Hone on *The Confession of Thomas Bedworth* on this early Victorian novel. Much more concretely, though, one can trace certain striking textual similarities between Dickens's novel and Hone's pamphlet.

Hone's description of the circumstances of Thomas Bedworth's murder of his mistress are tawdry compared to the highly charged, morally complex level of betrayal that leads to Sikes's murderous rage in *Oliver Twist*. Bedworth's wife has bigamously married someone else while he has been away at sea, so he turns instead to his wife's sister (Elizabeth Beesmore), who herself has been abandoned by her husband. Her husband returns, and Beesmore's sexual taunts about a possible reunion eventually provoke the brutal murder. Although Bedworth's confessional narrative is cheap compared to the fraught plotline surrounding Nancy's death, the sexualised nature of both murders none the less links them. This is the murder scene from Hone's pamphlet:

descending the stairs, he told her he wished to speak with her in the kitchen. – She replied, she must first put on his handkerchief, which, having done, they retired to the kitchen. Each remained for a moment in mute anxiety. – The unhappy woman, however, broke the pause, by clasping her right arm round his neck and embracing him, at the same time saying, with much agitation, 'Oh my dear Bedworth!' These were her last words, uttered in the last minute of her life. She kissed him during his conflict between jealous passion and strong affection: his injured regard and her perfidy rushed upon his mind; her deceptive embrace maddened him: whilst her kiss was warm upon his cheek, he suddenly drew the knife from his right hand pocket, and, as he supported her head with his left arm, he, by one rapid and determined cut on her throat nearly severed her head from her body! . . . He put the bloody knife in his pocket, whilst he looked at the blood rushing from her throat, and quitted the house.[13]

Nancy similarly makes a (more implicit) sexual appeal to Sikes immediately before her murder. She is described as 'lying half dressed' upon her bed when Sikes enters their room in Spitalfields, and she gives out an 'expression of pleasure at his return' as she raises herself up in bed to greet him (*Oliver Twist*, p. 395). Like Elizabeth Beesmore, Nancy is clasping her lover in her arms when he murders her, and both accounts give detailed descriptions of the attack:

The man struggled violently to release his arms, but those of the girl were clasped round his, and, tear as he would, he could not tear them away.
   'Bill,' cried the girl, striving to lay her head upon his breast . . . 'It is never too late to repent. They told me so – I feel it now – but we must have time – a little, little time!'
   The housebreaker freed one arm, and grasped his pistol . . . he beat it twice with all the force he could summon, upon the upturned face that nearly touched his own.
   She staggered and fell, nearly blinded with the blood that rained down from a deep gash in her forehead, but raising herself with difficulty on her knees, drew from her bosom a white handkerchief – Rose Maylie's own – and holding it up in her folded hands as high towards Heaven as her feeble strength would let her, breathed one prayer for mercy to her Maker.
   It was a ghastly figure to look upon. The murderer staggering backward to the wall, and shutting out the sight with his hand, seized a heavy club and struck her down. (pp. 396–7)

In many ways, of course, the affinities between the two texts serve to highlight important differences. Hone's is essentially the work of a hack writer, whilst Dickens's text is written by one who would come to be regarded as the greatest novelist in the country. Hone's pamphlet is morally crude, with Bedworth presented throughout as a repentant sinner who had been goaded to murder; Beesmore, as well as Bedworth's erring wife, is morally culpable. Dickens by contrast presents Nancy as a victim, Sikes morally unable to absorb that she has in fact shielded him from the law. Whilst Beesmore is an 'unhappy woman' with a 'deceptive embrace', Nancy is described throughout as 'the girl', and Sikes as 'the man', 'the housebreaker' and finally 'the murderer', thereby accentuating Nancy's vulnerability. Nancy's positioning as a melodramatic victim is confirmed by her importunate prayer as she dies clutching Rose Maylie's handkerchief; but more powerful is the bloody realism of the scene.

The differences aside, both Hone's pamphlet and Dickens's novel seem to draw on the raw material of street literature in the two murder scenes: a huge number of broadsides in the first half of the nineteenth century detailed the trial and sentencing of lovers or husbands who had killed their sweethearts or wives through sexual jealousy; witness statements in such broadsides always give detailed and often sensational accounts of the act of murder. These and other trials published as Broadsides had such a common cultural currency in both the early and mid-nineteenth century that both Hone and Dickens would have been aware of them.[14] Dickens's transformation of this raw material of popular culture is, though, characteristically remarkable. Hone's moral schema – whereby a sexually sinning woman is murdered by a jealous, morally wounded lover – is highly conventional; Dickens's negotiation of the same well-worn moral trope is anything but. For not only does he present the young girl as a victim, that girl is not an errant wife but a prostitute: the courage of Dickens's presentation of Nancy cannot be overstated. Christopher Herbert, writing about Mayhew's articles for the *Morning Chronicle*, has reflected that in the early and mid-Victorian periods 'much effort was invested by the upper classes, as Mayhew, Engels, Dickens and others testify, in engineering a way of life that would prevent the poor from ever crossing their field of vision'. Herbert argues that by determinedly looking at the poor, and insisting on their introduction into the 'field of vision' of all classes, Mayhew (and I would add Dickens) makes an 'heroic effort' on behalf of 'a distinct political agenda'.[15] It was an agenda that met with resistance. Lord Melbourne, Prime Minister when *Oliver Twist* was published, famously declared that 'It's all among Workhouses, and Coffin Makers, and Pickpockets . . . I don't *like* those things; I wish to avoid them; I don't like them in *reality*, and therefore I don't wish them represented.'[16] Melbourne was one of those who attempted to remove the poor from his 'field of vision'; Dickens's insistence on not only representing a prostitute, but on representing her sympathetically, is a radical cultural act of some significance.

The murders aside, there are many other, arguably more distinctive similarities between *The Confession of Thomas Bedworth* and Sikes's murder of Nancy. Full details of the disposal of the murder weapon are given in each case, and both murderers carefully dispose of bloodied clothing. The most striking similarity between the two texts is the account of each man's flight, his guilt and the apparitions of the murdered women. Both Hone and Dickens give a detailed topographical account of the murderers' flight across London, and both culprits leave and return to London several times, guiltily drawn back to the scenes of their respective crimes. Part of Hone's account reads as follows:

Bedworth's first steps of flight were directed into Spa Fields, where he remained until dark, and then returned into town. – Passing over London Bridge . . . He then wandered through the Borough, and over Blackfriars Bridge, and afterwards over Westminster Bridge, and thus roving about, he, by daylight, the following morning reached Regent's Park, where he threw the knife into the Canal. From the Regent's Park he pursued his way to Hampstead, where he passed the whole of that day about the fields, and where he also determined to pass the night . . .

Early on the following morning he pursued his route towards St Albans . . . At night he once more fled, for a hiding and resting place, to the fields . . . Unable to rest, he arose from the earth, left the sheep-pen, and walked towards Islington . . . and once more returned to London . . . (*Confession of Thomas Bedworth*, pp. 9–10)

Sikes's flight and wanderings are similarly meandering and troubled:

He went through Islington; strode up the hill at Highgate, on which stands the stone in honour of Whittington; turned down to Highgate Hill, unsteady of purpose, and uncertain where to go; struck off to the right again almost as soon as he began to descend it, and taking the foot-path across the fields, skirted Caen Wood, and so came out on Hampstead Heath. Traversing the hollow by the Vale of Health, he mounted the opposite bank, and crossing the road which joins the villages of Hampstead and Highgate, made along the remaining portion of the heath to the fields at North End, in one of which he laid himself under a hedge and slept . . .

He wandered over miles of ground, and still came back to the old place; morning and noon had passed, and the day was on the wane, and still he rambled to and fro, and up and down, and round and round, and still lingered about the same spot. At last he got away, and shaped his course for Hatfield.

(*Oliver Twist*, pp. 398–9)

Again, Dickens's account is more nuanced – the grim irony of the references to 'Dick Whittington' and the 'Vale of Health' is not lost on the reader – but the similarities are quite arresting, with both men ending up in St Albans at one stage in their respective journeys. And both men, as they wander, are full of guilt and struck with terror by the apparitions of the women they have murdered. Bedworth:

No new scene . . . or course which he pursued, could lighten the load of his crime, or chase away the guilty horrors which pursued him. On this night, while walking up Highgate Hill, the murdered woman again stood before him! Imagination may paint, if it can, the horrible feelings of Bedworth at this moment. She walked with him, side by side, until they reached the other side of the hill, and then taking the hand of the miserable man, placed it upon her severed throat, and groaned and moaned deeply! – Driven to despair, he fled into a field, where he threw himself down upon his face on some hay, hoping to elude at least the sight of his ghostly pursuer. (*Confession of Thomas Bedworth*, pp. 10–11)

Sikes:

Every object before him, substance or shadow, still or moving, took the semblance of some fearful thing; but these fears were nothing, compared to the sense that haunted him of that morning's ghastly figure following at his heels. He could trace its shadow in the gloom, supply the smallest item of its outline, and note how stiff and solemn it seemed to stalk along. He could hear its garments rustling in the leaves, and every breath of wind came laden with that last low cry . . .

At times he turned with desperate determination, resolved to beat this phantom off, though it should look him dead; but the hair rose from his head, and his blood stood still; for it had turned with him, and was behind him then . . .

[And] now a vision came before him, as constant and more terrible than that from which he had escaped. Those widely-staring eyes, so lustreless and so glassy, that he had better borne to see than think upon, appeared in the midst of the darkness; light in themselves, but giving light to nothing. There were but two, but they were everywhere. (*Oliver Twist*, pp. 402–3)

Dickens's rendering is much more powerful: whilst Hone's apparition is rather clumsily embodied, Dickens's merges menacingly with the wind and the leaves, and Nancy's glassy dead eyes synechdochally reprise the murder scene to chilling effect. All the same, the resonance between the two texts is remarkable. And Dickens's description of Sikes's hair as it 'rose from his head' in his full state of horror, as his blood 'stood still', vividly recalls Cruikshank's etching for the front cover of Hone's *Confession of Thomas Bedworth*: figure 10 could just as readily be a representation of Sikes as he is terrorised by the reproach of Nancy's unseeing eyes as of Hone's similarly haunted Thomas Bedworth.

Sikes's demise is much more sensational, and determinedly less conventionally moralistic, than Bedworth's: whilst the latter fully repents and

THE
POWER OF CONSCIENCE
EXEMPLIFIED IN THE GENUINE AND EXTRAORDINARY
CONFESSION
OF THOMAS BEDWORTH;
DELIVERED TO ONE OF THE PRINCIPAL OFFICERS OF NEWGATE, THE
NIGHT BEFORE HIS EXECUTION, ON SEPTEMBER 18, 1815, FOR THE
𝔐urder
OF ELIZABETH BEESMORE,
IN DRURY LANE.

RELATING HIS HORRIBLE SUFFERINGS
UNTIL COMPELLED TO SURRENDER TO PUBLIC JUSTICE BY THE CONSTAN
SUPERNATURAL VISITATIONS
OF THE MURDERED WOMAN, AND THE FREQUENT APPEARANCE OF HER
APPARITION.

FROM THE ORIGINAL PAPER,
NOW IN THE POSSESSION OF THE PUBLISHER.

Including interesting Particulars of BEDWORTH's former Life, his
behaviour before Execution, and *an original and full* Report of the
Common Serjeant's Address on passing Sentence.

LONDON:
PRINTED FOR Wm. HONE, 55, FLEET STREET.
By J. Swan, 76. Fleet Street.
PRICE SIXPENCE.
1815.

Figure 10 George Cruikshank, front cover illustration to William Hone, *The Power of Conscience*.

tamely turns himself in, confessing all, Sikes's dramatic last-ditch attempt to escape with his life founders on the ghastly reproach of Nancy's dead gaze and on his own ensuing psychological trauma. As he attempts to escape across the rooftops, Sikes attaches some rope to his body:

At the very instant that he brought the loop over his head, previous to slipping it beneath his arm-pits . . . at that very instant the murderer, looking behind him on the roof, threw his arms above his head and uttered a yell of terror.

'The eyes again!' he cried in an unearthly screech. Staggering as if struck by lightning, he lost his balance and tumbled over the parapet; the noose was at his neck; it ran up with his weight tight as a bow-string, and swift as the arrow it speeds. He fell for five-and-thirty feet. There was a sudden jerk, a terrific convulsion of the limbs, and there he hung, with the open knife clenched in his stiffening hand. (*Oliver Twist*, pp. 426–8)

Economically circumventing the paraphernalia of popular culture – the confession, the trial and sentencing, the dying last words – Dickens cuts straight to the execution, bringing retribution upon Sikes without the need of the lumbering mechanisms of law and order: the account of the flight, guilt and death of the murderer is all the more powerful for its relative economy.

It is well known that Dickens's public performances of his *Sikes and Nancy* reading were electrifying. Adding this reading to his repertoire in 1868, when planning his farewell tour, he thereby increased the popularity of this early novel still further. 'Never, probably, through the force of mere reading was a vast concourse of people held so completely within the grasp of one man,' *The Times* reported on 8 January 1869, following the first public performance.[17] Edmund Yates, his young colleague, described the performance thus:

gradually warming with excitement, he flung aside his book and acted the scene of the murder, shrieked the terrified pleadings of the girl, growled the brutal savagery of the murderer, brought looks, tones, gestures simultaneously into play to illustrate his meaning, there was not one, not even of those who had known him best or who believed in him most, but was astonished at the power and versatility of his genius.[18]

Clearly, then, Sikes's murder of Nancy remained central to Dickens's cultural imagination long after the novel's first publication.

There are needless to say many other popular sources for *Oliver Twist* beyond Hone's pamphlet. Its subtitle – *A Parish Boy's Progress* – suggests a debt to Hogarth's series of engravings, *The Harlot's Progress* and *The Rake's Progress*, which Dickens knew well.[19] The first novel to sustain a focus on a child-hero, *Oliver Twist* also draws in part on 'true-life' orphan tales that were popular in the period.[20] And as Lyn Pykett puts it: 'Like so many English novels of the eighteenth and nineteenth centuries, *Oliver Twist* is a romance about an orphan of mysterious parentage.'[21] Dickens's near-obsessive theatre attendance in the 1830s made it inevitable that he would also draw on the dramatic offerings of London's theatre land. Richard Brinsley Peake's melodrama from 1832, *The Climbing Boy; or, The Little Sweep*, would seem to be one such source, and resonates not only with *Oliver Twist* but also, to a lesser extent, with *The Pickwick Papers*.[22] The little sweep of Brinsley's title is a young boy of genteel family who has been forcibly separated from his mother and put to work as a chimney sweep. By a series of extraordinary coincidences he is finally restored both to her and to his rightful station in society.

In Peake's play the boy's grandfather, repenting of having disposed of his (as he thought) illegitimate grandson, belatedly seeks him out, but is told that 'The boy may [have been] sent to Botany Bay for picking pockets', a fate that Dickens would later reserve for Jack Dawkins in *Oliver Twist*.[23] His servant hides from his master the fact that he has 'sold the boy to a chimney sweep' (p. 6) (Mr Bumble memorably tries to effect just such a sale of young Oliver in Dickens's novel from 1837–9). The little sweep loses himself in a maze of chimneys during the course of his work in London, and half recognises a bedroom he finds himself in. His gaze alights upon a portrait on the bedroom wall:

[Boy:] Oh, goodness, how my heart beats! Now I know – now I am sure – that picture: (*kneels down and sobs.*) Yes! oh where is she now? (*Hysterically.*) Look at me! smile at me! remember me – mother! Mother! Mother! (Act 2, p. 9)

Heavily laden with melodramatic affect, the affinity between this episode and the less hyperbolic recognition scene in Brownlow's London house is very strong.

The figure of Jack Ragg in Brinsley Peake's play – a crossing sweeper who is the little sweep's one and only friend – also seems to have lodged himself in Dickens's creative imagination. Certain of his characteristics resurface in Sam Weller in *The Pickwick Papers* and in Jack Dawkins in *Oliver Twist*: Ragg's good-natured impudence and cockney slang is shared by both of Dickens's comic characters. The canting, hypocritical, Methodistical servant of the house, Jacob (who himself is a possible prototype for *Pickwick*'s Stiggins), objects to the crossing-sweeper wearing a hat in his master's house:

[JACOB:] This will never do. (*Takes Jack's hat off.*)
[JACK:] What? – O – ay, hang it up somewhere – there's a good boy. (Act 2, p. 13)

'None of your gammon, old cock' (Act 2, p. 15) is Jack's further riposte to Jacob's insolence. The benevolent master of the house, Mr Strawberry, admires 'the humour of the boy' (Act 2, p. 14) and takes Jack on as a footman, rather as Mr Pickwick takes on Sam.

In an attempt to get rid of the little sweep, the scheming Jacob plants his mistress's silver watch on the boy, so that Strawberry will believe him to be a thief, just as Brownlow is temporarily misled in *Oliver Twist*. And, finally, the play anticipates the episode in *The Pickwick Papers* when Pickwick is brought before Magistrate Nupkins stuck in a sedan chair: a similar fate befalls Jack Ragg, whose corpulence leaves him stranded in the sedan chair in which he has been hiding, and in which he is carried before a police constable.

It seems likely that Dickens would have seen *The Climbing Boy*: the Olympic Theatre in the Strand where it was first performed in July 1832 (running to 21 September) was literally round the corner from the young Dickens's lodgings. And the figure of the 'lost boy' sold as a chimney sweep resurfaces in 'The First of May' in *Sketches By Boz*, in which the legend of the boy 'stolen from his parents in his infancy, and devoted to the occupation of chimney sweeping' again recalls *The Climbing Boy*.[24] The play was a considerable popular success, surviving in theatre repertoires for nearly fifteen years;[25] and Dickens was clearly very familiar with Peake and his work. The novelist's amateur dramatic troop put on performances of Peake's plays (although not this one) on more than one occasion; Dickens corresponded with Peake concerning a benefit performance for Thomas Poole; and on the playwright's death he suggested to Macready that he might take part in a benefit performance for Peake's widow and children.[26]

That *The Climbing Boy* is a source for both *Oliver Twist* and *The Pickwick Papers* is unsurprising given that Dickens worked on them simultaneously in 1837.[27] And the theatrical borrowings are apt given that as he was writing both novels, Dickens was also superintending rehearsals for his own play, an unmemorable farce called *Is She His Wife? Or, Something Singular!*[28]

The most important single popular influence on *The Pickwick Papers* was the illustrator Robert Seymour. The first illustrator to work with Dickens on *Pickwick* – indeed the project originally belonged to him – Seymour took his own life after contributing just eight illustrations for the first five chapters of the novel. Seymour is as important as William Hone in understanding the popular cultural traditions out of which Dickens's novels grew, for he, like both Hone and Dickens, engaged with both radical and more broadly popular cultural markets, as of course did George Cruikshank, a pivotal figure in the Hone–Dickens nexus. It is in his *Humorous Sketches* published between 1834 and 1836 that Seymour's influence on early Dickens is initially in evidence. Whilst *Sketches by Boz* is modelled on the type of popular publication that comprised visual sketches with accompanying text, *The Pickwick Papers* has a more particular

I'm dem'd if I can ever hit 'em.

Figure 11 Robert Seymour, 'I'm dem'd if I can ever hit 'em', *Humorous Sketches*.

resonance with Seymour's work. Scene 17 from the *Humorous Sketches* features a bad shot with a rifle: the caption reads: 'I'm dem'd if I can ever hit 'em' (see figure 11).[29] In the prose sketch that accompanies the piece we learn that the gentleman with the gun, whose aim is so bad that he shoots through a cottager's windows while aiming for sparrows, has to wrestle with a 'vulgar peasant' who wishes to disarm him. This is strongly

Out!

So dont fatigue yourself. I beg, sir?

Figure 12 Robert Seymour, 'Out!', 'Andrew Mullins – An Autobiography',
in *Humorous Sketches*.

reminiscent of Mr Winkle's antics with a shotgun in *The Pickwick Papers* –
he injures Mr Tupman whilst ostensibly shooting at rooks, and Pickwick
attempts to disarm him. Another sketch – chapter 7 of the fictional
autobiography of one Andrew Mullins – features a village cricket match
(see figure 12) which, similarly, reminds us of a Pickwickian episode,
when the Dingley Dell team gamely take on the Old Muggletonians.[30]

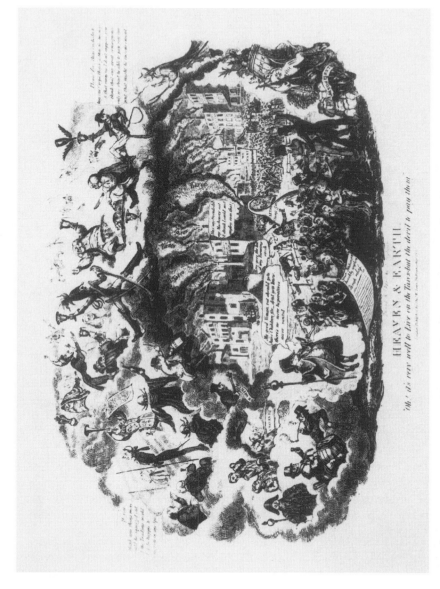

Figure 13 Robert Seymour, 'Heaven and Earth'.

Generally engaging with the broad popular market, Robert Seymour can also be identified as the artist who produced a memorable piece of anti-Poor Law propaganda in an 1830 engraving entitled 'Heaven and Earth'. Seymour's cartoon (see figure 13) prominently features an overweight, pompous figure of a parish beadle, immediately recognisable as a Bumble prototype. Seymour's engraving is one of a whole host of satirical and melodramatic illustrations from the 1830s and 1840s that would importantly shape – and subsequently be influenced by – Dickens's response to the New Poor Law in *Oliver Twist*. It is to these that I shall now turn.

THE LITERATURE OF THE ANTI-POOR LAW MOVEMENT

Seymour's engraving from 1830 anticipates both Dickens's political critique and the aesthetic mode of *Oliver Twist*. It has the Manichean structure of the melodrama: the morally repugnant, overfed and inebriated members of the middle and upper classes (the judiciary, the Duke of Wellington, the King, and venal parish officers) ostentatiously carouse in the 'heaven' of the title, whilst emaciated farmworkers, the unemployed, starving women, children and the elderly all huddle together below, on 'earth'. Central to the illustration is the figure of the parish beadle who, descending from on high on a cloud, delivers a message from 'heaven' for a particularly withered-looking mother and child: 'My good Voman, vot should you have Children for – don't you know, there's no more hoperatives never wanted.'[31] Seymour's is a satirical attack on the language of Malthusian political economy that would, four years after his cartoon was published, inform the provisions made in, and the general tenor of, the controversial New Poor Law of 1834. Characteristic too of the engraving is its preoccupation with consumption: it dramatically represents the consuming upper world in stark contrast to the starving bodies of the inhabitants of lower-earth, bodies that are being devoured by the juggernaut of political economy that enjoyed ideological currency in the 1830s and 1840s. The focus on women and children, and on the destruction of the working-class family, is also entirely typical of the literature and graphic art of the anti-Poor Law movement that would so powerfully influence, and in turn be shaped by, *Oliver Twist*.

There is considerable continuity between anti-Poor Law satire of the 1830s and the earlier graphic satire of the Regency period that I attended to in chapter 1.[32] Such continuity is vividly captured in an anti-Poor Law cartoon produced by C. J. Grant for *Cleave's Gazette of Variety* in 1837, in

THE POOR LAWS IN BRADFORD.

First Soldier. What d'ye say ye wont swallow 'em? How dare you presume to think that the Whigs don't know what is good for the welfare of the Bradford Paupers.

Second Soldier. It's plain we must *force* it down their throats with *Steel Lozenges*, and *Lead* Pills.

Third Soldier. The ignorant Boor has no idea of an independence of " Parochial Relief," or he'd never offer such resistance.

Figure 14 C. J. Grant, 'The Poor Laws in Bradford', *Cleave's London Satirist and Gazette of Variety* (9 September 1837).

which a gang of soldiers forces the New Poor Law down the throat of a pauper with their swords (see figure 14). This image strikingly echoes George Cruikshank's 'Steel Lozenges' illustration for William Hone's radical pamphlet from 1820, *The Man in the Moon*, in which yeomanry soldiers 'feed' the starving poor in St Peter's Fields with their swords (see figure 15). There is, then, a direct line of influence between Hone and Cruikshank in the Regency period, and Grant and other radical cartoonists and writers of the 1830s, the anti-Poor Law satirists owing a particularly strong debt to their early nineteenth-century forebears. William Cobbett is

STEEL LOZENGES

Figure 15 George Cruikshank, 'Steel Lozenges', in William Hone, *The Man in the Moon.*

likewise an important bridge between the Regency and the 1830s. Central to the protest against Peterloo and in support of Queen Caroline in 1819 and 1820 respectively, Cobbett was an equally significant figure in the anti-Poor Law movement: his 1835 pamphlet *Cobbett's Legacy to Labourers* was used as the basis for anti-Poor Law speeches right across the ensuing decade.[33]

Grant's 'Poor Laws in Bradford' illustration, like Seymour's seven years earlier, centres on the idea of consumption, a key concept in Malthusian political economy. The text below the cartoon reads as follows:

FIRST SOLDIER: What d'ye say ye wont [sic] swallow 'em? How dare you presume to think that the Whigs don't know what is good for the welfare of the Bradford Paupers.

SECOND SOLDIER: It's plain that we must *force* it down their throats with *Steel Lozenges*, and *Lead* Pills.

THIRD SOLDIER: The ignorant Boor has no idea of an independence of 'Parochial Relief,' or he'd never offer such resistance. [Emphases in original.]

Explicit in its echoing of Cruikshank's 'Steel Lozenges', Grant's text centres on what can legitimately be 'fed' to the poor: the nature of the workhouse 'dietary' and the total food-deprivation endured by those paupers who refused to enter the so-called 'poor law bastile' [sic] was one of the central preoccupations of the anti-Poor Law movement.

The bloated, overfed figure of the parish beadle, who contrasts ironically with the starving poor whom he disciplines, heavily populates anti-Poor Law literature of the 1830s and 1840s: Dickens was neither the first nor the last to focus on this much-derided lackey. The beadle originally derived from popular eighteenth-century representations, long predating Dickens's Bumble in *Oliver Twist* (1837–9) or his prototype in *Sketches by Boz* (1836). Up until the 1820s, though, the beadle had been represented textually and pictorially simply as a figure of chastisement. William Hogarth's is the best known popular eighteenth-century example of the beadle as an agent of punishment: in the second illustration from his *Industry and Idleness* series, the 'Idle 'Prentice at Play in the Churchyard', the parish beadle chastises an idle apprentice as he plays with his fellows on a tombstone. It was in the 1820s that the figure of the beadle first became a satirical target. An 1827 article on 'The Parish Beadle' in the *Gentleman's Pocket Magazine* is accompanied by two illustrations: the first is a reproduction of Hogarth's 'Idle 'Prentice' (see figure 16) and the second is an engraving by Cruikshank (see figure 17). In this second illustration Cruikshank became the first of the cartoonists to represent the lowly parish officer satirically, as a figure of both hate and fun.[34] It was this image of the Beadle as a corpulent, pompously attired, self-important petty official that established the satirical genealogy upon which Dickens and Cruikshank would together build a few years later, and which would be widely deployed by protestors against the New Poor Law.

A gentle lampoon of the parish beadle is to be found in John Poole's *Little Peddlington and the Pedlingtonians* (1839), a picaresque species of travelogue and close relative of Dickens's *Pickwick Papers*. Much harsher are C. J. Grant and Robert Seymour's cartoons from the 1830s that attack the beadle's role in the implementation of the new legislation relating to parish relief. In these cartoons the illustrators draw on both a radical satirical genealogy and a powerful melodramatic vocabulary that informed

THE GENTLEMAN'S
POCKET MAGAZINE.

PARISH BEADLES.

Figure 16 After William Hogarth, 'Idle 'Prentice at Play in the Church Yard', 1747.
Woodcut reproduction in *Gentleman's Pocket Magazine* (18 January 1827).

much of the literature and culture of the anti-Poor Law movement in the
1830s and 1840s, including Dickens's *Oliver Twist*.[35] Seymour's wood-
engraving from February 1836 for the *Figaro in London* (see figure 18)
contrasts the starvation regime imposed by the new legislation with the
sumptuous lifestyles enjoyed by its middle-class supporters. The large-
girthed beadle violently refuses outdoor relief to three generations of one
family; the ragged, emaciated family group, which is here shown protec-
tively huddled together, would be torn asunder were they to enter the
workhouse that lurks threateningly in the background. The skeletal, under-
nourished figures of the pauper family are also starkly contrasted with the
rotundity of the parish officers enjoying a drink in the 'New Poor Laws
Tavern' directly behind them. Again, a consumption trope is central to the
image's meaning: the unrestrained over-consumption of the portly Poor Law
officials is contrasted with the regulated dietary of the poor, their bodies
consumed by deprivation. This illustration was followed up a few months

Figure 17 George Cruikshank, 'Parish Beadle', *Gentleman's Pocket Magazine*
(18 January 1827).

later in the same penny weekly with a wood engraving by an unknown
illustrator that follows through the implied narrative of the initial cartoon:
here the Beadle oversees the brutal separation of (possibly the same) pauper
family as they enter the workhouse (see figure 19). As workhouse officers beat

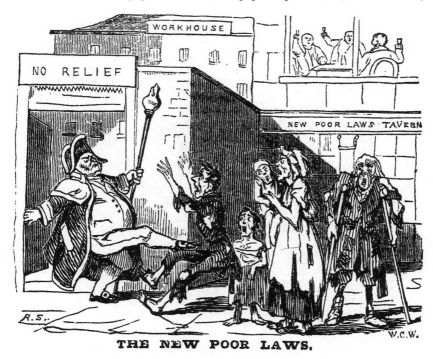

Figure 18 Robert Seymour, 'The New Poor Laws', *Figaro in London* (20 February 1836).

the distressed parents, the beadle looks on self-importantly, oblivious both to the weeping child who pleads with him for mercy and to the crying infant who has been left on the stone floor as its mother is dragged away. In both illustrations from *Figaro in London*, the perceived moral brutality of the New Poor Law is translated into literal physical violence, with the beadle kicking the frail-looking father in the first cartoon and overseeing his battering with a truncheon in the second. The bodiliness of the melodramatic mode – its reliance on physical gesture as well as on the spoken word – was well adapted to the contemporary onslaught against the 1834 legislation.

The New Poor Law's assault on the working-class family was further critiqued in the protest literature through its setting up of parish function-aries – and sometimes the legislation itself – as brutal surrogate parents. The beadle as an ogre-like child-snatcher features in an unattributed 1839 wood engraving from the cheap weekly newspaper *The Odd Fellow*, where the instantly recognisable parish official is shown forcibly removing terrified-looking children to the workhouse, with barely a glance over his shoulder at

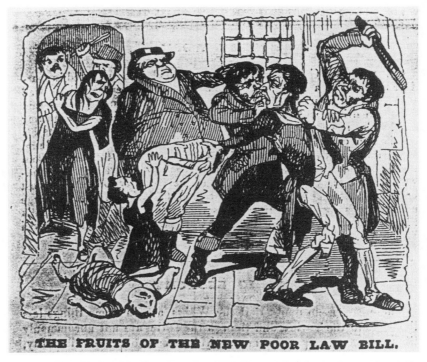

THE FRUITS OF THE NEW POOR LAW BILL.

Figure 19 'The Fruits of the New Poor Law Bill', *Figaro in London* (10 September 1836).

the church in the background (see figure 20). His grip on the children is tight, akin to the enforced hand-holding that Oliver Twist has to endure in the care successively of Bumble and Bill Sikes. In each case – and in a great deal of the literature and culture of the anti-Poor Law movement – what is being subjected to intensely critical scrutiny is the violent appropriation of children, interchangeably by a criminal (in the case of Bill Sikes) or by the parish (the beadle). The new legislation's assault on the working-class family was perceived by its critics to create a large number of effectively parentless children – something that Dickens was alert to in *Oliver Twist*, which is full of children necessarily living in 'alternative' family units.

The effects of the New Poor Law on children is also subjected to powerful criticism in an undated woodcut by C. J. Grant (probably *c.* 1834), called 'Effects of the New Bastardy Law'. Here the beadle oversees the removal of cartloads of apparently parentless infants to the workhouse (see

POOR LAW SKETCHES.—" A DOG IN OFFICE."

Figure 20 'Poor Law Sketches. – "A Dog in Office"', *Odd Fellow* (8 June 1839).

figure 21). The bastardy clauses of the New Poor Law were particularly controversial in that they now held unmarried mothers fully responsible for illegitimate pauper children, whereas the old Poor Law legislation was such that fathers had previously been pursued for maintenance.[36] The perceived effect of the new legislation was the creation of much larger numbers of fatherless pauper babies. The crudely satirical text accompanying Grant's undated woodcut reads as follows:

Awful fecundity – surely nothing is wanting to evince the *march of knowledge* among the young folks of the present day than this – Oh! Martineau and Malthus, what say you to this! O Tempore! O Mores!

Figure 21 C. J. Grant, 'Effects of the New Bastardy Law', *The Political Drama*.

I say, Sir John, there are a few specimens of *good breeding* at all events, exercised under the new Law.

Ha! ha! I suppose you would call this the *fruits* of the new Bastardy Law.

Delightful idea. The sensualist can now enjoy himself without the fear of *corroborative testimony*. [etc.] [Emphases in original.]

The high-sounding 'march of knowledge' ironically refers to the fact that the lewd-looking young men smoking casually in the background of the illustration have learnt from the legislation that they can impregnate as many young women as they please, as they will no longer be pursued for financial support. Far from teaching sexual continence to the poor, then, Grant implies that the bastardy laws encouraged the opposite, quite contrary to the wishes of the scions of political economy, the alliteratively-yoked Martineau and Malthus. Instead of limiting the reproduction of the poor and encouraging 'good breeding' (amongst the middle and upper classes), the new legislation, the image and the text imply, encourages *plentiful* breeding. The pauper babies who are the '*fruits* of the new Bastardy Law' at a glance resemble cabbages or melons that have been harvested for human consumption, and a cannibalism trope – the underbelly of untrammelled consumption – lurks here and elsewhere in the literature of the anti-Poor Law movement. Here the suggestion of cannibalism is only implicit; in *Blackwood's Edinburgh Magazine*, an upmarket Tory monthly, the need for the poor to consume themselves is made explicit in a satirical flourish modelled on Swift. The author of 'New Scheme For Maintaining the Poor' dismisses moral objections to cannibalism on the grounds that the law as it stands only prohibits the 'shedding of blood'. The writer argues that given that most workhouse inmates are elderly or infirm, rather than waste time and expense in burying them when they die, the surviving paupers could make a meal of their corpses:

Three-fourths of the inmates in a union poor-house may be put down as aged and infirm – the other fourth as children and idiots – so that the large majority being composed of the aged and infirm, it follows that there must be a rapid succession – that in the course of Nature they must die faster than any other portion of the population . . . I would have, then, those that drop off support those that live on; and I think, after the scheme had been in operation a little while, the supply would be regular and certain. There are but two prejudices to get over – the foolish and unphilosophical repugnance to any kind of flesh, and the very useless and wasteful one of burying the dead.[37]

The Swiftian *sang froid* of the high-brow *Blackwood's* satire transmutes into angry reportage in *The Book of the Bastiles* (sic), a contemporary anthology of anecdotal reports on the effects of the New Poor Law, published in 1841. Bursting with indignantly expressed 'facts', one extract from the *Book* recounts that Earl Stanhope, speaking in the House of Lords on 15 June 1839, 'related, that certain Guardians had told a poor woman, when she applied for relief, "to go home and make a pie of some of her children"'.[38] The cannibalism trope found expression, then, in a variety of anti-Poor Law texts: in comic satirical illustrations; in searing Swiftian satire; and in horrified witness statements.

The Book of the Bastiles, although some of the reportage is of dubious origin, importantly reaffirmed, in 1841, the central concerns of protesters against the New Poor Laws: there is a preoccupation with the literal starvation of the poor; with the Act's assault on the working-class family; and with the poor preferring to consider killing their children rather than take them into a workhouse. A representative sample confirms these recurrent tropes:

- In the parish of Bourne, in Lincolnshire, a poor man who was out of work applied to the Guardians of the poor for relief. They offered him admission into one of the Union workhouses. He declared he would *rather die* than enter such a place, and refused to accept the offer. Within a week afterward the man was found dead in a field, having absolutely chosen to submit to death by starvation than enter one of the workhouses established under the present system. [*Genl. Johnson at the Crown and Anchor*, 9 February 1838]

- The general feeling of the poor is, that they will *rather starve*, or *commit suicide*, than go into these prisons, and many are willing to emigrate. [*Extract of a letter from Mr John Perceval to Mr Oastler*, dated from Kent, 18 February 1838]

- The poor woman said, 'I only wish those who like the law may suffer under it as I have done. I would *sooner kill my children and hang myself than go in again* to be treated as I have been.' [*Extract of a Letter from a Southern County Correspondent to the Author*, dated 2 October 1840.]

- Mr Chappell related an anecdote of a man who was now in Knutsford gaol, for fetching his child into his bed, having heard it crying during the night, in another part of the workhouse in which he then was. [*Roworth's 'Observations on the New Poor Law'*, 1840][39]

The *Book of the Bastiles* includes contributions from Richard Oastler and the Tory *Times* as well as from Feargus O'Connor and the Chartist *Northern Star*, and the cross-class composition of the anti-Poor Law movement is something that would have greatly appealed to Dickens, concerned as he was to reach out to the largest possible popular audience. In an ostensibly unlikely alliance, Chartists and Tories united to form a truly popular front. The Chartists defended the interests of the poor and the dispossessed threatened by Malthusian political economy; whilst to the Tories the New Poor Law was an attack on traditional relations between rich and poor that had hitherto been based on patronage and charity.[40] The cross-class make-up of the anti-Poor Law movement meant that it had at its disposal an extraordinarily diverse print culture, ranging from the Tory *Times* and *Blackwood's Edinburgh Review* to the radical weekly *Cleave's Gazette of Variety*, the Chartist *Northern Star* and Gilbert À Beckett's comic penny weekly *Figaro in London*. Street literature too was used as a vehicle for anti-Poor Law argument. A broadside from *c.* 1836, *The New Poor Law Bill in Force*, draws on the cruder generic conventions of both satire and melodrama – such infinitely malleable modes in class terms – to articulate its own particular form of protest. The text of the broadside has a repeated chorus that is interspersed in the text, lending it the performative apparel of the melodrama proper. Appealing to a non-elite audience, the broadside focuses hyperbolically on the contrast between bloated parish officials and starving paupers, and also on the lewd potential of the bastardy clauses. The text proper (with the original lexical errors uncorrected) begins:

SPOKEN. – Now, Mr. *Blubberhead* the Beadle, fetch in the Overseers' and Churchwardens 12 bottles of the best Port Wine, yes Sir, and Blubberhead, is there any Vagrants outside wants examining? why, Sir, there is a wonderful lot of people outside, and I think they are all Bones, for there is very little flesh upon them. – Now, Mr. Blubberhead, the Beadle, let in one of those Rascals – Who are you pray, Why Sir, my name is John Pineway, who is been ill Seventeen long months, I have a Wife Confined, and eight Children Starving.[41]

Again there is a preoccupation with the bodily effects of consumption of various kinds: the parish officials are rendered full of 'blubber' because of their over-consumption of port wine, whilst the bodies of the starving poor are reduced to (unappealing and, it is implied, barely edible) mere bones. In relation to the paupers brought before the overseer, concerns about consumption are closely linked to concerns about lower-class sexuality and reproduction. The pauper family, with its pregnant wife and eight children, presents a contrast between sexual plenty and economic insufficiency. Malthusian economic theory held that 'a proportion of the population exceeds economic purpose, and thereby turns what had been the source of wealth – labour – into its parasite'.[42] Contemporary fears of working-class sexuality were closely linked, in Malthusian terms, to a fear that the offspring of the poor would consume too much food. Both food consumption and reproduction needed, then, to be firmly regulated, hence the preoccupation with the workhouse dietary and with the separation of husbands and wives in the workhouse so as to prevent further pregnancies. The perceived moral injustice of this was leapt upon by anti-Poor Law protestors: the broadside here referred to not only satirically attacks an overfed parish hierarchy but goes on provocatively to suggest that major beneficiaries of the bastardy clauses were parish officials who could themselves impregnate pauper women without sanction.

'I WANT SOME MORE': *OLIVER TWIST*

AND POLITICAL ECONOMY

Any reader with even the most cursory knowledge of one of Dickens's best-known novels will be familiar with the scene in *Oliver Twist*, memorably captured by Cruikshank (see figure 22), when young Oliver, 'desperate with hunger and reckless with misery' twice asks the master of the workhouse – 'a fat, healthy man' – for more: 'Please, sir, I want some more' (*Oliver Twist*, p. 15). A highly theatrical moment, perfectly adapted for theatre and film, Cruikshank's tableau remains firmly embedded in the British cultural imagination almost 170 years after the novel's first publication.[43] It is Dickens's astonishing ability to transform the raw material of popular culture that means that this moment of high drama is not only aesthetically and emotionally effective, but also crystallises one of the central debates in political economy that exercised both supporters of and protestors against the New Poor Law Act of 1834. The poor's status as consumers, and the amounts that the poor should be permitted to consume, are as central to Dickens's novel from 1837–9 as they were to the wider body of anti-Poor Law literature explored in the previous section.

Dickens also borrows and builds on many other features of anti-Poor Law literature from the 1830s: he responds to and develops the figure of the beadle in the laughably self-important and venal Mr Bumble; he emphasises the effects of the New Poor Law on children in particular; he focuses on the destruction of the working-class family; he explores the role of the surrogate parents spawned by the new legislation; he emphasises the causal link between poverty and crime; and he exploits to the full the capacity of melodrama and satire for both comic and radical expression.

Oliver's demand that he be given a second bowl of gruel provokes a dramatic reaction from the workhouse functionaries: the small boy is caned by the beadle as he washes outside in the stone yard, and is flogged every night in the dining hall 'as a public warning and example' (*Oliver Twist*, p. 18). The bodiliness of the melodrama is violently enacted in Dickens's novel. Mr Limbkins, one of the Board of Guardians, predicts, when he

Figure 22 George Cruikshank, 'Oliver Asking For More', 1837.

hears of Oliver's misdemeanour, that 'That boy will be hung' (p. 15). The exaggerated response to Oliver's desire to consume more gruel than allowed by the workhouse dietary derives from political economy's determination that the poor should not consume the nation's wealth. James Mill, a follower of Jeremy Bentham and one of the leading political economists of the early nineteenth century, argued that political economy was centrally concerned with 'two grand objects, the Consumption of the Community, and that supply upon which the consumption depends'.[44]

Beth Carney has remarked that the adherents of political economy had an ambivalent relationship with consumption in as much as that the desire to consume is what drives the free market; but, conversely, in a world of limited resources consumption is also a threat, because it cannot continue indefinitely without taking into account, in Mill's words, 'the supply upon which [it] depends'.[45] According to this model, then, the pauper is greedier than the rich man because the rich man contributes as well as consumes wealth, whereas the pauper claiming relief only consumes.

An important essay in support of the New Poor Law that adheres closely to the tenets of political economy was published in the *Quarterly Review* in 1835. The author, F. B. Head, posits the poor as devouring consumers, gobbling up the nation's wealth without contributing to it. Duplicating the methodology of the Poor Law commissioners who gathered anecdotal evidence in order to compile their report of 1834, the author of the satirically entitled 'English Charity' follows an assistant Poor Law commissioner around the country as the latter tries to set up the Poor Law Unions established by the New Poor Law. Mimicking the contemporary vocabulary of topography and travel, F. B. Head describes a workhouse in East Kent as '"a delightful retreat", splendidly contrasted with the mean little rate-paying hovels at its feet'. He notices the 'robust outlines' of 'able-bodied women' and 'a room full of sturdy labourers out of work' who had 'an over-fed, a mutinous, and an insubordinate appearance'.[46] Head goes on to identify the luxurious dietary at the paupers' disposal as the cause of such mutiny and insubordination:

Almost everywhere the Kentish pauper has what are called three meat-days a week, in many cases four meat-days, and in some cases five; his bread is many degrees better than that given to our soldiers; he has vegetables at discretion; and especially in the large workhouses, it is declared with great pride that 'there is no stinting', but that *we gives 'em as much victuals as ever they can eat.'* ... The general effect produced by this system may be sufficiently explained by a very few instances. Mr Curling, the governor of Margate workhouse, declared in our hearing:

'I am an eye-witness that, by over-feeding the pauper, we have made the labouring classes discontented.'[47]

Richard Ford similarly disputed Dickens's account of the starvation regime of the workhouse in a review of the novel that was deeply antagonised by the workhouse scenes. He too contended that the workhouse dietary was lavish: 'The besetting sin of "white-waistcoated" guardians is profusion, not parsimony ... After all, the proof of the pudding is in the eating: one week's poorhouse pot-luck fattens a pauper brat up to such a sucking-pig nicety, that its own parent, like Saturn, longs to eat it up with more than kisses.'[48] Whilst Ford viciously describes the pauper as the ultimate devouring consumer – licking its lips at the prospect of devouring even its own offspring – Dickens, like other anti-Poor Law writers, uses the cannibalism trope with a quite different objective. One remembers that Oliver's decision to ask for more gruel is taken under duress, after one of his fellow sufferers has declared that his hunger is so great that he may have to resort to eating one of their number:

Oliver Twist and his companions suffered the tortures of slow starvation for three months; at last they got so voracious and wild with hunger, that one boy, who was tall for his age, and hadn't been used to that kind of thing (for his father had kept a small cook's shop) hinted darkly to his companions, that unless he had another basin of gruel *per diem*, he was afraid he should some night eat the boy who slept next to him, who happened to be a weakly youth of a tender age.

(*Oliver Twist*, p. 14)

Here, then, Dickens anticipates and rebuts Ford's vituperative attack on the hungry poor – it is famine, not greed that leads to the most transgressive mode of consumption known to human kind. Levels of consumption are everywhere the object of Dickens's scrutiny in *Oliver Twist*: at Mrs Mann's Baby Farm Oliver and the other infants are 'without the inconvenience of too much food' (p. 6) and are locked into the coal cellar 'for atrociously presuming to be hungry' (p. 7). The Board of Guardians is comprised of 'fat gentlemen' (p. 11) who impose a starvation diet upon the workhouse inmates. Each pauper is permitted 'Three meals of thin gruel a day, with an onion twice a week, and half a roll on Sundays' (p. 13).

In mimicking the language of political economy, Dickens satirically undermines the famine regime of the workhouse even as he defends it in economic terms:

It was rather expensive at first, in consequence of the increase in the undertaker's bill, and the necessity of taking in the clothes of all the paupers, which fluttered loosely on their wasted, shrunken forms, after a week or two's gruel. But the number of workhouse inmates got thin, as well as paupers; and the board were in ecstasies. (p. 14)

Mrs Sowerberry, the wife of the undertaker to whom Oliver is apprenticed, is similarly set up as an object of Dickens's political critique as she weighs up the costs and benefits of taking Oliver into the family business in the crudest vocabulary of political economy. In response to her complaint that Oliver is 'very small', Bumble assures this 'short, thin, squeezed-up woman' that he will grow bigger. Her sharp reply is 'Ah, I daresay he will ... on our victuals, and our drink. I see no saving in parish children, not I; for they always cost more to keep, than they're worth' (p. 32). Although the undertaker's wife hardly needs further condemnation, Dickens makes his attack on political economy explicit at this early stage in the novel. Oliver's first meal at the Sowerberrys' consists of scraps that had been set aside for the dog. Dickens reflects:

> I wish some well-fed philosopher, whose meat and drink turn to gall within him, whose blood is ice, and whose heart is iron, could have seen Oliver Twist clutching at the dainty viands that the dog had neglected, and witnessed the horrible avidity with which he tore the bits asunder with all the ferocity of famine; there is only one thing I should like better; and that would be to see him making the same sort of meal himself, with the same relish. (p. 33)

Consumption in all its forms is thematically linked in *Oliver Twist* to transgression and to criminality. The squalling, hungry babies at Mrs Mann's Baby Farm are referred to as 'culprits' and as 'juvenile offenders against the poor laws' (p. 6); and Oliver's demand for more gruel in the workhouse leads to the reflection that 'That boy will be hung' (p. 15). In asking for more food, Oliver is behaving as a consumer: his punishment (the attempt to apprentice him to a chimney sweep) firmly puts him in his place as an object in the marketplace rather than the consuming subject he would like to be.

When Oliver furiously attacks Noah Claypole at the Sowerberrys' house, goaded to it by insults aimed at his dead mother, Bumble is quick, like the author of the earlier 'English Charity' essay, to blame pauperish insubordination on over-feeding. When Oliver boldly rebuffs the beadle's attempts to bully him into meekness, Mrs Sowerberry cries:

> 'Oh you know, Mr Bumble, he must be mad ... No boy in half his senses would venture to speak so to you.'
> 'It's not madness, ma'am,' replied Mr Bumble, after a few moments of deep meditation; 'it's meat.'
> 'What!' exclaimed Mrs Sowerberry.
> 'Meat, ma'am, meat,' replied Bumble, with stern emphasis. 'You've overfed him, ma'am. You've raised a artificial soul and spirit in him, ma'am, unbecoming a person of his condition, as the board, Mrs Sowerberry, who are practical philosophers, will tell you ... If you had kept the boy on gruel, ma'am, this would never have happened.' (p. 53)

Bumble here echoes Head's account of the 'overfed', 'mutinous' and 'insubordinate' inmates of a Kentish workhouse; but it is clear that Dickens's sympathy in the novel is all on the side of the downtrodden orphan driven half to madness by his brutal treatment.

The workhouse, with its designation of its pauper inhabitants as 'inmates' and with its restrictive codes concerning the freedom of paupers to return to their communities, was frequently associated with the prison, and this also played a part in coding paupers themselves as criminals: the logic of political economy (here strongly inflected with Benthamite utilitarianism) was such, its detractors would claim, that to be poor was a criminal offence. This elision of pauper and criminal also finds its way into anti-Poor Law literature. Again, from the *Book of the Bastiles*: 'Here is the appalling fact, that the New Poor-Law is indirectly demoralizing a very large proportion of children, whose destitute parents, *rather than encounter the persecutions of a Whig workhouse*, permit them to become habitual thieves.'[49]

Dickens is clear in *Oliver Twist* about the causal link between poverty and criminality, and deploys the consumption trope to demonstrate how closely hunger and crime were connected. It is the relatively luxurious level of food consumption enjoyed by Fagin's gang that initially entices young Oliver into London's criminal underworld. The Artful Dodger's first act, on meeting the half-starved Oliver at Barnett, is to feed him:

the young gentleman took him to an adjacent chandler's shop where he purchased a sufficiency of ready-dressed ham and a quartern loaf . . . Taking the bread under his arm, the young gentleman turned into a small public house, and . . . Here, a pot of beer was brought in by the direction of the mysterious youth; and Oliver, falling to, at his new friend's bidding, made a long and hearty meal, during the progress of which the strange boy eyed him from time to time with great attention.
(*Oliver Twist*, p. 61)

It is interesting that Jack Dawkins *purchases* food for Oliver (Roman Polanski's 2005 film adaptation has him steal it). It is as if even ill-gotten gains from criminal activity are somehow retrievable to the extent that they can be reinvested into a consumption economy.[50] And the first thing Oliver sees and smells when he arrives at Fagin's den for the first time is food and the suggestion of drink:

There was a deal-table before the fire, upon which was a candle stuck in a ginger-beer bottle; two or three pewter pots, a loaf and butter, and a plate. In the frying-pan which was on the fire . . . some sausages were cooking. (p. 64)

There is an implicit invitation to the reader to compare the meals that Jack Dawkins and Fagin offer to Oliver with the repast proposed by Mrs Sowerberry (the dog's leftovers – and her very name is suggestive of the kind of bitter sustenance Oliver will receive at the undertaker's house). All three, though, in the language of political economy, are investing in Oliver with an eye to the kind of return they might get. Mrs Sowerberry has no faith in her investment of food, but Jack and Fagin both see a potential return from Oliver in the context of London's criminal underworld. Despite the haphazard plotting of *Oliver Twist* compared to Dickens's later novels, there is a striking continuity between the 'workhouse' and the 'criminal-London' sections of the novel in that both are presented as operating according to the tenets of political economy.

Fagin is described by Bill Sikes as a 'covetous, avaricious, in-sa-ti-a-ble old fence' (p. 98); Fagin is driven by a desire to protect and increase his own wealth every bit as fierce as the boldest of the political economists. He may work in a criminal economy rather than a government-sanctioned one, but his desires and motivations are, the novel suggests, the same. The novel's refashioning of the self-seeking individualist, Noah Claypole, as 'Morris Bolter', similarly emphasises the grasping, all-consuming force of self-interest that characterises both the criminal underworld and the laws of political economy. When Jack Dawkins and Charley Bates desert Oliver and leave him to be arrested for a theft he did not commit, Dickens suggests that they are acting as good Benthamite citizens. In his *Book of Fallacies* Jeremy Bentham, one of the architects of political economy, had argued that 'In every human breast ... self-regarding interest is predominant over social interest; each person's own individual interest, over the interests of all other persons taken together.'[51] Fagin and his gang have bought wholesale into this aspect of Bentham's political and economic philosophy, adapting the logic of political economy to their own criminal marketplace. Dickens's satirical commentary on such a philosophy also caustically glances towards Thomas's Malthus's account of 'Dame Nature' in his essay on population that massively influenced the political economists of the early nineteenth century.[52] Dickens holds political economists such as James Mill, following Bentham and Malthus, theoretically responsible for London's criminal gangs. Reflecting on Dawkins's and Bates's desertion of Oliver he reflects that they:

> were activated ... by a very laudable and becoming regard for themselves; and forasmuch as the freedom of the subject and the liberty of the individual are among the first and proudest boasts of a true-hearted Englishman, so I need hardly beg the reader to observe that this action must tend to exalt them in the opinion of all public and patriotic men, in almost as great a degree as this strong proof of their anxiety for their own preservation and safety goes to corroborate and confirm the little code of laws which certain profound and sound-judging philosophers have laid down as the mainsprings of all Madam Nature's deeds and actions; the said philosophers very wisely reducing the good lady's proceedings to matters of maxim and theory, and ... putting entirely out of sight any considerations of heart, or generous impulse and feeling. (*Oliver Twist*, p. 94)

Dickens's objection here to a mechanical application of the tenets of political economy to human situations is thoroughly Carlylean; but it is consistent too with the general tenor of the literature of the anti-Poor Law movement which proliferated as the young novelist wrote *Oliver Twist*. The individualistic concern for 'number one', characteristic of Benthamite philosophy, is parroted by Fagin as he educates Noah Claypole in the ways of the criminal underworld: ' "Every man's his own friend," replied Fagin. "Some conjurors say that number three is the magic number, and some say number seven. It's neither, my friend, neither. It's number one" ' (p. 360). Antipathetic as he was towards aspects of Dickens's political critique in *Oliver Twist*, Richard Ford was quick to identify in Fagin's peroration 'the utilitarian principle of Mr Jeremy Bentham – *alias*, the golden rule of number one'.[53]

But Dickens does more than satirically undercut Benthamite philosophy in *Oliver Twist*; he actively resists it. Notwithstanding Fagin's gospel of 'number one', at least three members of the criminal gang in which Oliver finds himself regard themselves as part of an alternative family grouping, and are drawn back to the gang even against their own individual interests.[54] Nancy, offered the chance of a new life overseas, refuses it, explaining to Brownlow and Rose Maylie that:

> 'I must go home.'
> 'Home!' repeated the young lady, with great stress upon the word.
> 'Home, lady,' rejoined the girl. 'To such a home as I have raised for myself with the work of my whole life.' (p. 388)

And Sikes, at considerable risk to his own safety, seeks out and is given strength by the proximity of other men when he helps to put out a rural fire during his tormented wanderings: 'Any sound of men in that lonely place, even though it conveyed a real sense of alarm, was something to him' (p. 403); and 'oppressed by the fear of another solitary night' (p. 404) he decides to risk returning to London – 'There's somebody to speak to there, at all events.' He returns to one of the gang's lairs, exactly the place he will be hunted down, needing the kinship of his habitual companions; and he is uncharacteristically nonplussed by Charley Bates's rejection of him. As Charley shrinks from him Sikes nods, 'and made as if he would shake hands with him': ' "Why Charley!" said Sikes stepping forward. "Don't you – don't you know me?" ' (p. 422).

The proliferation of alternative families in *Oliver Twist* – Oliver finds a 'home' of various kinds at the Baby Farm (where he bonds with Little Dick), at the workhouse, with the Sowerberrys, with Fagin's gang, with Brownlow and with the Maylies – draws attention to the absence of conventional parent figures in the novel. Orphaned at birth, Oliver is 'parented' by a series of surrogates: Mrs Mann (her very name indicating her insufficiency in the maternal role); the Board of Guardians ('You know you've got no father and mother, and that you are brought up by the parish, don't you?' Bumble demands of Oliver (p. 12)); the grasping Sowerberrys; Fagin and Sikes (Sikes claims to be Oliver's father as he accepts a ride from a carter); the Maylies and Dr Losberne, who nurture Oliver back to life; and, finally, Brownlow (with Mrs Bedwin at his side), who formally adopts him.[55] In a novel that, curiously, so many critics have regarded as falling into two clear 'halves',[56] this parenting trope is thematically utterly central and importantly links the workhouse and criminal-London scenes. In *Oliver Twist* as in the literature of the anti-Poor Law movement, the New Poor Law itself is presented as at best an inadequate and at worst a malevolent institutional surrogate parent to the thousands of children that it forcibly removed from their mothers and fathers. Oliver and Little Dick are determinedly sentimentalised in their purity and untainted affections in contrast to the corrupted urban youth of Jack Dawkins, Charley Bates and Nancy. But they are all alike in their parentless status, and Dickens's sympathy clearly extends to the children of London's streets. The biggest question that the novel asks is whether the Poor Law, be it in its old or its new incarnation, is really a better 'parent' than Fagin and his criminal gang. It would have been a profoundly discomfiting question for supporters of political economy to have been asked.

The absence of parents in the novel is symptomatic of the absence of any traditional model of the family *at all* in its pages. The literature of the anti-Poor Law movement draws our attention to the destruction of the working-class family; in *Oliver Twist*, this process would seem to have reached its terminal point. The Sowerberrys are small tradespeople who keep servants; the abject Bayham family is reduced to pauperism. Refusing to enter the workhouse in the manner Dickens outlines above, and denied outdoor relief, Mr Bayham has to watch his wife literally die of starvation in a distressing scene that has its counterpart in many of the incidents recounted in Baxter's *Book of the Bastiles*. Oliver and Mr Sowerberry find the bereaved family in a rat-infested neighbourhood:

There was no fire in the room; but a man was crouching mechanically over the empty stove. An old woman, too, had drawn a low stool to the cold hearth, and was sitting beside him. There were some ragged children in another corner; and in a small recess opposite the door there lay upon the ground something covered with an old blanket . . .

'Ah!' said the man, bursting into tears, and sinking on his knees at the foot of the dead woman; 'kneel down, kneel down – kneel round her every one of you, and mark my words. I say she starved to death. I never knew how bad she was, till the fever came upon her, and then her bones were starting through her skin. There was neither fire nor candle; she died in the dark – in the dark. She couldn't even see her children's faces, though we heard her gasping out their names.'

(*Oliver Twist*, p. 41)

Dickens more usually alights – and would do so to strong emotional and moral effect in *A Christmas Carol* a few years later – upon the working-class family as a domestic refuge from the chill air of the world of political economy. Here, though, although the genuine feeling and bonds of love that the reader will later witness in the Cratchit family are not in doubt, in all other respects the working-class domestic unit is in tatters, deprived as it is of its life's blood – labour. The Bayhams represent what, in Dickens's view, might happen to those of the poor who reject the harsh regime of the workhouse; it is little wonder, the novel suggests, that Fagin's den might be deemed to offer a reasonable refuge to the orphans of the New Poor Law.

Dickens's satire on the New Poor Law, and on the tenets of political economy that spawned it, is hard-hitting; the conventions of melodrama are, though, equally important in reaching the broad popular audience which he wished to address. I would agree with Juliet John that Dickens had an ideological commitment to the aesthetics of melodrama, and to its 'working-class concerns as well as its emphasis on family and community'.[57] Melodrama had long been established, as we have seen, as an aesthetic of protest when Dickens began to negotiate its conventions in the interpolated melodramatic 'tales' of *The Pickwick Papers* and more full-bloodedly in *Oliver Twist*. Arguably this, his second novel, is the most melodramatic of them all: its narratives of dispersal and reunion and of domestic suffering; its representation of bodily violence and physical affliction; the criminal elements; the providential plotting and wild coincidences; the Manichean structure of good and evil; the lost will; old Sally's deathbed revelation; and Oliver's unexpected inheritance – all would, in the 1830s, have immediately aligned the novel with this hugely popular and potentially radical genre.

Broadly writing within the parameters of a popular aesthetic mode also helped ensure financial success for the young author, and Dickens shared with other of the anti-Poor Law writers and artists a willingness to embrace commercialism: this critique of political economy has, after all, its own external economic logic. C. J. Grant is an interesting comparative figure in this respect: firmly rooted, in his anti-Poor Law cartoons, in a popular radical tradition of protest, he at the same time was not averse to more purely commercial work, providing, for example, the illustrations for Edward Lloyd's and Thomas Peckett Prest's massively successful plagiarisms of *The Pickwick Papers* and *Oliver Twist*, the *Penny Pickwick* and *Oliver Twiss* 'By Bos', respectively.[58] Grant drew on early nineteenth-century popular radical political caricature, but was also able to take advantage of the rise of commercial populism towards the mid-century in the work he did for Edward Lloyd. Dickens, too, was quick to exploit the possibility of a mass readership. In Dickens's case, though, the coupling of popular radical cultural traditions to commercial populism was on a much grander scale than Grant or others could have dreamt of. The 'popular front' of the anti-Poor Law movement, with its literature circulated across establishment newspapers, high-brow quarterlies, middle-brow monthlies, penny weeklies and even street literature, was a textual field ripe for intervention from an up-and-coming young novelist who wished to write a commercially viable literature both about and for 'the People' in the broadest sense. *Oliver Twist*, published in the monthly *Bentley's Miscellany*, was not cheap; but it made itself available to an audience beyond the middle classes through its stage adaptations, pirated fictional pastiches and, later, through Dickens's own electrifying performances. Peter Ackroyd, writing about *The Pickwick Papers*, has illustrated other ways in which Dickens's fiction was circulated throughout the land:

the most important evidence for the success of Dickens's work is to be found in the report of one of his first biographers who, at the time of the novel's appearance, had visited a locksmith in Liverpool: 'I found him reading Pickwick . . . to an audience of twenty persons, literally, men, women and children.' It was hired by them all for two pence a day from the circulating library, because they could not afford a shilling for the monthly number, and the observer never forgot how these humble people, who themselves could not read, laughed with Sam Weller and cried with 'ready tears' at the death of the poor debtor in the Fleet prison. This was the audience which Charles Dickens had found – not only the judges and the doctors, but the labouring poor. By some miracle of genius he had found a voice which penetrated the hearts of the high as well as of the low. Truly he had created a national audience.[59]

Not all of Dickens's audience was, though, uncritically bound to him. *Oliver Twist*'s critics disputed its reliability as a critique of the New Poor Law, and most vocal of these was Harriet Martineau. Writing in 1849, Martineau, whilst acknowledging Dickens's genius, wished that he would refrain from 'the exhibition of human miseries as an artistical study'. She wished too 'that he had a sounder social philosophy' and complained that 'Another vexation is his vigorous erroneousness about matters of science, as shown in *Oliver Twist* about the new Poor Law (which he confounds with the abrogated old one).'[60] It is generally agreed that Oliver Twist, according to the novel's timescale, is born in 1828 under the old regime of parish overseers (some effort is made to pursue his missing father, which is suggestive of the old Settlement Laws). When Oliver returns to the workhouse from Mrs Mann's Baby Farm, aged eight or nine, he is entering a new regime with its attendant Board of Guardians.[61] Bumble the beadle survives the changing regime, and is promoted under the new one to master of the workhouse. Whilst Dickens *is* accurate in his recording of the ways in which many of the practices of the 'old' regime persisted under the new one, historical accuracy is not what drives his novel, nor the whole sea of anti-Poor Law literature that both inspired *Oliver Twist* and was greatly enriched by it. Whilst the scene in the novel in which Oliver is brought before the Board of Guardians was published in *The Times* as a social document (rather than as a piece of fiction) in the newspaper's campaign against the New Poor Law,[62] what propels Dickens's novel is not a factual history but an *imaginative* critique of political economy. It is political economy in general, rather than old or new Poor Laws in particular, which is the political spur to Dickens's creativity in *Oliver Twist*. Nor was he alone in his alighting upon the parish beadle as part of his critique: as we have seen, this easily identifiable, readily despised figure of scorn was vilified not just by Dickens but across a whole swathe of literature and visual culture that set itself against the new legislation. No matter that he became a redundant figure in the world of the New Poor Law – the satirical effect of Dickens's and others' attack upon this figure of petty officialdom is paramount. Dickens's critique of the New Poor Law can usefully be compared with William Cobbett's in this respect. Whilst Cobbett had shown himself as willing as the most popular writers to embrace melodrama in his political campaigns earlier in the century, in his *Legacy to Labour* from 1835 he carefully constructs a rational argument against the new legislation, an argument grounded in scripture and in moral and political philosophy. Dickens, by contrast, appeals to the emotions and intuitive morals of his readership, drawing heavily upon, as well as imaginatively extending, the themes, tropes and preoccupations of an existing literature of protest, as well as upon the aesthetic genres – satire and melodrama – that spoke most articulately to and about the poor and the oppressed.

The jovial 'happy ending' that characterises the final pages of *The Pickwick Papers* is by and large sustained in *Oliver Twist*, and the melo-dramatic expectations of its readers are satisfied with a restoration of moral order. Fagin, not Oliver (as predicted by the Board of Guardians and

Figure 23 John Leech, 'Ignorance and Want', 1843.

threatened by Fagin), is hanged; Sikes accidentally hangs himself in front of a baying mob; Dawkins is transported overseas; Monks dies a reprobate's death; Oliver is restored to the gentility of his birthright; and Rose Fleming marries Harry Maylie. But there are some characters who fall beneath the radar of the moral order of the melodramatic mode. Oliver's joy at his own restitution is marred by the death of Little Dick, whose appearance before his death – 'his young limbs had wasted away like those of an old man' (*Oliver Twist*, p. 138) – closely resembles the distressingly wizened appearance of the children both in Seymour's etching for *Figaro in London* in February 1836 (see figure 18) and, later, in John Leech's illustrations of 'Ignorance' and 'Want' in *A Christmas Carol* (figure 23). Nancy – the only one of Fagin's gang who helps Oliver, and who has retained a strong moral sensibility – dies a violent death; whilst Noah Claypole gets off scot free, morphing seamlessly into the role of police informer. In this as in all of his later novels Dickens interrogates and pushes at the boundaries of the melodramatic mode, at the same time as firmly committing himself to it.

More affirmatively, Charley Bates is reclaimed, his instinctual horror at Sikes's murder of Nancy rendering him recuperable in terms of the novel's moral economy. Charley, the reader is informed, decides to lead 'an honest life' and goes on to become 'the merriest young grazier in all Northamptonshire' (*Oliver Twist*, pp. 452–3). The affirmative mood survives in the first of Dickens's Christmas Books in the early 1840s (*A Christmas Carol*, 1843), and more problematically into his second (*The Chimes*, 1844).

The paternalistic structure that was a feature common to early nineteenth-century melodrama remains intact in *Oliver Twist*: it is the gentlemanly Brownlow who effects the despatch of the villainous Monks; who effectively seeks the punishment of the hateful Bumbles; and who claims Oliver as his own at the close.[63] The novel's paternalism persists in the first of Dickens's Christmas Books, but is vehemently challenged in the second. In *Barnaby Rudge*, though, Dickens's novel from 1841, paternalism is jettisoned entirely as a political structure of feeling. These and other popular political writings from the 1840s are the subject of the next chapter.

CHAPTER 4

Christmas is cancelled: Dickens and Douglas Jerrold writing the 1840s

DICKENS, JERROLD AND THE POPULAR RADICAL INHERITANCE

Early in November 1836, Dickens wrote to the popular playwright and journalist Douglas Jerrold to invite him to write for *Bentley's Miscellany*:

> Although I have not the pleasure of knowing you personally, I am on such intimate terms with your writings that I almost feel an apology to be unnecessary when I say that I intend calling on you tomorrow afternoon . . . in the hope that I may be able to obtain your promise of a paper for the first number of Mr Bentley's 'Wit's Miscellany'.[1]

In the event, Jerrold contributed neither to *Bentley's Miscellany* nor, later, to *Household Words*, even though Dickens coveted his services for both. This early letter none the less marks the beginning of a quite remarkable literary and political relationship between the two authors. The theatre was a shared passion, with Jerrold enjoying considerable renown as a popular playwright in the 1820s and 1830s, most notably with *Black-ey'd Susan* (1829) and *The Rent Day* (1832).[2] Dickens praised a production of *Black-ey'd Susan* in one of the various theatre reviews he wrote between 1835 and 1849, commenting on Jerrold's play that it 'is a remarkable illustration of what a man of genius may do with a common enough theme'.[3] Much the same could be said of a great deal of Dickens's writing, the two writers sharing an ability both to engage with and to energise popular cultural forms. A leading participant in the high-profile amateur dramatics that Dickens organised between 1845 and 1848, Jerrold was also a popular melodramatist in the theatre. Like Dickens, though, he was equally at home with a satirical pen in his hand, and this is the aesthetic mode that informs a great deal of Jerrold's most powerful journalistic writings from the 1840s. Their shared hatred of the workhouse system, their dislike of organised religion, their attacks on the judiciary and more generally their sympathy for the poor and for the oppressed: such preoccupations, as well as their shared commitment to satire and melodrama as aesthetic vehicles, and an at times savage humour, forged an unusually strong literary and political bond between the two writers in the wintry economic climate of the 1840s.[4]

Determinedly anti-establishment, one of the most powerful political structures of feeling that both Dickens and Jerrold would negotiate in the 1840s was paternalism. Often embedded in the melodramatic mode of writing embraced by both writers, and much in evidence in both *The Pickwick Papers* (1836–7) and *Oliver Twist* (1837–9), Dickens would be the first to cast off the politics of paternalism to dramatic effect in his novel from 1841, *Barnaby Rudge*. Endorsing paternalism just once more in *A Christmas Carol* (1843), in the figure of the newly benevolent and charitable Mr Scrooge, Dickens would determinedly renounce it once and for all in *The Chimes* (1844), never again championing paternalism as a panacea either for social injustice or the evils of poverty. Jerrold's writings in the 1840s are equally in dialogue with paternalistic politics: whilst an essay from 1843 written for the *Illuminated Magazine* firmly rejects the feudal past[5], his story serialised in *Punch* in the same year, *The Story of a Feather*, melodramatically espouses paternalism as a social cure-all.[6]

Both Dickens's and Jerrold's negotiation of paternalism will form a central strand of the second half of this chapter. It was not only the politics of paternalism that preoccupied these two popular writers of the 1840s, though: they were equally earnest in their denunciation of contemporary theories of political economy. This second major shared political concern, illuminated in relation to Dickens in my reading of *Oliver Twist* in chapter 3, can also be identified in Jerrold's attack on the New Poor Law in an essay published in January 1843. Leader writer for *Punch* in the first half of the 1840s, Jerrold wrote a whole series of radical essays under the guise of 'Q' that were politically hard-hitting and highly critical of the social and political status quo.[7] Fiercely anti-clerical and republican, Jerrold's journalism for *Punch* in the 1840s is also characterised by its attacks on Parliament, on the legal system and on those individuals whom he felt should be held to account for the sufferings of the poor. Thoroughly characteristic is 'The "Milk" of Poor Law "Kindness"', a 'Q' essay in which Jerrold uses as his starting point a report that at Bethnal Green workhouse 'An infant, only *five weeks old*, was separated from the mother, being occasionally brought to her for the breast.'[8] Jerrold's essay, in focusing on the separation of infants from their mothers in the workhouse, reprises one of the most recurrent and emotive themes of the literature of the anti-Poor Law movement that continued to flourish in the 1840s. The essay was accompanied by a Kenny Meadows illustration

PUNCH'S PENCILLINGS.——N°· LXII.

THE "MILK" OF POOR-LAW "KINDNESS."

Figure 24 Kenny Meadows, 'The "Milk" of Poor Law "Kindness"', *Punch, or,*
The London Charivari (4 January 1843).

(see figure 24) that depicts a Manichean opposition between good and evil
fundamental to popular melodrama. The pauper mother and her infant are
seated beneath a weeping angel who cannot bear to look on as the workhouse harridan, overseen by a grinning devil, rips the baby from its
mother's breast, the workhouse railings clearly visible in the background.
The presence of the angel suggests the iconography of Madonna and child,
implying a critique of contemporary Christianity that Jerrold also exploits
in his accompanying text. Jerrold's essay, though, shifts away from the
melodramatic mode of Meadows's illustration, adopting instead a harshly

satirical tone. Meadows's workhouse harridan transmutes, in Jerrold's text, into the New-Poor-Law-as-mother:

What a beneficent presence is this same Poor-Law, that it takes to its bosom babes and sucklings – that it lavishes upon callow infancy the tenderness, the love, the gushing kindness of maternal instincts! . . .
   Let us watch the outward development of the inward love beating in the heart of the Somerset-House automaton, the mother-in-law (for he was officially born of the statute) of Mr EDWIN CHADWICK. Her adopted babe of five weeks old screams for its natural parent; and the old hag – the childless SYCORAX, unblest even by a CALIBAN of her own – hobbles with the squalling nuisance, the pauper-brat, the law-made offal of the land, to its natural parent, who has offended the decencies of the land by adding to the list of GOD's helpless creatures, and who is therefore doomed to the hospitality of the Union.[9]

Meadows's baby-snatching harridan figuratively merges with the Poor Law itself, the 'Somerset-House automaton' whose 'gushing kindness' and 'maternal instincts' are heavily ironised. The Poor-Law-as-mother trope is extended in Jerrold's characterisation of the legislation as the 'mother-in-law . . . of Edwin Chadwick', Chadwick being the author of the Poor Law Report and so chief architect of the legislation. The consumption trope common to so much anti-Poor Law literature also resurfaces here in the description of the wailing infant as the 'law-made offal of the land' – the least desirable portion of the nation's biological produce, not worthy of consumption.

   The same trope is extended when the essay enters its most severely satirical phase as Jerrold reports on the refusal of a special festive dietary to workhouse inhabitants on Christmas Day in 1842:

There had been talk – a foolish rumour of foolish intention, to regale certain workhouse people with a gill or so of ale, and a slice of pudding . . . that Christmas might be to their senses something more than a name – that they might feel that a recollection of the Advent of Christ yet throbbed in the hearts of their richer fellow-Christians. But no! the Poor-Law – at least in the opinion of Lord Howick – was expressly passed to repeal the New Testament, and there should be no chance of the paupers running riot on the strength of illegally applied Christianity.[10]

Provocatively divorcing not only the Poor Law but also the government itself from Christianity, Jerrold here, like Dickens before him, draws on a common currency amongst anti-Poor Law protesters. In *Oliver Twist* Dickens had recounted how each workhouse boy was fed 'one porringer' of gruel at each mealtime 'except on festive occasions, and then he had two onions and a quarter of bread besides' (*Oliver Twist*, p. 14) *The Book of the*

Bastiles – the anthology of anti-Poor Law texts discussed in chapter 3 – similarly records a Christmas-related incident:

By Mr Walter. – Q. 'Supposing any charitable lady in the neighbourhood were desirous of giving the children a dinner on Christmas day, could you, as the chairman of the board, allow a thing of that sort to be done?' A. 'No, I could not.'[11]

The festive diet of the poor is also topical to Dickens's first two Christmas Books, *A Christmas Carol* and *The Chimes*, as I will illustrate in the next section.

Jerrold's satirical attack on the state's neglect of Christian principles is repeated across a great deal of his journalism from the 1840s. Characteristic too is the satirical attack upon responsible individuals – in this case Edwin Chadwick – as are the Shakespearean allusions, which reflect the largely middle-class readership he is addressing.

All these characteristics would also have been familiar to readers of Dickens. In *Oliver Twist* there is a satirical attack – typically a little more genial in tone than Jerrold's – on the lack of true Christian principles amongst those who profess themselves to be followers of the faith. ' "He's an out-and-out Christian," ' Charley Bates comments humorously about Sikes's dog, after which Dickens reflects mischievously that:

This was merely intended as a tribute to the animal's abilities, but it was an appropriate remark in another sense, if Master Bates had only known it; for there are a great many ladies and gentlemen claiming to be out-and-out Christians, between whom and Mr Sikes's dog there exist very strong and singular points of resemblance. (*Oliver Twist*, p. 148)

The comic hypocrisy of the wheedling Stiggins in *The Pickwick Papers*, the snivelling insincerity of the hateful Heep in *David Copperfield*, the air-filled emptiness of Chadband's pseudo-Christian rhetoric in *Bleak House* and the pompous hypocrisy of Pumblechook as he presides over Christmas dinner in *Great Expectations*; clearly Dickens was as alert as Jerrold to the mismatch between the profession and the practice of Christianity in the society he saw around him. The objects of his attack were more likely to be low church than high church, though, whilst Jerrold's preferred hate figures tended to be bishops and the higher clergy. In this way Jerrold's anti-clericalism perhaps had more in common with that of his popular radical forebears in the early years of the nineteenth century.

Jerrold's attacks on the clergy are arguably also closer in tone as well as in substance to the anti-clerical writings of Regency radicals. Whilst Michael Slater is quite right to have identified Rabelais as a major influence on Jerrold's satirical writings throughout his career,[12] it is worth remembering that Jerrold moved to London and became a printer's apprentice in January 1816. As we have seen in chapter 1, this was London's great age of radical satire, with William Hone, George Cruikshank, Thomas Wooler, William Cobbett and others furiously producing satirical pamphlets and news-papers that attacked the Church, the monarchy and the aristocracy on behalf of the poor and the oppressed. Jerrold was in many ways a scion of these popular radical writers of the second decade of the nineteenth century, and his subsequent influence on his friend and fellow writer, Charles Dickens, reinforces the younger writer's own links to Regency culture.

Jerrold's 'Q' articles from *Punch* in the first part of the 1840s are strewn with satirical attacks on greedy, bloated bishops on £10,000-a-year sti-pends. In 'The Corn Laws and Christianity' he attacks the Anglican episcopate in general terms;[13] in 'Wanted – Some Bishops!' he alights more particularly on Henry Philpotts, Bishop of Exeter. A favourite object of Jerrold's satire, Exeter is reported as having suggested, in response to the want and distress he witnessed all around him, that the country needed more bishops to guide it spiritually. 'All our sufferings arise from a dearth of Bishops,' Jerrold remarks, apparently deadpan. But what he really thinks about the efficacy of the bishopric in alleviating the miseries of the poor is revealed in the ensuing paragraphs, in which the proposed abundance of clergymen is contrasted ironically with their illiberality in matters of charity:

The Catholic Church has her hundred legends of the liberality of her saints, who have stripped themselves to clothe the naked pauper. But with all her triumphs – amidst all her relics, can she show the pawnbroker's duplicate of a Bishop's watch, left with the Lombardy merchant in default of ready money, for hard cash wherewith to the relieve the poor.

The satire of the final effusion in favour of more bishops is sharp:

Shall we deny to Henry of Exeter even a multitude of Bishops? Certainly not; and, therefore, let there be circulated throughout every village where a curate vegetates, handbills with these words –
'WANTED – SOME BISHOPS!'[14]

A few weeks later Jerrold compares the Archbishop of Bordeaux to a highway robber – his disrespect for the upper echelons of the Church knew no bounds.[15] It was a disrespect that persisted beyond his sinecure as leader writer for *Punch* in the early 1840s: his 'Hedgehog Letters' for *Douglas Jerrold's Shilling Magazine* include a satirical account of the debates in the Church concerning the wearing of surplices, with the Bishop of

Exeter once again the butt of Jerrold's wit.[16] He also includes in his weekly magazine a melodramatic tale, 'The Winter Robin', in which a clerical magistrate accosts a small child who is on her way home from the pawn shop, having pawned her dead mother's wedding ring in order to buy some food: 'Come, come, speak out child,' the clergyman berates her: 'Do you know who I am – eh? I am a clergyman and a magistrate . . . I allow no beggars in Rookfield! I send them all to prison!'[17] Jerrold's serially published novel, *St Giles and St James*, which appeared in *Douglas Jerrold's Shilling Magazine* between 1845 and 1846, similarly attacks the luxurious lifestyles of the higher Anglican clergy, represented here by one Rev. Dr Gilead of Lazarus Hall.[18] Jerrold's jeering attacks on bishops and the higher clergy resonate strongly with William Hone's attacks on the worldliness of the clerical magistrate in *The Political House That Jack Built* in 1819 and in his numerous other assaults on corrupt church functionaries.[19] They echo, too, the anti-clericalism of Thomas Wooler and William Cobbett in the same period. Wooler's essay from 1819, 'AFFECTATION OF CHRISTIANITY BY THE 'HIGHER ORDERS'', is characteristically jeering in tone:

Who would not imagine, from the mode in which our *lords* and *lordships*, bishops, deans, prebends, and priests, talk of Christianity, that it was a system of *exclusive preference of the rich*! – a religion of *pomp* and *circumstance*? – and something above the faculties of the 'lower orders' . . . Who would not imagine its FOUNDER to have been some purple-meek and lowly JESUS, who had nowhere to lay his head? Who went about doing good? Exhorting to temperance and charity, and setting the example of abstinence which he preached? . . . Their religion consists only in their emoluments – the *tythe laws* are their *Decalogue*; and the church dues all of gospel for which they care.[20]

The acerbic tone adopted by William Cobbett towards the clergy is similarly characteristic of Regency anti-clericalism:

It is very curious that, while we are so frequently told that the population of the *labouring classes* is too great and ought to be checked in its increase, we hear of no projects for checking the population of those who do not labour. The clergy, for instance, together with their off-spring, form a very numerous body. They receive a very large portion out of the fruits of the earth, and they contribute nothing that I can perceive, towards an increase of those fruits . . . Immense sums, out of the taxes, and raised upon our salt, soap, candles &c, have within these few years, been given to what is called the '*poor clergy*'! Immense sums, I say, to augment the maintenance of the poor clergy; and only last year, a *hundred and ten thousand pounds* was granted for this purpose, and I never heard that it was objected to by MR. BROUGHAM, who is so anxious to check the population of the labouring classes.[21]

Whilst Dickens tended to be more concerned with doctrinal cant than with the wealth of the clergy, his affinities to Cobbett are nonetheless very marked. The currency of Malthusian theories of population in the early nineteenth century is clearly evinced in Cobbett's diatribe. Brougham and Cobbett would go on to become two of the leading players in the debates for and against the New Poor Law of 1834, and are here shown to be engaged in a conflicted dialogue as early as 1819. Cobbett's implied support of those working-class families that wished to have children would be echoed down the years in *The Chimes*, Dickens's Christmas Book from 1844, in which the author stoutly defends early marriage amongst the poor. The Chartist *Northern Star* also supported the reproduction rights of the working classes, typically congratulating a weaver named Joseph Ashworth who had recently fathered triplets – expanding his family to thirty children – under the heading 'Anti-Malthusianism'.[22]

Cobbett was like Dickens in his caution around the subject of republicanism. Whilst Dickens's writings suggest that he had republican sympathies, they were not central to his agenda as a social critic and novelist. None the less, his *A Child's History of England* is, as John Lucas has noted, essentially a republican account of England, peopled with cruel and tyrannical monarchs and ending in 1688 in praise of Cromwell;[23] and his satirical portrait of the Prince Regent in the figure of Old Turveydrop in *Bleak House* is far from genial. Cobbett – unsurprisingly given the politically oppressive climate in which he was writing – was more careful still, publicly avowing in 1819 to have 'nothing to do with anyone' who declared 'for *Republican Government*'.[24] Douglas Jerrold's approach to republicanism was reckless in comparison, and has much in common with Thomas Wooler's and William Hone's writings against the monarchy. Michael Slater has described how Jerrold 'kept his hat firmly on his head when the Queen and Albert passed him, riding through Putney village in a "char-à-banc" attended by several courtiers'.[25] This republican stance was backed up by a number of essays written for *Punch*, perhaps most notably his 'Q' leader from 1843, 'A Royal Wife of – £3,000'.[26] In this essay Jerrold reports on Robert Peel's announcement that the Princess Augusta would shortly be married to the Duke of Mecklenburgh Streltz:

The Duke, however, wanted something more in his cup to make the draft palatable; in a word, the wife was very well – but, with the wife he wanted money ... The Princess Augusta ... will receive £3,000 a year from the taxes. This is moderate – very moderate indeed. How the young couple will be able to get on we know not ... Again, when we remember the immense sum of £10,000 was voted only for the education of the poor of all England, we are surprised at the magnanimity which contents itself with something less than a third of that amount.[27]

The jeering tone used to attack the wealth inequality between the monarchy and its subjects is worthy of William Hone's endless attacks on the gross luxury of the Prince Regent's lifestyle in the late 1810s, and of Thomas Wooler's comparison of the Prince Regent with an Eastern Mogul, an attack that landed Wooler in jail.[28] Leigh Hunt, too, while editor of the *Examiner*, found himself imprisoned from 1813 to 1815 for having likened the Prince Regent to a 'fat old Florizel of forty'.[29] The fierceness of Jerrold's satirical attacks on the monarchy in the 1840s binds him closely to his radical Regency forbears. Jerrold, of course, was writing for a rather different readership than Wooler, Cobbett and Hone in the 1810s: *Punch* was addressed to the middle classes, whilst Hone, Wooler and Cobbett were speaking to a wider popular audience. What Jerrold achieved in *Punch* in the early 1840s was to import a disreputable radical politics from an earlier period into middle-class Victorian culture.

Strong as the affinities undoubtedly are between Jerrold's journalism and that of the popular radical writers of the Regency period, his literary and political proximity to Dickens is stronger still.

JOURNALISM, JERROLD AND DICKENS IN THE 1840S

Two characteristic pieces of journalism from the 1840s, one by Jerrold and one by Dickens, vividly illuminate their shared political and literary temperament. Jerrold was heavily involved in journalism in the 1840s, as he would be for the rest of his life. As well as writing leaders for *Punch* in the early 1840s, he also edited the *Illuminated Magazine* and in 1845 and 1846 respectively set up two of his own journalistic ventures, *Douglas Jerrold's Shilling Magazine* and *Douglas Jerrold's Weekly Newspaper*. Dickens, whilst constantly projecting journalistic ventures during the 1840s, mainly concentrated in this period on the writing of fiction, focusing his journalistic efforts on writing for Albany Fonblanque's and subsequently John Forster's *Examiner*. His scattering of unsigned essays and squibs for this radical weekly is, though, of great interest for its profoundly anti-Tory stance, representing some of his most radically expressed opinions. Dickens's one foray into mainstream journalism in this decade as editor of the *Daily News* proved to be an abortive adventure, his editorship of the new paper lasting just eighteen days, and his overall involvement with the project ten weeks.[30]

Jerrold was full of satirical energy as he launched his weekly *Shilling Magazine* in 1845, and one of the strongest of his leading articles for the new periodical was a piece in the manner of Swift: 'Slavery: The Only Remedy for the Miseries of the English Poor, By a Philanthropist'. Both Jerrold and Dickens were influenced by the eighteenth century satirist, as well as by Hone and Wooler; Dickens owned Swift's complete works.[31] The title of Jerrold's essay is self-explanatory: with a sang-froid worthy of his fellow satirist from the eighteenth century, Jerrold proposes that enforced slavery would act as a ' "panacea" to the varied and bitter ills that beset three-fourths of the poor inhabitants of "The *United* Kingdom" ':

[T]he only way to permanently and efficiently remedy the complicated evils [of poverty] would be, to ENSLAVE *the whole of the people of England who have not property* . . .

The first great advantage would be, that the lower classes of society would be placed on an equality with the domestic animals; and by becoming property, become valuable and valued . . . Entire and complete slavery of the poor would put an end to all the discussions of their rights, and clearly and definitely work out the relative duties of all classes.[32]

Very much in the style of Swift's *Tale of a Tub* (1704), Jerrold here boldly and provocatively positions his persona against an abolitionist discourse that would have had a powerful currency amongst the middle- and lower-middle-class readers of *Douglas Jerrold's Shilling Magazine*. He also leans on some of the arguments from the literature of the anti-Poor Law movement that argued that prisoners were treated better than paupers: here it is slavery that is posited as preferable to the lot of the English poor. Here too Jerrold takes a side-swipe at contemporary political economy in his persona's reflection that as slaves the 'lower classes of society' would, 'by becoming property', at least 'become valuable and valued'. Writing two years after the Chartist petition of 1842 and in the years preceding the subsequent Chartist flashpoint of 1848, Jerrold clearly aligns himself, here, against capital and on the side of the disenfranchised who were clamouring for their 'rights'.

Writing in the year of the Chartist petition itself, Dickens similarly sets himself against the ruling political classes, identifying strongly with 'the vulgar men of toil and sweat, and want and rags' who are treated with disdain by 'the Landed Interest' and by 'Oppressive and unequal laws'. More complex than Jerrold's undoubtedly powerful satire, Dickens's 'Snoring for the Million', published in the *Examiner* in 1842, takes as its ostensible theme the contemporary vogue for the teaching of singing to the poor. The Privy Council's Committee on Education had decided in 1841 that:

Amusements which wean the people from vicious indulgences are in themselves a great advantage ... The songs of any people may be regarded as an important means of forming an industrious, brave, loyal and religious working class.[33]

As the practice of teaching the poor to sing increased, 'Singing for the Million' became a popular catchphrase, and it is this that is the spur to Dickens's satire. Clearly incensed as well as filled with a strong sense of the comic absurdity of the government's decision to respond to poverty with singing lessons, Dickens's retort is sharp:

The Government seeing the million with their mouths wide open, naturally thinks that they must want to sing; for it only recognizes two kinds of forks, the silver fork and the tuning fork, between which opposite extremes there is nothing. 'John,' said the frugal lady to her thirsty footman, 'when you go into the cellar to draw beer, be good enough to whistle all the time.' 'John,' says the Government to its starving servant, 'when you ramble up and down the market-places, dying of hunger, be careful, above all things, to sing perpetually.'

Inspired – he would have his readers believe – by the success of the government's singing programme, Dickens proposes that the scheme be extended: 'We desire to propound a system of Snoring for the Million.'[34] One can immediately distinguish the difference, in the 1840s, between Dickens and Jerrold, as well as the similarity. Both use satire as a vehicle with which to criticise the government's inadequate (as they saw it) response to poverty; and their proposed 'remedies' (enforced slavery on the one hand, mass snoring on the other) are patently (and determinedly) absurd. But whilst Jerrold's proposed 'antidote' is savage and harsh, Dickens's is ludicrous; Jerrold's satire is designed to stimulate righteous anger, whilst Dickens's provokes hilarity as well as indignation. Lurking in Dickens's satire is the belly laughter of Samuel Weller; Jerrold's is more bitter in tone.

The essential sobriety of Jerrold's satirical journalism is evinced again in a leading article he wrote for the *Pictorial Times* in 1843, ironically entitled 'The Beauties of the Police'. In it he begins with an anecdotal (and presumably fictional) account concerning the forcing apart of a man and his child in the Mile-End workhouse. Charged with begging in the street, the man, one 'Bull' (a byword for the patriotic English working man), is asked by the magistrate: 'Wherefore did you not go to the workhouse?' Bull explains that he had been in a workhouse, but had been separated there from his wife and child, and that any amount of suffering was preferable to that: 'He would risk starvation and the cold comfort of a stone-step for his bed; but, then, his child would be with him in his misery: they would not be separated like cattle in the pens of Smithfield.'[35] Father and child are none the less once more separated when the former is sent to the House of Correction. In describing the distress of the man and his daughter Jerrold's essay shifts rapidly between satire, melodramatic affect and then back to satire once again:

Bull, however, showed himself an incorrigible vagabond. When about to be torn from his child he writhed in agony, and the little girl, says the reporter, 'wept bitterly.' Notwithstanding, the culprit of poverty was taken away by the gaoler; taken to the House of Correction; there to dream a JACOB's dream, seeing the Poor Law Commissioners, like celestial presences, 'ascending and descending' for the especial relief and comfort of the English pauper.[36]

The melodramatic affect produced by the wrenching apart of the distraught father and his weeping child is lent realism by its being presented as reported speech ('wept bitterly'), throwing the tableau into vivid relief, set as it is amidst the unforgiving satire of Jerrold's bitter commentary.

The rapid shifts between satire and melodrama in Jerrold's essay are a feature, too, of the first two of Dickens's Christmas Books from the 1840s, *A Christmas Carol* (1843) and *The Chimes* (1844). Both works of fiction also incorporate material not only from Jerrold's 'Beauties of the Police' essay from 1843, but from his oeuvre more generally. It is to Dickens's Christmas Books from 1843 and 1844 that I will now turn.

WRITING CHRISTMAS: *A CHRISTMAS CAROL* AND *THE CHIMES*

John Forster, Dickens's first biographer, reflected in 1872 that his friend had 'identified himself' with Christmas and noted that 'its privilege to light up with some sort of comfort the squalidest of places, he had made his own'.[37] From the earliest days of his writing career, Dickens had alighted upon Christmas as a season of good cheer and fellow feeling in the midst of the national privations endured in the 1830s and 1840s. In his youthful collection of journalistic pieces, *Sketches by Boz* (1836), he had celebrated the pleasures of Christmas thus:

Christmas time! . . . There seems a magic in the very name of Christmas. Petty jealousies and discords are forgotten; social feelings are awakened, in bosoms to which they have long been strangers; father and son, or brother and sister, who have met and passed with averted gaze, or a look of cold recognition, for months before, proffer and return the cordial embrace, and bury their past animosities in their present happiness.[38]

In the 'good-humoured Christmas Chapter' of *The Pickwick Papers* Dickens similarly venerates Christmas as a 'brief season of happiness and enjoyment ... How many old recollections, and how many dormant sympathies, does Christmas time awaken!' (*Pickwick*, p. 361).

With the publication of *A Christmas Carol* in December 1843, Dickens was hugely successful in awakening such 'dormant sympathies' in a novella that warmly elaborates on his earlier Christmas themes. Lord Jeffrey, the former editor of the *Edinburgh Review*, wrote affectionately to Dickens on Boxing Day 1843: 'Blessings on your kind heart, my dear Dickens! . . . We are all charmed with your *Carol*, chiefly, I think, for the genuine *goodness* which breathes all through it, and is the true inspiring angel by which its genius has been awakened.'[39] Three months later, reviewing the *Carol* for *Fraser's Magazine*, Thackeray was almost as effusive:

Who can listen to objections regarding such a book as this? It seems to me a national benefit, and to every man or woman who reads it a personal kindness. The last two people I heard speak of it were women; neither knew the other, or the author, and both said, by way of criticism, 'God bless him!' A Scotch philosopher, who nationally does not keep Christmas Day, on reading the book, sent out for a turkey, and asked two friends to dine – this is a fact![40]

The access of feeling aroused across the country by Dickens's little book meant that it was quickly established as a national institution, even though initially it sold – by Dickens's standards – a relatively modest number of copies (about 15,000 by early 1844).[41] Dickens felt that commercially the book made him an insufficient return, expressing his surprise and disappointment in a letter to Forster from February 1844:

Such a night as I have passed! I really believed I should never get up again, until I had passed through all the horrors of a fever. I found the *Carol* accounts awaiting me, and they were the cause of it. The first six thousand copies show a profit of £230! And the last four will yield as much more. I had set my heart and soul upon a Thousand. What a wonderful thing it is, that such a great success should occasion me such intolerable anxiety and disappointment! My year's bills, unpaid, are so terrific, that all the energy and determination I can possibly exert will be required to clear me before I go abroad.[42]

Dickens's need to pay some hefty household bills partly explains the emergence of his Christmas Books as a genre. Writing five such books in total between 1843 and 1848, it was the first two that made the most impact on the national literary imagination: 'The popularity of the first two works in the annual [Christmas] series was unrivalled in English literature,' *Tait's Edinburgh Magazine* reflected in January 1849.[43]

But Dickens's need to make money coincided with a genuine desire to communicate his critique of political economy and account of poverty in

1840s England – via the powerful 'Christmas Book' format – to as wide a readership as possible. His original plan in the year that he published *A Christmas Carol* had been to write a political pamphlet provisionally entitled 'An Appeal to the People of England, on behalf of the Poor Man's Child', a project to which he makes reference in two letters to Dr Southwood Smith. Smith was one of the four Commissioners who had compiled the *Second Report of the Children's Employment Commission* that had been published in February 1843, and he had personally sent a copy of it to the young author, realising Dickens's importance as a disseminator of the ideas of the social reformers.[44] The *Second Report* made a powerful impression, detailing as it did the high numbers of children under seven years of age who worked ten to twelve hours a day across a whole range of employment fields.[45] Dickens intended to write a pamphlet that would, he told Southwood Smith on 6 March 1843, be 'very cheap' (and thus affordable to all), and would be signed (thus assuring a wide circulation). Four days later he wrote again, explaining to the Commissioner a change of direction:

Don't be frightened when I tell you, that since I wrote to you last, reasons have presented themselves for deferring the production of that pamphlet, until the end of the year. I am not at liberty to explain further, just now; but *rest assured* that when you know them, and see what I do, and where, and how, you will certainly feel that a Sledge hammer has come down with twenty times the force – twenty thousand times the force – I could exert by following my first idea.[46]

The 'Sledge hammer' was *A Christmas Carol*, and Dickens was surely right that this 'Ghostly little book', 'which shall not put my readers out of humour', as he describes it in his Preface, made a much bigger impact on behalf of the 'Poor Man's Child' than a cheap pamphlet could have done, albeit by a writer as famous as Boz. The currency of the *Carol* quickly spread beyond the written page, with various dramatized versions appearing at once, reaching out to non-reading as well as to literate audiences: by February 1844 at least eight theatrical productions had been staged.[47] Dickens himself went to and enjoyed Edward Stirling's adaptation at the Adelphi, which, like many subsequent productions ever since, included added songs in the manner of the melodrama proper. 'I saw the Carol last night,' he wrote to John Forster on 21 February 1844. 'Better than usual, and Wright seemed to enjoy Bob Cratchit, but *heart-breaking* to me.'[48] The *Carol* also became the mainstay of Dickens's public readings: it was the first public reading he ever gave (in 1853) and remained in his repertoire right up to his farewell performance in 1870, the year of his death. His first London performance of the *Carol* was recorded as an immense popular success:

We have rarely witnessed or shared an evening of such genuine enjoyment, and never before remember to have seen a crowded assembly of three thousand people hanging for upwards of two hours on the lips of a single reader . . . At the close there was an outburst, not so much of applause as of downright hurrahing, from every part of [the hall].[49]

This first London performance was for charity, but when Dickens turned professional in 1858 the *Carol* became, in its spoken version, a huge commercial success as well as a centrepiece of mid-Victorian popular culture.

The fate of Tiny Tim, and the scenes depicting the Cratchit family's brave attempts to maintain its working-class home in despite of the privations of poverty, are thematically central to the first of Dickens's Christmas Books. In imagining the death of Tiny Tim, and his family's brave but unavailing attempts to bear its grief ('"My little, little child!" cried Bob. "My little child!" He broke down all at once. He couldn't help it'),[50] Dickens dramatises to great emotional effect political economy's perceived assault on the working-class family. In using the supernatural 'ghostly' mechanism of the story's dream structure, though, he is able to resurrect Tiny Tim so that by the end of the tale what the reader has experienced is simultaneously an attack on and a defence and reaffirmation of working-class domesticity. As we have seen in chapter 3, protecting the integrity of the working-class family had been a central concern of the anti-Poor Law movement, and it is a concern that is expressed with great poignancy in *A Christmas Carol*. Here Dickens is able to sustain the Cratchits' nurturing family home notwithstanding the deadly apparitions of 'Ignorance' and 'Want' that lurk allegorically in the background. It is this dual vision that ensured the popularity of this, Dickens's first Christmas Book: his attack on political economy and the individualism that went with it is hard-hitting; but it is seasonally ameliorated by his Bacchanalian vision of plenty at Christmas time.

The kindness and beneficence that so many commentators identified in *A Christmas Carol* are a rarer commodity in the writings of Douglas Jerrold. None the less, the more sombre of the two writers significantly influenced Dickens's first Christmas Book. The Magistrate's heckling of 'Henry Bull' in 'The Beauties of the Police', written earlier in the same year – 'Wherefore did you not go to the workhouse?'[51] – is echoed by Scrooge a few months later when asked to give alms for the poor at Christmas:

'Many thousands are in want of common necessaries; hundreds of thousands are in want of common comforts, sir,' [said the gentleman].

'Are there no prisons?' asked Scrooge.

'Plenty of prisons,' said the gentleman, laying down the pen again.

'And the Union workhouses?' demanded Scrooge. 'Are they still in operation?'
'They are. Still,' returned the gentleman, 'I wish I could say they were not . . .'
'I wish to be left alone,' said Scrooge. '. . . I help to support the establishments
I have mentioned: they cost enough: and those who are badly off must go there.'
'Many can't go there; and many would rather die.' (*Carol*, p. 12)

Here Dickens deftly suggests a correspondence between workhouses and
penitentiaries at the same time as condemning the individualism associated
with political economy ('"I wish to be left alone," said Scrooge,' and further
on in the conversation he asserts that: '"It's enough for a man to understand
his own business, and not to interfere with other people's"' (p. 12)). In
Oliver Twist such individualism is framed in terms of Fagin's philosophy
of 'number one', which he teaches to his criminal apprentices; here its
endpoint is – in the nightmare vision of the 'Last of the Spirits' – a
wretchedly lonely death for Scrooge, as lonely as that endured by Fagin
in the earlier work of fiction. The parallel is not incidental.

Dickens extends his critique of political economy with the appearance
of the third spirit, who in a series of tableaux repeatedly, and ironically,
hurls Scrooge's own vocabulary back at him. In the final tableau of the
series, the increasingly uneasy man of business asks the Spirit what will
become of the ghostly apparitions of 'Ignorance' and 'Want'. The two tiny
children allegorically figured in John Leech's illustration (see figure 23) are
wizened and old before their time, closely resembling the verbal description
of Little Dick in *Oliver Twist* (see page 104) and Robert Seymour's etching
of pauper children for *Figaro in London* (see figure 18). Dickens's accompanying text combines a melodramatic rhetoric of good and evil with a
sober satire on the language of political economy:

They were a boy and girl. Yellow, meagre, ragged, scowling, wolfish; but prostrate,
too, in their humility. Where graceful youth should have filled their features out,
and touched them with its freshest tints, a stale and shrivelled hand, like that of
age, had pinched, and twisted them, and pulled them into shreds. Where angels
might have sat enthroned, devils lurked, and glared out menacing . . .
Scrooge started back, appalled . . .
'Have they no refuge or resource?' cried Scrooge.
'Are there no prisons?' said the Spirit, turning on him for the last time with his
own words. 'Are there no workhouses?' (pp. 62–3)

In the last of Dickens's Christmas Books, *The Haunted Man*, Dickens
similarly presents 'A bundle of tatters, held together by a hand, in size and
form almost an infant's, but, in its greedy, desperate little clutch, a bad old
man's . . . A baby savage, a young monster, a child who had never been a

child'.[52] In the final and arguably the gloomiest of Dickens's Christmas Books, the 'young monster' is real enough; here, though, the disturbing apparitions disappear as the story resolves into a Bacchanalian feast of plenty at Christmas time.

In resolving the Cratchits' poverty by having Scrooge provide them with a sumptuous Christmas lunch, Dickens asserts the right of the poor to eat – a right (in the language of political economy) to take part in the process of consumption from which, according to Benthamite economics and Malthusian theories of population, they should be excluded. In this way it shares one of the central themes of *Oliver Twist*.

The abundance that characterises the lasting impression of *A Christmas Carol* perhaps rather surprisingly would seem to owe a debt to a satirical utopian fantasy that Douglas Jerrold had written for the *Illuminated Magazine* in August 1843. As Michael Slater has noted, Jerrold's 'The Chronicles of Clovernook' is 'exactly similar in its vision of a world of joyous abundance' to the vision in Dickens's story of the jovial 'Ghost of Christmas Present'.[53] Jerrold's Rabelais-influenced 'Hermit of Bellyfulle' is discovered surrounded by a cornucopia of foodstuffs – eggs, hams, sausages, ales, wines – in a vision comparable to Dickens's 'Ghost of Christmas Present' on his throne of 'turkey, geese, game, poultry, brawn, great joints of meat, etc.' (*Carol*, p. 43).[54] Jerrold's serialised 'Chronicles' imagine, in Michael Slater's words, an:

hierarchical, but wholly benevolent society, a glorified mirror-image of contemporary England, where 'the state with paternal love watched . . . at the very cradles of the poor', where bishops 'from their tenderness, their piety, their affection towards their flocks, were looked upon as the very porters to heaven', not envied but 'looked upon as men, who having put into a lottery, had had the luck to draw a prize', and the poor 'were always treated with a softness of manner that surprised me.' The characters of the nobility of As-You-Like are expressed by their titles – the Duke of Lovingkindness, the Marquis of Sensibility, the Earl of Tenderheart, and so on.[55]

Jerrold's is a nostalgic rural vision of an imaginary feudal past in which the rich nurture the poor, and all enjoy an abundance of food that could only have been dreamt of in the so-called hungry 1830s and '40s. The nostalgia – which was utterly alien to Dickens's social and political imagination – is coupled with a paternalistic social vision which, when Jerrold and Dickens were writing, was under threat from the new social relationships forged by nineteenth-century industrialism and commerce. The paternalism, if not the nostalgia, of Jerrold's 'Chronicles of Clovernook' is to a certain extent carried over into *A Christmas Carol*. The Cratchit family is rescued from hunger and death by a newly benevolent Scrooge – by the Christian charity that he had set himself against at the start of the story.

The power of kindness and benevolence – a simple, New Testament Christianity – and Dickens's belief, in 1843, in the efficacy of individual charity in ameliorating poverty and social division, firmly underpin the paternalistic narrative of *A Christmas Carol* and give it its 'Christmas' mood. An 1844 reviewer for the *Westminster Review* – a high-brow monthly and mouthpiece for political economy – described the paternalism of Dickens's earlier fiction in less than sympathetic terms, also implicitly criticising the melodramatic mode he engaged with across his oeuvre: 'In most of Dickens's works there is to be found some old gentleman with surplus cash going about redressing the evils which some other old or young gentleman goes about perpetrating' – Brownlow and the Cheeryble brothers, Fagin, Monks and Ralph Nickleby are the examples he gives.[56] The reviewer greatly simplifies the political complexion of Dickens's early writings: the Fleet Prison scenes in *The Pickwick Papers* are beyond amelioration; the Bayham family, as well as Nancy, are beyond the reach of any number of Brownlows in *Oliver Twist*; and the allegorical figures of 'Ignorance' and 'Want' in *A Christmas Carol* are clearly much more than a fictional phantasm as far as Dickens was concerned (one could go on). The reviewer also conveniently fails to mention *Barnaby Rudge* (1841), which cannot be recuperated in the way described. He is right, though, that Dickens does in certain of his earlier works of fiction cling, at the level of plot, to a paternalistic structure of feeling. It is a structure of feeling that would be challenged in his next Christmas Book, and in a way that thoroughly discomfited some of his readers.

Writing to Forster in the autumn of 1844, Dickens was clearly fired up as he composed *The Chimes* while living in Genoa:

I am in a regular, ferocious excitement with *The Chimes*; get up at seven; have a cold bath before breakfast; and blaze away, wrathful, red-hot, until three o'clock or so . . . I am fierce to finish it in a spirit bearing some affinity to those of truth and mercy, and to shame the cruel and canting.[57]

'Ferocious', 'wrathful', 'red-hot', 'fierce' – the anger that Dickens felt towards the 'cruel and [the] canting' who ensured, as he saw it, that the lot of the poor was not improved, is plain enough. So too is his strong sense of the instrumentality of his writing at this period: his aim was to 'shame' those he held responsible for poverty and oppression. *The Chimes* affected him forcibly: he wrote to Forster again on 3 November to tell him that in finishing the story he had had 'what women call "a real good cry!"'[58]

Dickens's friends and associates were equally enthusiastic about his second Christmas Book. In advance of publication, Dickens gave a private reading of the story at which Douglas Jerrold, Thomas Carlyle and the actor William Charles Macready amongst others were present. Dickens's illustrator, Daniel Maclise, reported 'shrieks of laughter . . . floods of tears', and Dickens wrote to his wife that Macready had been 'undisguisedly sobbing, and crying on the sofa, as I read'. When Forster had read the story to the popular writer and journalist (and Dickens plagiarist) Gilbert À Beckett, the latter had 'cried so much, and so painfully, that Forster didn't know whether to go on or stop'.[59]

Although brimming o'er with Jerroldian satire, *The Chimes* is as full of the emotional affects of melodrama as *A Christmas Carol*: in the *Carol* it is the affecting death of Tiny Tim that forms the central melodramatic tableau; in *The Chimes* it is the imagined repentance and death of Lilian Fern, and the nightmare of Meg Veck's suicide and drowning of her baby, that are the vehicles for a melodramatic rhetoric designed to move its readers to social action.

The Chimes was a commercial success: Dickens's net profit on the first edition of 20,000 copies was £1,065 8s 2d.[60] The pecuniary success did not ensure continued popularity, though. Neither the dramatised version by Gilbert À Beckett and Mark Lemon that Dickens sanctioned (staged at the Adelphi two days after publication) nor his own public reading of it that he experimented with in 1858 achieved the level of popularity enjoyed by *A Christmas Carol*. The relative failure of the theatrical adaptations alone would partly explain why *The Chimes* did not reach out to such a large popular audience as effectively as the *Carol* had done. But this can also be explained by the distinct change of tone between the first and the second of Dickens's Christmas Books. All the same, the publication of *The Chimes* in December of 1844 caused something of a critical storm: one commentator writing at the end of that month remarked that it was 'attacked and defended with a degree of ardour which scarcely any other subject is capable of inspiring'.[61] The monthly *Union Magazine* had warned that, 'were it not a shilling book, and unlikely, therefore, to be read by those whom it professes to school in their interests, we should pronounce it one of the most mischievous ever written'.[62] The Chartist *Northern Star* was on the other side of the critical debate, applauding the way that 'Mr Dickens throw[s] the weight of his great name into the scale on poverty's side'.[63] Dickens's own sense of the purposeful instrumentality of his second Christmas Book was confirmed in a letter to Forster from Lady Blessington, who predicted that 'this book will melt hearts and open purse strings . . . I was embarrassed to meet the eyes of my servants, mine were so red with tears.'[64]

The attacks in *The Chimes* on the vocabulary of political economy and on the social mores that went with it are more highly charged, and more bitter in tone, than in *Oliver Twist* or *A Christmas Carol*. The story begins with its main protagonist, Toby (known as 'Trotty') Veck, at his post as a ticket-porter and eating his modest lunch of tripe. Dickens was as interested as Henry Mayhew in the range of employments undertaken by the poorest of the poor in London, and he presents Trotty's humble pursuit with gentle dignity. The ticket-porter's meal is rudely interrupted with the approach of one 'Alderman Cute' and 'Mr Filer', the latter interrogating him about his diet as well as relieving him of his food. Eating 'tripe', Mr Filer contends, is an economically wasteful indulgence, and he 'proves', by statistical analysis, the patent untruth that in eating tripe Toby Veck is 'robbing' it from widows and orphans:

'But who eats tripe?' said Mr Filer, looking round. 'Tripe is without exception the least economical, and most wasteful article of consumption that the markets of this country can by possibility produce. The loss upon a pound of tripe has been found to be, in the boiling, seven eighths of a fifth more than the loss upon a pound of any other animal substance whatever. Tripe is more expensive, properly understood, than the hothouse pineapple . . .

    'Who eats tripe?' said Mr Filer, warmly. 'Who eats tripe?'

    Trotty made a miserable bow.

    'You do, do you?' said Mr Filer. 'Then I'll tell you something. You snatch your tripe, my friend, out of the mouths of widows and orphans.'

    'I hope not, Sir,' said Trotty, faintly. 'I'd sooner die of want!'[65]

By ridiculing through parody Filer's economic logic (and by revealing him as an hypocrite – as he lectures Toby Veck, he eats most of the poor man's lunch), Dickens was hitting back at the Benthamite *Westminster Review*, which had greatly irritated him by arguing – apparently in total seriousness – that according to the laws of political economy some poor person must have gone 'without turkey and punch in order that Bob Cratchit might get them – for, unless there were turkeys and punch in surplus, some one must go without'.[66]

In *The Chimes* Toby Veck internalises Filer's attack on him, and the remainder of the story comprises an unravelling of Filer's Benthamite account of poverty, and a reaffirmation of Dickens's more generous view, a benevolent account of the poor in tune with the 'Christmas' theme of his book.

The influence of Douglas Jerrold is everywhere apparent in *The Chimes*; Dickens had often been in touch with him during the composition of his first two Christmas Books. He had posted a copy of *A Christmas Carol* to his friend in January 1844,[67] and in November of the same year invited him to his private reading of the story. The satirical attacks on Alderman Cute and Sir Joseph Bowley, and the melodramatic tableau in which the repentant Magdalen, Lilian Fern, returns to Meg Veck to die at her feet, all resonate strongly with Jerrold's 1840s journalism and fiction. Dickens's Alderman Cute is modelled on Sir Peter Laurie (1778–1861), a well-known Middlesex magistrate who was celebrated for his bluff jocularity and his ability (as he saw it) to talk to offenders in their own language. Dickens parodies Laurie's fake camaraderie as the magistrate berates young Meg Veck for intending to get married, warning her that the poverty of her projected marriage will drive her to desperation:

'All young mothers, of all sorts and kinds, it's my determination to Put Down . . . And if you attempt, desperately, and ungratefully, and impiously, and fraudulently attempt, to drown yourself, or hang yourself, I'll have no pity on you, for I have made up my mind to Put All Suicide Down . . . So don't try it on. That's the phrase, isn't it! Ha, ha! Now we understand each other.' (*The Chimes*, p. 113)

Douglas Jerrold had long been infuriated by Laurie's bluffly expressed campaigns to 'Put Down' various transgressions of the poor, attacking him in *Punch* as early as 1841.[68] It was, though, Laurie's determination severely to punish attempted suicide amongst the poor that most infuriated both Jerrold and Dickens. In a 'Q' leader called 'Peter the Great' from 1844, Jerrold mockingly praises Sir Peter as 'a very great man' for the harsh sentences he imposed on the very poorest, most vulnerable members of society:

ELIZABETH MORRIS, a poor seduced creature, is charged before the Knight [Peter Laurie] with having taken poison; whereupon his philosophy is immediately exhibited . . .
'Sir Peter said he should send her to the Old Bailey for attempted suicide. It was a fit case for trial, *and he had no doubt she would be transported*. HE HAD PUT AN END TO PERSONS ATTEMPTING TO DROWN THEMSELVES; HE WOULD NOW TRY THE SAME CURE FOR ATTEMPTED POISONING. He had no doubt that those who took poison did not do so for the purpose of self-destruction, but for the purpose of exciting sympathy; and such morbid charity was more calculated to do injury than anything else.'
Wise man – good man – great man! . . . He will, in a word, make death respectable, by placing it out of the reach of the poor and desperate . . . LAURIE WILL PUT AN END TO SUICIDE![69]

The satirical interplay between Jerrold and Dickens that produced the figure of Alderman Cute in *The Chimes* is clear. Both were also outraged by the sentencing to death of a seamstress, one Mary Furley, for attempted suicide and the 'wilful murder' of her baby; it is the Furley case that inspired Meg Veck's story in *The Chimes*. Driven to desperation by her experiences in a workhouse, and having been robbed of her meagre earnings from slopwork, Furley had tried to drown herself and her child in the Thames. She was pulled out alive, but the child did not survive. After the jury had found her guilty, Justice Maule told her that 'Your act, which would have been at any time cruel, is rendered more so by the fact of the crime being committed by you – the mother of the child.'[70] Mary Furley was sentenced to hang on 16 April 1844, but after a public outcry the sentence was commuted to seven years' transportation. In their journalism, whilst Jerrold had commented on the 'atrocious cruelty' of Furley's treatment, Dickens had satirised the pompous High Toryism of those who supported the original sentence.[71] It is in *The Chimes*, though, that the Furley story is most fully realised.

Harangued for eating lunch by the odious Filer and Cute, Toby Veck is further browbeaten by a 'Crimes' column of a newspaper in which he reads of a 'woman who had laid her desperate hands not only on her own life but on that of her young child'. Diminished by the harsh view of the poor that Filer and Cute have impressed upon him, Toby thinks the worst of the desperate young mother: '"Unnatural and cruel!" Toby cried. "... None but people who were bad at heart: born bad: who had no business on the earth: could do such deeds ... We're bad!"' (*The Chimes*, p. 133). It is from this state of mind that Veck's nightmare vision emerges. In his dream, Meg and her fiancé Richard do not marry, the latter having been persuaded by political economists that he could do better by himself, unencumbered by a wife, much as Scrooge eschews marriage in favour of business in the first of the Christmas Books. The unmarried Meg ekes out a meagre living as a sweated seamstress whilst Lilian Fern, the niece of a country labourer whom the Vecks had welcomed into their humble home, is driven by poverty into prostitution. Meg eventually marries a much-diminished Richard, whose death leaves her and her baby destitute. Before she confronts the horror of her own situation, though, Meg is faced (as is Toby Veck, who looks on helplessly) with the fate of Lilian Fern, who returns to her friend to die. Here Dickens carefully stages the familiar story of the repentant Magdalen, filling it with all the emotional affects available to the melodramatic mode, in what is a highly visual as well as a very declamatory tableau:

She saw the entering figure; screamed its name; cried 'Lilian!'
It was swift, and fell upon its knees before her: clinging to her dress.
'Up, dear! Up! Lilian! My own dearest!' ...

'Never more, Meg. Never more! When I first looked into your face, you knelt before me. On my knees before you, let me die. Let it be here! . . . Forgive me, Meg! So dear, so dear! Forgive me! I know you do, I see you do, but say so Meg!'

She said so, with her lips on Lilian's cheek. And with her arms twined round – she knew it now – a broken heart.

'His blessing on you, dearest love. Kiss me once more! He suffered her to sit beside His feet, and dry them with her hair. Oh Meg, what Mercy and Compassion!'

As she died, the Spirit of the child returning, innocent and radiant, touched the old man [the watching Toby Veck] with its hand, and beckoned him away. (p. 157)

The emotional affects of the scene attracted the critics' attention, ameliorating as it does the bitter satire of other phases of the story. The anonymous reviewer for *The Times* commented that it was 'one of the most pathetic and heart-stirring' scenes 'that ever were written'.[72] It is a highly stylised, theatrical tableau with great popular currency – the figure of the repentant prostitute was very familiar to the nineteenth-century cultural imagination. Dickens draws explicitly on the Bible's Book of Luke (7:38), but also on a comparable tableau in a serialised novel that Douglas Jerrold wrote for *Punch* in 1843. Jerrold's *Story of a Feather* has at its centre a young feather-dresser, Patty Butler who, like Meg Veck after her, offers comfort to a repentant prostitute. Jessy (the Magdalen figure) is, like Lilian Fern, 'country born; my childhood was one long happy holiday . . .' Repentant before she dies, she throws herself at Patty Butler's feet:

'. . . will you forgive me – forgive the wretched Magdalen – and – yes – pray for me?'

Saying this, Jessy, in a passion of grief, dropped upon her knees. Patty, starting from her chair, and hiding her face in her hands, sobbed –

'I do forgive you – I pray for you – I – God in heaven bless and strengthen you!'[73]

The melodramatic theatricality of each of the two tableaux owes much both to Jerrold's playwright sensibility and to Dickens's own highly developed theatrical mode of fiction writing. In both cases the popular appeal of this particular scene was assured.

Unlike *A Christmas Carol* there is no kind 'old gentleman with surplus cash' to help the likes of Toby and Meg Veck and William and Lilian Fern out of poverty. The change in consciousness that led Scrooge into more charitable ways in the *Carol* is confined in *The Chimes* to humble Toby Veck. As he sees his daughter contemplating her own and her baby's death by drowning in his dream vision, Toby Veck recognises that she is motivated by a desire to protect her baby daughter from a future akin to Lilian Fern's: 'Oh, God be thanked! She loves her child!' (*The Chimes*, p. 166). The freeing of Toby from the ideological constraints of political economy leads, at the level of plot, to the happy marriage of Meg Veck and Richard, her fiancé, and to wedding festivities on New Year's Day. There is no sense, though, that the Filers and the Cutes have in any way adjusted their harsh view of the poor, and this partly accounts for this story's more sombre tone in comparison with the *Carol*.

Along the same lines, one of the important differences between Jerrold's *Story of a Feather* and Dickens's *The Chimes* is that, whilst Jerrold retains a paternalistic structure of feeling in his narrative, Dickens not only rejects but is highly critical of paternalism in his second Christmas Book. Jerrold's Patty Butler is engaged to be married to a young curate, Inglewood, who becomes consumptive. His life is saved by the benevolence of his old employer, one Earl Blushwood, who pays for his convalescence in Madeira. The same benevolent aristocrat also provides him with a curacy on his return to England, thus ensuring the happiness and healthfulness of Patty's marriage. Meg and Richard, by contrast, can only rely on the goodness of their own kind. Dickens values the solidarity of the poor – the Vecks help the Ferns, and the kindly shopkeeper, Mrs Chickenstalker, stands by all of them, and on one level *The Chimes* can be said to be a stalwart defence of working-class community and of the right of the poor to marry. In *The Chimes* as in the *Carol*, the working-class family is at once assaulted and then reconstituted, and always defended. What is different is the explicit attack on a paternalism that in the *Carol* had retained Dickens's respect. Here it is attacked in the figure of 'Sir Joseph Bowley, Member of Parliament'. Sir Joseph's brand of paternalism demands complete and utter dependency on the part of the poor and derives not a little from the 'Young England' Toryism of Benjamin Disraeli. When Toby takes a message to his London home, Sir Joseph imposes upon him his vision of the relationship between the rich and the poor:

'Your only business, my good fellow,' pursued Sir Joseph, looking abstractedly at Toby; 'your only business in life is with me. You needn't trouble yourself to think about anything. I will think for you; I know what is good for you; I am your perpetual parent. Such is the dispensation of an all-wise Providence!'

(*The Chimes*, p. 121).

Dickens ironically reveals Bowley's gentry-paternalism to be of the most tight-fisted kind as the MP announces the nature of his New Year bountifulness: 'Once every year, myself and friends will address him [the poor man] with the deepest feeling. Once in his life, he may even perhaps receive; in public, in the presence of the gentry; a Trifle from a Friend' (p. 122).[74]

In *The Chimes*, then, Dickens plays off Filer's political economy against Bowley's paternalism and finds both wanting. As anti-Tory as it is anti-Benthamite, *The Chimes* is perhaps the most avowedly radical of Dickens's works of fiction.

The sideswipe at what he regarded as Bowley's empty paternalistic rhetoric is matched in *The Chimes* by an attack on the Tory reverence for the past and its more feudal social and political arrangements. The 'red-faced gentleman in the blue coat' who accompanies Filer and Cute at the start of the story berates 'such degenerate times as these', refusing to 'take an interest in a fellow like this [Toby Veck]' (p. 110). The red-faced gentleman blames Toby's poor appearance on the passing of 'The good old times, the grand old times, the great old times' (ibid.). Dickens's satirical attack, in *The Chimes*, on a nostalgic vision of the past had been anticipated in the series of squibs he had written for the *Examiner* in 1841. Signed 'W', they were intended to assist the Liberals in their opposition to Robert Peel's Tory interregnum of that year.[75] Peel, who took power from the aristocratic Whig Prime Minister, Lord Melbourne, was loathed by his opponents partly because of his involvement at the level of government in the repressive measures of 1819 that had resulted in Peterloo, as discussed in chapter 1. There was a genuine fear amongst Liberals and Radicals that there could be a return to the dark days of Lord Liverpool's Regency administration. In response Dickens, as John Drew has put it, conducted in the early 1840s 'a kind of one-man guerrilla warfare against the return of the bad old Tory days'.[76] The most memorable of the three squibs written for the *Examiner* is 'The Fine Old English Gentleman', which comprises not only an assault on Peel's Toryism and its antecedent Liverpool administration, but also on Disraeli's 'Young England' manifesto which the younger politician celebrates in *Sybil, or The Two Nations*, a novel that would be published in 1845, just a few months after *The Chimes*. The biting satire of Dickens's poem is given popular power by his melding of it to the stanzaic pattern and metrical arrangement of a popular song by Purday. Purday's song had been sung after a toast at a recent dinner in Gloucestershire at which a Tory peer had welcomed 'the return of the good old English times, when the nobleman afforded advice to his tenants, and identified himself with them'.[77] Dickens's 'song' has, clearly, a quite different view of the past:

The Fine Old English Gentleman
(To be said or sung at all Conservative Dinners)
I'll sing you a new ballad, and I'll warrant it first rate,
Of the days of that old gentleman who had that old estate;
When they spent the public money at a bountiful old rate
On ev'ry mistress, pimp, and scamp, at ev'ry noble gate,
  In the fine old English Tory times;
  Soon may they come again!
The good old laws were garnished well with gibbets, whips and chains,
With fine old English penalties, and fine old English pains,
With rebel heads, and seas of blood once hot in rebel veins;
For all these things were requisite to guard the rich old gains
  Of the fine old English Tory times;
  Soon may they come again!
. . .
Those were the days for taxes, and for war's infernal din;
For scarcity of bread, that fine old dowagers win;
For shutting men of letters up, through iron bars to grin,
Because they didn't think the Prince was altogether thin,
  In the fine old English Tory times;
  Soon may they come again![78]

The sixth stanza (the last one quoted here) refers specifically to the imprisonment of Leigh Hunt, then editor of the *Examiner*, for his attack on the Prince Regent as a 'fat old Florizel of forty'. In its direct attack on the Liverpool administration, adapted into a popular song form, it echoes in a very direct way the nursery-rhyme satires of William Hone discussed in chapter 1. Similarly 'The Quack Doctor's Proclamation' directly attacks Robert Peel, who had recently given a speech in Tamworth in which he had expressed support for a sliding scale of tax on corn (as opposed to its total abolition, as demanded by the Anti-Corn League):[79]

> Homeopathy too, he has practised for ages;
> (You'll find his prescriptions in Luke Hansard's pages)
> Just giving his patient when maddened by pain –
> Of Reform the ten thousandth part of a grain.[80]

In setting himself against the politics of the past in the 1840s, Dickens distances himself from Thomas Carlyle's political thought which was otherwise, in its suspicion of Benthamite statistics, its hatred of the so-called 'cash-nexus' and its sense of impending social conflagration a significant influence on Dickens's fiction.[81] Whilst Jerrold's fiction tended to preserve the paternalism of the politics of nostalgia, he was at one with Dickens in his journalism on the subject. In May 1843 Dickens had written to Jerrold congratulating him on his 'Elizabeth and Victoria' essay that had appeared in Jerrold's *Illuminated Magazine*. Jerrold's essay attacks the myth of the 'good old days' and reflects on the harsh punishments and tortures meted out in Tudor times. The main gist of the essay is to point out that that even the poorest Victorians were better off than Elizabethan peasants.[82] Writing in admiration of Jerrold's essay, Dickens espouses his own contempt for the Tory politics of nostalgia:

If ever I destroy myself, it will be in the bitterness of hearing those infernal and damnably good old times, extolled. Once in a fit of madness, after having been to a Public Dinner which took place just as this Ministry came in, I wrote the Parody I send you enclosed, for Fonblanque. There is nothing in it but wrath; but that's wholesome – so I send it to you.[83]

The parody in question was 'The Fine Old English Gentleman'.

The 'wrath' that Dickens describes in this letter to Jerrold finds its way into *The Chimes*, and it is partly this that led commentators to reflect that it was a more politically committed work of fiction than anything he had written previously. The review for the *Economist* is typical in its detection of a thoroughgoing political response to the 'Condition of England':

The *Chimes* is a picture of the condition of England, and an earnest exhortation to all classes to amend it, by giving to the meanest of our brethren their rightful share in the advantages of society. The author has been heretofore merely a novelist – in the *Chimes* he is a political philosopher and a social reformer. His book is a political and social essay of intense interest.[84]

The political commitment may have been new, but the 'wrath' that finds its way into *The Chimes* was present too in a novel that he had published three years before his second Christmas Book. Angry, afraid and as alert to the political and social conditions of its day as anything that Dickens would ever write, *Barnaby Rudge* is a much overlooked novel, central to Dickens's political imagination in the early 1840s.

BARNABY RUDGE AND THE CRISIS OF PATERNALISM

Written in the crisis year of 1841, *Barnaby Rudge: A Tale of the Riots of Eighty* bears the ideological scars of the troubled moment in British history when it came into print. With the Poor Law agitations of the late 1830s rumbling on, and merging with the Chartist riots of 1839, further political disturbance ensued upon the formation of the Anti-Corn Law League in 1839 and the attempted assassination of Queen Victoria in 1840. As he fired off his wrathful anti-Tory squibs for Fonblanque's *Examiner* in August 1841, Dickens reflected on his political opinions at the time in a letter to Forster: 'By Jove how radical I am getting! I wax stronger and stronger in the true principles everyday.'[85] At the same time as he spontaneously (and anonymously) let off steam in the *Examiner* Dickens was hard at work on the long-delayed novel about the Gordon Riots of 1780, *Barnaby Rudge*. Originally conceived (but not written) in 1836, the novel's appearance was postponed by Dickens's preoccupation with, severally, *The Pickwick Papers* (1836–7), *Oliver Twist* (1837–9), *Nicholas Nickleby* (1838–9) and *The Old Curiosity Shop* (1840–1).

By the time he came to write *Barnaby Rudge*, Dickens was famous for his novels of contemporary life that attacked social injustice: *Oliver Twist* had taken the part of the anti-Poor Law protestors, *Nicholas Nickleby* had launched an attack on the Yorkshire Schools, and *The Old Curiosity Shop* contained many moving encounters between Nell and the starving inhabitants of the Black Country. Following swiftly upon these earlier novels, *Barnaby Rudge* was bound to be political. But it was not contemporary in the way that his earlier novels are, as Dickens ostensibly concerns himself with a period of English history sixty years in the past. His readers and critics did not thank him for this. Kathryn Chittick has noted that the novel 'went almost totally unnoticed' by critics, whilst Paul Schlicke has reflected that those notices it did get 'ranged from the negative to the severe'.[86]

Serialised weekly in Dickens's short-lived magazine venture, *Master Humphrey's Clock*, and following hard upon the heels of *The Old Curiosity Shop*, sales fell from 70,000 copies for the first instalment to 30,000 for the last.[87] Whilst certainly qualifying *Barnaby Rudge* as a popular novel, the sales were well below what Dickens had enjoyed as he wrote the history of Little Nell, which, by the time the series of weekly instalments came to an end, was selling 100,000 copies a week.[88] Whilst Ruskin regretted what he regarded as the novel's 'diseased extravagance' and 'violence of delineation', the diarist Henry Crabb Robinson, who thought better of it, reflected that 'Dickens will lose popularity with the saints, for he too faithfully exposes cant', remarking on Dickens's scathing presentation of anti-Catholic Protestantism in the figure of Sir Chester and his evil sidekick, Gashford.[89]

What is certain is that the historical setting of *Barnaby Rudge* marks it off from the novels that had earned Dickens fame and popular success. It is worth quoting Ruskin once more in this regard, for if he was too harsh (I think much too harsh) on Dickens's novel from 1841, he was right when he reflected after Dickens's death that one of the hallmarks of his work is its modernity. *Oliver Twist* had been the most contemporary novel ever to have been written, and Ruskin is surely right in his assertion that:

Dickens was a pure modernist – a leader of the steam and whistle party *par excellence* – and he had no understanding of any power of antiquity except a sort of jackdaw sentiment for cathedral towers . . . His hero is essentially the iron-master; despite *Hard Times* . . . his distrust of nobility and clergy.[90]

John Bowen is right that the fictional landscape of *Barnaby Rudge* has none of 'the vivid life of contemporary England that had made him famous'.[91] But Dickens's fifth novel none the less reflects, through the distortions of an historical magic lantern, the troubled social and political landscape of the early Victorian period every bit as powerfully – or more so – as his earlier writings had done. As Peter Ackroyd has reflected:

although *Barnaby Rudge* is an historical novel it is one, which, like all good historical novels, is actually concerned with its own time. His interest in the London mob which had rampaged through the streets of London and set fire to Newgate prison, for example, must have been considerably increased by the fact that now in his own period Chartism and the Chartists seemed about to provoke civil rebellion of a similar kind.[92]

John Bowen has interestingly reflected on the troubled evolution of *Barnaby Rudge* that, whilst when Dickens set out as a young novelist in 1836 he could have expected that the writing of an historical novel would earn him respect, by 1841, when he came to complete it, he himself had established a much more contemporary mode for the nineteenth-century novel, exceeding even Walter Scott's popularity. He was, though, saddled with the novel's already established historical frame.[93]

In 1841, then, we find an author who has no respect (or at least no reverence) for the past writing an historical novel. The historical novel was, in Franco Moretti's words, 'the most successful form of the century', with Harrison Ainsworth and Bulwer Lytton, as well as Walter Scott before them, both selling extremely well by writing within this well-established and highly regarded genre.[94] Dickens's more ambivalent relationship to the historical genre leads him to combine it with those aspects of the melodrama that he had negotiated so successfully in his earliest work. The return from the dead of one assumed to be long ago buried; the criminal elements of the plot; the aristocratic seduction of a poor girl; the last-minute reprieve from a hanging; the return of the long-lost lover from overseas; the lovers parted through force of circumstance; the clear delineation of 'good' and 'bad' characters in a Manichean moral order; the emigration trope; and the restoration of moral order at the close – all these ingredients would have been as apt in a stage melodrama as in an historical novel, Dickens once again working with the aesthetic tools to which he knew he owed so much of his power as a writer.[95] He also negotiates the Gothic mode, the first part of the novel reading as a murder mystery laden with ghostly hauntings rather than as an historical narrative in a traditional sense.

Dickens's somewhat uneasy position as heir to the popular historical novel (in terms of literary genealogy he was a recalcitrant 'son' to Walter Scott, the 'father' of the genre) corresponds with a more generalised uneasiness between fathers and sons in *Barnaby Rudge*.[96] For this is a novel in which personal battles between fathers and sons act as a metaphor for a negotiation of – and finally a rejection of – paternalism at a political level. Private conflicts between father and son duplicate in the domestic realm the attempts violently to overthrow the established social order. As Ben Winyard has put it, 'The modes of injustice and repression in the first half of the novel – fathers obstructing the ascension of youth to adulthood and the exclusion of the majority from property and power – lead to an explosion of frustration during the Gordon Riots.'[97]

The connection between parental tyranny and the despotism of state paternalism is most fully fleshed out in the figure of Sir John Chester, MP. The veneer of Augustan gentlemanliness that veils his hypocrisy, avarice and cynical immorality only serves to accentuate them. Living the life of a gentleman, Chester is in fact penniless, having spent the family money on a life of luxury and idleness.[98] He cynically tries to manipulate his legitimate son, Edward, into a profitable marriage to retrieve the family's position. When Edward professes his love for Emma Haredale, Chester initially affects a sentimental, urbane and thoroughly moral stance: '"My good fellow," said his smiling father, "you quite affect me. Go on, my dear Edward, I beg"' (*Barnaby Rudge*, p. 132). Edward protests against his own gentlemanly upbringing when his father discloses the parlous state of the family finances, and recoils utterly from his father's insistence that he should make a financially advantageous marriage. It is at this point that the mask of Augustan civility is dropped, and Chester's moral cynicism is revealed:

'... you must do as I did ... you must marry well and make the most of yourself.'
'A mere fortune hunter!' cried the son, indignantly.

'What in the devil's name, Ned, would you be!' returned the father. 'All men are fortune hunters, are they not? The law, the church, the court, the camp . . . what but fortune hunters are they filled with? . . . If you are squeamish and moral, Ned, console yourself with the reflection that at the worst your fortune-hunting can make but one person miserable or unhappy. How many people do you suppose these other kinds of huntsmen crush in following their sport – hundreds at a step? Or thousands?' (*Barnaby Rudge*, p. 135)

Dickens was at one with Chester in his estimate of the law, the Church, and the court; what is criticised here is the cynicism of Sir John's willingness casually to condone thoroughgoing immorality not only in the institutions of Church and state but in the private sphere as well. His sneering description of his own son as 'squeamish and moral' forces home Dickens's estimate of the urbane eighteenth-century gentleman.

Sir John Chester's favourite reading matter is Lord Chesterfield's (1694–1773) *Letters to His Son Philip Stanhope* (1774), which in David Roberts's words 'proved easy to caricature: self interest above morality, adultery above marriage, cynicism above patriotisim, breeding above all'.[99] Lord Chesterfield represented for Dickens the worst kind of degenerate aristocracy (he had read and reacted angrily to the lord's unscrupulous worldly advice), and his attack on him in the fictional figure of Sir John Chester is savage.[100] Whilst Sir John's treatment of Edward is cruel, his response to Hugh, his illegitimate son from the lower orders, is altogether more sinister. Provoked by his father to raze the Catholic Haredale's residence, Hugh's filial amenability propels him to the gallows.

The critique of paternalism in *Barnaby Rudge* is cross-class. John Willet, the landlord of the Maypole Inn, refuses to admit his grown-up son Joe to adulthood, humiliating and emasculating him at every turn. Highly critical of this more humble father-figure, Dickens undercuts the ostensible presentation of the Maypole as a nostalgic rural idyll by revealing it to be a place of atrophy, inertia and oppression, only kept alive by the simmering frustrations of the son unable to escape the smothering paternalism of his father.[101] It is no surprise, given the novel's rejection of paternalism, that the Maypole should be destroyed in the wake of the onrushing mob, its master left dazed and reduced. Even Gabriel Varden, ostensibly the moral centre of the novel (it was originally to have had his name as the title), is in one very particular sense an oppressively paternalistic figure. Without a son of his own Varden's ridiculing of Sim Tappertit, and his denial of his assistant's social and sexual identity as he fixates on Varden's daughter, contribute to Tappertit's aggrieved redirection of his energies into insurrectionary activities. And it should not be forgotten that it is Varden who forges the great locks and keys that deny freedom to the prisoners of Newgate, suggesting complicity with the power and authority of the state. Varden is meekness itself, though, compared to the melodramatic villainy of Rudge, a gothically symbolic figure in Dickens's panoply of troubled father–son relationships.

Dickens's highly critical account of domestic paternalism through the figures of John Chester and John Willet, and of father-and-son relationships more generally, is paralleled with a sneering stance towards those figures of male authority who represent state paternalism. The scorn that Dickens feels for eighteenth-century paternalistic government is funnelled through his attack on Sir John Chester: the affected sentimentalism and urbanity of public politics barely veiled, in Dickens's view, the want and distress, and the harsh penal codes over which it presided. In the figure of the country magistrate who threatens Barnaby and his mother with prosecution when they refuse to sell Barnaby's pet raven, Grip, to him, Dickens attacks the magistracy of the eighteenth century in what must be one of the angriest 'out-takes' from his entire fictional oeuvre. His description of this bullying, brutal figure, resonates strongly with the 'Fine Old English Gentleman' whom he berated in the *Examiner* at almost exactly the same time:

Now, this gentleman had various endearing appellations among his intimate friends. By some he was called 'a country gentleman of the true school', by some 'a sporting gentleman,' by some 'a fine old country gentleman,' by some 'a thorough-bred Englishman,' by some 'a genuine John Bull;' but they all agreed in one respect and that was, that it was a pity there were not more like him, and that because there were not, the country was going to rack and ruin every day. He was in the commission of the peace, and could write his name almost legibly; but his greatest qualifications were, that he was more severe with poachers, was a better shot, a harder rider, had better horses, kept better dogs, could eat more solid food, drink more strong wine, go to bed every night more drunk and get up every morning more sober, than any man in the county . . . He had no seat in Parliament himself, but he was extremely patriotic, and usually drove his voters up to the poll with his own hands. (*Barnaby Rudge*, p. 390)

Anticipating the Tory rhetoric of the 'red-faced gentleman in the blue coat' who would later appear in *The Chimes*, the harshly satirical tone adopted here bespeaks Dickens's simultaneous rejection of and sense of scorn towards the politics of pre-reform Britain, of the landed gentry, and of those representatives of the law who abrogated their moral responsibilities.

For the country magistrate's blather is far from harmless: it is his lies that result in Barnaby being sentenced to death.

Highly critical of representatives of the legal system in this as in other of his novels, Dickens emphasises the feebleness and inefficacy of the civil magistracy: the Lord Mayor of London, Chief Magistrate of the city, refuses to intervene as the mob – with the misguided Barnaby at its centre – rampages through London. An elderly gentleman urges the magistrate to take action:

'Now, you hear this, my Lord?' – said the old gentleman, calling up the stairs, to where the skirt of a dressing gown fluttered on the landing place. 'Here is a gentleman here, whose house was actually burnt down last night.'

'Dear me, dear me,' replied a testy voice, 'I am very sorry for it, but what am I to do? I can't build it up again. The chief magistrate of the city can't go and be a rebuilding of people's houses, my good sir. Stuff and nonsense!' (p. 507)

The young Joe Willet's voice merges with Dickens's own as he looks on helpless whilst the mob turns its attention to the house and law library of Lord Mansfield: 'What's a magistrate in this case, but an impertinent, unnecessary, unconstitutional sort of interference? . . . Damn the magistrates!' (p. 483).

It is important to note here that at this early stage in Dickens's writing career it is not 'law' *per se* that antagonises him, but its misapplication and its inefficacy. Indeed he bewails the burning of Lord Mansfield's legal collection, lamenting the destruction of 'the great Law Library, on almost every page of which were notes in the Judge's own hand, of inestimable value' (p. 551). At the start of the 1840s there is a sense that the young author believed that the legal system could be reformed; it would take more than another decade for his disenchantment with it to become total. In *Barnaby Rudge* in 1841, the objects of Dickens's legal critique are corrupt or inefficient *individual* agents of the law; in *Bleak House* in 1852–3 his object is the entire edifice of the legal system and its institutions. The result in the later novel is a relentlessly sombre vision of English society at the start of a decade that was supposed to usher in the so-called 'age of equipoise'.

But the view from 1841 is bleak enough: the paralysis and brutality of the law is matched by indiscriminate mob violence. In *Barnaby Rudge* as in *A Tale of Two Cities* nearly two decades later, Dickens shows himself to be both fascinated and repelled by a political crowd that is represented simultaneously as both an irresistible force of nature and as a debased, contaminating power. Dennis, Hugh and Sim Tappertit – the leaders of the mob – are described as 'wallowing, like some obscene animals, in their squalor and wickedness on two heaps of straw' (p. 432). Of the riotous behaviour of the crowd, Dickens reflects that 'The contagion spread, like a dread fever: an infectious madness' (p. 438). On the very same page, though, the mob is described as resembling 'rivers as they roll towards the sea' – an altogether natural metaphor suggestive of the inevitability of their onrush towards the Houses of Parliament. In describing the horrible fascination with which rumours about the rioters were received among the London populace, Dickens remarks on 'that appetite for the marvellous and love of the terrible which have probably been among the natural characteristics of mankind since the creation of the world' (p. 446). The energy of the vocabulary and syntax used to describe the wrecking of the Maypole Inn conveys an immense sense of movement and power to the extent that the reader senses Dickens's own 'love of the terrible' that draws him towards the mob:

Yes. Here was the bar – the bar that the boldest never entered without invitation – the sanctuary, the mystery, the hallowed ground: here it was, crammed with men, clubs, sticks, torches, pistols; filled with a deafening noise, oaths, shouts, screams, hootings; changed all at once into a bear-garden, a mad-house, an infernal temple: men darting in and out, by door and window, smashing the glass, turning the taps, drinking liquor out of China punchbowls . . . clambering in at the windows when there were doors wide open; dropping out of windows when the stairs were handy; leaping over the banisters into chasms of passages: new faces and figures presenting themselves every instant – some yelling, some singing, some fighting, some breaking glass and crockery, some laying the dust with the liquor they couldn't drink, some ringing the bells till they pulled them down, others beating them with pokers till they beat them into fragments: more men still – more, more, more – swarming on like insects: noise, smoke, light, darkness, frolic, anger, laughter, groans, plunder, fear, and ruin! (p. 450)

The extraordinary heaping up of nouns ('men, clubs, sticks' and so on) and of verbs presented in the present continuous form ('darting', 'clambering', 'smashing', 'yelling', 'singing' and so on) creates an immense sense of over-crowded, irresistible movement. The use of the present continuous tense produces a sense of immediacy, as if the action were in the present – very reminiscent of Carlyle's account of the Fall of the Bastille in his history of the French Revolution. And the jostling of positive energy ('leaping', 'singing', the description of the 'laughter' of the riot as conveying a sense of 'frolic') with negative ('smashing', 'fighting', 'swarming', 'plunder, fear and ruin') creates a 'Janus-faced' effect in Dickens's presentation of the riot. So too does the affirmation with which the paragraph begins ('Yes'), and the (albeit ambivalent) gasp of distress with which it closes ('ruin!').

Dickens would use comparable imagery and syntax in his rendering of the French revolutionary mob in *A Tale of Two Cities*, which also importantly deploys a natural metaphor in its description of the revolutionaries: one of Hablot Browne's illustrations is called 'The Sea Rises', and Dickens describes the onrush towards the Bastille as resembling 'the force of the ocean' and as 'the sea that rushed in' (*Two Cities*, pp. 224–6).

The conflictual political structure of feeling that underpins *Barnaby Rudge* creates a dark, troubling and troubled novel that the highly staged, theatrical denouement – Dolly Varden and Emma Haredale's rescue from sexual danger by Joe Willet and Edward Chester, and Barnaby's last-minute reprieve from hanging – does little to assuage. Dickens's political unease in this novel partly arises from the general disquiet concerning the Chartist outbreaks of 1839. The Reform Act of 1832 had not enfranchised the majority of the British people, firmly excluding the working classes from the suffrage. The broad conception of 'the People' with which Dickens works in his fiction fully embraces the working classes and the poor more generally, so that one would expect him instinctively to side with those who questioned whether the 1832 legislation had really improved the lot of the vast body of wage-earners whom it did not enfranchise. He knew – and his novels of the 1830s and early 1840s articulate this forcibly – that it had not. Chartist demands – universal male suffrage, the secret ballot, the payment of Members of Parliament, the abolition of the property qualification for MPs, equal constituencies and annual elections – were constitutional. They gathered momentum, though, through the activities and literature of the anti-Poor Law movement, and through the growing public clamour for factory reform. Dickens sympathised with the broad thrust of these working-class grievances, and in his fiction – *Oliver Twist*, *Nicholas Nickleby*, *A Christmas Carol* and *The Chimes* in particular – he strongly sides with that section of 'the People' that had been excluded from the franchise in 1832. His literary imagination had clearly been unsettled, though, by the Chartist disturbances in Birmingham and Newport in 1839, and he would never give unreserved public support to the Chartist movement.[102] At the same time, however, he was deeply unhappy at the return to Toryism signalled by the election of Robert Peel's administration in 1841; his conflicted political feelings at this period explain the political ambivalence of *Barnaby Rudge*.

Notwithstanding the caution with which he approached the Chartist movement, in the early and mid-Victorian period Dickens was writing in precisely the same cultural landscape and publishing environment, and had the same social preoccupations concerning poverty and social distress, as the many hundreds of Chartists who took up the pen to further their cause. Like Dickens and Jerrold, Chartist writers such as Ernest Jones, W. J. Linton, Thomas Cooper, Thomas Martin Wheeler and Thomas Doubleday used fiction and journalism as a vehicle for their social and political beliefs in an attempt to persuade their readers to take ameliorative social action and, in the case of the Chartists, to support the Charter. The following chapter will trace the significant continuities that existed between the literary and journalistic projects of Chartism, of Dickens and of Douglas Jerrold in post-Reform Britain.

Popular and political writing in the radical press: from Douglas Jerrold to Ernest Jones, Chartist

POPULAR AND/OR RADICAL? THE RISE OF THE COMMERCIAL NEWSPAPER PRESS IN THE 1840S

The 1840s witnessed a quite remarkable expansion of the popular press in Britain. In the decade during which Dickens would contribute radical squibs to the *Examiner* and abortively launch the *Daily News*, and Jerrold would temporarily dominate *Punch* and then go on to launch his own newspapers, a new type of literary subculture was forming itself for working men and women: 'penny bloods', plagiarisms of mainstream fiction (not least of Dickens's novels), and translations of risqué continental fiction. Both Louis James and, more recently, Ian Haywood, have identified the 1840s as the decade that witnessed the advent of a truly mass-circulation literature.[1] It was within this context that Douglas Jerrold and Charles Dickens made their way in journalism and fiction writing in the 1840s and beyond, and it was a context that demanded that they attend to the new publishing conditions that increasingly prevailed.

Central to the development of mass-circulation literature was the rise of the commercial newspaper press: *Lloyd's Weekly Newspaper* (established in November 1842 as *Lloyd's Illustrated London Newspaper*), the *News of the World* (launched in October 1843 by John Browne) and *Reynolds' Weekly Newspaper* (first edition published in May 1850).[2] Partly at least assisted by the radical reduction in stamp duty (the tax on newsprint) in 1836,when it was reduced from 4d to 1d per copy, by the mid-1850s the newspaper press was increasingly in the grip of the new commercial press barons. In 1854 the organ of the establishment, *The Times*, averaged sales of 50,000–60,000 copies; *Punch*, broadly middle class and diversely radical, typically sold 40,000 copies a week. Meanwhile the new mass-market weekly, *Lloyd's*, regularly sold 96,000, *Reynolds'* 49,000 and the *News of the World* 100,000 copies. Staggeringly, by 1855 George Reynolds's *Reynolds' Miscellany* was selling 200,000 copies a week.[3]

While the contours of this new commercial newspaper landscape were gradually forming themselves, Dickens abortively tried to enter the market as editor of the newly established *Daily News* in 1846, a (later very successful) project which would go on to be edited by Dickens's friend, John Forster. Politically announcing itself as resoundingly liberal, Dickens's first and only editorial for the newspaper made clear his alertness to the fact that what was being played out in the 1840s (and of course beyond) was a battle over the meaning and constitution of a 'popular' readership and its associated periodical and newspaper press. Dickens's stated aim in the *Daily News* was to contribute towards establishing the 'bodily comfort, mental elevation, and general contentment of the English people'.[4] Who, exactly, comprised 'the English people' in this and in other newspapers and periodicals of the period? What constituted the 'popular' press in the 1840s, and how did it relate to radical politics and culture? These are the questions that will be addressed in this and the next chapter.

Dickens's acute consciousness of a newly 'massified' commercial print culture at the mid-century is made clear in his 'Preliminary Word' to *Household Words* in 1850, which I shall discuss in chapter 6. Dickens's cultural centrality to the commercial as well as to the popular press of the period is evinced by the way that Edward Lloyd and George Reynolds, the two most successful commercial newspaper men of the Victorian age, embarked on their massively successful journalistic careers by issuing plagiarised 'penny' versions of Dickens's novels. Whilst Lloyd pirated (for example) *The Penny Pickwick*, the *Pickwickian Songster* and *Oliver Twiss*, Reynolds enjoyed great success with his *Pickwick Abroad*.[5] Whilst such plagiarisms provoked, in Richard Altick's words, 'Dickens's almost apoplectic wrath',[6] they also confirmed him as a commercially massively successful writer as well as a popular one, a writer much emulated by a rising generation of commercial publishers keen to attend to the reading habits and preferences of an expanding non-elite customer base. All three, too, embraced radical as well as popular culture: whilst Lloyd's and Reynolds's motivations were primarily commercial, their newspapers, where they commented on political issues, could broadly be described as taking a radical stance.

E. P. Thompson long ago reflected that in the 1840s 'the popular press – the publications of Cleave, Howitt, Chambers, Reynolds and Lloyd – came from [a] Radical background.'[7] As I have argued in the Introduction and in chapter 1, in the Regency England of William Hone and Thomas Wooler the popular and the radical were overlapping categories to the extent that 'popular radicalism' has become a generally accepted historiographical descriptor for the radical activities and publications of the 1810s. The rise of the mass-market commercial newspaper press in the 1840s led – eventually – to a bifurcation of the popular and the radical press to the extent that the very meaning of the word 'popular' becomes contested. William Hone's pamphlets of the 1810s were 'popular' not only because they sold well, but because they announced themselves as constituting the culture of 'the People' against a broadly defined 'old corruption'. Arguably, the popularity of the *News of the World* in the 1840s hinged on its sensational headlines ('EXTRAORDINARY CHARGE OF DRUGGING AND VIOLATION' is emblazoned across its first edition[8]) rather than any claim to represent an authentic culture of 'the People'. The process of bifurcation from the 1840s onwards was, though, gradual, and never complete. Whilst – I argue – Dickens would supremely transcend the split between the 'popular' and the 'radical' at the mid-century, many other literary and journalistic careers were, equally, sharply defined by the new commercial conditions of the newspaper market from the 1840s, and by the contested meanings in this period of a 'popular' readership. Not least of these was Douglas Jerrold, and it is to his role as an editor and journalist in the 1840s that I will initially direct my attention.

DOUGLAS JERROLD, JOURNALIST AND EDITOR: FROM *PUNCH* TO *LLOYD'S WEEKLY NEWSPAPER*

Ian Haywood's characterisation of the weekly *Punch; or, The London Charivari* as a 'polite' magazine, full of 'genteel satire' is, as far as its early years were concerned, wide of the mark.[9] Whilst it avoided the scurrility and sexual innuendoes usually associated with comic papers in the early Victorian period, *Punch* had, in its rich use of caricature and parody, more than a little in common with the popular radical publications of William Hone in Regency England. Like Hone's *Political House That Jack Built* from 1819, *Punch*, in its early years, physically juxtaposed political caricature with parodic literary material. In Richard Altick's words, *Punch* is a close relative to Hone's pamphlets in 'its intermingling of parodies of literary material and caricatures of public men that were essentially graphic parodies of the real persons'.[10] Hone's chief caricaturist had been George Cruikshank, who, although he declined an invitation to join the *Punch* team in the 1840s, wielded a massive influence on John Leech, one of its lead artists.[11] It was the Swiftian rage and seething indignation of Douglas Jerrold, though, that more obviously leads the reader to detect echoes, in early editions of *Punch*, of its unruly antecedents from Regency England.

High-minded and politically earnest, the *Shilling Magazine* welcomed non-elite contributors, and a number of radicals wrote for it too, including the journalists R. H. Horne and William Howitt (both of whom would go on also to write for Dickens's *Household Words*), Goodwyn Barmby, the radical utopianist, and Thomas Cooper, the Chartist.[18] Jerrold himself determinedly persisted with the satirical vein that he had established in his 'Q' contributions for *Punch*, which I discussed in chapter 4. His 'Hedgehog Letters', 'Containing the Opinions and Adventures of Juniper Hedgehog, Cabman, London; and written to his relatives and acquaintances, in various parts of the world', continued his satirical attacks on the social injustices he saw all around him. His targets included a bishopric heedless of the deprivations of the poor, the government's own contumely, a bloated monarchy, legal injustices, and the cruelty of the New Poor Law.[19] The Swiftian 'Slavery: The Only Remedy for the English Poor, By a Philanthropist', discussed in chapter 4, is characteristic of the general political tenor of *Douglas Jerrold's Shilling Magazine*.

Jerrold's combination of campaigning journalism, stories, history and romance in his *Shilling Magazine* enjoyed reasonable commercial success, with a healthy circulation of about 9,000 copies a month. But it was a minnow in comparison with the sales figures generated by the mass-market newspaper press that began to emerge at this period, and eighteen months after the first number of the *Shilling Magazine* had appeared, Jerrold decided to launch a sister publication aimed at a bigger audience, *Douglas Jerrold's Weekly Newspaper*. The motivation for this was purely commercial, and there is an interesting correspondence between Dickens and Jerrold concerning the latter's need to provide for his and his family's future, and an acknowledgement that he was launching the weekly newspaper purely for financial purposes. Jerrold had written to Dickens that:

This newspaper ... is hard to work; but it is *independence* ... I have a feeling of dread – a something almost insane in its abhorrence of the condition of the old, worn-out literary man ... flung upon literary funds while alive, with the hat to be sent round for his coffin and his widow.[20]

Dickens and Jerrold were alike in their dread of penury, both having not only suffered from domestic debt (in Dickens's case not his own but his father's), but also having assisted with cap-in-hand collections for the widows of both William Hone and Richard Brinsley Peake. Dickens's response to his friend's launch of *Douglas Jerrold's Weekly Newspaper* was generous:

I am truly pleased to receive your good account of that enterprize. I feel all you say upon the subject of the literary man in his old age, and know the incalculable benefit of such a resource. You can hardly fail to realize an independent property from such success; and I congratulate you upon it, with all my heart and soul.[21]

There are considerable overlaps between Jerrold's *Shilling Magazine* and his *Weekly Newspaper*. An 1846 *Weekly Newspaper* article that Jerrold commissioned Eliza Meteyard to write on 'The Poor Law in St Pancras Parish' complains of the poor sanitary conditions 'where fever and rheumatism may sprout'.[22] Charges of cruelty and the mismanagement of the poor are reported a week later in an unsigned article on 'The Treatment of the Poor in Marylebone Workhouse'.[23] Jerrold's frontal assaults on the bishops continue unabated in an unsigned essay on 'The Poor Man's Church and its Rich Bishops' that complains that 'The Society for the Diffusion and the Aggrandizement of Bishops, otherwise called the Ecclesiastical Commissioners, can afford, it seems, to build palaces for the accommodation of prelates.'[24] The *Weekly Newspaper* also includes serious reportage of Chartist activities, expressing support for the 'conscientious chartist'[25] and complaining of the harshness of the sentences meted out to Ernest Jones and four other Chartists in July 1848 (they were sentenced to two years' imprisonment).[26] Jerrold hired Thomas Cooper, the Chartist poet and writer of fiction, to write a weekly 'Eyewitness' column which sought to verify 'The Condition of the People of England':

What is the *real* life of 'the masses'? – how are the people fed; clothed; housed? what is the nature and kind of their labour? – how long are their days of work, and frequent their holidays? [&c][27]

A few weeks after the paper's launch Cooper was, for example, reporting on the living conditions of Leicester stockingers in a manner strongly redolent of anti-Poor Law reportage:

One man ate a raw potato for sheer hunger ... a woman who had subsisted a whole day on cold water, bared her breast to give her infant its expected nourishment – but there was no milk, and while the child screamed with hunger and impatience she fainted.[28]

Clearly Jerrold's political sympathies and commitment did not change as he embraced the weekly newspaper market. What did change, though, was the overall composition and cultural profile of his newspaper columns. His support for the poor and the oppressed never wavered, but alongside social and political articles Jerrold also introduced sensationalist news reportage that would never have found column space in either the *Shilling Magazine* or in *Punch*. The 'Crimes and Casualties' columns of *Douglas Jerrold's Weekly Newspaper* include lurid headlines such as 'Extraordinary Strangulation', 'Shocking Suicide and Triple Murder', 'Assassination in Norfolk' and 'Dreadful Doings at Hertford', clearly modelled on similar columns in the highly successful *News of the World*.[29] In this way, then, Jerrold simultaneously attempted to produce a newspaper that was popular both in the sense that it was genuinely *of* 'the People' and, at the same time, produced matter likely to appeal to an increasingly 'massified' reading public. The newspaper is representative of the 'uneasy mixture' that Raymond Williams has identified in modern popular culture:

Popular culture is always an uneasy mixture of two very different elements; the maintenance of an independent popular identity, often linked with political radicalism, resistance to the establishment, and movements for social change; and ways of adapting, from disadvantage, to a dominant social order, finding relief and satisfaction or diversion inside it.[30]

Jerrold's 'uneasy mixture' initially sold well, notching up 20,000 weekly sales at 6d a copy at the start.[31] But after two years it began to falter in the face of the ever-expanding power of the biggest of the weeklies. At 6d *Douglas Jerrold's Weekly Newspaper* was not particularly cheap: Dickens's weekly *Household Words* was priced at 2d, *Chambers's Edinburgh Journal* was 1½d and *Figaro in London* along with the ocean of other penny weeklies was cheaper still. Jerrold's weekly newspaper folded in 1848, surviving the *Shilling Magazine* by a year. Four years later, in 1852, Jerrold accepted an invitation to take over as editor of *Lloyd's Weekly Newspaper*, a move that at once both solved his perennial money problems (his salary was £1,000 per annum)[32] and completed his journey from popular radical journalism to the mass-market newsprint of Edward Lloyd and G. W. M Reynolds. Jerrold by no means abandoned his political commitment in his new role: *Lloyd's* was a newspaper that could readily accommodate his radical temperament. Jerrold's first leading article characteristically attacks bishops, and a second leader attacks the Tory Solicitor General.[33] But it is true to say that the emphasis was on more lurid and sensational newsprint, a journalistic strategy that meant that by the time of his death in 1857 *Lloyd's*, under Jerrold's stewardship, was notching up 182,000 weekly sales.

Jerrold's journalistic career across the 1840s and 1850s tells a wider story about the relationship between the popular and the radical press in the first half of the nineteenth century. What I want to emphasise here is the *fluidity* of the popular and radical newspaper and periodical press at the mid-century, Jerrold's own traversing of the cultural field typifying the constant shifting of the meaning and content of the popular press and, more specifically, its relationship to radical culture. The overlaps between popular and radical journalism that had been commonplace in the Regency London of William Hone by no means abruptly disappeared: in 1845, for example, Jerrold had handed over the editorship of the *Illuminated Magazine* to the Chartist W. J. Linton; and Thomas Cooper's reporting for *Douglas Jerrold's Weekly Newspaper* bolstered the radical profile of a weekly that was determined to appeal to a mass readership. More strikingly, perhaps, the editors of the biggest Chartist newspaper, the weekly *Northern Star*, were confident in 1844 that their readers were not only also perusing the novels of Charles Dickens, but the satirical weekly *Punch*, too. In a review of the second of Dickens's Christmas Books, *The Chimes*, the reviewer joins Dickens and Jerrold in their twin-pronged attack on Sir Peter Laurie, a London magistrate whom Jerrold had satirized in the pages of *Punch* and Dickens in *The Chimes*:[34]

Our readers who are also readers of *Punch* – and we expect but few are otherwise – must be pretty well acquainted with the doings of Peter the Great (ass), who hesitates at nothing, and is omnipotent at '*putting down*' all delinquents ... It strikes us we have ere now seen [in *The Chimes*] the original of *Alderman Cute*, presiding at the City Mansion House Police Court: but doubtless Alderman Sir Peter Laurie can say whether we are right.[35]

The (quite understandable) desire to impose some kind of order on the truly massive, protean body of writing that constitutes the Victorian periodical and newspaper press has, I think, sometimes led cultural historians too readily to lay down rigid boundaries between 'popular', 'radical' and 'progressive', and 'middle-class' and 'working-class' publications. Whilst Brian Maidment distinguishes sharply between what he calls 'Magazines of Popular Progress' and penny weeklies, Ian Haywood produces a meticulous taxonomy that places '*Eliza Cook's Journal* (1849–54), *Douglas Jerrold's Shilling Magazine* (1845–7) and even *Tait's Edinburgh Magazine* and *Household Words*' beyond the pale of his genealogy of popular radical publications and writers, describing them instead as 'polite journals of popular progress' whose mission was to 'use popular culture to disseminate a liberal philosophy of graduation and class conciliation.'[36] Whilst I would suggest that there was a greater overlap between the penny weeklies and 'magazines of popular progress' than Maidment allows, my argument with Haywood concerns not his generalised account of the particular political complexion of Jerrold's *Shilling Magazine* or of

Dickens's *Household Words*, but the more general tendency towards a rigid set of taxonomies along political lines. Such a taxonomy has the effect, on the one hand, of occluding the instability of the 'popular' and the 'radical' as categories in the period; and, on the other hand, of stifling the highly charged political contestation of the very conception and category of the 'popular' that was so characteristic of the periodical and newspaper market of the 1840s and early 1850s.

The politically non-aligned Douglas Jerrold (like Dickens, he never pledged his allegiance to any particular political party) was by no means alone in negotiating the tensions that developed between the popular and the radical press at the mid-century. The myriad of Chartist journalists and newspapers that came to the fore from the late 1830s similarly had to contend with the struggle for the 'popular' that was a direct consequence of the rise of the commercial newspaper market in the 1840s. It is to the journalistic project of Ernest Jones, the firebrand of late Chartism, that I shall now direct my attention. The aim of the second half of this chapter is, firstly, to reinforce my contention that the cultural category of the 'popular' was an intensely contested political field at this period; and, secondly, to draw attention to the work of a significant radical mid-century writer whose serially published works of fiction enter into a dialogue with popular melodrama in a politically complex way matched only – later in the decade – by Dickens.

ERNEST JONES, CHARTIST JOURNALISM AND POLITICAL MELODRAMA

The rapid expansion of the popular press in the 1840s was a mixed blessing for those Chartist activists who wished to use the pen to persuade the people of the rightness of their cause. The first radical movement that had to contend with the new commercial popular press of the nineteenth century, Chartist writers and journalists were able, like their commercial counterparts, to take advantage of the substantial reduction in stamp duty in 1836. Chartist journals and newspapers proliferated, publishing not only political argument and reportage but also a rich vein of fiction and poetry. At one point, there were more than fifty Chartist newspapers and journals, and many times that number of Chartist scribes who sought to give political direction to a huge, broadly non-elite readership. Most of the Chartist periodicals were short-lived, but the largest of them, the *Northern Star*, had at its peak a circulation of 50,000 and survived for fifteen years from 1837 to 1852.[37]

Chartist literature was generically diverse. Many Chartist newspapers ran a poetry column as well as publishing short stories and longer serialised novels. Chartist poets proudly inherited the Romantic lyric from Shelley, as well as songs, hymns and broadsides from a popular oral tradition. Chartist writers of fiction availed themselves of fable, allegory, melodrama and the *bildungsroman* in their particular fashioning of a Chartist aesthetic.[38] Broadly, there were two main aesthetic trajectories within Chartist literature: a high-cultural Romanticism and a more populist melodramatic vein.[39] Responding to the inexorable soaking up of non-elite readers by *Lloyd's Weekly Newspaper* and the *News of the World*, from the late 1840s an increasing number of Chartist writers began to write populist novels in serial form, exploiting the conventions of popular melodrama for a political analysis of class conflict and economic inequality.[40]

At the centre of the Chartist turn to the 'popular' was Ernest Charles Jones. As a scion of the Chartist movement Jones has a somewhat surprising genealogy. Born in Berlin in 1819, where he lived until his family returned to England in 1838, Jones, known to his relatives as 'Carl', was the son of one Major Charles Jones. Jones senior had fought at Waterloo and was equerry to the Duke of Cumberland, the uncle of Queen Victoria who would eventually become King Ernest I of Hanover. Jones the Chartist revolutionary was, then, the godson of a Prussian king. Yet it is his aristocratic connections that helped fashion Ernest Jones, in Patrick Joyce's words, as 'the suffering gentleman leader ... a surrogate for a dispossessed people'.[41] Jones, like Feargus O'Connor before him, and like his contemporary and rival, G. W. M Reynolds, lived out his political career 'as a romantic hero', 'exiled and spurned by [his] own sort, doing battle in the cause of [his] similarly exiled but poor fellow m[e]n'.[42]

Jones's turn to fiction was most sustained after his incarceration in Mill Bank jail as a political prisoner from 1848 to 1850, after which time he wrote two novels in quick succession, *De Brassier: A Democratic Romance* (1851) and *Woman's Wrongs* (1852). He also resumed his journalistic career within Chartism, and took to the road once more as a political orator. Jones was one of the most astonishingly diverse of Chartism's scribes: as well as a notable poet and writer of popular melodramatic novels, he was a quite brilliant political essayist and orator and an indefatigable editor of a total of eight Chartist newspapers between 1847 and 1860: *The Labourer* (1847–8) (with Feargus O'Connor); *Notes to the People* (1851–2); *The People's Paper* (1852–8); *The Chartist Circular* (1858); *The London News* (1858); *The Cabinet Newspaper* (1858–60); *The Penny Times* (1860); and *The Weekly Telegraph* (1860). The diversity of Ernest Jones's literary contribution to the Chartist movement had its roots in the hybridity of his own cultural background. An English boy in Germany, by the age of eleven he could speak English, German, French and Italian. As a master of many tongues he found it easy to adopt and adapt a multitude of literary discourses. Something of a literary ventriloquist, he was able to mimic and reproduce a variety of literary genres. This is significant, too, in relation to his political career, during which he engaged, at different times but with equal facility, with a panoply of political discourses: Disraelian Toryism in the late 1830s and early 1840s, O'Connorite Chartism with its Romantic preoccupation with ownership of land in the late 1840s, Marxist socialism in the 1850s and, finally, Liberal Reformism in the 1860s. Some commentators have used the various changes of direction in Jones's political career to suggest that his involvement in Chartist politics between 1846 and 1858 was somehow inauthentic or sham. Miles Taylor's unsympathetic biography regards Jones as a political cross-dresser and shameless opportunist.[43] The problem I have with this reading of Jones and his politics is that it suggests that the sudden immersion in Chartist politics was an easy option. Ernest Jones could have had a lucrative career not only as a barrister, but alternatively as a journalist: he was a talented writer, sufficiently well connected to have found openings on high-profile London journals. And politically he could have joined the Christian socialists, or the mainstream middle-class radicals such as John Bright, John Cobden and John Stuart Mill, or Disraeli's 'Young England' movement. Any of these alternatives would have harmonised more readily with his background than the plunge into Chartism. The Ernest Jones archives in Manchester and New York have convinced me of the authenticity of his commitment to Chartism from 1846 through to its death throes in 1858. Imprisoned for two years from 1848 to 1850, Jones spent the whole of the 1850s in near poverty and watched his wife and children suffer as he tried to keep his various Chartist newspapers afloat and Chartism itself alive. An opportunist would almost certainly have changed direction after 1850. Instead, Jones turned down a relative's offer of £2,000 on his release from prison, an offer dependent on his giving up his Chartist involvement.

It was in the Chartist press that Jones published his most significant and interesting novels: *The Maid of Warsaw* (1854) began life as *The Romance of a People* in *The Labourer*; whilst *De Brassier* (1851) and *Woman's Wrongs* (1852) were both initially published in *Notes to the People*. Like most Chartist periodicals and newspapers, the ones that Jones edited were radically under-funded: they were not commercial enterprises, but political ones. He was all too aware, though, of the need to negotiate the 'popular' in his writings, in order to hang onto a non-elite readership which might otherwise desert the Chartist press. Highly conscious of the commercial press with which his own radical newspapers were in competition, to a certain extent Jones attempted to emulate the mix of radical politics and populist newsprint of which his rival, G. W. M. Reynolds, was such an adept exponent.[44] As Jones was launching his *People's Paper* in 1852, a friend urged him to advertise with handbills and posters similar to those that had been used to advertise *Reynolds' Weekly* and *Lloyd's*: 'If you get any posters out this week, I advise you to have them the same as Lloyds, Reynolds, &c.'[45] Jones's awareness of the need to appeal in his political writing to a popular non-elite readership is illustrated throughout the 1850s. The front-page article for the first edition of his *People's Paper* promises to mix politics with entertainment:

A continuous course of exposure of the great State monopolies of England will be published. We begin with the State Church, and can promise our readers some curious revelations under this head.

Features of Romance will not be wanting to temper and to harmonise the more stern and serious portions of the *People's Paper*, and to commend it as a household companion of the leisure hour.[46]

Similarly, in an advert for one of the last of his radical newspapers, *The Penny Times*, Jones promised that the paper would be 'racy' and 'amusing' as well as 'useful' and 'instructive'. Its 'Contents' list features 'Foreign News', 'Police Reports', 'Parliament', 'Sporting News', 'Markets', 'Fun', 'Romance and Housewife's Corner' and 'Useful Information'.[47]

Conscious as he was of the necessity to retain a popular readership for the radical press, Jones attempted, most notably in his *Notes to the People*, to tread a fine line between a populist and a radical journalistic approach. Jones had an ambivalent attitude to popular literary forms. In his Preface to *De Brassier: A Democratic Romance*, he insisted on the efficacy of popular fictional conventions in advancing social revolution, and there is something of an echo here of Dickens's popularist reform-ist philosophy that had been articulated in *Household Words* two years before:

Rowland Hill said, when setting his psalms to opera melodies, 'he did not see why the devil should have all the good tunes to himself.' Rowland Hill was right, (always supposing that the others did belong to the devil).

In like manner I do not see why Truth should always be dressed in stern and repulsive garb. The more attractive you make her, the more easily she will progress. Let the same moral be conveyed in a tale, and preached in a sermon, the former will make ten proselytes, when the latter will secure but one.[48]

Less than a year later, though, his attitude seems to have shifted somewhat. Referring specifically to Reynolds's newspaper, and echoing the tone (if not exactly the content) of an attack that Dickens had made in *Household Words* two years earlier, Jones is unable to contain his contempt:

Democracy is too pure and holy to come bound up and classified with the Newgate calendar. We cannot afford to spend our time every Saturday night in endeavouring to dig a few stray gems of liberty from a dense morass of moral filth. When we sit down to the feast of democracy we must not have the table spread with garbage. The man whose taste has led him to dish up Chartism with such trash; and he who is satisfied with it, have alike mistaken their mission, and the nature of the principles they have adopted.[49]

Jones's understanding of the potential political pitfalls of an increasingly 'massified' culture enabled him to sidestep them. In each of *The Maid of Warsaw*, *De Brassier* and *Woman's Wrongs* he manipulates and adapts the ingredients of popular melodrama in order to forge a radical political aesthetic.

Jones's own speeches and essays, as well as his works of fiction, were strongly marked by a melodramatic rhetoric. His famous 'Blackstone Edge' speech, which gave rise to the poem of the same name, is replete with the stark moral oppositions, and the preoccupation with the suffering body of the poor, which are so typical of the melodramatic mode:

They say we are too ignorant to enjoy the franchise; we, ourselves, do not know what we want. Does a man know what he wants when he is starving? And sees the rich rolling in riotous profusion? He'll tell you he wants food – but then, they say that's all his folly – it's the *workhouse* that he wants! Does a man know what he wants when he is sinking with over-work, that the healthy may enjoy their sumptuous indolence? He'll tell you he wants some hours of rest; but then, they say that's idleness and crime! It's the *gaol* that he wants.[50]

Never afraid of melodrama, Jones claimed in a letter written in 1855 that he wrote some of his prison poems, including 'The New World', with his own blood, having been denied the luxury of pen and ink.[51] The bodiliness of the melodramatic aesthetic – here expressed in an extreme form – meant that the writing of melodramatic fiction came easily to one of Chartism's most able scribes.

Melodramatic writing of the nineteenth century consistently urged the need for radical change in the lives of the powerless and the oppressed, and in this at least it is inherently radical. As Simon Shepherd puts it:

Melodrama may be said to construct excitement out of the possible alter-nations between being trapped by circumstances and being able to change them ... Melodrama's excitement may be said to relate to a fantasy of *agency*, the possibility of being able single-handedly to challenge authority and change it.[52]

In traditional melodramas, though, individual lives are changed for the better through chance or sheer good luck. A classic instance of this kind of plot device can be found in *Oliver Twist*, in which Oliver is rescued from poverty and criminality by his chance meeting with Mr Brownlow: his secret identity as the son of the well-to-do is revealed and he is able to escape the harsh city, retreating to the countryside. Such a plot device was indeed borrowed by some Chartist writers of melodrama. In Thomas Cooper's short story 'Seth Thompson, the Stockinger' Seth and his family, after many years of semi-starvation in the slums of Leicester, are saved by the chance arrival, *deus-ex-machina* fashion, of a long-lost (wealthy) uncle.[53] Ernest Jones, in common with other determinedly radical exponents of the genre (not least Dickens himself in the 1850s), eschewed the 'happy endings' of mainstream melodrama in his own writings, rejecting individual betterment and insisting on the necessity of wider social and economic change.

Melodrama was a heterogeneous form, variously drawing on popular crime narratives, Gothicism, tragedy, romance and even satire. Alert to this heterogeneity, Jones mixes his own melodramas with political analysis and quasi-historical reportage. The initial title of *De Brassier: A Democratic Romance* was *The History of a Democratic Movement, compiled from The Journal of a Democrat, the Confessions of a Demagogue, and the Minutes of a Spy*, manifestly drawing attention to itself as a heteroglot form. This, the first of Jones's novels to have been written after his release from prison in 1850, has all the hallmarks of radical melodrama. Its opening focuses on a seamstress and a young child, her niece, who are helplessly starving in a garret. Jones draws on literary Gothic as he details the 'moaning' wind and the 'flickering moonlight' through the rattling windows; the 'dark column of smoke' from a factory chimney nearby is 'like an eternal offering to the god of evil'.[54] The mode of excess characteristic of melodrama has the seamstress 'bur[ying] her face sobbing in her hands' as 'the tears course down [her] cheeks' (*De Brassier*, p. 35). The arrival home of her brother, the unemployed Charles Dalton, heralds another 'whirlwind of passion' as 'he shook before the faint cries of that starving child like an oak beneath a whirlwind; a wild expression danced within his eyes' (p. 40). Dalton's wife has died in a workhouse, and he, like Dickens's Betty Higden in *Our Mutual Friend* some fourteen years later, regards a return to the 'Poor Law

Bastile' as a fate quite literally worse than death: ' "we won't go to the workhouse! We'll die first!" ' (p. 39). The exclamatory syntax and heightened emotion of melodrama are equally present in Jones's narratorial interventions as he urges the rich to have pity on the poor: 'one moment stolen from pride and vanity, one small dole from all those riches, would save lives, oh! How precious and how dear!' (p. 47) The extreme violence characteristic of many melodramas manifests itself in the brutality of the police as they arrest the protesting Charles Dalton: 'he was stricken down . . . at the blow of the baton the blood streamed from the deep cleft in his head' (p. 48).

But Jones was too subtle a writer, and too politically alert, simply to reproduce melodramatic conventions. In *De Brassier* he borrows heavily from melodrama at the same time as he manipulates and interrogates the crime narrative at the heart of the melodramatic plot. Such an interrogation enables a politicising of his analysis of social and economic oppression beyond the confines of an orthodox melodramatic rhetoric. Melodrama readily incorporated elements of popular crime fiction; crime is in many ways the perfect ingredient of melodrama, as it has an immediate dramatic impact, it creates dramatic conflict and thereby implies resolution. It also often makes a *physical* impact, readily melding with melodrama's aesthetic of the body. Typical ingredients of melodramatic crime narratives of the nineteenth century included the seduction of a working-class girl by an aristocratic villain, and a near-obligatory trial scene, in which unjust accusations are made, so that a revelation of the truth is needed to save the hero or heroine from punishment. An acted-out confrontation between the guilty and the innocent parties was also a common trope. All of these – and more – can be promptly identified in *De Brassier*. The seamstress victim is sexually threatened, first by the overseer of the workhouse, and thereafter by a corrupt aristocratic second son, Simon De Brassier. An heroic artisan Chartist plots to save her. Charles Dalton collapses – apparently dead – in a set-piece trial scene, and returns to exact his revenge on his oppressors.

Beginning with these staple ingredients, Jones manipulates them so as to maximise their radical political affects. He reinterprets the criminal elements characteristic of popular melodrama so as to interrogate its politics and to produce a more complex, more nuanced political fiction than would be possible if the moral and dramatic structures of classic melodrama were reproduced wholesale.

Central to the plot of *De Brassier* are two criminal acts of vengeance. The first of these contains all the ingredients of classic melodrama,

consisting as it does of a melodramatic confrontation between an aristocratic seducer – the debauched, decadent Walter de Brassier – and his
victim, Lucy, also known as 'Maline', who is presented as a fallen woman
turned femme fatale. Lucy has set Stanville Hall, Walter de Brassier's
ancestral home, on fire, and the crippled old aristocrat becomes engulfed
in the flames:

> He rolled himself on to the ground – and half crawling, half staggering, dragged
> himself towards the valet's room. He cast his frenzied glance towards the bed –
> and there, in virgin white, partly shrouded by the dark red draperies, sat a female
> figure –
>   Walter de Brassier staggered as if stricken by a sudden blow.
>   'Lucy!' but the word died on his tongue.
>   'Yes! Lucy!' cried Maline, without moving from the spot, and casting the glance
> of her scorn and hatred on the abject wretch that crawled on the ground before her
> feet. The paralysis of disease had been superseded by the paralysis of fear! 'Yes!
> Lucy! the girl you seduced from happiness – you lured to crime – you left to
> destitution – and you condemned to vice! Do you remember me!' . . .
>   'Mercy!' he shrieked – 'help! help!' but the dull roaring of the flames answered
> him alone. (pp. 223–4)

This is classic melodrama, with an admixture of Gothic thrown in for good
measure; its political impact is limited by its conventionality.

The second, related act of vengeance in the novel forces the reader to
reappraise the somewhat hackneyed scenario I have just quoted, and to see
it anew as having a political significance. This second act of vengeance
consists of an attack by an ostensibly politically motivated mob on a
mansion housing the wicked bourgeois industrialist – Henry Dorville –
who has robbed the hapless Charles Dalton of his means of earning a living.
The mysterious leader of the mob sets Dorville's mansion on fire and
the factory owner dies of his burns. Jones deliberately duplicates the plot
here – both acts of vengeance circle around arson attacks on rich men's
mansions – so as to invite the reader to compare the two scenarios. The
mysterious stranger who leads the attack on Dorville's mansion turns out
to be Charles Dalton, returned from the dead to avenge himself on the
employer who starved and incriminated him. The fictional device of one
returning from the dead, or from overseas, is, again, a highly conventional
melodramatic trope: similar devices are used in Gaskell's novels *North and
South* (1854–5) and *Sylvia's Lovers* (1863–4). But what is important here is
that Jones's juxtaposition of these two acts of vengeance draws attention
to the fact that they both result from the exploitation of one class by
another.

Hackneyed as the fallen-woman story may be, it has a political resonance that Jones brings out by juxtaposing it with a more obviously political act of class vengeance. The personal tragedies of melodrama are shown to be profoundly political. In this way Jones draws attention anew to the *political* dimensions of the personal dramas at the core of so many melo-dramatic plots. Through repetition – they were very widely circulated in mid-nineteenth century English culture – such plots could tend to lose their radical effects, audiences becoming so accustomed to melodrama's rhetoric as to be unable to retain a sense of its political motivation. Jones, though, recovers the initial political impetus of melodrama.

De Brassier remained unfinished when Jones, probably tired of this first foray into popular melodrama of the domestic variety, turned his attention to *Woman's Wrongs: A Novel in Four Books*, which has considerably more political weight than its predecessor. In *De Brassier*, Jones's engagement with the 'Woman Question' only extends to representing the wrongs of the seamstress and of the fallen woman. In *Woman's Wrongs*, though, he is self-consciously writing within an established political tradition, at the same time as retaining those elements of popular melodrama deemed essential to attract a wide readership. This was not the first time, though, that Jones had focused on the oppression of women in his fiction: his earlier novel, *The Maid of Warsaw*, is powerfully punctuated by a series of atrocities directed at women, whom Jones's narrative seeks to defend and transform into heroines. In this his first attempt at writing a determinedly populist novel, begun before his incarceration in Millbank gaol, Jones leans heavily on Gothic in his account of Poland's defeat by Russia in the early 1830s, an episode in Eastern European history that had been the initial impetus for Jones's political radicalism. Starting life as 'The Romance of a People', serialised in the *Labourer* from 1847 to 1848 and eventually published in complete form as a one-volume novel, *The Maid of Warsaw*, in 1854, this early novel makes evident the Romantic trajectory of Jones's earlier writ-ings. *The Maid* is a fairly typical example of that sub-genre of melodrama loosely known as Romantic melodrama, which was characterised by Eastern locations, and, typically, an 'exotic' cast of characters (often including Magyars, Tartars and so on).[55] Replete with Gothic castles, dungeons and dangerous moonlit expeditions, *The Maid of Warsaw* is peopled by heroic Polish noblemen and women who fight off the maraud-ing Russian counts and commanders. *The Maid of Warsaw* is a powerful, romantic evocation of Poland's heroic last stand against the Russians, but it is problematic in terms of its gender politics. For in this particular formulation of Romantic melodrama, 'woman' figures solely as a trope.

A series of horrific rapes litter the narrative, as Russian soldiers pillage their way through Poland, the violated bodies of Polish girls representing the wider rape of their nation. In this novel, women exist not as a discrete oppressed group, but as synechdoches for their forlorn, oppressed country. It is only when Jones turned to a class- and gender-based politics after 1848, and to a more domestic melodramatic vocabulary, that he was able to apprehend women as oppressed social and political subjects in their own right.

1851, the year in which Jones began to serialise *Woman's Wrongs* in *Notes to the People*, witnessed the presentation in the House of Lords of the first petition for universal female suffrage.[56] It was also the year in which Harriet Taylor published her radical essay on the 'Enfranchisement of Women' in the *Westminster Review*.[57] The title of Jones's novel pays homage to Mary Wollstonecraft's *The Wrongs of Woman, or Maria. A Fragment* (1798), while also echoing Charlotte Tonna's elaboration of *The Wrongs of Woman* in 1843–4.[58] Jones clearly took an interest in the 'Woman Question': later in his career he was invited to women's suffrage meetings in Manchester and availed himself of a copy of the prospectus of the Manchester Ladies' College in 1868.[59]

Some critics have regarded Chartist melodramas as irredeemably sexist. Anna Clark, for example, argues that in their desire for social and sexual respectability Chartists became locked into a restrictive language of domesticity that was supported by the conventions of domestic melodrama. A typical melodramatic Chartist plot has a working-class female victim rescued from an aristocratic sexual predator by virtuous Chartist manhood, the typical denouement involving a reassuring vision of future domestic bliss brought about by manhood suffrage.[60] Chartist men demanded full political rights to enable them to speak for themselves in the public arena. Although there were thousands of female Chartists, fundamentally they had a supplementary role in the movement, protesting on behalf of their men and their families rather than as independent political subjects. Chartist women were often posited by Chartist rhetoric as melodrama's victims; this does not mean, though, that melodrama has no force as a feminist medium. Judith Walkowitz has commented that one of the benefits of melodrama as a genre for a feminist perspective is that in the nineteenth century it inserted gender into the discussion of class politics.[61] Both Martha Vicinus and E. Ann Kaplan have remarked that melodrama particularly appealed to female audiences, writers and performers precisely because it foregrounded issues of gender and power, and highlighted the role of the heroine, however passive and suffering she might be.[62] Dickens would, between 1851 and 1853, manipulate the female character types of melodrama to extraordinary effect so as to present, in *Bleak House*, a cross-class account of women's wrongs.[63] Jones achieves the same in his novel from 1852, *Woman's Wrongs*.

In *Woman's Wrongs*, his composite novel from 1852, Jones writes within an established proto-feminist tradition. As early as 1840, Chartist Reginald Richardson had written a pamphlet while in prison called 'The Rights of Woman', pre-empting Jones's tribute to Wollstonecraft by some twelve years.[64] In the first of the stories in *Woman's Wrongs*, 'The Working Man's Wife', the main female protagonist and her daughters are archetypal figures from melodrama: Margaret Haspen, whose husband is unemployed, is a helpless, hapless, economically dependent figure. Her older daughter is seduced by her father's ex-employer, the evil industrialist Barrowson, and turns to prostitution. The main contours of the story are as follows: John Haspen, a factory hand, is thrown out of work; his wife gives birth in utter penury. Consumed by rage and a sense of injustice, Haspen eventually murders his ex-employer. His wife attempts to conceal evidence of the murder, is discovered in this and hanged for her part as an accomplice to the murder. Jones resolutely refutes the typically ameliorative character-istics of melodrama: there is no stroke of good fortune to rescue the Haspens, and even the younger of the two daughters, it seems, will be forced into prostitution at the story's close.

The main villain of the piece is not the aristocratic seducer whom one finds in other Chartist tales, such as Thomas Frost's *The Secret* or Reynolds's *Mysteries of London*, but is one Barrowson, a working man turned industrialist, rather in the style of Dickens's Josiah Bounderby.[65] In this regard, Jones's political melodrama is thoroughly modernised, apprehending the rising bourgeoisie, rather than the aristocratic land-owners, as the bearers of social and economic power in mid-Victorian industrial society. Within the parameters of the melodramatic narrative, Jones insists on a brutal realism, emphasising the domestic squalor endured by the working classes.

Jones, then, as a writer of radical melodrama, manipulates and refor-mulates its codes so that his fictions reveal the deprivation that the more affirmative, and more conventional, political melodramas tended to efface. An important element in Jones's reformulation of radical melo-drama is the use of pastiche and parody in order to reveal the limitations of a genre he is not afraid to engage self-consciously with: only Dickens, in his two great social novels of the 1850s, *Bleak House* and *Little Dorrit*, matches the sophistication of Jones's dialogue with the melodramatic mode.

Elsewhere in his journalism Jones, like his contemporaries Douglas Jerrold and Charles Dickens, drew on the tradition of radical satire that had had such a strong currency in the radical press of the 1810s and 1820s.[66] In the final pages of 'The Working Man's Wife' he injects an element of satire and parody into an otherwise apparently straightforward melodramatic scene. The scene is a thoroughly staged one, drawing heavily on Newgate fiction; but the narrative voice here is unstable, shifting between, on the one hand the unabashed emotional affects of melodramatic hyperbole and, on the other hand, a satirical performance of that excess. The shifts are carefully crafted in order to make the reader reappraise the social and political significance of an otherwise highly conventional, formulaic fictional scene. In the final section of the story, sub-headed 'An Execution', Jones simultaneously aligns himself with the rhetoric of melodrama and sustains a critical distance from it. Like Dickens before and after him, he exploits the strong cultural currency of execution scenes from broadside literature to powerful literary and political effect.[67] In this final tableau Margaret Haspen is hanged alongside one Latchman, as Jones invites the reader to compare the significance and emotional affects of the two executions. The excited onlookers at the hangings are heavily criticised by Jones, who creates a pathos with the arrival of Margaret's two daughters – the youngest of whom, Mary, cries out, begging her mother not to die, not to leave them. Her mother's corpse dangling in front of her, Mary is led away sobbing by her older sister, Catherine, who is in turn comforted by her fellow prostitutes, her only friends. The scene closes with two cane-twirling young shopmen smirking knowingly about the probable fate of the youngest daughter – ' "Luckily for her, she's pretty!" '[68]

The staginess is clear: Latchman, the convicted criminal, is presented as a showman – ' "Ladies and Gentlemen!" ' – and Jones refers to the hangings as 'this dread drama'. It is in fact an extraordinarily self-reflexive piece of writing, satirical and parodic as well as melodramatic. The onlookers at the hanging respond to the imminent death of Margaret Haspen as to a spectacle or an entertainment, akin to the Old Bailey crowd in *A Tale of Two Cities*. Such onlookers are rather like the readers of Newgate fiction, which Jones mimics here. But the mimicry is self-conscious and critical, for readers of Newgate fiction formed part of the target audience of Jones's popular radical fiction. At the beginning and end of this final section of the story, Jones asks his readers to consider their own role as passive onlookers at the death of Margaret Haspen. The self-reflexivity of the following extract anticipates the Brechtian 'alienation effect', as Jones repeatedly criticises the spectators who, by implication, are synonymous with his own readers, who are also onlookers at Margaret's death:

An execution was to take place at Newgate . . . Before daybreak, the people began to assemble . . . They came, as they would to the public-house, seeking something to drown thought for a few hours. They came, as they had gone the previous evening to the playhouse, to get the amusement of one excitement more! . . .

. . . Whilst this was going on in the open air . . . a harrowing scene was enacting in the prison – [where] in a dull, dead cell, lay Margaret. The door opened, and a young woman entered, bearing a child in her arms.

'Mother! Mother!' cried an agonising voice! 'My poor mother!' . . .

Meanwhile, the crowd without became impatient for the sight – some wanted their breakfast – some had to go to work – some felt cold and tired – and the show delayed. At last, Latchman appeared. Hopelessness and certain death had given courage to his craven heart. He advanced with a firm step; bowed gracefully around; talked unconcernedly to the hangman; and, with a theatrical pronunciation, turning to the multitude said –

'Ladies and gentlemen! I trust I have made my peace with earth and heaven! I forgive all my enemies! And I die full of hope!'

Whereupon something like an approving murmur ran along the crowd; isolated cries were raised of, 'Well done, old boy!' 'Spoken like a trump!' and then his neck was broken – the people being edified by his behaviour, and learning to believe that . . . hanging was not so very bad, and that a murderer could die in a very comfortable manner.

But the next act of this dread drama was approaching. Intense, breathless attention riveted the crowd, when Margaret appeared! Suffering and agony had ennobled her otherwise common face – death clothed it with interest – sorrow touched it with beauty! She spoke no word! . . . [but] merely rested her eyes for a few moments reproachfully on the multitude below, and then raised them mournfully to heaven.

At this moment a piercing shriek rang over the crowd, and below, close in front of the drop stood Catherine and Mary. The latter was raised high in her sister's arms, and stretched her little hands upward to her mother.

'Mother!' cried the child, 'you must not die! Stay with me, mother. Mother! What will become of me? What shall I do without you?'

'God pity you!' cried Margaret, and writhed her pinioned arms in vain . . .

Another moment, and her lifeless corpse was dangling in the air before that careless myriad of spectators.[69]

The self-reflexivity and performative character of the passage are most obvious when Latchman theatrically takes to the stage during his execution, the performativity of his hanging enabling the onlookers (and the reader) to distance themselves from what is actually happening to him. There is a constant shifting from such distancing devices to the full-blooded hyperbole and emotional affects of melodrama, the effect of which is to jerk the reader into a sense of realism in relation to the melodramatic moments. I am referring here to a realism of affect, rather than to a representational realism. Jones is fully aware – as his readers at the time would have been – that he is drawing on the narrative tropes of Newgate fiction. He is not asking his readers to 'believe in' the scene at the level of incident, but he *is* asking them to respond to the emotional affects of the scene and, thereafter, to act upon the injustices meted out to the Margaret Haspens of mid-nineteenth-century Britain.

Margaret Haspen and her daughters have little or no agency. While Latchman takes control of his own death, Margaret is the passive, speechless, suffering victim, her only utterance being one of the pitying mother for her child as Jones blesses her with angelic maternal status. Margaret, as she looks up to heaven, becomes an iconographic figure of suffering and martyrdom. Her baldly described lifeless dangling corpse, though, acts as a sharp corrective to the saccharine affects of the previous sequence.

'The Working Man's Wife' closes with a prostitution trope that Jones does not confine in the novel as a whole to working-class women. In the subsequent stories – 'The Young Milliner', 'The Tradesman's Wife' and 'The Lady of Title' – he extends the prostitution trope across all social groups. As a composite work of fiction, then, *Woman's Wrongs* presents a cross-class analysis of female oppression that posits women as an oppressed group in their own right, and not just as adjuncts to working-class men. Jones's analysis is indebted to Marx's and Engels's accounts of prostitution: they apprehended the prostituted woman as the archetypally commodified body, and Jones was influenced in this as in other areas of his political thought by the two German theorists.[70] His deployment of the prostitution trope makes it clear that the wrongs of woman are gender specific, and not simply an extension of the class politics that other Chartist writers of melodrama favoured over and above sexual politics. In 'The Tradesman's Daughter', a young woman, socially and sexually stifled by years of working long hours keeping accounts in her father's shop, is married off to her father's business partner, even though she clearly lusts after her cousin, a penniless young writer. In 'The Lady of Title', the Lady in question is sold off in marriage to her father's political rival, a pawn in the political machinations of the aristocracy.

It is the first two stories of *Woman's Wrongs* that are most powerfully realized, though, perhaps indicating Jones's greater commitment to the plight of non-elite women, whatever his broader sympathies. In 'The Young Milliner', which is one of numerous 'seamstress' stories from the mid-century, the starving seamstress at the centre of the tale resists the advances of an aristocrat's footman only to succumb to a sexually attractive young medical student.[71] One of the interesting things about this story is that Anna, the seamstress, is clearly and deliberately presented as a desiring sexual subject: no passive object of desire, she stares longingly out of her garret window hoping to catch the glance of the impecunious medical student who lives in the attic opposite. She actively participates in their lovemaking, which is staged not as a seduction scene but as a romantic, erotic consummation. Charles Trelawney, the medical student, is not wealthy, but poor – temporarily at least – and in turn it is made clear that he not only desires Anna but also grows attached to her. The point that Jones seems to be making is that in different economic circumstances this is a cross-class relationship between a man and a woman that need not have turned out to be the exploitative one that it does in fact become. At the very least, Trelawney is a far cry from the villainous aristocratic seducers of conventional melodrama. He and Anna set up home together, but he finds that he cannot stay with her – and certainly cannot legitimize their relationship – without being financially cut off by his middle-class parents. Trelawney ultimately abandons Anna, who then goes the way of many a seduced seamstress in nineteenth-century fiction: she gives birth to a sickly child, and they both die.

As in 'The Working Man's Wife', Jones opts for a sensational close to 'The Young Milliner'. Dying in hospital, Anna's body is appropriated by the authorities for scientific purposes. When Trelawney attends an anatomy lecture at London University, the body on the slab is revealed as Anna's: he screams and faints with shock. The Burke and Hare-like close resonates with contemporary fears surrounding the Anatomy Act that had found its way into the statutes in 1832, not long before the passage of the New Poor Law Bill in 1834. While dead paupers were not automatically handed over to the medical authorities for dissection, the Act did allow workhouses to sell unclaimed bodies to the medical schools.[72] In other words, while the final tableau of Jones's tale is sensationalist, it none the less draws on the very real fear amongst the poor that even their dead bodies were not their own property. More important in political terms is the fact that the final violation of Anna's body on the dissection slab properly completes a process of objectification in a narrative in which the female protagonist begins as a desiring subject and ends as a prostituted commodity. It is only when Trelawney is forced to 'see' (anew) Anna's violated body that he is able to register his own role in that process.

Jones's *Notes to the People*, which he replaced with the *People's Paper* in 1853, represents an heroic attempt to yoke serious, purposeful radical journalism to popular cultural production. It was in *Woman's Wrongs* that Jones was most successful in the attempt to blend radical politics with a popular aesthetic, and it remains an important text in the tradition of popular radicalism.

He was by no means alone in the attempt. Alongside Jones stood that other quite extraordinary Chartist, G. W. M. Reynolds. Exiles from the upper and middle classes respectively, both men were rather glamorous figures within late Chartism. Suffering financial distress as young men, both became journalists, with Reynolds's journalistic influence extending well beyond his death (*Reynolds' Weekly Newspaper* remained a considerable force in the 1960s). The differences between the two men are, though, as significant as their similarities. By 1850 George Reynolds was a very rich man, benefiting hugely from his role in the development of the commercial popular press in the middle years of the nineteenth century. Reynolds was the first editor of the *London Journal* (1845–1912), a paper aimed at a semi-literate readership, which, after a shaky start, went on to establish profits of between £10,000 and £12,000 per annum. He subsequently founded his own *Reynolds' Miscellany of Romance, General Interest, Science and Art* (1846–9), which sold 30,000 current numbers and 10,000 back numbers each week; he then went on to the even more successful *Reynolds' Weekly Newspaper*, launched in 1850.[73] By 1850, Reynolds was living in a large country house, whilst Ernest Jones was spending his second year in prison, jailed for sedition in July 1848. Jones never made enough from his newspaper editing to support his family, sending them the odd pound here and there, even this often borrowed.[74]

Jones's political project of wedding radical politics to nineteenth-century populist cultural forms was at once smaller in scale (in a material sense) than Reynolds's, and more politically focused. Alert as he was to the need to borrow some of the journalistic apparel of the popular commercial press, the driving force behind Jones's journalistic enterprises remained political. Determined to steer Chartism to the left after 1848, commercial viability was an economic necessity rather than, as for Reynolds, an end in itself. Although Jones and Reynolds would seem to have had a shared political commitment, Reynolds proved to be a ruthless commercial rival. With hindsight, Jones was never a threat to George Reynolds's commercial enterprises, which made Jones's struggling newspapers look like very small fry. Jones's *Notes to the People*, for example, which ran from 1851 to 1852, had a circulation in the low two thousands;[75] similarly, the *People's Paper* advertised average weekly sales of 2,684 in 1854.[76] This made them the most successful of the Chartist newspapers to have been spawned by the radical revival of 1848. They were, though, positively dwarfed by *Reynolds' Weekly*'s circulation of 49,000 in 1855 and 60,000 in 1860.[77] But this did not dissuade Reynolds from driving his smaller rival out of business. In October 1858, when Jones was standing as a Radical MP for Nottingham, Reynolds publicly accused him of political insincerity and of embezzling funds donated to his struggling *People's Paper*, and had bill posters distributed across Nottingham to this effect.[78] Jones successfully sued Reynolds for libel, but in the process the *People's Paper*, Jones's most politically radical journalistic project, closed down because of cash-flow problems during the court case.[79]

Reynolds is as significant a figure as Jones in the political and cultural history of the popular radical press, as Ian Haywood's, Rohan McWilliam's and Anne Humphery's scholarship has amply demonstrated.[80] That Jones and Reynolds ended up as bitter rivals is testament to the intensity of the battle for the twin fields of the popular and the radical at the mid-century, as the commercialisation of the newspaper market accelerated in pace. To some extent Jerrold was a victim of that process, 'in harness', in Michael Slater's words, to Lloyd's gargantuan newspaper at the end of his life.[81] Whilst for Edward Lloyd the hiring of Jerrold was a bid for respectability, for Jerrold it was something of a compromise.

Dickens did not, of course, watch from the sidelines as the contestation of the popular as a category reached boiling point. In 1850 he made his own intervention in the popular market with the launch of his cheap weekly magazine, *Household Words*. It is the cultural and political significance of this project that forms the focus of the following chapter.

CHAPTER 6

Household Words, *politics and the mass market in the 1850s*

DICKENS, G. W. M. REYNOLDS AND 'THE PEOPLE'

The launching of *Household Words* in March 1850 brought to fruition Dickens's long-standing desire to enter the periodical market. His motivations were commercial, cultural and political. Long aware of the financial precariousness of novel writing, Dickens was, like his friend Douglas Jerrold, haunted almost throughout his life by the proximity of debt amongst family and friends. A letter to Angela Burdett Coutts in April 1850 reveals the novelist's desire to establish a secure income from his new publishing project:

The Household Words I hope (and have every reason to hope) will become a *good property*. It is exceedingly well liked, and 'goes', in the trade phrase, admirably . . . and although the expences [sic] of such a venture are necessarily very great, the circulation much more than pays them, so far. The labor, in conjunction with Copperfield, is something rather ponderous; but to establish it firmly would be to gain such an enormous point for the future (I mean *my* future) that I think nothing of that. It is playing havoc with the villainous press.[1]

Dickens was a little optimistic about the impact that *Household Words* would have on G. W. M. Reynolds's sales figures, but it is certainly to his bitter rival that he refers in the final sentence above. Reynolds's sensationalist *Mysteries of London* (1844–8) and *Mysteries of the Courts of London* (1848–55) were huge commercial successes, with the latter selling in excess of a million copies; whilst *Reynolds's Miscellany* (1846–9) had outsold all of G. W. M.'s rivals in the penny weekly market.[2] *Reynolds's Weekly Newspaper*, which would go into production in May 1850 (hard on the heels of *Household Words*), rapidly became one of the most successful of the mass-market Sunday newspapers.[3]

That Dickens also refers indirectly (but unmistakably) to Reynolds as a rival in his Preliminary Word to the first edition of *Household Words* is a clear indication that they were broadly (and very consciously) competing within the same literary market and for the same section of the reading public. Dickens's popular reach was much greater than Reynolds's – his aim was to appeal to a cross-class readership, whilst Reynolds exclusively targeted readers from the working classes. Dickens was, though, as interested as his commercial rivals in communicating with and influencing the rapidly growing body of literate consumers from the non-elite classes of society, as his Preliminary Word makes clear: 'We hope to be the comrade and friend of many thousands of people, of both sexes, and of all ages and conditions, on whose faces we may never look.'⁴ And he positions the new periodical very carefully within the existing cheap weekly magazine market:

Some tillers of the field into which we now come, have been before us, and some are here whose high usefulness we readily acknowledge, and whose company it is an honour to join. But, there are others here – Bastards of the Mountain, draggled fringe on the Red Cap, Panders to the basest passions of the lowest natures – whose existence is a national reproach. And these, we should consider it our highest service to displace!⁵

The attack on Reynolds was repeated in the *Household Narrative* for April 1851, a monthly supplement to *Household Words* that contained a digest of the month's main news. Again Reynolds, who had recently taken part in the production of the newly radicalised Chartist programme of 1851, is vilified as a promoter of 'debased' literature for the masses: 'Let us note it as a characteristic circumstance that the name first affixed to this Chartist programme is that of a person notorious for his attempts to degrade the working men of England by circulating among them books of a debasing tendency'.⁶ It is interesting that Dickens repeatedly attacks G. W. M. Reynolds rather than Ernest Jones in the early 1850s: it was, after all, Jones who had been the leading figure in manoeuvring Chartism to the left at the Chartist Convention of April 1851. Dickens's targeting of Reynolds suggests that it was not so much (or not only) the radicalisation of Chartism that troubled him in the early 1850s as its coupling with the (as he saw it) cheap sensationalism of Reynolds's newsprint, quite different in timbre to Jones's *Notes to the People*.⁷ It was the combination of Reynolds's commercial success and his potentially massive cultural influence on the working classes that perplexed the editor of *Household Words*. Jones himself expressed concern about the nature of Reynolds's cultural influence in the following year, as we will recall from chapter 5 of this study. Jones's view as a fellow Chartist was that 'We cannot afford to spend our time every Saturday night in endeavouring to dig a few stray gems of liberty from a dense morass of moral filth. When we sit down to the feast of democracy we must not have the table spread with garbage.'[8]

What was being contested by Dickens, Jones and Reynolds in the early 1850s was the very meaning of the 'popular' as a category. What constituency of readers might properly be addressed as 'the People' nearly two decades after the great Reform Act of 1832, and what might be written for and read by them? What might be the relationship between culture and politics in the periodical press? Dickens had long been alert to the fact that the political opinions and cultural tastes of a rapidly expanding number of readers in mid-century Britain were increasingly being formed not only by novel reading but also by the periodical and newspaper press. He had been dismayed, on his first trip to America, by the general tenor and quality of the available newsprint. In the 'New York' chapter of *American Notes* he demands rhetorically whether there are any 'amusements' in that city and reflects with disgust on:

the fifty newspapers, which those precocious urchins are bawling down the streets, and which are kept filed within, what are they but amusements? Not vapid waterish amusements, but good strong stuff; dealing in round abuse and blackguard names; pulling off the roofs of private houses, as the Halting Devil did in Spain; pimping and pandering for all degrees of vicious taste, and gorging with coined lies the most voracious maw; imputing to every man in public life the coarsest and the vilest motives; scaring away from the stabbed and prostrate body-politic, every Samaritan of good conscience and good deeds; and setting on, with yell and whistle and the clapping of foul hands, the vilest vermin and worst birds of prey.[9]

There is a real sense of consternation, here, about the role of the press in a democratic society; it would have been partly this that acted as a spur to Dickens as he persistently expressed a desire to conduct a periodical publication of some kind. On returning from America in 1842 he had tried to enlist the support of the 'Whig doyenne', Lady Holland, in a bid to relaunch the recently defunct *Courier* newspaper:[10]

Perhaps you are aware that the Courier newspaper (formerly on the Whig side, and recently Conservative) is just now dead, and incorporated with the Globe. If I had been aware of its condition (which my absence from Europe prevented) I should have put myself into instant communication with the leaders of the Liberal party, and made proposals to them for saving the Paper – nailing the true colours to the mast – and fighting the battle staunchly, and to the Death.[11]

This venture failing to gain support, Dickens was tempted in 1845 to take on the arduous role of editor of a new daily newspaper – the *Daily*

News – with a news-gathering staff of some seventy to a hundred.[12] Having overseen its launch, the novelist bowed out, the duties of such a role too onerous for one with Dickens's commitment to the writing of fiction. He was still projecting some kind of journalistic project in the second half of the 1840s, though, writing to Forster in November of 1846 that he would like, one day, to establish 'a kind of *Spectator* (Addison's) magazine – very cheap, and pretty frequent'.[13] In 1849 he relayed to his publishers, Bradbury and Evans, that he persisted in his desire one day to establish 'that long-deferred-but-never-sufficiently-to-be-considered-and-never-to-be-approached-though-not-yet-planned-or-named-Periodical, as shall carry us to Chambers-like profits at a hand gallop'.[14] It was with the launching of *Household Words* in 1850 that his ambition was finally realised.

Dickens's marking out of his territory in the Preliminary Word to the new magazine, with its excoriating attack on Reynolds's publications, succeeded in drawing ire from his biggest publishing rival. *Reynolds' Weekly Newspaper*'s jeering dismissal of Dickens as 'That lickspittle hanger-on to the skirts of Aristocracy's role "Charles Dickens, esq." – originally a dinnerless penny-a-liner on the *Morning Chronicle*' confirms that Reynolds was keenly aware that what was taking place at the start of the 1850s was nothing less than a culture war.[15] Although Dickens had a number of friends with titles, his politics were entirely antithetical to the aristocracy. His satirical lampoon of Sir Joseph Bowley in *The Chimes*; his harsher satirical portrait of Sir John Chester in *Barnaby Rudge*; the dismal atrophy of Chesney Wold and its aristocratic remnants in *Bleak House*, not to mention the 'Coodles' and 'Doodles' who people Parliament in that same novel – clearly Reynolds is wide of the mark concerning Dickens's inclinations towards the aristocratic classes. This has not, though, prevented subsequent critical accounts from positioning *Household Words* as a paternalistic project designed to stifle – or at least to circumscribe – the culture of the masses. Most recent amongst these is Ian Haywood's account of Dickens's weekly magazine in his otherwise admirable study of nineteenth-century popular literature. Haywood posits that the 'explicit political motivation' of *Household Words* was to launch 'a major counter-revolution' against such cheap publications as those circulated by Reynolds, Lloyd and others, 'with the aim of regulating and pacifying the common reader'.[16] I want to argue quite differently that, far from being a species of Althusserian state apparatus, Dickens's cultural and political project in *Household Words* was to bridge – in a manner more imaginative, if not more lucrative, than anything ever conceived of by Reynolds – the incipient chasm that was opening up between popular and radical culture from the 1840s onwards. By determinedly pursuing a broad popular readership at the same time as promoting a politics of social reform, and by insisting on sustaining an inclusive conception of 'the People', Dickens's journalism persists with an older conception of 'popular' culture (a culture 'of' the people) that was gradually being superseded, from the 1840s, by a commercial culture produced 'for' a mass-market populace. In a stroke of journalistic genius Dickens positions *Household Words* between, on the one hand, a tradition of 'miscellanies' aimed at a broadly defined popular audience and, on the other hand, the tradition of campaigning journalism associated with William Cobbett, Thomas Wooler and William Hone earlier in the century. William Hone had himself moved between these two journalistic mediums, shifting from producing radical satirical pamphlets and his Cobbett-esque *Hone's Weekly Register* in the 1810s to editing a series of popular miscellanies (the *Everyday Book* (1825), the *Table Book* (1827), and the *Year Book* (1832)) in the next two decades. Dickens's decision to combine the two journalistic traditions within a single publication means that *Household Words* is a political and cultural hybrid, and in important ways a unique weekly magazine of the period. Dickens's ambition in *Household Words* was nothing less than to wed an eighteenth-century conception of 'the People' as a political entity to the emergent nineteenth-century category of the 'populace' in a commercial culture.

The first edition of *Household Words* included two pieces that between them comprise a cultural and political manifesto: the Preliminary Word already mentioned and the first instalment of a two-part article, 'The Amusements of the People'. Not only does Dickens distinguish his journal from Reynolds's and other such cheap magazines and newspapers, he also sets *Household Words* apart from those journals of 'improvement' and 'popular progress' with which it has often been subsequently compared: 'No mere utilitarian spirit, no iron binding of the mind to grim realities, will give a harsh tone to our Household Words . . . [but it will] cherish that light of Fancy which is inherent in the human breast'.[17] Dickens may have wished for Chambers-like profits, but not at the expense of bowing to its utilitarian and materialistic profile. *Chambers's Journal* would have been particularly familiar to the editor of *Household Words* given that his sub-editor, W. H. Wills, had worked on it between 1842 and 1845.[18] Dickens was emphatic about the quality of 'Fancy' with which he wished to invest his own magazine, and his subsequent reference in the Preliminary Word to the 'thousand and one tales' that he felt the modern world had to tell fleetingly glances towards his beloved *Arabian Nights*, a composite text that would become central to his editorial policy. John Drew has written interestingly about Dickens's rewriting of a submission by Henry Morley that had described a visit to a smelting works in the East End of London. Dickens found the article too baldly informative and utilitarian and complained in a letter to the man who would become one of *Household Words*'s most important political writers that a more attractive, more literary style was required so as to attract 'the mass of readers'.[19] This is an important letter both in its expression of confidence in the ability of 'the mass of readers' to relish good writing and in its consciousness of the culture war that he was fighting against Reynolds and his ilk:

The indispensable necessity of varying the manner of narration as much as possible, and investing it with some little grace or other, would be very evident to you if you knew as well as I do how severe the struggle is, to get the publication down into the mass of readers, and to displace the prodigious heaps of nonsense and worse than nonsense, which suffocate their better sense. I know of such 'perilous stuff' at present, produced at a cost about equal to the intrinsic worth of its literature, and circulating six times the amount of Household Words.

My confidence in the ability of such people to receive and relish a good thing, is so far from being in the least shaken by this knowledge that I only feel the more strongly that the good thing must be done at its best.[20]

Dickens here expresses concern about the ideological function of the cheapest magazine literature, which (as he saw it) kept the aspirations of 'the mass of readers' low, and their horizons limited, 'suffocat[ing] their better sense'. That his is an altogether fair assessment of Reynolds's journalistic projects is unlikely – Ian Haywood, Rohan McWilliam and Anne Humpherys have all engagingly argued otherwise – but, clearly, this was Dickens's view of the political function and cultural danger of the lowest end of the newspaper and magazine market at the time.[21]

Dickens's revision of Morley's essay resulted in a co-authored leader, 'Discovery of a Treasure Near Cheapside', in which, in John Drew's words, 'a dreamer descends into a metropolitan Aladdin's Cave, couched in allusions to Grimm's fairytales, classical mythology, *Gulliver's Travels*, *Candide* and *Arabian Nights*'.[22] Dickens's and Morley's final fusion of interesting information about an industrial process with literary allusions to such disparate fantastical texts as Swift's *Gulliver's Travels* and the *Arabian Nights*'s Aladdin, to classical mythology and to Grimm's fairytales indicates a talent, akin to that of William Hone in the Regency period, to traverse high- and low-cultural boundaries in the production of a properly 'popular' literature.

The embrace of both high and low culture – and more especially an endorsement of the latter – is equally a feature of 'The Amusements of the

People'. This manifesto-like essay that is introduced in two parts in the first and third editions of *Household Words* reveals the hybridity of Dickens's cultural project as editor, a hybridity that allowed him to address, engage with and influence a diverse cross-section of 'the People'. There is in 'The Amusements of the People' an ostensibly competing set of cultural discourses that enter into dialogue with one another. In one respect the essay presents itself to a middle-class readership as a window onto the culture of the lower orders. Dickens introduces his readers to one 'Joe Whelks, of the New Cut, Lambeth', who, although not a great reader, loves going to the Victoria Theatre.[23] There is something of Mayhew in Dickens's desire to draw the attention of the middle classes to the culture of non-elite peoples, although in Dickens's case it is presented with much greater affection. He directs us to observe the Victoria Theatre's audience of mechanics, their wives and babies ('the pit was a perfect nursery'), and even pickpockets – whom he assures us are there to watch the entertainment rather than to 'work' – with a kindly eye.[24] The essay also, though, has an 'improving' motif, consonant with the project of the so-called 'polite journals of popular progress' of the period. In the second of the two essays Dickens urges that the culture of 'Joe Whelks' and his like should, firstly, be regarded as legitimate and, secondly, be improved upon. At this point in the essay a species of cultural paternalism is at work:

> Ten thousand people, every week, all the year round, are estimated to attend this place of amusement [the Britannia Saloon, Hoxton, East London] . . . The people who now resort here, *will be* amused somewhere. It is of no use to blink that fact, or to make pretences to the contrary. We had far better apply ourselves to improving the character of their amusement.[25]

The project of cultural improvement is, though, undermined from within by the two essays' irrepressible enthusiasm for and commitment to the culture of the non-elite classes of society. In the first of the two essays Dickens tells his readers that such classes have 'an innate love . . . for dramatic entertainment'.[26] In the second essay, though, he asserts that theatrical entertainment has an appeal that extends well beyond the cultural horizons of 'Joe Whelks': 'We have already intimated that we believe a love of dramatic representations to be an inherent principle in human nature.'[27] He extends the point by comparing the kind of melodramatic entertainments favoured by 'Joe Whelks' with the performances of Italian opera favoured by the middle and upper classes. In insisting on the similarities between the two theatrical modes, Dickens implies that the theatrical entertainments put on at the Victoria Theatre and the Britannia

Saloon, far from needing improvement, are already valid cultural forms. Having outlined the sensational plotline of *Eva Betrayed, or The Lady of Lambythe*, avidly followed by the Britannia faithful, he reflects that:

It is but fair to MR WHELKS to remark on one curious fact in this entertainment. When the situations were very strong indeed, they were very like what some favourite situations in the Italian Opera would be to a profoundly deaf spectator. The despair and madness at the end of the first act, the business of the long hair, and the struggle in the bridal chamber, were as like the conventional passion of the Italian singers, as the orchestra was unlike the opera band, or its 'hurries' unlike the music of the great composers. So do extremes meet; and so there is some hopeful congeniality between what will excite MR WHELKS, and what will rouse a Duchess.[28]

Given the choice of going to watch a melodrama or an Italian opera, Dickens would have certainly opted for the former, as his visits to the Victoria and the Britannia and a whole host of other 'illegitimate' theatres in London would suggest. And the delight and gusto with which he narrates the denouement of *Eva the Betrayed* suggests a level of engagement well beyond that of the cultural investigator:

But when the Hunchback made himself known, and when More did the same; and when the Hunchback said he had got the certificate which rendered Eva's marriage illegal; and when More raved to have it given to him, and when the Hunchback (as having some grains of misanthropy in him to the last) persisted in going into his dying agonies in a remote corner of his cage, and took unheard-of trouble not to die anywhere near the bars that were within More's reach; MR WHELKS applauded to the echo. At last the Hunchback was persuaded to stick the certificate on the point of a dagger, and hand it in; and that done, died extremely hard, knocking himself violently about, to the very last gasp, and certainly making the most of all the life that was in him.[29]

The somewhat headlong punctuation of Dickens's description of the denouement comically conveys the pell-mell action of the melodrama; its recreation of the melodrama's dramatic affects is also suggestive of unalloyed enjoyment. Here as in his novels Dickens relishes the bodily violence of the melodrama and embraces it with considerable brio. If he felt a need to improve upon the melodramatic plotline of *Eva the Betrayed*, it is in his novels that he does so, and most extraordinarily in *Bleak House, Hard Times* and *Little Dorrit*, the subject of the final chapter of this study. As elsewhere in his journalism and fiction, in 'The Amusements of the People' Dickens demonstrates his commitment to the theatre and its aesthetic grammar, and it is the wide cultural reach of the nineteenth-century theatre that partly explains its appeal for him.

If *Household Words* announces itself, in 'The Amusements of the People' as a culturally hybrid project, delightedly celebrating as well as ostensibly wishing to improve upon popular culture, then this hybridity is also evident in the material appearance of Dickens's two-penny weekly. Lorna Huett's excellent essay on *Household Words, All The Year Round* and the mass-market periodical press has described how Dickens deliberately shaped his periodical – in terms of its physical appearance – in opposition to the older, more established highbrow monthly and quarterly reviews addressed to a more leisured and secure upper class.[30] At two-pence, *Household Words* positioned itself at the upper end of the cheap weekly market, but without putting itself beyond the reach of the readers of penny blood fiction and the penny weeklies. Visually it announced itself as belonging to the cheap end of the periodical market: it was printed on a single sheet of poor-quality paper, which was of a similar size to that used by Lloyd and Reynolds in their magazines and in the production of penny blood fiction. As Huett puts it: 'Consisting as it did of this single folded sheet, the journal would physically have resembled either a penny blood or a miniaturised newspaper, though its lack of illustration would have made it visually distinct from either of these.'[31]

Contrarily, Robert Chambers had decided in 1844 that he wished to distance his own cheap weekly from the lowest end of the market, explaining in an Address to Reader that he was responding to readers' complaints that 'its large size ... [caused] inconvenience of such bulky volumes in a library'.[32] The smaller format that he subsequently adopted lent it a more middle-/upper-class appearance, clearly targeting this more leisured body of readers. The first incarnation of Chambers's 1½d weekly, with its large pages and three columns of type, had 'effectively damned itself to appear inelegant and plebeian in the eyes of its more aspirational readers'.[33]

Dickens, chameleon-like, negotiated both ends of the periodical market in the material production of *Household Words* and, later, *All the Year Round*. The weekly numbers resembled cheap penny weeklies and penny bloods, but they were subsequently bound up into paper-covered monthly parts and, thereafter, hard-bound as semi-annual indexed volumes, 'ready for inclusion in the most respectable library'.[34] On the one hand, Dickens was maximising the commercial potential of his magazine in adopting the publishing practices of both ends of the market. On the other hand, he thereby fulfilled his political and cultural commitment to address 'the People' in its widest sense, as well as answering his own clarion call, in 'The Amusements of the People', for cheap, good-quality entertainment for all.

In terms of content, too, *Household Words* and *All the Year Round* played an important role in renegotiating the cultural boundaries of the mass-market periodical. By including serialised fiction Dickens was taking a risk, inasmuch as, by so doing, he was clearly identifying his magazine with the cheapest end of the periodical market. *Chambers's Edinburgh Journal* was reluctant to publish much fiction in weekly parts, and the reason for this was that the weekly serial was becoming, at the mid-century, associated with the 'lower' end of the market.[35] By including good-quality, original fiction in *Household Words* (Elizabeth Gaskell contributed a four-chapter story spread across its first three numbers), Dickens was boldly opening up new markets – including the middle-class one – for the weekly serial, rendering it more respectable than it had hitherto been. As Joanne Shattock has remarked, it was with the establishment of the *Cornhill* and the *Fortnightly* in 1860 that the publication of serial fiction in periodicals became fully respectable.[36] Dickens initiated this process in *Household Words*.

Explicitly committing himself to popular culture in 'The Amusements of the People', Dickens was at pains as editor to include in the pages of his magazine extensive coverage of the subjects of popular melodrama. The next section of the chapter will concern itself with *Household Words*'s negotiation of the melodramatic mode.

HOUSEHOLD WORDS'S MELODRAMATIC SUBJECTS

In January 1850, two months before the launch of *Household Words*, Dickens urged upon Elizabeth Gaskell his earnest hope that she should contribute a 'short tale' to the new magazine:

> My Dear Mrs Gaskell,
>   You may perhaps have seen an announcement in the papers, of my intention to start a new cheap weekly journal of general literature? . . . there is no living English writer whose aid I would desire to enlist, in preference to the authoress of Mary Barton (a book that profoundly affected and impressed me). I venture to ask whether you can give me any hope that you will write a *short* tale, or any number of tales, for the projected pages.[37]

Gaskell agreed, and her four-chapter story, 'Lizzie Leigh', was serialised across the first three editions of the new journal. Andrew Sanders has remarked on the strongly theatrical content of the first number of *Household Words*,[38] and in 'Lizzie Leigh' Dickens imports into the keynote edition of his magazine a staple figure from the melodrama – the 'fallen woman'. A few days after writing to Elizabeth Gaskell, Dickens penned a letter to Angela Burdett Coutts, the millionaire philanthropist with whom he worked so closely on the 'Urania Cottage' project, the 'Home for Homeless Women' that had been established in 1847.[39] He commends Burdett Coutts for the 'moral bravery' of her philanthropic efforts on behalf of homeless women (often but not always prostitutes) and discusses his intention of exploring this theme in *Household Words*:

It is difficult to approach, in pages that are intended for readers of all classes and all ages of life; but I have not the least misgiving about being able to bring people gently to its consideration. You will observe that I am endeavouring to turn their thoughts a little that way, in Copperfield. And I hope before I finish the story, to do something strongly suggestive, in that kind of preparation.[40]

Gaskell's 'Lizzie Leigh' brings the plight of the 'fallen woman' to the attention of Dickens's magazine readers right from the start: the first instalment of the story is given pride of place as the first item after the editor's Preliminary Word. The story embraces the traditional opposition between country and city that was familiar to the melodrama: Gaskell's central protagonist is a counterpart to the farmer's daughter, Anna, who is the central subject of Ernest Jones's 'Milliner's Tale', discussed in the previous chapter. 'Lizzie Leigh' tells the tale of a young country girl who goes out to service in Manchester, becomes pregnant and, losing her place, resorts to prostitution. She abandons her baby into the nurturing arms of a woman who (coincidentally) goes on to be courted by Lizzie's older brother. The child dies in a domestic accident in its adopted home, and the story focuses strongly on Lizzie's maternal grief. In its sympathy for Lizzie, and in the tenderness of the scenes between the magdalen Lizzie and virginal Susan, there are strong echoes of the most powerful tableaux of *The Chimes*.[41] Dickens's enthusiasm after reading the first two chapters was unreserved: 'I think it *excellent* ... It interested me greatly, as I read it. And it made me cry – which I mention because I take that to be indisputable proof of its effect.'[42]

The coincidence at the level of plot on which melodrama so often depends, and the sudden swings between good and bad fortune, happiness and grief, which are similarly characteristic of the genre, confirm 'Lizzie Leigh', like *Mary Barton* before it, as a clear example of this popular genre which Dickens embraced throughout his writing career, in his journalism as in his fiction. That Lizzie's older brother should have alighted upon Susan as a lover – the very woman to whom she had anonymously entrusted her child – is entirely coincidental. And just as it seems that Lizzie will be reunited both with her own mother and with her infant child, the latter falls down stairs at night and dashes her head onto the stone floor.

Although eschewing Dickens's advice that she should kill Lizzie off ('I seem to see through that means, a forcible lesson on the postponement of forgiveness'[43]), Gaskell equally eschews the happy endings of mainstream theatrical melodramas. The story closes with Lizzie, living in seclusion in a rural spot, weeping over her dead child's grave.

Dickens is kinder to Martha, the prostitute figure from *David Copperfield*, who not only emigrates to Australia but happily marries there. He had discussed the possibility of such an outcome for 'fallen women' in a letter to Angela Burdett Coutts, in which he is clearly responding to a suggestion by her that marriage for such women in a new country would be morally unacceptable. His rejoinder was cautious but firm:

I am not quite sure that perfect penitence in these women – in the best of them I mean – would lead them in all cases not to Marry; for I can certainly (I think) descry a kind of active repentance in their being faithful wives and the mothers of virtuous children; but in all other respects I most certainly concur with you.[44]

Dickens and Burdett Coutts's 'Home for Homeless Women' finds its way into the pages of *Household Words* in an essay of that title in April 1853. The essay has a strongly utilitarian cast in its emphasis on the discipline and reformation of the 'inmates', each of whom he presents to the reader as a 'case' – 'Case number twenty-seven', 'Case number thirteen', and so on.[45] With an eye to his middle-class readers, the essay is cautious in its presentation of the homeless women, with only one of them being referred to as euphemistically having '[gone] wrong'.[46] Nonetheless, what Dickens – like Gaskell before him – achieves in the essay is determinedly to bring into view (in much the way as he did in *Oliver Twist*) the poor, the downtrodden and the exiled, and to demand sympathy on their behalf. 'Case number thirteen' could equally have made an appearance in Baxter's *Book of the Bastiles* more than ten years before:[47]

Case number thirteen was a half-starved girl of eighteen whose father had died soon after her birth, and who had long eked out a miserable subsistence for herself and a sick mother by doing plain needlework. At last her mother died in a workhouse, and the needle work 'falling off bit by bit,' this girl suffered, for nine months, every extremity of dire distress. Being one night without any food or shelter from the weather, she went to the lodging of a woman who had once lived in the same house with herself and her mother, and asked to be allowed to lie down on the stairs. She was refused, and stole a shawl which she sold for a penny. [The girl ends up in prison.][48]

Dickens's journalistic ploy of introducing melodramatic subjects into his campaigning journalism is a common rhetorical manoeuvre in

Household Words. In his account of a visit to a Ragged School in 'A Sleep to Startle Us' in March 1852, he combines a quite brisk, utilitarian-inflected account of the more positive aspects of the school with an affecting tableau of a dying child, which altogether unsettles what could otherwise have been an upbeat account of efforts to improve the education of the poor and to ameliorate the effects of poverty and ignorance. Early in the essay he notes affirmatively the quiet orderliness of the 'Industrial School' apprentices as they learn the tailoring trade and admires the effectiveness of efforts to ventilate the dormitory using simple but efficient technology.[49] The narrative is, though, sharply disrupted towards the close by a poignant tableau in which a very sick young boy suddenly appears alongside a dying elderly man, both having recourse to the school out of desperation. It is as if Jo the Crossing Sweeper from *Bleak House*, which Dickens had begun writing a few months before, erupts before both the reader's eye and that of the investigative journalist, totally changing the perspective of the account:

> Beside this wreck [of an old man], but all unconnected with it and with the whole world, was an orphan boy with burning cheeks and great gaunt eager eyes, who was in pressing peril of death too, and who had no possession under the broad sky but a bottle of physic and a scrap of writing. He brought both from the house-surgeon of a Hospital that was too full to admit him ... a creature, surely, as forlorn and desolate as Mother Earth can ever have supported on her breast that night. He was gently taken away, along with the dying man, to the workhouse; and he passed into the darkness with his physic-bottle as if he were going to the grave.[50]

Dickens's certainty that neither 'Mother Earth' nor anyone else will be able adequately to support the desperately sick child on that or on any other night casts a desolate gloom over what in other respects presents itself as a progressive essay campaigning for better education for the poor. In so doing, it undermines the ostensibly utilitarian impulse with which Dickens begins his essay. In many respects melodrama, with its insistence on 'la voix du sang' and on the importance of emotional affect, is *the* anti-utilitarian aesthetic, which would also explain the power of Dickens's melodramatic protest against the utilitarian New Poor Law in *Oliver Twist.*[51]

Emotionally affecting tableaux of sick and dying children are everywhere to be found in the pages of *Household Words.* Just as the diminutive figures of Little Nell, Tiny Tim, Paul Dombey and Jo the Crossing Sweeper haunt the pages of Dickens's fiction, so too do such figures memorably people his journalism. Orphans and lost and sick children were a staple of theatrical melodrama, and Dickens is, as usual, finely attuned to the affective power of popular cultural tropes. This is another reason for his enthusiasm for Gaskell's 'Lizzie Leigh', which features a moving deathbed tableau, as Lizzie's dead infant is wept over by both its adoptive and its biological mother. Dickens's sweetly sentimental (and, it has to be said, thoroughly anodyne) 'A Child's Dream of a Star', from April 1850, recounts the deaths of three children – the young sister, the baby brother and, later in life, the maiden daughter of the central protagonist – all of whom are welcomed into heaven as angels by the first of the children to die. The story ends with the death of the boy at the centre of the story, who is now an old man: the deathbed tableau, with the well-loved father surrounded by his grieving, loving children, is an instantly recognisable sentimental scene. Dickens establishes the deathbed tableaux of a series of children in this soft-focused essay – 'the sister [who] drooped' and the baby brother who 'while yet he was so little that he never had yet spoken word ... stretched his tiny form out on his bed, and died' – only subsequently to darken them, and inflect them with a serious social critique in future essays.[52]

One of these is a leading article from 1852 co-authored with Henry Morley, which hails the recent opening of the Great Ormond Street hospital for sick children. Combining praise for the new hospital with a grim reflection on the unacceptably high mortality rates amongst the children of London, the essay is in one sense a utilitarian plea for sanitation projects, for the funding of medical research and for greater investment into the medical treatment of children. Grimly relating to their readers the fact that by the age of eleven one-third of London's children are dead, Dickens and Morley's diagnosis of the problem is consonant with that of the sanitary reformers:

Our children perish out of our homes; not because there is in them an inherent dangerous sickness ... but because there is, in respect of their tender lives, a want of sanitary discipline and a want of medical knowledge ... We fail to prevent disease; and, in the case of children, to a much more lamentable extent than is well known, we fail to cure it.[53]

Much more memorable than the sanitary and medical analysis, though, is the appearance, in an imaginary sequence, of now-dead children who had lived in the environs of Great Ormond Street before it became synonymous with the children's hospital of that name. Dickens and Morley reflect upon the 'Many, far too many, pretty house-fairies [who] had vanished from before it, and left blank spaces on the hearth, to be filled up nevermore.'[54] One such dead child leaps out from the page in an embodiment of Tiny Tim, whom Dickens had written about so affectingly nearly a decade before:

'And I,' said another shadow, 'am the lame and mis-shapen boy who read so much by the fireside, and suffered so much pain so patiently, and might have been as active and as straight as you, if any one had understood my malady; but I said to my fond father carrying me in his arms to the bed from which I never rose: "I think, O dear Papa, that it is better I should never be a man, for who could then carry me like this, or who could be so careful of me when you were gone!"'[55]

Dickens's interest in and commitment to projects for social improvement led him in May 1850 to visit the Marylebone workhouse with Jacob Bell, the prospective Member of Parliament for St Albans. Having attacked the Poor Laws old and new in *Oliver Twist*, and the institution of the workhouse that was their embodiment, Dickens revisits the subject just over a decade later. Although he finds one or two things to commend – the calm and purpose of the children's school rooms the main one of these – he is perplexed by the lack of play facilities, by the inappropriateness of the paupers' Sunday sermon and by the utter dejection of the elderly male paupers, who are barely able to connect with the world. Most arresting of all, though, is his encounter with the wardswoman, or nurse, in the so-called 'itch ward' of the workhouse.[56] In an affecting tableau, in which the woman weeps over the body of a dead baby, Dickens thoroughly humanises the pauper woman at the same time as taking a side-wipe at those political economists who had made a social monster out of pauperism. He reflects on the pitiful state of the humans he encounters in the workhouse that 'the dragon, Pauperism, [is] in a very weak and impotent condition; toothless, fangless, drawing his breath heavily enough, and hardly worth chaining up'.[57] Not worth chaining up at all, in the itch ward, where Dickens quickly discounts the wardswoman's slatternly appearance so as to reveal the tender humanity veiled by her slovenly dress. The wardswoman was:

herself a pauper – flabby, raw-boned, untidy – unpromising and coarse of aspect as need be. But, on being spoken to about the patients whom she had in charge, she turned round, with her shabby gown half on, half off, and fell a-crying with all her might. Not for show, not querulously, not in any mawkish sentiment, but in deep grief and affliction of the heart; turning away her dishevelled head; sobbing most bitterly, wringing her hands, and letting fall abundance of great tears, that choked her utterance.[58]

It transpires that the wardswoman is grieving for a foundling baby in her care who 'had died an hour ago'. The figuration of the woman's grief through bodily gesture – the wringing of the hands, the turning away of her dishevelled head – is thoroughly melodramatic, as is the heightened emotionalism of the tableau. Once again, a melodramatic tableau disrupts the measured essay on social reform. The visceral nature of Dickens's sympathy for the poor and the oppressed is suggested by his impulsive and entirely characteristic attempt to help this individual woman in some way. He wrote to Jacob Bell, who had accompanied him on the visit to the workhouse:

Mr Dear Sir,

I have thought a great deal about that woman, the Wardswoman in the Itch Ward, who was crying about the dead child. If anything useful can be done for her, I should like to do it. Will you bear this in mind, in confidence, and if you can put me in the way of helping her, do me the kindness of telling me how it can be best done?[59]

There is something of the kindness and benevolence of Mr Jarndyce, from *Bleak House*, in Dickens's instinctive sympathy for the poor. It is his personal proximity to the kind of benevolence represented by Jarndyce which means that he could never be full-bloodedly utilitarian in his social thinking. At the same time, though, he was fully aware that private charity – part and parcel of a paternalistic social code that he had already discarded in 1841, with the publication of *Barnaby Rudge* – was never going to be a panacea for social ills. It was for this reason that he was committed to administrative, political and social reform, aware as he was that it was only at the level of national and local government that substantial social change could be brought about. At the end of his essay on the Ragged School, a movement to which he was personally committed and on whose behalf he had personally sought to bring about action, Dickens's indignation that it is left to private individuals to try to correct society's ills bursts through his account of the visit to the school in Farringdon Road:

It was an awful thing, looking round upon those one hundred and sixty-seven representatives of many thousands, to reflect that a Government, unable, with the least regard to truth, to plead ignorance of the existence of such a place, should proceed as if the sleepers never were to wake again. I do not hesitate to say – why should I, for I know it to be true! – that an annual sum of money, contemptible in amount as compared with any charges upon any list, freely granted in behalf of these Schools, and shackled with no preposterous Red Tape conditions, would relieve the prisons, diminish county rates, clear loads of shame and guilt out of the streets, recruit the army and navy, waft to new countries, Fleets full of useful labor, for which their inhabitants would be thankful and beholden to us.[60]

It was his determination to try to bring about major structural change at both local and national levels of government that steered Dickens towards schemes for social and sanitary improvement, sometimes utilitarian in character. His frustration at the stymieing effects of governmental bureaucracy led him both to individual efforts – trying to help the weeping wardswoman in the workhouse – and to a connection with philanthropic work such as that undertaken by Angela Burdett Coutts. But he knew that in the end such efforts would not be enough to tackle the enormity of the social problems that he saw around him. It was this perception, combined with his enthusiastic embrace of modern technology and engineering, that led him to commit himself to a politics of national progress as he launched *Household Words* in 1850. In the next section of the chapter I will examine the nature of Dickens's commitment to progress and to modernity in his journalism from the 1850s, demonstrating the ways in which such a commitment very quickly came under pressure as he entered the sixth decade of the nineteenth century.

HOUSEHOLD WORDS AND THE POLITICS OF PROGRESS

Dickens was consistently opposed to a politics of nostalgia; to this extent his embrace of modernity was enduring. His bitter satirical attack on the politics of the past in *Barnaby Rudge*, and his lampooning of the same in the figure of Sir Joseph Bowley in *The Chimes*, was often repeated in dialogue with his friends. His biographer John Forster recounted how the novelist confided to him that 'the greatest mystery in all the earth, to me, is how or why the world was tolerated by its Creator through the good old times, and wasn't dashed to fragments'.[61] Dickens's discarding of the past in the 1840s was matched by a generally optimistic embrace of the future, despite his anger at the social abuses and deprivation that he saw around him. The final sentences of his travelogue *Pictures From Italy*, published in 1846, posit a vision of modernity and progress against the 'miseries and wrongs' of Italy and its 'barbarized' language:

And let us not remember Italy the less regardfully, because, in every fragment of her fallen Temples, and every stone of her deserted palaces and prisons, she helps to inculcate the lesson that the wheel of Time is rolling for an end, and that the world is, in all great essentials, better, gentler, more forbearing, and more hopeful as it rolls![62]

Five years later the novelist was writing determinedly to W. H. Wills concerning 'the distribution of Titles in England':

It would be a very remarkable thing to take the list of the House of Peers, the list of Baronets and Knights, and (without personality) divide the more recent titles into classes and ascertain what they were given *for*. How many chemists, how many men of science, how many writers, how many aldermen

How much intellect represented.
How much imagination represented.
How much learning.
How much expression of the great progress of the country – How much of Railway construction, of Electric Telegraph discovery, of improvements in Machinery, of any sort of contribution to the happiness of mankind.[63]

His desire to modernise the demographic make-up of government and the peerage combines in this letter with an enthusiastic embrace of 'the great progress of the country', which for Dickens was embodied by the railway, the electric telegraph, and by 'improvements in Machinery'. His enthusiasm for 'social wonders' and his belief in progress find their way into the 'Preliminary Word' of *Household Words* in March 1850: 'We seek to bring into innumerable homes, from the stirring world around us, the knowledge of many social wonders, good and evil, that are not calculated to render any of us ... less faithful in the progress of mankind, less thankful for the privilege of living in this summer-dawn of time.'[64] Dickens's view of progress was never wholly benign – he is cognisant here of the 'evil' as well as of the 'good' that can be born of modern 'social wonders' – but the general tone is determinedly upbeat. Only nine months later, though, Dickens would compose, in 'A December Vision', in Michael Slater's words a 'powerful and menacing denunciation of the failure of the great institutions of Victorian society to address the terrible problems of mass poverty and deprivation'.[65] By 1854, nearly a year after the completion of *Bleak House*, his faith in progress would seem to have taken such a battering that in 'To Working Men' Dickens finds himself desperately haranguing his readers – of all classes – into taking action to avoid complicity with 'wholesale murder': 'It behoves every journalist ... to warn his readers, whatsoever be their ranks and conditions, that unless they set themselves in earnest to improve the towns in which they live, and to amend the dwellings of the poor, they are guilty, before GOD, of wholesale murder.'[66] In 1856, when he was halfway through the composition of *Little Dorrit*, he presents his readers with a phantasmagoric social vision in 'A Nightly Scene in London'. The poor and the oppressed are represented metaphorically in this *Household Words* essay as 'five bundles of rags' and, more ominously, as 'Five awful Sphinxes'.[67]

What was it that punctured the forward-looking optimism that characterises the 'Preliminary Word' to *Household Words* in 1850? By tracing the responses in Dickens's cheap weekly magazine to the Great Exhibition and to factory legislation, this final section of the chapter will begin to establish a context for the writing of Dickens's great social novels of the 1850s, *Bleak House*, *Hard Times* and *Little Dorrit*.

In an essay written a few months before the Great Exhibition of 1851, Dickens expresses his enthusiasm for the British engineering feats that went into the building of the London and North Western Railway:

> To bring it to its present state of working efficiency, a thousand ingenious problems have been studied and solved, stupendous machines have been con-structed, a variety of plans and schemes have been matured with incredible labour: a great whole has been pieced together by numerous capacities and appliances, and kept incessantly in motion.[68]

The 'stupendous machines', 'incredible labour', the 'great whole' and incessant motion that Dickens so admires here may lead one to expect that he would wholeheartedly have embraced the Great Exhibition of 1851, a spectacle that patriotically asserted Britain's right to be regarded as the so-called 'workshop of the world'. This, though, was not the case. Dickens had been a member of the Working-Class Committee, which was to look into the role of, and arrangements for, the working classes during the Exhibition. Peter Ackroyd has speculated that it was set up so as to ward off the possible danger the lower classes may have posed were they actively excluded from participation.[69] After four months, though, Dickens was instrumental in disbanding the committee when it became clear to him that it had not been set up in good faith and that no special attention was actually going to be paid to the needs of the 'lower orders'.[70]

Ambivalence towards the Great Exhibition can be traced in the pages of *Household Words*. Deborah Wynne has reflected that Dickens would have been all too aware of the great public interest in the Exhibition and so would have had to be cautious about criticising it in his magazine.[71] His single contribution on the subject is a jointly authored laudatory piece, 'The Great Exhibition and the Little One', in which he and Richard Horne compare the Great Exhibition favourably with a small exhibition at the Chinese Gallery, Hyde Park Place, the large one showing off Britain as a progressive nation 'moving in the right direction towards some superior condition of society', and the small one revealing China as 'an odd, barbarous ... eccentric nation'.[72] Whilst articles by W. H. Wills and Charles Knight written in January and May 1851 are generally positive about the Exhibition, subsequent essays are irreverent.[73] Henry Morley's 'What Is Not Clear about the Crystal Palace' comprises a series of ima-ginary letters from assorted individuals expressing their views about the future of the Crystal Palace. One, from a 'young lady', gushingly requests that it be turned into a shopping mall:

Dear, dear Mr Conductor, – Mama tells me that people are at a loss what to do with the Crystal Palace, if they do not take it down. Do, please, dear, dear sir, put in a word for those lovely shawls, and those sweet muslin dresses. It is so tiresome having to shop in those nasty streets, where people smoke and push about; and it's so dusty always that one cannot see for dust, or else so dirty, that one is knee-deep in puddle. Oh the dear Exhibition, where you look at all the shops, and need not buy![74]

George Sala's 'The Foreign Invasion', published later in the year, openly mocks British fears that the Exhibition would attract 'nasty, dirty, greasy, wicked, plundering, devastating, murdering, frog-eating, atheistical foreigners' who would leave in their wake an 'England unchristianised; the Archbishop of Canterbury guillotined in Lambeth walk'.[75] Sala's hyperbole and Morley's 'girlish' babble contrast sharply with those articles published earlier in the year that purported to convey a more uncritically patriotic account of the Exhibition.

Dickens's editorial obligations towards the Crystal Palace were relatively short-lived: its closure on 15 October 1851 he described to Angela Burdett Coutts as 'an event for which I am fervently thankful'.[76] Much more persistent throughout the 1840s and 1850s were debates about working conditions in factories and about the legislation that was passed to ameliorate them. It was this, rather than ambivalence about the Great Exhibition, that most thoroughly tested Dickens's embrace of progress and industrial modernity.

Dickens's stance towards modern manufacture and industry was unstable. Peter Ackroyd has convincingly argued that before he went to the USA in 1842, the novelist's position was quite close to the anti-manufactory bias of men like Lord Shaftesbury; but that on his return, having been enthused by the well-run Lowell factory system and its care towards its employees, and having been convinced that its success was due in no small part to the relationship between the North American factory system and public institutions of state, his attitude shifted. Instead of regarding industrialists as responsible for poor working conditions and exploited labour, he 'came to believe that the twin evils of protectionism and aristocratic government were the real enemies of progress. Flunkies, corn laws, nepotism, red-tapeism of all descriptions became his principal targets both in his journalism and in his fiction'.[77] Whilst I would broadly agree with Ackroyd's account, I would qualify it with the reflection that in the first half of the

1850s Dickens's support of industry and its leaders came under severe pressure to the extent that, by February 1856, with the publication of Henry Morley's essay on 'The Manchester Strike', Dickens was instructing his main political lieutenant to argue that 'Unwholesomely cheap production is a perversion of the common law of trade', and that free competition puts unskilled workers at an unfair disadvantage.[78] The final chapter of this book will include an analysis of the instability of Dickens's view of the manufactory as embodied by Mr Rouncewell, the upright ironmaster in *Bleak House* (1852–3), and by Mr Bounderby, the vicious factory owner in *Hard Times* (1854). Here, though, I want to trace Dickens's shift in sympathy towards poor industrial workers and against the manufacturing interest in *Household Words* in the first half of the 1850s, and in particular his and Henry Morley's very public falling-out with Harriet Martineau over factory legislation.

Household Words was unusual amongst high-circulation family weeklies in the extent to which it sought to shape its readers' political opinions.[79] Edgar Johnson long ago characterised Dickens's magazine as a crusading, politically driven reformist project:

Hardly a week goes by in which it is not attacking some abuse. It consistently opposes racial, national, religious and class prejudices. It crusades against illiteracy and in favour of . . . public education and free elementary and industrial schools. It crusades for proper sewage disposal, cheap and unlimited water supply, and the regulation of industries. It demands the replacement of slums by decent housing, pleads for the establishment of playgrounds for children, and advocates systematic municipal planning . . . It insists that industrialists must not be allowed to mutilate and kill their labourers in order to save the cost of preventing accidents. It scandalously affirms that working men have the right to organise into unions, and calls upon the working class to use its power to turn the 'Indifferents and Incapables' out of Downing Street and Westminster.[80]

Like Mayhew, Dickens enquires into the actual state of the poor, actively seeking out workhouses, gin shops, prisons, hospitals and factories. Politically much harder-edged than *Howitt's Journal*, with which it is often compared, it is in its enquiry into industrial working conditions that *Household Words* provoked the anger of supporters of the factory system.

John Drew has commented that Dickens was far from sanguine about the direction to be taken by the reshuffled coalition Tory administration of 1854, and was rapidly becoming 'much more convinced of the evils of *laissez-faire* political economy'.[81] Whilst the factory inspectors had issued a circular on 31 January 1854 stating that they would 'compel every shaft of machinery at whatever cost and of whatever kind, to be fenced off', this was by no means everywhere complied with. Factory owners formed a National Association of Factory Occupiers, subscriptions to which were used to pay the fines of offending manufacturers, thereby effectively neutralising the legislation.[82] It is in this context that between 22 April 1854 and 28 July 1855 Dickens published five essays by Henry Morley that championed the need to enforce those sections of the 1844 Factory Act that required factory owners to fence their machines safely. The essays are hard-hitting in the emphasis they place upon the deaths and mutilations caused by non-compliance with the law. The first of the series, 'Ground in the Mill', published in the same issue as the fourth instalment of *Hard Times*, sets the general tone of Morley's contributions:

Perhaps it is not good when a factory girl, who has not the whole spirit of play spun out of her for want of meadows, gambols upon bags of wool, a little too near the exposed machinery that is to work it up, and is immediately seized, and punished by the merciless machine that digs its shaft into her pinafore and hoists her up, tears her left arm at the shoulder joint, breaks her right arm, and beats her on the head.[83]

The melodramatic bodiliness of Morley's attack on errant factory owners was bound to jar with Harriet Martineau's utilitarian cast of thought. 'Ground in the Mill' was followed up with a further series of essays about industrial accidents and their causes, and with the instalment of *Hard Times* in which Stephen Blackpool is fatally injured in a factory accident. Late in 1855 Martineau responded with a pamphlet, *The Factory Controversy: A Warning Against Meddling Legislation*, which launched a ferocious attack on Dickens and his journal.[84]

The public argument between Martineau, Dickens and Morley was particularly fraught given that the author of *Illustrations of Political Economy* (1832–4) had been a regular contributor to *Household Words* since its inception. Although one may imagine that the author of *Oliver Twist* and the champion of political economy could never have had much in common, Martineau and Dickens's 'temporary and uneasy' five-year alliance was initially based, probably, on their shared opposition to American slavery and on a broad faith in progress.[85] Although she would (rather confusingly) later deny it in her *Autobiography*, Martineau contributed a long series of articles to *Household Words* between October 1851 and May 1852 that concerned themselves with modern manufacturing processes and in particular women's role in them. The essays uncritically celebrate industrial procedures as 'magic' and full of 'wonders'.[86] The sharply contrasting tenor of Henry Morley's subsequent essays demonstrates the manner in which *Household Words* stages competing accounts of industrial modernity in the 1850s. Martineau's attack on Dickens's support for 'meddling legislation' was vehement and personal. Offered to and rejected by the *Westminster Review*, it was accepted with alacrity by the National Association of Factory Occupiers, who paid the author 100 guineas for the honour of publishing it. In it she accuses Dickens, as Morley's editor, of: 'unscrupulous statement, insolence, arrogance and cant, to which the door is opened when meddling legislation is accorded to the pseudo-philanthropy which is one of the disgraces of our times'.[87] Dickens himself she dismisses as a 'humanity-monger', full of 'unfairness and untruth'.[88]

Morley sent the pamphlet to Dickens, who was in Paris at the time, and the former drafted a response to Martineau that would be published in *Household Words* in January 1856. 'Our Wicked Mis-Statements', whilst stating from the outset the authors' 'respect for Miss Martineau, won by many good works she has written, and many good deeds she has done',[89] is none the less firm in its rebuttal of her accusations:

[M]ight we not say, very fairly, that a writer who believes in his heart that resistance to a given law dooms large numbers of men to mutilation, and not few to horrible deaths, may honestly speak with some indignation of the resistance by which those deaths are produced; and that the same right to be angry is not equally possessed by an advocate who argues that the deaths cannot be helped, and that nobody has a right to meddle specially in any way with a mill-owner's trade?[90]

Martineau had written her last *Household Words* essay in January 1855 (sharing column space with Elizabeth Gaskell's *North and South*); she would contribute no more. Morley and Dickens's essay was followed two weeks later by 'The Manchester Strike', an essay in which Dickens had intervened editorially, insisting that Morley make it more sympathetic towards the striking spinners and piecers of one of Britain's major industrial cities. Their wages had been reduced at a time of rising prices, and Dickens wrote to Wills on 6 January 1856 that Morley's article could not be allowed to convey the view that 'all strikes among this unhappy class . . . are always necessarily wrong':

Nor can I possibly adopt the representation that these men are wrong because, by throwing themselves out of work, they throw other people, possibly without their consent. If such a principle had anything in it, there would have been no civil war; no raising by Hampden of a troop of Horse, to the detriment of Buckinghamshire Agriculture; no self sacrifice in the political world. And O Good God when Morley treats of the suffering of wife and children, can he suppose that these mistaken men don't feel it in the depths of their hearts, and don't honestly and honourably – most devoutly and faithfully – believe – that for those very children when they shall have children, they are bearing all these miseries now![91]

Morley complied with Dickens's request, and the result – a critique of liberal economics – shows the distance that Dickens had travelled since launching *Household Words* in 1850.

He had not arrived at this position all at once, though, and it was not a stance adopted in response to Harriet Martineau's intemperate outburst alone. From December 1850, less than nine months after the magazine's launch, *Household Words*'s columns would be punctuated by a series of increasingly bleak visions written by Dickens himself. The first of these is 'A December Vision' (December 1850), a haunting essay that gloomily anticipates *Bleak House*. Belligerent interventions such as 'To Working Men' (October 1854) and 'A Nightly Scene in London' (January 1856) were accompanied by a series of essays in which increasingly harsh attacks on government are made, and in which a bitter satirical vein is introduced into the journal's pages: the three-part 'The Thousand and One Humbugs' (April–May 1855), 'The Toady Tree' (May 1855), 'Cheap Patriotism' (June 1855) and 'Our Commission' (August 1855), will all be examined in the following chapter. The melodramatic content and tone of many *Household Words* essays and works of fiction are counterbalanced by a progressively mordant satirical mode of expression in these essays from the mid-1850s. Both would also inform the fictional texture of Dickens's great social novels published between 1852 and 1857, in a two-way process that makes Dickens's fiction and journalism in this decade deeply intertwined.

Dickens's attacks on Government in 1854 and 1855 were positioned in *Household Words* alongside the usual miscellany of essays: on cooking, on gambling, on travel, on rubbish, on the railway as a subject of poetry, on life in a small town, on fairy tales and so on; and alongside poetry and serialised fiction. Sometimes, as in the case of Elizabeth Gaskell's *North and South*, the issues addressed in Dickens's and Morley's political essays resonate and enter into dialogue with other contributions to the magazine. In a general way, though, *Household Words* stays true to its status as a miscellany throughout the 1850s, combining campaigning political journalism with matter designed to amuse and to inform. Dickens's combining of a political and cultural embrace of 'the People' with a commercial magazine enterprise addressed to a mass-market populace was hugely successful: whilst never remotely matching Reynold's sales figures, *Household Words* did, in Dickens's own words, become 'a *good property*'.[92] At the same time it addressed a much broader cross-section of 'the People' than any of Reynolds's ventures could hope to do, the latter more narrowly addressed to a lower-class readership. The first edition of *Household Words* sold in the region of 100,000 copies, with subsequent numbers settling down at on average 38,500 sales. These figures were handsomely augmented by the sale of monthly parts at nine-pence and six-monthly bound volumes at 5s 6d, and by the publication of the monthly *Household Narrative* (1850–5) and the enormously successful Extra Christmas Numbers (1850–8), which themselves sold over 80,000 copies. At the end of its first year the magazine turned in a profit of £1,715, which rose to £2,270 after three years.[93] Dickens's combining of political intervention, popular entertainment and commercial enterprise would, like his simultaneous embrace of melodramatic and satirical aesthetics in his journalism, be carried forward to quite startling political and aesthetic effect in each of *Bleak House, Hard Times* and *Little Dorrit,* the subject of my final chapter.

CHAPTER 7

Flunkeyism and toadyism in the age of machinery: from Bleak House to Little Dorrit

In March 1850 Dickens's newly launched weekly magazine had struck an optimistic note, confidently embracing progress as the keynote of the new decade. Privileged to be living in 'this summer dawn of time', Dickens promised to communicate to his readers the 'many social wonders' of the modern world, and to promulgate a faith 'in the progress of mankind'.[1] Only nine months later, though, an altogether more sombre note is struck, Dickens having found himself unconvinced – irked even – by the patriotic and (as he saw it) self-satisfied preparations for the Great Exhibition of 1851.[2] In the leading article for the 14 December 1850 edition of *Household Words* Dickens presents to his readers a bleak 'December Vision' that powerfully anticipates the major themes and preoccupations of the novel that he would begin to write a year later, *Bleak House*. In the 'vision' of the title the writer recounts how he has seen 'a mighty spirit, traversing the earth'. The 'spirit' is not, though, benign, but is akin to a noxious vapour fatally infecting all who encounter it. Its shadow has ominously darkened the faces 'of young children lying asleep, and they awoke no more . . . It revealed itself to the baby on the old crone's knee and left the old crone wailing by the fire.'[3] Heedless of age or social class, the spirit finds its way into the homes of every rank, uniting 'the People' in a manner not conceived of by the promoters of the Great Exhibition:

But, whether the beholder of [the Spirit] were, now a King, or now a labourer, now a Queen, or now a seamstress; let the hand it palsied be on the sceptre, or the plough, or yet too small and nerveless to grasp anything: the Spirit never paused in its appointed work, and, sooner or later, turned its impartial face on all . . . I saw the rich struck down in their strength, their darling children weakened and withered, their marriageable sons and daughters perish in their prime.[4]

Dickens establishes the source of this all-encompassing vision of death as the 'dull low howl' of 'Ignorance', in the 'Thirty thousand children' who have been 'hunted, flogged, imprisoned, but not taught – who might have been nurtured by the wolf or bear, so little of humanity had they, within or without them'.[5] In 'Ignorance' Dickens both looks back to the grotesque apparitions of 'Ignorance and Want' in *A Christmas Carol* and forward to Jo the Crossing Sweeper in *Bleak House*, the desolate and destitute boy who will unintentionally infect the beloved Esther Summerson with smallpox.[6] He anticipates *Bleak House* too in the dismal vision he presents in the essay of that 'portion of the [legal] system called EQUITY, which was ruin to suitors . . . a byword for delay, slow agony of mind, despair, impoverishment, trickery, confusion, insupportable injustice'.[7]

Not only anticipating the first of his great social novels of the 1850s, 'A December Vision', with its grimly assorted scenes of human distress, can also be read as a bleakly critical commentary on the smugness that Dickens felt pervaded the preparations for the Great Exhibition in Hyde Park. Dickens's human exhibits suggest a country far from at ease with itself: 'prisoners wasting in jail; mad people babbling in hospitals; suicides chronicled in the yearly records; orphans robbed of their inheritance; infants righted (perhaps) when they were grey'.[8]

Three issues later, another leading article in *Household Words* makes Dickens's stance towards the Great Exhibition more explicit:

I have seen . . . a project carried into execution for a great assemblage of the peaceful glories of the world. I have seen a wonderful structure, reared in glass, by the energy and skill of a great natural genius, self-improved; worthy descendant of my saxon ancestors: worthy type of ingenuity triumphant! Which of my children shall behold the Princes, Prelates, Nobles, Merchants, of England, equally united, for another Exhibition – for a great display of England's sins and negligences, to be, by steady contemplation of all eyes, and steady union of all hearts and hands, set right?[9]

In an extraordinarily compressed form Dickens presents, in this brief extract from 'The Last Words of the Old Year', much of the content (the 'great display of England's sins and negligences') as well as the entire structure of feeling of *Bleak House*. For *Bleak House* demands nothing less than that the whole of society – 'your Majesty, my lords and gentlemen . . . Right Reverends and Wrong Reverends of every order . . . men and women, born with Heavenly compassion in your hearts' – should unite to 'set right' the terrible wrongs anatomised in the novel's pages.[10] And Joseph Paxton, the 'great natural genius, self-improved' who designed the Crystal Palace, very probably provided Dickens with the original for Mr Rouncewell the ironmaster,[11] in many ways an exemplary figure in a novel that has at its core a residual faith in reform, modernisation and progress.

A number of critics have apprehended *Bleak House* as a riposte to the Great Exhibition of 1851.[12] Chris Vanden Bossche has also suggested that the 'House' of the novel's title might gesture towards the lethargic and corrupt House of Commons that is frequently satirised in its pages.[13] Sambudha Sen, looking back to Dickens's antecedents in Regency England, has speculated that one of the originals for *Bleak House* is William Hone's *Political House That Jack Built*, the satirical pamphlet that has been examined in chapter 1 of this study. Jack's 'House', built by 'the People' has, like the Houses of Parliament, been stuffed full of 'vermin' (Whigs and Tories) who do nothing to aid the people on whom they depend for their sinecures.[14]

The popular tradition of radical satire with which this study began continues to resonate in the pages of *Bleak House*, with its lampooning assaults on aristocratic government and in its more extended satire on Chancery. The mood of the satire has, though, generally changed. Some of the hilarity of Sam Weller persists – in the Sol's Arms's parodic and disrespectful performance of Nemo's Inquest, and in Guppy's marriage proposal to Esther, which is hedged around by a fear of a Breach of Promise suit – but elsewhere the satire is often altogether more sombre.[15] The extended satire on Chancery that pervades the entire novel is altogether bleaker in tone than anything William Hone wrote.

The popular radical inheritance is none the less clear. Hone's love of nicknaming – 'Dr Slop', 'Derry Down Triangle' and 'The Doctor' in *The Political House That Jack Built* – is shared by Dickens and is displayed in *Bleak House* in the satirical contempt he shows for the Boodles, Coodles, Doodles, Foodles, Goodles, Hoodles, Noodles and Quoodles and so on, intermarried members of the aristocracy who preside in perpetuity over Parliament. '[M]y Lord Boodle', one of Sir Leicester Dedlock's house guests, complains to old baronet 'with astonishment' that:

Supposing the present Government to be overthrown, the limited choice of the Crown, in the formation of a new ministry, would lie between Lord Coodle and Sir Thomas Doodle – supposing it to be impossible for the Duke of Foodle to act with Goodle, which may be assumed to be the case in consequence of the breach arising out of that affair with Hoodle. Then, giving the Home Department and the Leadership of the House of Commons to Joodle, the Exchequer to Koodle, the Colonies to Loodle, and the Foreign Office to Moodle, what are you to do with Noodle? You can't offer him the Presidency of the Council; that is reserved for Poodle. You can't put him in the Woods and forests; that is hardly good enough for Quoodle. What follows? That the country is shipwrecked, lost, and gone to pieces (as is made manifest to the patriotism of Sir Leicester Dedlock), because you can't provide for Noodle!'[16]

Preoccupied as it is with an incestuous circulation of power between a small group of aristocratic families, Parliament pays no attention to the distresses of 'the People', disdainfully dismissive of their claims and regarding them as mere bit-part players in the political process: 'A People there are, no doubt – a certain large number of supernumeraries, who are to be occasionally addressed, and relied upon for shouts and choruses, as on the theatrical stage' (*Bleak House*, p. 191). Dickens holds aristocratic government to account for Tom-all-Alone's – a synechdoche in the novel for poverty, ignorance and unsanitary distress: '[Each] human wretch comes and goes, fetching and carrying fever, and sowing more evil in its every footprint than Lord Toodle, and Sir Thomas Doodle, and the Duke of Foodle, and all the fine gentlemen in office, down to Zoodle, shall set right in five hundred years – though born expressly to do it' (p. 257). Dickens's frustration with the inertia and stasis of parliamentary politics is given vent when he comments ironically on a policeman's insistence that Jo the crossing sweeper must 'move on': 'Do you hear, Jo? It is nothing to you or to any one else, that the great lights of the parliamentary sky have failed for some years, in this business, to set you the example of moving on' (p. 308). For Jo, we are told, there is 'no thoroughfare in any direction' (p. 309); the fear deeply embedded in the novel is that the same may eventually be true of the whole nation.

If Dickens's attacks on aristocratic government in *Bleak House* (and, later, in *Little Dorrit*) reinforce his connection to the Regency radicalism of William Hone, so too does his deployment of biblical parody in the novel. Hone, as I described in chapter 1, was tried for (and cleared of) seditious blasphemy following the publication of a series of biblical parodies in 1817. In the first of the trials in December 1817 (as in the subsequent ones), the text of the parodies was read out in court as evidence against Hone and caused much hilarity. The text included a parodic Ten Commandments:

I. Thou shalt have no other Patron but me . . .
V. Honour the Regent and the helmets of the Life Guards, that thy stay may be long in the Place, which the Lord thy Minister giveth thee.
VI. Thou shalt not call starving to death murder.
VII. Thou shalt not call Royal gallivanting adultery.[17]

It also included a parody on the Lord's Prayer that brilliantly combines a satirical assault on the corruption, venality and idleness of Parliament with an implied interrogation of the integrity of the Church, closely entangled as it was with the state:

Our Lord who art in the Treasury, whatsoever be thy name, thy power be prolonged, thy will be done throughout the empire, as it is in each session. Give us our usual sops, and forgive us our occasional absences on divisions; as we promise not to forgive them that divide against thee. Turn us not out of our places; but keep us in the House of Commons, the land of Pensions and Plenty; and deliver us from the People. Amen.[18]

Dickens's biblical parodies in *Bleak House* are thoroughly worthy of Hone, although altogether more sombre in tone. His rehearsal of the Lord's Prayer as Jo lays dying I will give an account of further on. Here I want to comment on the parody of the funeral service from the Book of Common Prayer that shapes the chapter in which the Inquest into Captain Hawdon's death takes place. The very title of the chapter – 'Our Dear Brother' (an echo of 'Our dear brother here-departed' from the funeral service) – gestures ironically towards the fact that Hawdon was 'dear' to very few, when alive, and estranged from the woman whom he loved.[19] His wretched, solitary death in Krook's squalid lodgings is carefully juxtaposed with the tender phrases of the funeral service. The chapter culminates with an account of Hawdon's burial in a shallow grave in a city graveyard in which Dickens mounts a three-pronged attack on unsanitary city burial grounds, on uncompassionate burials, and on those responsible. The satirical accretion of 'our dear departed brother' has the effect of an ironic liturgy:

the body of our dear departed brother [is carried] to a hemmed-in churchyard, pestiferous and obscene, whence malignant diseases are committed to the bodies of our dear brothers and sisters who have not departed; while our dear brothers and sisters who hang about official backstairs – would to Heaven they *had* departed! – are very complacent and agreeable ... With houses looking on ... here, they lower our dear brother down a foot or two; here, sow him in corruption, to be raised in corruption: an avenging ghost at many a sick bedside: a shameful testimony to future ages, how civilisation and barbarism walked this boastful island together. (*Bleak House*, p. 180, emphasis in original)

The parodic echoing of the book of Corinthians – the original reads 'sow him in corruption, to be raised in incorruption'[20] – provocatively transforms biblical metaphor into a plea for sanitary reform, Hawdon's inadequately interred corpse all too likely to spread disease across the city. The reference to 'this boastful island' is another sideswipe, probably, at the Great Exhibition; and the 'shameful testimony' is a self-referential glance towards Dickens's own novel, itself a form of testimony to 1850s Britain.

Bleak House centrally concerns itself with the validity of various forms of social and legal 'testimony', and not least in this same chapter, in which Jo's testimony at Hawdon's Inquest is rejected by the coroner on the grounds that he doesn't know his catechism.[21] Jo's testimony to the Inquest has an affective force: 'He wos wery good to me, he wos' is the young boy's emotional refrain in relation to Hawdon. It is the kind of testimony that Dickens values:

Jo, is it, then? Well, well! Though a rejected witness who 'can't exactly say' what will be done to him . . . in greater hands than men's, thou art not quite in outer darkness. There is something like a distant ray of light in thy muttered reason for this:
    'He wos wery good to me, he wos!' (*Bleak House*, p. 180)

Jo's affection for Nemo has more of a Christian 'light' about it, for Dickens, than the expansive religious performances of Mr Chadband and Mrs Pardiggle, mercilessly lampooned elsewhere in the novel.

Memorable as Dickens's biblical parody is, the main satirical focus of the novel is Chancery, that 'vastly ceremonious, wordy, unsatisfactory, and expensive' embodiment of what Mr Jarndyce calls 'Wiglomeration' (p. 121); an arm of government and law that the novel holds directly responsible for the deaths of Tom Jarndyce, Mr Gridley, Miss Flite and Richard Carstone, and for the miseries and anxieties endured by many more. Again favouring Hone's penchant for nicknames in his account of 'Mr Tangle [the barrister who] knows more of Jarndyce and Jarndyce than anybody. He is famous for it – supposed never to have read anything else since he left school' (p. 18), Dickens massively increases the power of Chancery as the novel's central satirical symbol by setting alongside it a series of satirical mirrors. The main one of these is Krook's bottle and rags warehouse, a grotesque satirical reflection of Chancery, where everything is 'wasting away and going to wrack and ruin' (p. 70). It has 'the air of being in a legal neighbourhood', and 'There was a little tottering bench of shabby old volumes, outside the door, labelled "Law Books, all at 9d"' (p. 68). And the central irony is, of course, that notwithstanding the fact that the warehouse mirrors the all-consuming non-productivity of Chancery ('Everything seemed to be bought and nothing to be sold there', (p. 67)), it is in Krook's squalid and shambolic chambers that the Will that resolves the Jarndyce and Jarndyce case is found, rather than amongst the pomp and the overpaid lawyers of Chancery proper.

Miss Flite's room in Krook's lodgings itself holds a forlorn mirror up to Chancery proceedings, the life cycle of her caged birds serving as a sombre allegory on the fate of Chancery suitors. Her collection of birds – which she says she will free when she finally receives her judgement – has, Krook jeers, 'died over and over again' (p. 74) while Chancery ponderously deliberates on her case. Miss Flite and Mr Gridley will themselves, like the birds, die before the Chancellor pronounces. The Smallweeds' sifting of Krook's papers and rubbish after his death mimics the lawyers' sifting of Chancery papers: ' "They are still at it, sir," says Mr Guppy, "still taking stock, still examining papers, still going over the heaps and heaps of rubbish. At this rate they'll be at it these seven years" ' (p. 631).

Most dramatically, the spontaneous combustion of Mr Krook violently mirrors the self-consumption of the Jarndyce and Jarndyce case, which is eaten up from within by its own rottenness and rancour, lost in the rancid ocean of its own costs. The spontaneous combustion is also a symbolic displacement of the novel's desire to see Chancery blown up. As Robert Tracy has remarked, many of Dickens's readers would have remembered that Parliament had burnt down in 1834.[22] It is the emotionally hyperbolic Lawrence Boythorn who freely articulates the novel's wish (on one level at least) that the atrophying institutions of government simply be swept away:

'Nothing but a mine below it on a busy day in term time, with all its records, rules, and precedents collected in it, and every functionary belonging to it also, high and low, upward and downward, from its son the Accountant General to its father the Devil, and the whole blown to atoms with ten thousand hundredweight of gunpowder, would reform it in the least!' (*Bleak House*, p. 144)

One of the political shifts between *Bleak House* and *Little Dorrit* is the sense that in the later novel Boythorn's position teeters on the brink of becoming Dickens's own.

The satire of *Bleak House* combines the high energy levels of the Regency satires of William Hone with a more dour satirical scrutiny of government and its institutions. One of the significant developments in *Bleak House*'s satire is the shift from a focus on individuals to a more structural social and political critique. Whereas Hone, for example, tended to focus his attacks on identifiable corrupt individual representatives of Church and state, such as Sidmouth, Canning and Castlereagh, Dickens's two great social novels of the 1850s propose a more thoroughgoing critique, less concerned with culpable individuals than with the entire fabric of a diseased and paralysed political state. The whole edifice of government and its institutions begins to come under scrutiny in *Bleak House*; Dickens's forensic satirical gaze will be even more probing in *Little Dorrit*. Earlier in his novelistic career Dickens had quite often attacked identifiable individuals: Magistrate Fang, in *Oliver Twist*, is modelled on Allan Stewart Laing (1788–1862), a police magistrate who had been attacked as excessively severe in Gilbert A Beckett's satirical weekly *Figaro in London*;[23] and Alderman Cute, in

The Chimes, is modelled on Sir Peter Laurie (1778–1861), a well-known Middlesex magistrate who was celebrated for his bluff jocularity and his ability (as he saw it) to talk to offenders in their own language.[24] Whilst certain individuals can be identified amongst *Bleak House*'s panoply of characters – neither Leigh Hunt, who served as a model for Harold Skimpole, nor Walter Savage Landor, the original of Lawrence Boythorn, were at all happy about Dickens's casting[25] – such individuals are not the main target of Dickens's satire. Not even the Lord High Chancellor himself is held responsible for Chancery's wrongs. Apparently modelled on Lord Lyndhurst, in whose Court of Chancery the young Dickens had worked as a reporter in the late 1820s, the Chancellor is figured as a benign individual, 'courtly and kind' (*Bleak House*, p. 45), 'affable and polite' (p. 47).[26] Notwithstanding his benignity, Dickens reflects that none the less 'The Lord High Chancellor, at his best, appeared so poor a substitute for the love and pride of parents' (p. 45). Like the New Poor Law in *Oliver Twist*, Chancery is an inadequate institutional parent; but the Chancellor himself, unlike the malevolent Mr Bumble or the Board of Guardians, is not a melodramatic villain living off the fat of the land – it is an unreformed Chancery, rather than the individual figure of the Chancellor, which the novel blames.

Notwithstanding the shift towards a structural critique of society, *Bleak House* is as heavily populated by the individual character types of melodrama as any of Dickens's earlier works of fiction, and it is his negotiation of this other popular radical aesthetic that I will now examine.

DICKENS'S DIALOGUE WITH MELODRAMA IN *BLEAK HOUSE*

Bleak House draws on a medley of popular cultural forms: the ominous ghost walk at Chesney Wold nods towards the Gothic tradition; the emergence of Inspector Bucket to unravel the mystery of Tulkinghorn's death and Lady Dedlock's disappearance anticipates the development of detective fiction across the second half of the nineteenth century; and the eruption of the murderess Maria Manning from the novel's pages, in the shape of Hortense, suggests an indebtedness to street literature, Manning having been the 'star' of many a broadside. All these popular cultural modes are wedded in the novel to the melodrama: a secret birth, family mysteries, a contested will, a shipwreck and the return of a long-lost lover from overseas, strongly virtuous and downright malevolent characters, a strong sense of the forces of good set against the forces of evil, heightened emotion, a domestic 'happy ending' – the raw ingredients of popular melodrama are as evident in this novel from 1852–3 as they were in *Oliver Twist* fifteen years before.

In this mature political novel, though, Dickens does not simply reproduce the ingredients and the structures of feeling of popular melodrama. The aesthetic contours of melodrama are deftly manipulated in *Bleak House* in a variety of ways that suggest that Dickens is interrogating the efficacy of the melodrama as a mode of expression capable both of anatomising the wrongs of 'the People' and of demanding that they be addressed.

One such challenge to the melodramatic mode resides in the fact that the main source of evil in this novel is not a 'bad' individual character but a government institution. Whereas in earlier novels such as *Oliver Twist* and *Nicholas Nickleby* it is by and large 'good' and 'bad' individuals that shape the moral parameters of the novel, in *Bleak House* the villain of the piece is Chancery, a mechanism of the state: 'this High Court of Chancery, most pestilent of hoary sinners' (*Bleak House*, p. 14). The result is unsettling, for the focus on good and evil individuals in earlier popular radical melodrama meant that evil could be overcome by good through the endeavour of heroic individuals. In *Bleak House*, though, Gridley, Miss Flite, Richard Carstone and John Jarndyce are all powerless in the face of the (faceless) power of Chancery.

The dehumanised agency of Chancery – '"My lord!" Maces, bags, and purses, indignantly proclaim silence' (p. 18) – is opposed by Dickens with melodramatic characterisations and realisations. The battered, disease-ravaged bodies of the novel's children, its dead babies, the physical violence wreaked on Jenny and on her opposite in the social scale, Mr Tulkinghorn; Dickens determinedly opposes the bodiliness of the melodramatic mode to the objectifying and dehumanising processes of Chancery. It is the physical wreckage of Jo the crossing sweeper's body that most powerfully insists that the reader prioritise the visceral morals of the melodrama over and above the dry inhumanity of Chancery's legalese. Jo's deathbed scene is a close relative to the many moving tableaux devoted to dead and dying children that fill the pages of *Household Words*, discussed in chapter 6. Here Dickens builds on the familiar tableau of the deathbed scene to extraordinary emotional and moral effect. Although contemporary critics found much to complain of in *Bleak House*, Dickens's account of Jo's death generally drew approbation, with Dean Ramsay declaring to John Forster that 'To my mind, nothing in the field of fiction is to be found in English literature surpassing the death of Jo!'[27] The review in the *Athenaeum*, whilst generally negative, reflected that 'The dying scene, with its terrible morals and impetuous protest, Mr Dickens has nowhere in all his works excelled.'[28]

The title of the chapter in which Jo dies is, like the one that sees Nemo buried, ironic. 'Jo's Will' draws attention to Jo's vulnerability and lack of status (what legal person would ever heed a will made by this poor illiterate boy?); it also, though, indicates Dickens's much greater valuing of Jo's dying wishes over and above the legal document (the Jarndyce Will) on which the main plot of the novel hinges. Although one effect of Dickens's parodic reprise of the melodramatic plot device of the will is to emphasise Jo's powerlessness and lack of agency, Dickens by no means leaves it at that. For the coming together of Mr Woodcourt, Mr Jarndyce, Mr Snagsby, soldier George and Phil Squod around Jo's deathbed marks a moment in the novel when Dickens forces upon the reader – to great emotional effect – Jo's humanity. His deathbed attendants represent a broad cross-section of 'the People' as Dickens conceived of that category – a gentleman, a doctor, a legal stationer, a discharged soldier, a shooting gallery assistant. Their sympathy for, and recognition of, the crossing sweeper's plight, and their attentiveness to what he says; all are testimony to Dickens's determined embrace of Jo as one of 'the People'. Jo's remorse at having infected Esther with the smallpox virus, and his observation that Mr Woodcourt and Mr Jarndyce have both wept over her illness, give him a moral and emotional dimension that distinguishes him from the visions of 'Ignorance' and 'Want' of *A Christmas Carol*.

Jo's deathbed scene gains power through its gathering together of a whole multitude of the novel's motifs into what Martin Meisel has described as a form of 'montage'.[29] The scene's emotional affects are also heightened through Dickens's rapid alternation between the melodramatic pathos of Jo's dying wish and a venomous satirical reprise concerning Chadband's empty religious proselytising; the juxtaposition of pathos and satire sharpens the rhetorical effect of both. Mr Snagsby, the kindly law stationer whose best effort is to offer Jo a series of half crowns, is summonsed to the dying boy's bedside, as he has a dying wish that he wants to relate:

'What I wos a thinkin on, Mr Sangsby,' proceeds Jo, 'wos as you wos able to write wery large, p'raps?'

'Yes, Jo, please God,' returns the stationer.

'Uncommon precious large, p'raps?' says Jo, with eagerness.

'Yes, my poor boy.'

Jo laughs with pleasure. 'Wot I was a thinkin on then, Mr Sangsby, wos, that when I was moved on as fur as ever I could go and couldn't be moved no furder, whether you might be so good p'raps, as to write out, wery large so that anyone could see it anywheres, as that I wos wery truly hearty sorry that I done it and that I never went fur to do it; and that though I didn't know nothink at all, I knowd as Mr Woodcot once cried over it and was allus grieved over it, and that I hoped as he'd be able to forgiv me in his mind. If the writin could be made to say it wery large, he might.'

'It shall say it, Jo. Very large.'

Jo laughs again. 'Thankee, Mr Sangsby. Its wery kind of you, sir, and it makes me more cumfbler nor I was afore.' (*Bleak House*, p. 731)

Jo's moral awareness and sympathy are poignantly combined with a child-like apprehension that the writing of his apology in a large hand will increase its effectiveness. The boy's repeated assertion throughout the novel that 'I don't know nothink!' here comes to a poignant climax when Jo shows himself to have a quite remarkable knowledge after all; not of letters or of scripture, but of people's feelings and of their sufferings, an intuitive moral sensibility that Dickens valued above all other forms of knowledge.

Jo's heavily laboured breathing is figured throughout the scene through the twin metaphors of 'moving on' and 'the cart': '"Draw breath, Jo!"' Woodcourt urges him. ' "It draws," says Jo, "as heavy as a cart."' He might add, 'and rattles like one'; but he only mutters, '"I'm a moving on, sir"' (p. 728). Three pages later 'that cart of his is heavier to draw, and draws with a hollower sound' (p. 731); there is a reference on the next page to 'the cart so hard to draw' (p. 732); until 'The cart had very nearly given up' and 'The cart is all shaken to pieces' (p. 733) The continual iteration, throughout the novel, that Jo must, in the vocabulary of the police, 'move on', is here semantically recast as Jo prepares to 'move on' in the most final of ways.

Allan Woodcourt's attempt to teach Jo the Lord's Prayer as he draws his last breaths is at once poignant and sharply discomfiting:

'Jo! Did you ever know a prayer?'
'Never know'd nothink, sir.'
'Not so much as one short prayer?'
'No, sir. Nothink at all. Mr Chadbands he wos a prayin wunst at Mr Sangsby's and I heerd him, but he sounded as if he wos a speakin' to his-self, and not to me . . . *I* never knowd what it wos all about.' . . .
'Jo, my poor fellow!'
'I hear you, sir, in the dark, but I'm a gropin – a gropin – let me catch hold of your hand.'
'Jo, can you say what I say?'
'I'll say anythink as you say, sir, for I knows it's good.'
'OUR FATHER.'
'Our Father! – yes, that's wery good, sir.'
'WHICH ART IN HEAVEN.'
'Art in Heaven – is the light a comin, sir?'
'It is close at hand. HALLOWED BE THY NAME!'
'Hallowed be – thy –'
The light is come upon the dark benighted way. Dead!

Dead, your Majesty. Dead, my lords and gentleman. Dead, Right Reverends and Wrong Reverends of every order. Dead, men and women, born with Heavenly compassion in your hearts. And dying thus around us, every day.

(pp. 732–4)

The satirical accretions around religion and prayer in the course of the novel here come to a climax: as well as knowing that Esther's illness caused much sadness, Jo also knows that Chadband's prayers are self-serving. The poignancy of Woodcourt's simple, well-meant attempt to teach Jo the Lord's Prayer as he dies none the less leaves the reader feeling profoundly uncomfortable given the adjacent satire on Chadband's prayer-making. This is nothing if not the most discomfiting of novels.

The intervention of the narrator at the close of the chapter sharply removes the reader from the tableau, reminding us that it *is* a tableau, an effect, a rhetorical set piece. Drawing attention to the performed, staged nature of Jo's death has a reality effect. And whilst in *A Christmas Carol* Dickens's weeping readers could blame the Scrooges of the world for the plight of the Cratchit family, ten years later they are forced to look at themselves – it is 'us' around whom such children die every day. More important still, Jo himself is one of 'us'.

Jo's deathbed scene, along with Esther's emotionally fraught reunion with her long-lost mother, is a melodramatic set piece in a novel in which Dickens frequently challenges the melodramatic mode even as he embraces it. One of the ways in which the novelist enters into a dialogue with melodrama is through his negotiation of domesticity. Domesticity as a panacea and cross-class emollient is deeply embedded in the melodramatic aesthetic; in his deployment of the domestic trope Dickens is writing within a firmly established cultural tradition. His configuration of domesticity is, though, more disruptive and generally more troubled than at first perhaps meets the eye. *Bleak House* begins and ends with domestic harmony: the touching domestic scene at the entrance to the lodge keeper's cottage at Chesney Wold and the domestic harmony of the Bagnets and soldier George at the close. The domestic bliss of the second Bleak House is the other closing set piece of the novel. But these domestic scenes *are* very staged and self-conscious, as is the whole of Esther Summerson's narrative. Esther's self-sacrificing, self-effacing femininity is archly *performed* in the novel, drawing attention to itself through its confinement to Esther's part of the narrative. The new Bleak House at the novel's close is presented to us almost as a stage set, it is painstakingly crafted (by Mr Jarndyce, as a proxy for Dickens), and thereby draws attention to itself as a constructed 'object'. It is, in Esther's words, 'a cottage, quite a rustic cottage of doll's rooms ...' – almost literally a doll's house (p. 962).

Undoubtedly, domesticity is presented to the reader as a refuge from the madness, disease and death of the rest of the novel. It is, though, emphatically revealed as a fragile refuge. For beyond the walls of Bleak House sheer domestic hell reigns virtually supreme: in the coldly unloving environment of Esther's childhood home; in the squalor and brutality of Tom-all-Alone's; in the domestic violence of the brickmaker's hovel; in the mistrust and discomfort of the Snagsby home; in the tight-lipped, childless *sang froid* of the Dedlock residences; in the chaos and neglect of the Jellyby house; in the straitened circumstances and self-delusion of the Carstone apartments; and in the sad, crazy solitude of Miss Flite's room.

If Dickens's deployment of the domestic trope serves to highlight by contrast the madness and misery of the world beyond it, rather than shut it out, then his account of femininity at the mid-century is also more interrogative, more enquiring than many critics have allowed for. The publication of *Bleak House* in 1853 coincided with the rise of first-wave feminism in Victorian England and drew sharp criticism from John Stuart Mill, who thought it 'done in the very vulgarest way – just the style in which vulgar men used to ridicule "learned ladies" as neglecting their children and household'.[30] It is Dickens's satirical account of Mrs Jellyby to which Mill objects, the champion of 'Telescopic Philanthropy' later dropping this project in favour of agitating for women's political rights. Dickens's satire is harsh, and yet it could be argued that Mrs Jellyby's endless writing of letters (she seems to spend most of her time opening her mail), her setting up of committees and societies and other such institutional paraphernalia simply mimic the (patriarchal) mechanisms of Chancery, which are shown in the novel to be so pointless and destructive: like Krook, she is said to live amidst 'waste and ruin' (*Bleak House*, p. 480).

Mill, though, had a point. Mrs Jellyby is a satirical portrait, another political lampoon, and one that is not sympathetic to the early claims of women's rights activists.[31] But the satire is played off against a range of *melodramatic* female character types which tell an entirely different story, one that promotes a powerful critique of women's oppression at the mid-century. The domestic angel that forms part – the least knowing part – of Esther Summerson's self-identity is a near relation to the heroine of domestic melodrama, and many of the other female figures in the novel have melodramatic antecedents: the imperious Lady Dedlock echoes the archetypal fallen woman; the French maid, Hortense, is the deadly foreign

murderess, who has her counterpart in Ernest Jones's *De Brassier:
A Democratic Romance*;[32] Jenny the brickmaker's wife is the victim of
domestic brutality; young Charley the orphan mother. These types,
though, are not fixed in the novel. Lady Dedlock, the Lady of the
Manor, merges, towards the novel's close, with the archetypal figure of
the prostitute who drowns herself in the Thames: the 'doubling' of aristocratic lady and forsaken prostitute is carefully staged. As Esther and
Inspector Bucket search London for Lady Dedlock, Esther spots a poster,
on a 'mouldering wall' by the Thames, on which she can discern the words
'FOUND DROWNED', which fills her with 'an awful suspicion shad-
owed forth in our visit to that place':

> A man yet dark and muddy in long, swollen sodden boots and a hat like them, was
> called out of a boat, and whispered with Mr Bucket, who went away with him
> down some slippery steps –as if to look at something secret that he had to show.
> They came back, wiping their hands upon their coats, after turning over some-
> thing wet; but thank God it was not what I feared! (*Bleak House*, p. 869)

There is a whole series of mistaken female identities in the novel.
Mistaken identity is, of course, a staple ingredient of melodrama, but it
has a profound implication for Dickens's class-inflected account of
femininity in *Bleak House*. Lady Dedlock is mistaken – designedly so –
for Hortense, her maid; Jo mistakes Esther for Lady Dedlock, and
Esther mistakes her own dead mother for Jenny, the brutal brickmaker's
wife:

> On the step at the gate, drenched in the fearful wet of such a place, which oozed
> and splashed down everything, I saw, with a cry of pity and horror, a woman lying
> – Jenny, the mother of the dead child . . . She lay there, who had so lately spoken to
> my mother. She lay there, a distressed, unsheltered, senseless creature . . . I passed
> on to the gate, and stooped down. I lifted the heavy head, put the long dank hair
> aside, and turned the face. And it was my mother, cold and dead. (pp. 913–15)

The drowned prostitute, the brutalised brickmaker's wife, the dead Lady of
the Manor: all converge in Esther's 'feverish, wandering journey' in search
of her mother (p. 904). Both Jenny, the brickmaker's wife, and Lady
Dedlock, the wife of a baronet, have lost their babies: the one to poverty
and disease, the other to the moral codes of social propriety. Their equality
in victimhood is dramatically expressed in the above scene, Dickens
engaging here and throughout the novel in a cross-class account of
women's oppression.

The anti-aristocratic temper of *Bleak House* allies its structure of feeling to that of popular melodrama, traditionally peopled by villainous

aristocrats. But although Dickens is severe in his contemplation of the aristocratic government of the Coodles and Doodles; and as contemptuous of the effete dandyish hangers on at Chesney Wold as he is of Mr Turveydrop's mimicking of an aristocratic lifestyle; in Sir Leicester Dedlock Dickens resists a by now old-fashioned figuring of the aristocrat as villain. Whilst he lampoons Dedlock's fear of modernity; and whilst he is critical of his complicity with the deadening parliamentary deadlock of Doodles and Coodles and with bribery and corruption in the electoral process; in the personal realm – the realm in which the aristocrat in a melodrama would reveal his villainy – the old baronet is presented as loyal and forgiving, and utterly gentle.

The anti-paternalism of the novel similarly sets it against the dominant structure of feeling of mainstream popular melodramas. The Lord High Chancellor has already been described as 'so poor a substitute' in his quasi-parental role in relation to Richard and Ada; Mr Jarndyce's genial paternalism is demonstrably insufficient to rescue Richard from Chancery's grip; and Mr Rouncewell, in many ways the novel's social and moral touchstone, firmly rejects Sir Leicester's patronage, firstly by making his own way in industry rather than enter into service at Chesney Wold, and secondly by removing Rosa from the estate so as to educate her to live amongst the rising middle classes.

The failure of paternalism in the novel goes hand-in-hand with a commitment to progress and modernity, even in the face of the apocalyptic potential of Tom-all-Alone's. The primal mud and fog at the start of *Bleak House* is as antithetical to the optimistic 'progress' motif of the Preliminary Word to *Household Words* as it is to the Great Exhibition. And there is no doubt of the novel's very real fear that governmental paralysis will have explosive social consequences:

not an ignorance, not a wickedness, not a brutality of his committing, but shall work its retribution, through every order of society, up to the proudest of the proud, and to the highest of the high. Verily, what with tainting, plundering, and spoiling, Tom has his revenge. (p. 710)

But there is a belief in the novel – a belief that is severely under pressure, almost to the point of breaking; but a belief none the less – in the power of progress, reform and industrial modernity. In 'A December Vision' Dickens hangs on to a visionary glimpse of 'Certain lawyers and laymen ... [who] said to one another ... We must change this'.[33] And he is on Ada's side in *Bleak House* when she reflects that 'an honest judge in real earnest' ought to be able to establish justice in Chancery (p. 78).

To this extent there is some internal resistance in the novel to its own structural critique, and this explains Dickens's enduring commitment to the melodrama, a cultural mode that foregrounds the actions of individuals. When Mr Jarndyce blames Mr Gridley's plight on 'the system', Gridley himself begs to disagree:

Mr Jarndyce said that he condoled with him with all his heart, and that he set up no monopoly, himself, in being unjustly treated by this monstrous system.

'There again!' said Mr Gridley, with no diminution of his rage. 'The system! I am told, on all hands, it's the system. I mustn't look to individuals . . . But if I do no violence to any of [the lawyers in Chancery], there – I may! . . . I will accuse the individual workers of that system against me, face to face, before the great eternal star!' (p. 251)

Gridley's refusal to blame 'the system' *tout court* is a manifestation of Dickens's own reluctance to tie himself to a thoroughgoing systemic account of political paralysis and inertia, social deprivation and distress. For a full-blooded structural critique crucially cedes the social and political agency of 'the People'. Dickens isn't ready for this in *Bleak House*, which is why he turns on his readers after Jo's death in a vehement denunciation of all those who can and should do something to help. In remarking that children like Jo are 'dying thus around us every day' (p. 734), Dickens aligns himself with the 'us' of his readership – all those whom he believes could, like him, do something to effect change: *Bleak House* is his own contribution to that process.

Mr Rouncewell, the ironmaster, the epitome of industrial modernity, provides the reader of *Bleak House* with a glimpse of Dickens's progressive ideal. Full of movement and vigour, Rouncewell's rapid traversing of the country is sharply contrasted with Sir Leicester's sedentary repose:

'In these busy times, when so many great undertakings are in progress, people like myself have so many workmen in so many places, that we are always on the flight.'
. . . Sir Leicester sits down in an easy chair, opposing his repose and that of Chesney Wold to the restless flight of ironmasters. (p. 451)

The effects of industrial modernity are presented in an altogether less sanguine way in *Hard Times*, the novel that Dickens would write immediately after *Bleak House*. Mr Rouncewell, the upright ironmaster, grotesquely transmutes into the cruel and bombastic factory owner, Bounderby, in a novel in which Dickens appears to do a complete *volte face*. In the next section of this chapter I will provide a context for understanding this temporary abatement of Dickens's enthusiasm for modern industrialism.

HARD TIMES AND HOUSEHOLD WORDS

Bleak House was commercially a massively successful novel that the critics on the whole tended to dislike. The reviewer for the *Athenaeum* complained that in reading the novel 'the reader might be excused for feeling as though he belonged to some orb where eccentrics, Bedlamites, ill-directed and disproportioned people were the only inhabitants.'[34] Walter Bagehot summed up reviewers' political unease with the novel when he complained that 'the real tendency of [Dickens's] exhortations is to make men dissatisfied with their inevitable condition, and what is worse, to make them fancy that its irremediable evils can be remedied'.[35] The government institutions that were the target of *Bleak House*'s uncompromising satire were largely stewarded by the middle and upper ranks of society. It was this that made it such uncomfortable reading for reviewers, who by and large were firmly rooted in those social groups. Dickens's wider readership clearly felt differently. With the serialised monthly shilling parts averaging sales of 34,000, its circulation was, in Dickens's own words, 'half as large again as Copperfield!'[36] It was a success in the theatre, too, becoming 'among the half dozen most frequently dramatized of Dickens's novels and stories'.[37] The level of Dickens's popularity by now somewhat troubled the intelligentsia, with George Henry Lewes veering towards the pompous in his admonition to 'My Dear Dickens' that '[Your] magnificent popularity carries with it a serious responsibility.'[38] Dickens meanwhile had hoped that after the effort of *Bleak House* he could 'do nothing in that way for a year'.[39] The commercial vacillations of the highly competitive cheap weekly periodical market, though, decreed otherwise. Hard on the heels of *Bleak House*'s completion in August 1853, Dickens would be told that sales of *Household Words* had fallen precipitously during the six months leading up to September 1853. Whereas six-monthly profits had previously averaged between £900 and £1,300, they had now dropped to £527 15s 10d.[40] Bradbury and Evans proposed that Dickens address the crisis by writing a new novel, to be published weekly in the magazine, and he duly set to work. The first instalment of *Hard Times* was published in the 1 April 1854 edition of *Household Words*; the last on 12 August 1854.

It is only possible to understand the contemporary significance of *Hard Times* by reading it week by week as it appeared in *Household Words*. It appeared on the front page of each edition of the magazine, and Peter Ackroyd has commented that visually it resembled 'a cross between a journalistic report and an editorial'.[41] *Hard Times* is arguably the Dickens novel most firmly rooted in contemporary 1850s Britain.

Bleak House has a complex double timescale, with certain aspects locating it in the 1820s or 1830s, and others – the plea for Sanitary Reform, for improved education, for the reform of Chancery – making it the most topical of contemporary works of fiction.[42] The double (or continuous) timescale of *Bleak House* is highly effective in making the reader reflect on the level of political representation that had been achieved (or not) since the Reform Act of 1832. *Little Dorrit*, too, has a double time scale: whilst it is explicitly set in 1825/6 (the opening words of the novel are 'Thirty years ago'), a savage satire on the state of contemporary government and its institutions fills many of its pages. *Hard Times*, though, is firmly rooted in the quotidian of the 1850s, and of all Dickens's novels it is the one most contiguous (materially as well as thematically) to his journalistic project.

In one sense *Hard Times* is a reprise, in the form of a fable, of the debate between utility and the imagination that Dickens had set up in the very first edition of *Household Words*. In 'The Amusements of the People', which I discussed in detail in chapter 6, he plays off the theatrical amusements of 'Joe Whelks' and his ilk against the instruction offered by the 'Polytechnic Institution in Regent Street'. The essay's central argument is that:

The Polytechnic Institution in Regent Street, where an infinite variety of ingenious models are exhibited and explained, and where lectures comprising a quantity of useful information on many practical subjects are delivered, is a great public benefit and a wonderful place, but we think a people formed *entirely* in their hours of leisure by Polytechnic Institutions would be an uncomfortable community.[43]

And so it proves in the case of Bitzer in *Hard Times*.

There is an implied dialogue, in *Household Words*, between essays such as those by Charles Knight that are packed full of 'useful' information (his 'Illustrations of Cheapness' series traces the production processes and properties of various commodities such as 'The Lucifer Match' and 'The Steel Pen'),[44] and other more 'fanciful' contributions, such as Dickens's own 'A Child's Dream of a Star'.[45] Charles Knight, a regular contributor to *Household Words*, superintended the publications of the Society for the Diffusion of Useful Knowledge, which published in Anne Lohrli's words 'numerous serials and compilations of information, instruction, and diversion, designed to make good reading cheaply available to the masses'.[46] Although Knight and Dickens were quite close, *Hard Times* is without doubt in one sense a riposte to the extremes of utility upon which Dickens seems to have felt that Knight's publications sometimes foundered. *Knight's Store of Knowledge For All Readers: Being a Collection of Treatises in Various Departments of Knowledge* actually contains – in all earnestness – the absurdly literal definition of a horse that young Bitzer parrots in *Hard Times*.[47] Asked by Gradgrind to define a horse, the apotheosis of Utilitarian education responds:

'Quadruped. Graminivorous. Forty teeth, namely twenty-four grinders, four eye-teeth, and twelve incisive. Sheds coat in the spring; in marshy countries, sheds hoofs too. Hoofs hard, but requiring to be shod with iron. Age known by marks in mouth.' Thus (and much more) Bitzer.[48]

Dickens's satire on the extremes of a Utilitarian education by no means indicates that he was anything other than an enthusiastic supporter of the modernisation of the education system, as his plea on behalf of the Ragged Schools in 'A Sleep to Startle Us', and the campaigning that he did on their behalf, makes plain.[49] Instinctively of the modernisers, it was the 'unreasonable disciples of a reasonable school, demented disciples'[50] amongst both the political economists and the Utilitarians that Dickens vehemently objected to. In *Hard Times* Mr Jupe's playfully named pet dog, 'Merrylegs', epitomises Dickens's response to the extremes of utility and pragmatism that he detected as a most unwelcome aspect of the modernisation process.

Another such aspect was the extreme of laissez-faire political economy whereby account books, as Dickens saw it, took precedence over humans. Charles Knight seems to have been concerned, on reading *Hard Times*, that Dickens was attacking men such as he (which he was), fearing that Dickens had set him down as 'a cold-hearted political economist'.[51] Dickens's response was to reassure him that:

Indeed there is no fear of my thinking you the owner of a cold heart . . .

My satire [in *Hard Times*] is against those who see figures and averages and nothing else – the representatives of the wickedest and most enormous vice of this time – the men who, through long years to come, will do more to damage the real useful truths of political economy, than I could do (if I tried) in my whole life.[52]

It was his hostility towards this extreme, and against those modernisers who 'push arithmetic and political economy beyond all bounds of sense',[53] that propelled the writing of *Hard Times*; and in this sense it is firmly allied to the social thought of Thomas Carlyle, to whom the novel is dedicated. The type of political economy that metonymically reduces workers in factories to the status of 'the Hands' and turns a blind eye to factory accidents (*Hard Times*, p. 66 and passim); and the Utilitarian spirit that reduces Sissy Jupe to 'girl number twenty' and a horse to a graminivorous quadruped (p. 12); these are determinedly yoked together in *Hard Times*, and both are found wanting. The 'severely workful' (p. 28) profile of

'Coketown' is countered in the novel by 'Sleary's Horsemanship' and the circus (chapter 6) in much the same way that Dickens had earlier countered the 'Polytechnic Institution in Regent Street' with the theatrical amusements of 'Joe Whelks' in his 'Amusements of the People' essay.

None of this, though, altogether explains the shift in Dickens's presentation of the factory owner from the upright and worthy ironmaster, Mr Rouncewell, in *Bleak House*, to the 'Bully of humility', Mr Bounderby, in *Hard Times* (p. 20). There is a very particular explanation for this shift: it was specifically the resistance of factory owners in the 1850s to legislation relating to the fencing of machinery that so that angered Dickens. His instinctive anger on behalf of the men, women and children who were being horribly injured at work led to his creation of the hyperbolically evil Bounderby: 'A big, loud man, with a stare and a metallic laugh . . . A man with a great puffed head and forehead, swelled veins in his temples . . . A man who could never sufficiently vaunt himself a self-made man' (p. 20). Once again, Dickens's visceral response to the sufferings and injustices of the poor led him to continue to embrace the melodramatic mode and its character types.

The formation of the National Association of Factory Occupiers in 1854, whose main raison d'être seemed to be to circumvent factory legislation, was a direct spur to Dickens's novelistic imagination.[54] The very close relationship between the ongoing social and political debates in *Household Words* and Dickens's writing of *Hard Times* means that it is politically the most localised of his novels.[55] It is also very different from both *Bleak House* and from *Little Dorrit* in its political configuration of social class. Whereas *Bleak House* and *Little Dorrit* determinedly reinvoke an eighteenth-century radical concept of 'the People' in which the lower and middle classes are joined together against the aristocracy (and more particularly aristocratic government), *Hard Times* centrally concerns itself with class conflict between the working and the middle classes. There is an oscillation in the radical culture of the mid-nineteenth century – not least amongst the Chartists – between a negotiation of 'the People' as a concept and a more oppositional account of class conflict.[56] Dickens's social novels of the 1850s likewise try to reach an accommodation between class conflict and the broader radical category of 'the People'.

Hard Times is Carlylean in its attack on the cash-nexus, its incipient fear of the working-class mob and its anti-Utilitarianism; but in other respects it owes as great a debt to the popular radical culture of the early nineteenth century as does *Bleak House*. One of its early reviewers objected (as did others) to the didactic strain of *Hard Times*, dismissing it as: 'a mere dull melodrama, in which character is caricature, sentiment tinsel, and moral (if any) unsound. It is a thousand pities that Mr. Dickens does not confine himself to amusing his readers, instead of . . . trying to instruct them.'[57] The irony is, of course, that in writing a 'melodrama' Dickens was drawing on a popular form of entertainment that may well have been expected to 'amuse' his readership; and the whole thematic thrust of the novel is in favour of 'amusement' over and above 'instruction'. *Hard Times* is indeed indebted to popular melodramas of the nineteenth century: the seduction trope played out in James Harthouse's dalliance with Louisa Bounderby; the wrongful accusation of Stephen Blackpool that necessitates a defence made by a virtuous young woman; the mistaking of identity that leads Mrs Peglar, Bounderby's long-suffering mother, to be misapprehended as a criminal; and Bounderby's disputed will – all these are immediately recognisable plot devices from melodrama.

The highly compressed, fable-like quality of *Hard Times* means that its debt to melodrama is very visible. Here as elsewhere in his fiction, though, Dickens transforms familiar melodramatic plotlines in a manner that allows him both to connect with popular culture and to rewrite it for a wider readership. The middle-class readers of *Household Words* wanted to read something superior to the melodramas enthusiastically consumed by 'Joe Whelks', and in *Hard Times* Dickens once more simultaneously embraces and builds upon the basic ingredients of popular culture. One such instance of Dickens's ability at once to identify with and to transform popular culture is the strange, hallucinatory sequence in the novel in which Stephen Blackpool has a nightmarish vision of the course of his tragic life. The vision culminates in a melodramatic tableau that clearly draws on Newgate fiction; but it is at the same time a highly complex, imaginatively resonating piece of writing:

He thought that he, and some one on whom his heart had long been set – but she was not Rachael, and that surprised him, even in the midst of his imaginary happiness – stood in the church being married. While the ceremony was performing, and while he recognised among the witnesses some one whom he knew to be living, and many whom he knew to be dead, darkness came on, succeeded by the shining of a tremendous light. It broke from one line in the table of commandments at the altar, and illuminated the building with words. They were sounded through the church, too, as if there were voices in the fiery letters. Upon this, the whole appearance before him and around him changed, and nothing was left as it had been, but himself and the clergyman. They stood in the daylight before a crowd so vast, that if all the people in the world could have been brought together into one space, they could not have looked, he thought, more numerous; and they all abhorred him, and there was not one pitying or friendly eye among the millions that were fastened on his face. He stood on a raised stage, under his own loom; and, looking up at the shape the loom took, and hearing the burial service distinctly read, he knew that he was there to suffer death. In an instant what he stood on fell below him, and he was gone. (*Hard Times*, p. 86)

At the start of the passage Stephen revisits his marriage ceremony in a long-gone happy past. His present desire for his wife's death, and his feelings of guilt in relation to this, produce the blazing religious experience in the church in which the table of commandments fills the building with fiery light and sound. Stephen then imagines himself exposed in front of a huge, malevolent crowd, in a phantasmagoric scenario that blends the Day of Judgement with a Newgate hanging, the clergyman from the church now about to preside over his hanging instead of his marriage. The reader is left to infer that in the interim Stephen has murdered his wife. In this highly compressed, delirious sequence, Dickens traces Stephen's adult life, from his youthful hope of marital happiness through to his present desire to see his wife dead. His hanging at the end of the dream sequence would have been immediately recognisable to Dickens's readers as deriving from Newgate fiction; but in *Hard Times* he doesn't allow such a simple melo-dramatic plotline to take hold of the novel. Stephen doesn't murder his wife, but steels himself to endure the prison house that is his marital tie, and – coinciding with the topical themes of the novel – he dies in a factory accident.

Whilst Dickens does partially accede, in the novel, to the happy, emollient endings of popular melodrama – the virtuous simplicity of Sissy Jupe utterly defeats James Harthouse, Thomas Gradgrind (like Mr Dombey before him) has a 'change of heart' and becomes a better parent, and Bounderby and Mrs Sparsit get their just deserts – the figure of Louisa Bounderby disallows a full melodramatic close. The most interest-ing figure in the novel, Louisa is left troublingly bereft at the close: 'Herself again a wife – a mother – lovingly watchful of her children . . . Such a thing was never to be' (p. 287). The happy ending of popular melodrama is reserved for the more two-dimensional Sissy Jupe – 'happy Sissy's happy children loving her; all children loving her' (p. 287).

Louisa never quite fits the melodramatic script. Mrs Sparsit plots a melodramatic denouement for her, imagining for the unhappy young wife a staircase down which she is inevitably to slide to seduction, elope-ment and perdition. Louisa, though, unknowingly confounds Mrs Sparsit's melodramatic script, for she is not in fact rushing headlong into sexual and social disgrace but, rather, to the refuge of her father's house. Louisa doesn't become a melodramatically fallen woman, but neither is she rescued by a virtuous hero: her father is as broken and confused by her predicament as she is. It is, then, partly in his treatment of Louisa that Dickens moves beyond the simple aesthetic contours of popular melo-drama: neither a straightforwardly 'good' nor a 'bad' character, but with the potential to be either, Louisa is not a character prototype from melo-drama but is a product – the most interesting product in this novel – of a particular system of education and ethics that is heavily criticised in the novel.

The commercial impact of *Hard Times* on *Household Words* was entirely positive. In March 1854, the month before the serialised novel began to appear, *Household Words*'s profits had fallen even lower than before; by contrast, the six months to September 1854 saw an increase in profit of 237 per cent.[58] *Little Dorrit*, which began to appear in monthly shilling parts in December 1855, would be even more commercially successful, and even less politically popular with the critics.

Whilst *Hard Times* insists on valuing popular culture, it is the paucity of cultural life in *Little Dorrit* that contributes to the deeply sombre complexion of Dickens's novel from 1855 to 1857. The culture of the poor is represented by the down-at-heels theatre where Fanny Dorrit is a dancer and where her broken old uncle plays the clarinet. Entirely lacking the *joie de vivre* of the theatres frequented by 'Joe Whelks', its dreariness is matched in the novel by the dull routines of the European Grand Tour, where the middle and upper classes seek their cultural experiences. Once a glamorous cultural rite of passage, the Tour in *Little Dorrit* is peopled by a motley assortment of people largely escaping from social difficulties in their homeland: hard-up refugees from the upper classes such as Henry Gowan; those like the Dorrits who feel they lack social credibility in British high society; the lonely and direc-tionless Arthur Clennam, returning from exile in China; and a criminal in the garb of a gentleman. It is with Dickens's most comprehensive – and his politically most hard-edged – satire on aristocratic government, its institutions and the high society that it sustains, that this book will close.

CHOLERA, THE CRIMEA, AND INTERNATIONAL FINANCE

On 28 March 1854, two days before the appearance of the first instalment of *Hard Times* in *Household Words*, the Crimean War broke out, a two-year long catastrophe that Dickens would witness with a mixture of fury and disgust. In August and September of the same year the terrible, unsanitary conditions in which London's poor were still forced to live triggered an epidemic of Asiatic cholera in the capital city. The previous outbreak of the disease had been in 1849; in this latest epidemic over 10,000 people died, and some of the poorer areas south of the river were so badly affected that they had to be cordoned off.[59] Meanwhile, governments came and went with – as far as Dickens could see – little being done to improve the sanitation and housing of the poor.[60] Dickens's frustration at the failure of successive government administrations on both the domestic and the international front combined in his imagination with a perceived spread of financial chicanery in the City. In 'Gone to the Dogs', a *Household Words* essay from March 1855, he writes of an 'eminent person – with indefinite resources in the City, tantamount to a goldmine – who had the delightful house near town . . . half-a-dozen carriages', whose wealth transpires to have been a mere chimera: 'Ruined . . . gone to the Dogs!'[61] Here Dickens at once recalls George Hudson, the 'Railway King' who lost his vast fortune in 1849, and eerily anticipates John Sadleir, the banking swindler whose eventual come-uppance in 1856 destroyed the livings of large numbers of investors.[62] The avoidable cholera epidemic, the disastrous consequences of administrative failings relating to the conduct of the war in the Crimea and the spread of large-scale financial malfeasance: these are the sources of *Little Dorrit*'s political nihilism.

On 7 October 1854, less than two months after the final instalment of *Hard Times* had been published in *Household Words*, Dickens addressed the magazine's leading article 'To Working Men'.[63] Appealing to a particular social group rather than to 'the poor' more generally, it is significant that Dickens directly appeals to that body of men amongst whom large numbers had been seeking the franchise under the banner of Chartism. Dickens's leading article fully recognises the political agency of working(-class) men and pleads with them to take unspecified direct action to force the government to improve the living conditions of the poor. He urges upon working men that they need to 'beware of being led astray from their dearest interests, by high political authorities', and makes an attack, which will be repeated in *Little Dorrit*, on the incestuous and unproductive power struggles in Parliament that divert attention from the scandalous conditions in which the poor are forced to live. In what must be the most anti-paternalist piece of non-fiction writing ever to have been inked by Dickens, he urges upon working men that they must take the initiative and lead the middle classes in an uprising of 'the People'[64] against the inertia of government: 'The whole powerful middle class of this country, newly smitten with a sense of self-reproach . . . is ready to join them. The utmost power of the press is ready to assist them. But the movement, to be irresistible, must originate with themselves, the suffering many.'[65]

Dickens's millionairess friend, Angela Burdett Coutts, had clearly expressed consternation about the political tenor of this essay, which could after all be interpreted as proposing outright revolt amongst working men. Coutts's letter has not survived, but Dickens's response to it has, and in it he politely refuses to take up a more conciliatory stance. Having repeated the demand that the poor at the very least be given sanitary conditions in which to live, he reiterates that it must be the working people themselves who take action:

a worthless Government which is afraid of every little interest . . . will never do these things for them or pay the least sincere attention to them, until they are made election questions and the working-people unite to express their determination to have them, or to keep out of Parliament by every means in their power, every man who turns his back upon these first necessities.

Cholera itself he presents as an agent of revolution:

Let it come twice again, severely, – the people advancing all the while in the knowledge that, humanly speaking, it is, like Typhus Fever in the mass, a preventable disease – and you will see such a shake in this country as never was seen on Earth since Samson pulled the Temple down upon his head.[66]

The plight of London's poor is revisited in 'A Nightly Scene in London', in January 1856, shortly after *Little Dorrit* had begun to appear in monthly shilling parts. During one of his regular night walks, Dickens comes upon five women heaped up in the street outside a workhouse, unable to get shelter for the night. In a nightmarish metonymy of 'five bundles of rags', the women already have the appearance of the dead: 'five dead bodies taken out of graves, tied neck and heels, and covered with rags'.[67] Resembling Amy Dorrit's and Maggy's shelterless walk through the city at night, during which they encounter a 'poor lost creature' who utters 'a strange wild cry' as she disappears into the 'ghastly dying of the night',[68] Dickens's night-time encounter provokes from him an ominous warning of imminent social catastrophe: 'Five awful Sphinxes by the wayside, crying to every passer-by, "Stop and guess! What is to be the end of a state of society that leaves us here!"'[69] The ominous political note struck here will resonate too in the pages of Dickens's novel from 1855 to 1857.

In the spring and summer of 1855, as ideas for *Little Dorrit* began to form themselves in Dickens's mind, he followed up his 'Gone to the Dogs' *Household Words* essay with a further series of articles that sharply strike the satirical chord that would reverberate throughout the entire novel. Dickens had never, since his early days as a parliamentary reporter for the *Morning Chronicle*, had much faith in Parliament and the political process on which it was built, as is attested in his early satirical account of the corrupt machinations at the Eatanswill Election in the *Pickwick Papers*. But the catastrophic mismanagement of the Crimean War, which had led to huge numbers of unnecessary deaths amongst the British regiments, gave a new impetus and a much harder edge to his long-standing contempt for the parliamentary process. The first of his 1855 satires, 'A Thousand and One Humbugs', recalls William Hone's Regency parodies in its combining of children's nursery literature with savage political satire. In Dickens's parody of 'The Merchant and the Genie' from the *Thousand and One Nights* (also known as the *Arabian Nights*), Lord Aberdeen, who had been forced from office in February in 1855 as a direct consequence of the Crimean debacle, is figured as 'the Addled', whilst his replacement in government, Lord Palmerston, becomes 'The Grand Vizier Parmarstoon (or Twirling Weathercock)' who is 'stricken in years' (Palmerston was a septuagenarian).[70] Far from convinced that the change of government would effect beneficial changes in the country at large or in its conduct of the war, Dickens's view of the Aberdeen–Palmerston transition is expressed in a trading metaphor in 'Our Commission':

[It is] a peculiarity of the Public-Office trade that the wholesale dealers were constantly retiring from business, and having successors. A new dealer came into possession of the already adulterated stock, and he, in his turn, infused into it a fresh quantity of Noodledom from his own private store. Then, on his retirement, came another dealer who did the same.[71]

Little Dorrit's 'Circumlocution Office' is anticipated in 'Cheap Patriotism', an essay in which, in the persona of a superannuated civil servant, Dickens describes a series of government ministers who are incapable of seeing anything beyond the labyrinthine administrative overprovision of their own departments. The sarcastically named 'Sir Janus Jasper' (whose name suggests he could have walked straight out of one of William Hone's satires), reflects on his office:

that there are forty-seven clerks in the Department, distributed through four classes, A, B, C, and D. This Department must be consolidated, by the reduction of those forty-seven clerks to thirty-four – in other words, by the abolition of thirteen juniors – the substitution of two classes and a Remove for four – and the construction of an entirely new system of check, by double entry and countersign.[72]

In private, Dickens dropped the satirical mask. Writing to his friend, the actor Macready, in October 1855, Dickens despairs of the possibility of social and political progress:

What with teaching people to 'keep in their stations', what with bringing up the soul and body of the land to be a good child, or to go to the beershop, to go a-poaching and go to the devil; what with having no such thing as a middle class (for though we are perpetually bragging of it as our safety, it is nothing but a poor fringe on the mantle of the upper); what with flunkeyism, toadyism, letting the most contemptible lords come in for all manner of places, reading *The Court Circular* for the New Testament, I do reluctantly believe that the English people are habitually consenting parties to the miserable imbecility into which we have fallen, *and never will help themselves out of it* . . .

In No. 3 of my new book [*Little Dorrit*] I have been blowing off a little of indignant steam which would otherwise blow me up, and with God's leave I shall walk in the same all the days of my life; but I have no present political faith or hope – not a grain.[73]

'No. 3' of *Little Dorrit* included the satirically entitled chapter, 'Containing the whole Science of Government', and it is with this that my reading of the novel will begin.

LITTLE DORRIT, SATIRE AND ARISTOCRATIC GOVERNMENT

Arthur Clennam, having visited the father of his mother's seamstress in the Marshalsea debtors' gaol, decides to try to unravel William Dorrit's financial affairs so as to ascertain which of his creditors are detaining him in the prison. Instructed to find his way to the Circumlocution Office, the department of state that ought to be able to assist him, he is met, on numerous occasions, with an enervating concoction of official incompetence, indolence and downright insolence. As he witnesses the 'imposing coming of papers' and the 'imposing going of papers' to and from the office, he is breezily told that 'I can give you plenty of forms to fill up. Lots of 'em here. You can have a dozen if you like. But you'll never go on with it' (*Little Dorrit*, p. 130). The various clerks he encounters advise Arthur to 'keep on writing' (p. 131) but, lacking Mrs Jellyby's epistolary zeal, he eventually gives up on the attempt to elucidate the extent of William Dorrit's debt. He is again defeated when he takes up where Mr Meagles left off in trying to get a patent for Daniel Doyce's industrial invention; the dead-end of the Circumlocution Office (like the other central symbol of the novel – the gaol) acts as a metaphor for the political cul-de-sac in which Dickens deemed his country to be trapped in 1855.

The inertia and lack of action in the Circumlocution Office is inimical to Dickens's passion for movement and industry: 'Whatever was required to be done, the Circumlocution Office was beforehand with all the public departments in the art of perceiving – HOW NOT TO DO IT' (p. 119).[74] Hereditary patronage is another target of Dickens's satire. Sir Tite Barnacle, the reader is told, is the Minister of State for the Circumlocution Office: 'As a Barnacle he had his place, which was a snug thing enough; and as a Barnacle he had of course put in his son Barnacle Junior, in the office' (p. 112). Lord Decimus Barnacle, more senior still, uses his power of aristocratic patronage in a blatantly corrupt political manoeuvre, this time to install the near-imbecile Mr Sparkler, the stepson of the financier Mr Merdle, into high governmental office. In a novel in which Dickens's political antennae are once again alert to the inefficacy and corruption of aristocratic government, the Doodles and Coodles of *Bleak House* are here recast as the Barnacles and Stiltstalkings. Here as in the earlier novel the country is in the grip of a small group of talentless, titled nonentities who with astonishing contumely dismiss as 'mob' the entirety of the middle and lower classes of society:

It was agreed that the country (another word for the Barnacles and Stiltstalkings) wanted preserving, but how it came to want preserving was not clear. It was only clear that the question was all about John Barnacle, Augustus Stiltstalking, William Barnacle and Tudor Stiltstalking, Tom, Dick, or Harry Barnacle or Stiltstalking, because there was nobody else but mob. (p. 333)

Not only aristocratic government, the whole of (high) 'Society' is condemned in *Little Dorrit*. The insolence of the faded lower branches of the aristocracy towards the wealth-producing middle classes particularly enrages Dickens. Mrs Gowan, 'the relict of the deceased Commissioner of nothing particular' (p. 411), discusses her son's imminent engagement to Pet Meagles: 'He picked the people up at Rome, I think?' she enquires of an affronted Arthur Clennam, who replies:

'Excuse me, I doubt if I understand your expression.'
'Picked the people up,' said Mrs Gowan ... 'Came upon them. Found them out. Stumbled against them.'
'The people?'
'Yes. The Miggles people.' (p. 335)

One of the things that *Little Dorrit* satirically strips bare is the way in which the language of 'Society' conceals actual social and economic relations. The superficial, mannered verbal exchanges between the upper echelons are full of form without meaning; the polite grammar of high society semantically dislocates linguistic signifiers in order to permit a series of social fictions to be played out. William Dorrit is enabled, by his adoption of the genteel manners of high society, to act out the fiction of being a gentleman of leisure even as he is imprisoned in the Marshalsea; Mr Merdle is enabled – through the polite manners of others – to sustain the fiction of being the most important, richest man in Britain.

Dickens's attack on high society and aristocratic government in *Little Dorrit* is accompanied by a continued resistance to patriarchy and to paternalism.[75] In *Dombey and Son*, published in monthly shilling parts between 1846 and 1848, Dickens had proposed a critique of the patriarchal violence of commercial society, a violence shockingly funnelled into the deeply distressing moment in the novel when Dombey strikes out at his loving daughter, Florence, thinking her in league with his wife Edith, whom he has purchased in marriage much as he would have purchased any other item of property.[76] Dickens continued his assault on the patriarchal organisation of commercial (and in this novel industrial) society in *Hard Times*, in which Louisa Gradgrind is passed as a chattel between her father and Josiah Bounderby. In *Bleak House* and in *Little Dorrit*, though, neither commerce nor industry are the objects of Dickens's anti-patriarchal and anti-paternalist critique, but, rather, the aristocracy and its mimics, and grubbing rentiers such as Mr Casby.

William Dorrit is lampooned by Dickens for his posturing as a paternalistically benevolent gentleman, the 'Father of the Marshalsea': 'Perhaps you are aware – my daughter Amy may have mentioned – that I am Father of this place' (*Little Dorrit*, p. 97) he tells a bemused and embarrassed Arthur Clennam on his first visit to the debtors' gaol. Dickens's likening of Dorrit to Lord Chesterfield is particularly damning, given the author's loathing of the eighteenth-century aristocrat: 'He would have comported himself towards any Collegian who might have looked in to ask for advice, like a great moral Lord Chesterfield.' (p. 247)[77] Dorrit's patronage of the long-term workhouse inmate, Old Mr Nandy ('my old pensioner' (p. 392)), is similarly ridiculed:

Mr Dorrit was in the habit of receiving this old man [in his shabby room in the Marshalsea], as if the old man held of him in vassalage under some feudal tenure. He made little treats and tea for him, as if he came in with his homage from some outlying district where the tenantry were in a primitive state. (pp. 387–8)

William Dorrit's 'paternal entrance[s]' around the Marshalsea like a 'benignant father' (p. 242) are paralleled in the novel by the social and economic fiction played out in Mr Casby's stately perambulations around Bleeding Heart Yard. 'Patriarch was the name which many people delighted to give to him,' (p. 160) the reader is told. With his 'shining bald head . . . and the long grey hair at its sides and back, like floss silk or spun glass, which looked so very benevolent because it was never cut' (p. 160), Casby passes himself off as a species of Jarndyce: 'father to the orphan and a friend to the friendless' (p. 161). In reality he is a patriarch more in the bullying, pitiless Bounderby mode, his employee, Mr Pancks, being delegated to ventriloquise the actual social and economic relationship between Casby and the inhabitants of Bleeding Heart Yard. It is a relationship based on hard-nosed liberal economics:

'You're not going to keep open house for all the poor of London,' pursued Pancks. 'You're not going to lodge 'em for nothing . . .'
  Mr Casby shook his head, in placid benignant generality.
  'If a man takes a room of you at half-a-crown a week, and when the week comes round hasn't got the half-crown, you say to that man, Why have you got the room, then? If you haven't got the one thing, why have you got the other?' (p. 171)

Mr Meagles's paternalism is presented more benignly in the novel: the sensible, intelligent banker is instrumental in securing Arthur Clennam's release from the Marshalsea and restoring him to his position at 'Doyce and Clennam'. More ambivalent is the presentation of Mr Meagles's fostering and employment as a servant of the Foundling child, Tattycoram. For even though Dickens explicitly defends the Meagles's paternalistic embrace and rechristening of Harriet Beadle (her Foundling name), asserting that their 'motives and actions' had been 'perverted' (p. 349) by Miss Wade's ungenerous account of them, the older woman's accusations none the less have a certain spiteful power, whatever the novel's explicit stance:

'See there,' [Miss Wade says to Tattycoram]. 'Here is your patron, your master. He is willing to take you back, my dear, if you are sensible of the favor and choose to go. You can be, again, a foil to his pretty daughter, a slave to her pleasant wilfulness, and a toy in the house showing the goodness of the family. You can have your droll name again, playfully pointing you out and setting you apart . . .' (p. 348)

Here as elsewhere Dickens is in dialogue with paternalism even in its more benign forms. Mr Meagles is by no means the moral centre of the novel and is in many ways a rather pathetic figure, having lost one daughter in infancy and the other to the dubious cares of the indolent, impoverished son of the aristocracy, Henry Gowan. In so far as the novel has a moral centre, it is to be found in the ostensibly secondary figure of Daniel Doyce, the small-scale factory man and inventor of industrial machinery. Both Doyce in *Little Dorrit* and Rouncewell in *Bleak House* are kept to the margins of novels that remain at best uncertain that modern industry coupled with ethical social relationships can act as a curative to the systemic canker of the institutions of government and, in *Little Dorrit*, of international finance. It is Dickens's account of industry and international finance in *Little Dorrit* and, finally, his melodramatic response to both, that the last section of the chapter will explore.

INDUSTRY, INTERNATIONAL FINANCE AND THE END OF MELODRAMA

In June 1855, Dickens made a speech to the Administrative Reform Association in the Theatre Royal at Drury Lane. In it he expressed his frustration at the petty machinations and supine indifference to 'the People' of the House of Commons:

It is said that it is proposed by this association to exercise an influence, through the constituencies, on the House of Commons. I have not the least hesitation in saying that I have the smallest amount of faith in the House of Commons at present existing, and that I consider the exercise of such influence highly necessary to the welfare and honour of this country.[78]

Dickens went on in the same speech to complain of the alacrity with which Parliament passed 'bills which cramp and worry the people, and restrict their scant enjoyments', whilst hindering attempts to pass 'measures for their real interests'.[79] Although he was a keen supporter (and member) of the Administrative Reform Association, Dickens differed from it in one important respect. As Trey Philpotts has remarked, whilst the Administrative Reform Association identified ability with commercial expertise, Dickens (in *Little Dorrit* at least) identifies it with engineering prowess.[80] It is for this reason that it is Daniel Doyce, rather than Mr Meagles with his 'scoop and scales' or Mr Merdle with his imaginary millions, who represents Dickens's ideal in *Little Dorrit*.

Little Dorrit expresses distaste for the kind of commercial enterprise – nebulously defined shipping and trading – conducted by the Clennam family. Arthur Clennam describes his twenty-year exile in China as a process in which he had been 'Trained by main force; broken, not bent … always grinding in a mill I always hated' (p. 35). The novel's distaste for the type of international commerce with which the Clennam family has been involved is further expressed through the descriptions of the Clennam household as an unproductive, distorted mechanical environment: 'Morning, noon, and night, morning, noon, and night, each recurring with its same accompanying monotony, always the same reluctant return of the same sequences of machinery, like a dragging piece of clockwork' (p. 361). Flintwinch, Mrs Clennam's side-kick, a monstrous surrogate father figure in the Clennam home who tries to exert patriarchal control over Arthur on his return, is described as an 'eccentric mechanical force', 'like some screw machine' (p. 382). Flintwinch – as his very name suggests – is a deeply unpleasant piece of machinery in the service of what turns out to be a corrupt house.

By contrast, Daniel Doyce's branch of industry, with which Arthur Clennam decides to throw in his lot, is described in entirely positive terms. Daniel Doyce is 'a smith and an engineer', who many years ago has 'perfect[ed] an invention' (p. 134). Book 1, chapter 23, entitled 'Machinery in Motion' – an apotheosis of Dickens's enthusiasm for industry – celebrates Doyce's workshop in Bleeding Heart Yard with its 'benches, and vices, and tools, and straps, and wheels' (p. 284). Mr Pancks's essential integrity and good nature are indicated by repeated descriptions of him as an industrious and busy little piece of machinery. He is a 'steam tug' which 'steamed out of [its] little dock' (p. 170); he is 'always in a hurry' and takes 'in his victuals much as if he were coaling; with . . . a puff and a snort occasionally, as if he were nearly ready to steam away' (p. 173).

Doyce's workshop is located in Bleeding Heart Yard, which is also home to the sympathetically presented Plornish family. Kindly but poor, the Plornish family is a close relative to the Toodles in *Dombey and Son*, and to the Cratchits in *A Christmas Carol*. 'Bleeding Heart' is a massively suggestive name that simultaneously suggests the suffering of those who are being bled dry by the rentier Casby and an emotional warmth not to be found elsewhere in the novel. This is where the beating heart of the city is – in Doyce and Clennam's workshop and in the warmth and generosity of the Plornish household. These, for Dickens, are 'the People': a coming together of middle-class industrialists and the respectable working classes. It is not, though, an exclusive conception: John Baptist Cavalletto, the reformed small-time Italian smuggler who is badly injured by a mail carriage in the London streets, also finds a friendly home in the Yard and employment with Clennam. And Amy Dorrit's sympathetic response to a young prostitute in the street at night suggests that Dickens's embrace of 'the People' extends beyond the inhabitants of the Yard: in *Little Dorrit* and *Bleak House* as in *Oliver Twist*,

Dickens's sympathetic gaze reaches out to the inhabitants of London's streets.

But the endeavours and good intentions of the people of Bleeding Heart Yard have to contend with urban unemployment as well as with the heartless rentier class represented by Casby. ' "All such things as jobs," said Mrs Plornish [whose husband has spent time in the Marshalsea], "seems to me to have gone underground, they do indeed" ' (p. 152). Dickens is accurate in his depiction of a metropolitan environment with scant employment opportunities for the lower classes. Despite claims to the contrary, urban unemployment remained high throughout the first half of the nineteenth century.[81] 'Mr Plornish didn't know who to blame for it' (p. 158), we are told; and whilst Dickens certainly does have a clearer sense of who is responsible, the novel is not sanguine about the possibility of overcoming weak and corrupt government. In *Little Dorrit* as in *Bleak House* there is a sense that removing individual 'bad' or ineffectual people from various offices of state will not act as a social and political curative, and in this particular sense they differ from the radical satires of William Hone in Regency England. Trey Philpotts and Claudia Klavner have both argued that one should be careful, in reading *Little Dorrit* as an extended satire on the system of government and on international commerce (which it undoubtedly is), not to read it as a renunciation of political agency. *The Times* had averred in May 1855 (and Dickens would have concurred) that 'To lay all the blame on the system is not to escape from blaming individuals; it is to inculpate most heavily the living and the dead.'[82] Philpotts argues that: 'Blaming the system means blaming the individual politicians and military leaders at the head of the system, whom *The Times* (and Dickens) unfailingly associate with the aristocracy.'[83] But whilst Aberdeen and Palmerston loom large in Dickens's satirical journalism of the 1850s, and are clearly identifiable as individuals, the same is not true in *Little Dorrit*, in which there is no lampooning of individual parliamentarians. And the internal melodramatic pressure on the systemic account of social injustice in *Bleak House*, which I discussed earlier in the chapter, is weakened in *Little Dorrit*; it is this that makes it an altogether bleaker political novel.

Beyond the pages of *Little Dorrit*, Dickens did still believe, in the 1850s, that Parliament and its processes could be reformed: this is why he took to a political stage for the first time in his address to the Administrative Reform Association in 1855; this is why he became an active member of the association. As he put it in 'To Working Men' when complaining of the persistent failure of governments to improve the unsanitary living conditions of the poor: 'any working man of common intelligence knows perfectly well, that one session of parliament zealously devoted to this object, would secure its attainment'.[84]

He believed too that industry and its processes could be managed humanely and fairly: Mr Rouncewell in *Bleak House* and Daniel Doyce in *Little Dorrit* are more representative of Dickens's response to industry than *Hard Times*'s Bounderby. His savage satirical account of Bounderby comprises an honest acknowledgement that unscrupulous and uncaring factory owners did exist; but it is not typical of Dickens's general attitude towards manufacturing industry.

What is really menacing about *Little Dorrit* – and most intractable politically – is its representation of the spectre of international finance with its seemingly arbitrary and insubstantial systems of debt and credit that can wreck lives in an instant. Money and wealth, debt and credit in *Little Dorrit* are unstable, insubstantial categories.[85] Mr Merdle's 'worldwide commercial enterprise' is an altogether nebulous affair – 'nobody knew with the least precision what Mr Merdle's business was except that it was to coin money' (p. 417): only Doyce's machines and mechanical inventions, and Pancks's bodily mimicking of a steam tug, are as tangible and real as the poor people's 'unconditional money down' (p. 298).

Mr Pancks, surprised that Arthur Clennam is willing to act as guarantor for young Cavalletto when he applies to rent a lodging at Bleeding Heart Yard, comments laconically on the lack of creditworthiness amongst the Yard's tenants: '"As to being a reference," said Pancks ... "Look at your tenants down the Yard here. They'd all be references for one another, if you'd let 'em. What would be the good of letting 'em? It's no satisfaction to be done by two men instead of one"' (p. 292). If Pancks (and probably Clennam) is sure that Cavalletto is penniless, nobody knows how much money the great financier, Mr Merdle has got: his sumptuous lifestyle and massive business investments are entirely dependent on his being credited as a successful financier:

'I am told,' said Bishop magnate to Horse Guards, 'that Mr Merdle has made another enormous hit. They say a hundred thousand pounds.'
    Horseguards had heard two.
    Treasury had heard three. (p. 267)

'These Merdle enterprises', as the financier's mysterious business dealings become known (p. 607), are presented in the novel as a dangerous canker, an epidemic infection spreading every bit as quickly as the cholera in London in 1854. Even Mr Pancks, used to dealing in the certainties of 'unconditional money down' (p. 298), falls prey to the 'infatuation' (p. 608) with financial speculation: 'I've gone into it,' Pancks explains to the trusting Arthur Clennam. 'I've gone into it. I've made the calculations. I've worked it. They're safe and genuine' (p. 609). 'In these moments,' Dickens reflects, 'Pancks began to give out the dangerous infection' (p. 609).

Dickens's critique of corrupt international financiers in *Little Dorrit* – Merdle turns out to have been a swindler on a grand scale, and to be worse than penniless at the time of his death, despite the luxurious lifestyle that he has been sustaining – is lent force by being satirically mirrored by William Dorrit's chimerical relationship to debt and credit. Even as he is incarcerated in the Marshalsea gaol, Dorrit sustains the financial fiction that his daughters, Amy and Fanny, are ladies of leisure; and they collude with his insistence that their economic labour (Amy as a seamstress, Fanny as a member of a dancing troupe) should remain invisible to him. He sustains the fiction of his family's creditworthiness when, in a polite note to Arthur Clennam, he postures as a free agent in the liberal economy of mid-nineteenth century England. The note – apparently written in all earnestness, deluded as Dorrit is by the intensity of his personal financial fiction – requests that Clennam forward him £3 10s, explaining that he is 'most unexpectedly finding himself in the novel position of having been disappointed of a remittance from the City on which he had confidently counted' (p. 279). Even at his richest, Dorrit remains obsessed with maintaining 'the family credit' (p. 509). The novel presents it as a nebulous notion, one that all too soon melts into air when Dorrit breaks down mentally and imagines himself back at the Marshalsea. When he is revealed to have little in the way of 'family credit' after all, his newly found admirers quickly melt away, as does his very fortune.

William Dorrit's misperception/misrepresentation of his actual social and economic position whilst incarcerated in the Marshalsea is characteristic of the gaol's prisoners, many of whom 'had come to regard insolvency as the normal state of mankind, and the payment of debts as a disease that occasionally broke out' (p. 103). Dorrit's older children, Fanny and Tip, are similarly dislocated from the usual debt and credit systems of a liberal economy, being always 'ready to beg or borrow from the poorest, to eat of anybody's bread, spend anybody's money, drink from anybody's cup and break it afterwards' (p. 250). This is a fair description too of the great financier Merdle's *modus operandi* in the commercial market: both decline to play by the rules that govern liberal economics.

Little Dorrit is, though, far from a paean in praise of liberal economics, as Dickens's treatment of the hateful Casby, who squeezes every last penny out of the inhabitants of Bleeding Heart Yard, attests. Pancks's ventrilo-quising of Casby's position is not endorsed by the novel: 'Take all you can get and keep back all you can't be forced to give up. That's business' (p. 97). Arthur Clennam takes the opposite stance when he is bankrupted by Merdle's swindling speculations, willingly giving up all he has to his creditors, and protecting his partner, Daniel Doyce, as far as he is able. Nor are Casby's inferred orders to Pancks – '[don't] hear of anything but unconditional money down' (p. 298) – heeded by the poor in their trans-actions with one another. Highly valued in *Little Dorrit*, as in Dickens's other works of fiction, is the gift economy that exists amongst the poor: Mr and Mrs Plornish's corner shop in Bleeding Heart Yard with its provision of groceries on (probably never repaid) credit; the generous Mrs Chickenstalker's 'loaning' of provisions from her grocery shop in *The Chimes*; the kindly turnpike-man's proffering of bread and cheese to Oliver as he crawls, starving, towards London, and the old lady who likewise '[takes] pity on the poor orphan, and [gives] him what little she could afford – and more' (*Oliver Twist*, p. 59); the Vecks' housing of the unknown Ferns in *The Chimes*; Liz and Jenny's sheltering of Jo in *Bleak House*; the endless acts of generosity amongst the poor that are everywhere figured in Dickens's fiction are for him a highly valued informal sector of the debt and credit economy.

As well as valuing the informal gift economy of the poor, *Little Dorrit* also negotiates liberal economic theories of credit across social classes. The middle-class Arthur Clennam stands surety for the injured ex-smuggler, John Baptist Cavalletto, even though the Italian man's credit-rating in a liberal economic market is desperately low. Clennam knows little about him other than that he is a foreigner in a strange land in need of assistance, but his giving of credit to Cavalletto is amply repaid. Dickens's resistance to the cash-nexus in his negotiation of the debt and credit economy in *Little Dorrit* is, of course, thoroughly Carlylean; less so is his belief in the possibility of social and economic agency amongst the poor.

Notwithstanding Dickens's localised challenges to the cash-nexus in *Little Dorrit*, the small acts of economic kindness amongst the lower and the middle classes in the novel are dwarfed by the calamitous collapse of the Merdle house of cards. Once again it is the larger social and financial currents that politically preoccupy – and dismay – Dickens in *Little Dorrit*.

Whereas in *Bleak House* the strong melodramatic contours of the novel act as a form of internal resistance to its politically gloomy systemic critique of government and its institutions, in *Little Dorrit* the force of Dickens's melodramatic plotting and characterisation is greatly reduced. An aesthetic mode that since the early years of the century had been a powerful vehicle for social and political critique was by 1857 losing some of its force. Dickens's increasing conviction that endemic weakness and atrophy in government combined with the powerful machinations of corrupt international finance were the source of England's social ills, led to an attenuation of his belief in the power of individual agency upon which melodrama centrally depends.

That there are melodramatic ingredients in abundance in *Little Dorrit* is not in doubt. The secret, hidden will, Rigaud's criminal blackmailing and the convoluted anterior plot to the novel are all highly characteristic of the melodrama. The novel's two 'Books' – 'Book the First: Poverty' and 'Book the Second: Riches' – structurally mimic the sudden reversals of fortune characteristic of the melodramatic mode. But the force of the melodramatic contrast is weakened by the fact that the two conditions are shown to be remarkably alike: William Dorrit is as anxious about maintaining the 'family credit' when he is a rich man as he was when a prisoner in the Marshalsea, and just as afraid of being socially 'found out'. A sudden inheritance is no longer the social panacea that it was in traditional melodramas.

Dickens can be as subtle in his manipulation of the melodramatic mode in *Little Dorrit* as anywhere else in his fiction. As Clennam wanders through the city on the first evening of his return home, he is haunted by a damp bill poster, 'a wretched little bill, FOUND DROWNED, was weeping on the wet wall; he came at last to the house he sought' (*Little Dorrit*, p. 46). This small detail is a brilliantly economic gesture, on Dickens's part, towards the story of Arthur's mother that guiltily haunts the home he is about to return to. Arthur, like Esther Summerson, is of illegitimate birth, and as in *Bleak House* the plot of *Little Dorrit* hinges on the secret of his parentage. The huge difference, though, is that in *Little Dorrit* the melodramatic plotline no longer dominates the novel's narrative contours, nor does it give meaning to its themes. In *Oliver Twist*, the secret of Oliver's birth, and his rescue by the paternalistic Mr Brownlow, are utterly central to the novel's meanings and to its overall structure; and in *Bleak House* Dickens's cross-class account of women's oppression depends on the secret of Esther's birth. In *Little Dorrit* by contrast the melodramatic plot line is deeply buried, entombed even, in the novel's structure, to the extent that it is almost impossible to retrieve it. As Joel Brattin has put it, the plot 'pivots on the extraordinarily unlikely point that a man might plausibly leave a substantial legacy to his brother's son's lover's former friend's brother's younger daughter.'[86] This central melodramatic plotline is essentially redundant, a redundancy that is confirmed by Amy Dorrit's burning (using Clennam himself as her proxy) of the will that gave her £1,000: it is as irrelevant to her future with Clennam as it is to the much larger critique of government and international finance that is the novel's major concern.

Engulfed as it is within Dicken's large-scale satire on government and international finance, the domestic melodrama of the Clennam family secret and of Amy Dorrit's lost inheritance becomes dependent for its moral and aesthetic force on the villainous figure of Rigaud/Blandois. It is the blackmailing Blandois, with his pantomimically evil appearance ('When Mr Rigaud laughed ... His moustache went up under his nose, and his nose came down over his moustache, in a very sinister and cruel manner' (p. 20)) who forces Mrs Clennam's hand and leads her to disclose to Amy Dorrit the secret of the hidden will. Blandois also serves as a melodramatic embodiment of all the moral canker anatomised in the wider body of the country which he invades: the rottenness, torpor and imbecility of aristocratic government, the cruelty and dishonesty of those like Mrs Clennam who profess to live by religion, the idle viciousness and insolence of the lower aristocracy who parasitically live off sinecures, the moral squalor of city financiers, the heartlessness and dishonesty of land-lords, the brutality of husbands to their wives.

In a traditional melodrama, the death of Rigaud would signify the restoration of moral order. In *Little Dorrit*, though, it is no longer able to perform such a function. Rigaud is an embodiment of pure evil and his villainy is clearly written on his body, a traditional melodramatic device in one of the most bodily of aesthetic modes. But the evil that Dickens saw all around him in the middle of the 1850s was not always so tangible nor so easily purged, particularly in the field of international finance and spe-culation. If melodrama is, as Peter Brooks has put it, a 'drama of morality' which 'strives to find, to articulate, to demonstrate, to "prove" the existence of a moral universe', then one can see why it is coming under such pressure in a novel such as *Little Dorrit*.[87] The fear that corruption is not always visible and readily dealt with is everywhere present: the grubbing Casby's 'physiognomical expression seemed to teem with benignity' (p. 162); Mrs Clennam's Calvinistic sabbatarianism masks outright dishonesty, sexual jealousy and moral canker; while the glittering surface of the Merdles' social life covers up a chasm of misery and despair that will soon engulf all those who trusted in Merdle's chimerical 'Investments'. Pancks's determi-nation, when he cuts off Mr Casby's benevolently flowing locks, that his employer's immorality should be revealed through his bodily appearance is a melodramatic gesture of defiance that offers momentary comic relief to the poverty-stricken inhabitants of Bleeding Heart Yard. But the novel's close is able to offer little more than such localised reassurance.

Arthur Clennam is released from the debtors' prison at the end of *Little Dorrit*, with Mr Meagles paternalistically entering his prison cell like 'a sunbrowned and jolly father' (p. 854). Meagles is able partially to restore Clennam's fortunes as Jarndyce was able to set Allan Woodcourt on his feet in *Bleak House*; there *is* an albeit localised residual paternalistic structure of feeling in both novels, and it has its roots in the melodramatic mode that has underpinned much of the literary critical analysis of this study. But such a structure of feeling is eclipsed in *Little Dorrit* by the larger structures of decadent government and international finance. The Barnacles remain in office at the novel's close, and there is no sense that the death of Merdle signifies a purging of the corrupt world of the international money markets. The very low key of the novel's closing lines suggests as much, as Amy and Arthur 'Went down into a modest life of usefulness and happiness'. They disappear, supporting each other, diminutive figures descending 'down into the roaring streets' (p. 859). But nothing, structurally, has changed: the individual narratives of the domestic melodrama are swallowed up by the uproar of a decadent and decaying capital city.

The decay at the heart of Britain's capital city is symbolised in the novel by the dramatic physical collapse of the Clennam house. The collapse dramatically gestures not only towards the purging of the domestic misery of Arthur Clennam's upbringing, but also towards the end of the 'House of Clennam' as a commercial enterprise, the 'House' symbolising the rottenness of Britain's commercial culture in general. It may also nod towards the House of Commons that Dickens explicitly reviled in 1855 in his speech to the Administrative Reform Association. In *Bleak House* it is left to Lawrence Boythorn to express the opinion that the only possible proper action to be taken in relation to Chancery would be to put 'a mine below it on a busy day in term time, with . . . the whole blown to atoms with ten thousand hundredweight of gunpowder' (*Bleak House*, p. 144). In *Little Dorrit* the whole movement of the novel tends towards the collapse of 'the House' and all that it symbolises. As George Bernard Shaw put it: 'whilst you laugh at Sparkler or young Barnacle, Dickens is in deadly earnest: he means that both of them must go into the dustbin if England is to survive.'[88] For Shaw the political logic of the novel was such that it seemed to him to be 'a more seditious book than *Das Kapital*'.[89]

Some of the reviewers for the highbrow periodical press came to the same conclusion as Shaw about the political tenor of *Little Dorrit*. James

Fitzjames Stephen objected to Dickens's lack of respect for the aristocracy: 'We wish he had dealt as fairly and kindly with the upper classes of society as he has with the lower';[90] and even more to the novelist's wholesale attack on the House of Commons. Of the chapter 'Containing the Whole Science of Government' Fitzjames Stephen complains that: 'It means, if it means anything, that the result of the British constitution, of our boasted freedom, of parliamentary representation, and of all we possess, is to give us the worst government on the face of the earth – the clatter of a mill grinding no corn, the stroke of an engine drawing no water.'[91] Fitzjames Stephen feared the novel's political impact on the 'poor and uneducated [who] take such words in their natural and undiluted strength'.[92] Others simply dismissed the attack on government in the novel as weak: 'What can be weaker in itself, to say nothing of the total want of art in connecting it with the story, than the intended satire on the Circumlocution Office?'[93]

Dickens's readers begged to disagree. Bradbury and Evans had printed 32,000 copies of the first number of *Little Dorrit*, but the demand was such that two reprintings, of 3,000 each, were needed that same month, and by February 1856 40,000 copies had been sold.[94] By May 1856, circulation had outstripped that of all the earlier novels.[95] The discrepancy between the critical and the public reception of *Little Dorrit* would seem to suggest that the intelligentsia of the 1850s was somewhat out of step with the cultural interests and political concerns of 'the People' whom Dickens was addressing. It is utterly characteristic of the novelist himself that he was not.

Notes

INTRODUCTION: DICKENS AND THE POPULAR
RADICAL IMAGINATION

1. Letter to C. C. Felton, 2 March 1843, Pilgrim Letters, vol. III, p. 454.
2. Ibid., p. 453.
3. Dickens was characteristically swift to go to the assistance of Hone's family after his death: he arranged a gift of fifty pounds from the Royal Literary Fund for 'the Wife and Family of poor Hone of the Every day Book ... They are very poor and he was not a common man.' Letter to John Black, 15 November 1842, Pilgrim Letters, vol. III, p. 373.
4. Joss Marsh is one of only two other critics to have recognised the affinity between Hone and Dickens, casting the latter as 'the rich relation of the "seedy" bookseller'. Joss Marsh, *Word Crimes: Blasphemy, Culture and Literature in Nineteenth-Century England* (Chicago and London: Chicago University Press, 1998) p. 51. Hers is a suggestive but tantalisingly brief comparison. Sambudha Sen alludes to Hone and others as one of Dickens's radical forbears in '*Bleak House* and *Little Dorrit*: The Radical Heritage', *English Literary History* 65 (1998), 945–70. Ben Wilson's recent biography of Hone does no more than nod towards the Regency writer's relationship with Dickens. See Ben Wilson, *The Laughter of Triumph: William Hone and the Fight for the Free Press* (London: Faber and Faber, 2005).
5. 'The Works of Charles Dickens', *London and Westminster Review* 27 (July 1837), 194–215, 213. Lyn Pykett, *Charles Dickens* (Basingstoke: Palgrave, 2002), p. 39: '*Pickwick* is perhaps a belated version of the those picaresque novels by Henry Fielding and Tobias Smollett, which Dickens read so avidly in his childhood and youth.' Pykett also identifies the 'criminal' elements in *Oliver Twist* as having their source in Defoe, Smollett and Fielding (p. 45).
6. Sylvia Manning, *Dickens as Satirist* (New Haven: Yale University Press, 1971), p. 234.
7. On the occasion of Dickens's death Anthony Trollope reflected that 'he was a radical at heart, believing entirely in the people, writing for them, speaking for them, and always desirous to take their part'. Anthony Trollope, 'Charles Dickens', in Stephen Wall (ed.), *Charles Dickens: A Critical Anthology* (Harmondsworth: Penguin, 1970), p. 182. A little later, Louis Cazamian

characterised Dickens as a Christian Socialist ('Dickens's Christmas Philosophy', in Wall, *Charles Dickens*, pp. 240–3); whilst George Bernard Shaw averred that *Little Dorrit* was 'a more seditious book than *Das Kapital*' (Foreword to *Great Expectations* (1937), repr. in Dan H. Laurence and Martin Quinn (eds.), *Shaw on Dickens* (New York: Frederick Ongar Publishing, 1985), p. 51). T. A. Jackson's *Charles Dickens: The Progress of a Radical* (1937; repr. New York: International Publishers, 1987) was published in the same year as Shaw's Foreword to *Great Expectations*.

8. Humphry House, 'The Changing Scene' in *The Dickens World* (London: Oxford University Press, 1941).

9. John Lucas, 'Past and Present: *Bleak House* and *A Child's History of England*', in John Schad (ed.), *Dickens Refigured: Bodies, Desires, and Other Histories* (Manchester and New York: Manchester University Press, 1996), pp. 136–56.

10. Paul Schlicke, *Oxford Reader's Companion to Dickens* (Oxford and New York: Oxford University Press, 1999), p. 449; Stephen Gill, Introduction, in Charles Dickens, *Oliver Twist* (Oxford: Oxford University Press, 1999), p. vii.

11. Anthony Trollope, *The Warden* (London: Longman & Co., 1855), chapter 15. Review of the *Library Edition of Charles Dickens's Works, Saturday Review* 5 (8 May 1858), in Wall, *Charles Dickens*, p. 122.

12. Walter Bagehot, 'Charles Dickens', *National Review* 7 (October 1858), in Wall, *Charles Dickens*, p. 123.

13. Schlicke, *Oxford Reader's Companion to Dickens*, p. 488.

14. Richard D. Altick, *The English Common Reader: A Social History of the Mass Reading Public, 1800–1900* (1957; repr. Chicago and London: Chicago University Press, 1963), p. 2.

15. Arnold Kettle, 'Dickens and the Popular Tradition', in David Craig (ed.), *Marxists on Literature: An Anthology* (1975; repr. Harmondsworth: Penguin, 1977), pp. 214–44, p. 220.

16. Ibid., pp. 227–9.

17. See Patrick Joyce, *Visions of the People: Industrial England and the Question of Class, 1840–1914* (Cambridge: Cambridge University Press, 1991) and *Democratic Subjects: The Self and the Social in Nineteenth-Century England* (Cambridge: Cambridge University Press, 1994). See also Gareth Stedman Jones, 'The Language of Chartism', in James Epstein and Dorothy Thompson (eds.), *The Chartist Experience: Studies in Working-Class Radicalism and Culture, 1830–1860* (London: Macmillan, 1982), pp. 3–58.

18. *Hard Times* is unusual in the Dickens canon in its pitting of the lower and the middle classes against one another in the industrial dispute at the centre of the novel. For a full discussion see chapter 7.

19. Ian Haywood, *The Revolution in Popular Literature: Print, Politics and the People* (Cambridge: Cambridge University Press, 2004), p. 163.

20. E. P. Thompson, *The Making of the English Working Class* (1963; repr. Harmondsworth: Penguin, 1978), p. 693.

21. I use the lower case when using 'radical' adjectivally; and the upper case ('Radical') when using it as a noun.

22. Lord Byron to John Cam Hobhouse, 22 April 1820, *'Between Two Worlds':
Byron's Letters and Journals*, ed. Leslie A. Marchand (London: John Murray,
1977), p. 81. My thanks to Martin Dzelzainis for directing me to Byron's
account of the term 'radical'.

23. [Thomas Wooler], 'TRIAL EXTRAORDINARY: MR CANNING VERSUS THE
RADICAL REFORMERS', *Black Dwarf, A London Weekly Publication* 4:15 (19
April 1820), 537–40, 537–8. Canning was a Cabinet minister.

24. Charles Dickens, *Little Dorrit*, eds. Stephen Wall and Helen Small (1855–7;
repr. London and New York: Penguin Books, 2003), p. 224.

25. Peter Ackroyd, *Dickens* (1990; repr. London: Minerva, 1991), p. 774.

26. There is a growing body of scholarship pertaining to melodrama. I have found
the following particularly helpful: Michael R. Booth, *English Melodrama*
(London: Herbert Jenkins, 1965); Peter Brooks, *The Melodramatic
Imagination: Balzac, Henry James, and the Mode of Excess* (New Haven: Yale
University Press, 1976) and 'Melodrama, Body, Revolution' in J. Bratton,
J. Cook, C. Lethal (eds.), *Melodrama: Stage, Picture, Screen* (London: British
Film Institute, 1994), pp. 11–24; Anna Clark, *The Struggle for the Breeches:
Gender and the Making of the British Working Class* (London: Rivers Oram
Press, 1995); Elaine Hadley, *Melodramatic Tactics: Theatricalized Dissent
in the English Marketplace, 1800–1885* (Stanford: Stanford University
Press, 1995); H. Islemann, 'Radicalism in the Melodrama of the Early
Nineteenth Century', in M. Hay and A. Nikolopolon, *Melodrama:
The Cultural Emergence of a Genre* (New York: St Martin's Press,
1996); Thomas Laqueur, 'The Queen Caroline Affair: Politics as Art in the
Reign of George IV', *Journal of Modern History* 54 (1982), 417–66; Martin
Meisel, *Realisations: Narrative, Pictorial and Theatrical Arts in Nineteenth-
Century England* (Princeton: Princeton University Press, 1983);
Simon Shepherd and Peter Womack, *English Drama: A Cultural History*
(Oxford: Blackwell, 1996), chapter 8; Martha Vicinus, '"Helpless and
Unfriended": Nineteenth-Century Domestic Melodrama', *New Literary
History* 13 (1981), 127–43; Judith Walkowitz, *City of Dreadful Delight:
Narratives of Sexual Danger in Late-Victorian London* (London: Virago
Press, 1992).

27. Brooks, 'Melodrama, Body, Revolution', p. 15.

28. Ibid., p. 17.

29. Brooks, *Melodramatic Imagination*, pp. 12–13.

30. Letter to Henry Carey, 24 August 1854, Pilgrim Letters, vol. VII, p. 405.
Emphasis in original.

31. Harriet Martineau's series of short stories, *Illustrations of Political Economy*
(London: Charles Fox, 1834), had set out a Malthusian economic agenda,
whilst Benjamin Disraeli's *Sybil; or, The Two Nations* (1845; repr. London:
David Bryce, 1853) is a manifesto for his Tory 'Young England' group in
Parliament.

32. William Cobbett, 'To the Reformers of Leeds, Preston, and Botley,' *Cobbett's
Weekly Political Register*, 35:16 (21 Dec. 1819), 484–503, 501.

33. Quoted in Ackroyd, *Dickens*, p. 746.
34. 'Cobbett's Evening Post,' *Cobbett's Weekly Political Register* 35:19 (5 January 1820), 639–42, 639. Emphases in original.

CHAPTER 1: POPULAR RADICAL CULTURE IN REGENCY ENGLAND: PETERLOO AND THE QUEEN CAROLINE AFFAIR

1. For an account of the political context of 'Peterloo' see especially Thompson, *Making of the English Working Class*, pp. 46–60, 764–5, 779–80.
2. James Chandler, *England in 1819: The Politics of Literary Culture and the Case of Romantic Historicism* (Chicago: Chicago University Press, 1998), pp. 3, 16.
3. A number of eyewitness accounts of the catastrophe in St Peter's Field are available. See for example: *An Impartial Narrative of the Late Melancholy Occurrences in Manchester* (Liverpool: Henry Fisher, 1819) (this is an anthology of contemporary eyewitness accounts); Samuel Bamford, *Passages in the Life of a Radical* (1884; repr. Oxford: Oxford University Press, 1984), pp. 151–2; Francis Braton (ed.), *Three Accounts of Peterloo by Eyewitnesses: Bishop Stanley, Lord Hylton, and John Benjamin Smith* (Manchester: Manchester University Press, 1921). Robert Patten gives the number of dead as eleven: see Robert Patten, *George Cruikshank's Life, Times and Art, Vol. 1: 1792–1835* (London: Lutterworth Press, 1992), p. 153; Thompson, *Making of the English Working Class*, p. 754, also puts the number at eleven and notes that by the end of 1819, 421 claims had been made to the Peterloo Relief Commission for relief of injuries suffered, and that 'more than 100 of the injured were women or girls'.
4. Asa Briggs, *The Age of Improvement* (London: Longmans, Green, 1959), p. 208.
5. Thompson remarks that 'For a time, ultra-Radicals and moderates buried their differences in a protest movement with which many Whigs were willing to associate', *Making of the English Working Class*, p. 756.
6. R. or possibly G. Cruikshank, 'Massacre at St Peter's or "BRITONS STRIKE HOME"!!!', in Dorothy George, *Catalogue of Political and Personal Satires: Preserved in the Department of Prints and Drawings in the British Museum* (London: British Museum, 1935–54). The cartoon is catalogued as B. M. 13258.
7. Thomas Wooler, 'Manchester Tragedy – A Horrible Farce,' *Black Dwarf. A London Weekly Publication* 3:35 (1 September 1819), p. 565. Emphases in original.
8. Iain McCalman, *Radical Underworld: Prophets, Revolutionaries, and Pornographers in London, 1795–1840* (Oxford: Clarendon Press, 1993), p. 110.
9. James Epstein, *Radical Expression: Political Language, Ritual and Symbol in England, 1790–1850* (New York: Oxford University Press, 1994), p. 35.
10. Marcus Wood, *Radical Satire and Print Culture, 1790–1822* (Oxford: Clarendon Press, 1994), p. 3. Wood is one of a small but gradually enlarging group of literary and cultural historians to argue for the political and cultural

significance of the Hone/Cruikshank partnership in Regency England, and of Hone's work at this period in particular. See also Anne Bowden, 'William Hone's Political Journalism, 1815–1821', unpublished PhD thesis, University of Texas at Austin (1975); Epstein, *Radical Expression*; Frederick William Hackwood, *William Hone: His Life and Times* (London: T. Fisher Unwin, 1912); David A. Kent and D. R. Ewen, *Regency Radical: Selected Writings of William Hone* (Detroit: Wayne State University Press, 2003); Marsh, *Word Crimes*; Patten, *George Cruikshank's Life*, vol. I, 1992; Edgell Rickword, *Radical Squibs and Loyalist Ripostes* (Bath: Adams and Dart, 1971).

11. William Hone, *The Whole Proceedings Before the Coroner's Inquest at Oldham, &c. on the Body of John Lees, who Died of Sabre Wounds at Manchester, August the 16, 1819* (London: W. Hone, 1820).

12. For fuller publication details see Bowden, 'Hone's Political Journalism', pp. 243–4, 287; Thompson, *Making of the English Working Class*, p. 719; Hackwood, *William Hone*, p. 191. George Lawley, in his unpublished monograph on the Cruikshank/Hone connection, puts the figure lower, at forty editions in six months. See G. J. Lawley, *Cruikshank Album* (Berg Collection, New York Public Library), vol. II, p. 118. Richard Altick puts the figure at 100,000 sales: see Altick, *The English Common Reader*, p. 382. Kent and Ewen, *Regency Radical*, p. 20, also claim that the *Political House* was 'the single most popular pamphlet of political satire in the entire period (100,000 were printed).' Patten, *George Cruikshank's Life*, vol. I, p. 165, writes that 'at least 40 editions were exhausted in six months, and Hone had to apologise to customers for not fulfilling the orders promptly'.

13. Wood, *Radical Satire*, p. 215.

14. Patten, *George Cruikshank's Life*, vol. I, p. 157.

15. Wellington features on the frontispiece to the pamphlet; Robert Gifford, the Attorney General, figures in the sixth plate; Nadin, the much-hated and feared chief of police in Manchester in the seventh plate; the three government ministers figure in plate 10. In this plate (p. 48), Castlereagh is the horridly grinning figure in the middle; Canning is on his right and Sidmouth to the left.

16. *The Political House That Jack Built* (London: William Hone, 1819) reproduced in Edgell Rickword, *Radical Squibs and Loyalist Ripostes* (Bath: Adams and Dart, 1971), pp. 35–58, pp. 48–9. Emphases in original.

17. I am indebted to Marcus Wood's study, *Radical Satire*, chapter 5, for the identifications of Cruikshank's caricatures. Wood in turn was informed by Bowden, 'Hone's Political Journalism'.

18. McCalman, *Radical Underworld*, pp. 117, 123.

19. Patricia Anderson, *The Printed Image and the Transformation of Popular Culture* (Oxford: Oxford University Press, 1990), p. 36.

20. Anne Bowden appends a good range of such imitations to her PhD thesis. See Bowden, 'Hone's Political Journalism', Appendices III–XI, pp. 451–64.

21. *The Political House*, in Rickword, *Radical Squibs*, pp. 44–5. Emphasis in original.

22. In the original of 'The House That Jack Built' it is a priest:

> This is the priest all shaven and shorn
> That married the man all tattered and torn
> That kissed the maiden all forlorn
> That milked the cow with the crumpled horn
> That tossed the dog
> That worried the cat
> That killed the rat
> That ate the malt
> That lay in the house that Jack built.

23. One of many imitations can be found in *The Queen That Jack Found* (London: John Fairburn, 1820), p. 3. This shilling pamphlet is sometimes attributed to Hone, but Bowden lists it as an imitation. See Bowden, 'Hone's Political Journalism', Appendix VIII.
24. Royal Archives, 51382 9a)/18; quoted in Patten, *George Cruikshank's Life*, vol. I, p. 164.
25. Quotation from a Letter to 'Childs', 24 November 1819. In Lawley, *Cruikshank Album*, vol. II, p. 118.
26. Kent and Ewen, *Regency Radical*, p. 21, write that the Regent considered prosecution but was talked out of it by Lord Eldon and the Solicitor General. See also Patten, *George Cruikshank's Life*, vol. I, p. 165, who reflects that 'Another courtroom defeat would have been ruinous for the government.'
27. *The Political House*, pp. 46–7. Emphasis in original.
28. See footnote 22 for the original.
29. A letter from Lord Sidmouth to the Earl of Derby, dated 21 August 1819, requests that the Prince's thanks be passed on to the magistrates:

> My Lord, –
> Having laid before the Prince Regent the accounts transmitted to me from Manchester, of the proceedings at that place on Monday last; I have been commanded by his Royal Highness to request that you will express to the Magistrates of the County palatine of Lancaster, who attended on that day, the great satisfaction derived by his Royal Highness from their prompt, decisive, and efficient measures for the preservation of the public tranquillity.

> Included in *An Impartial Narrative*, p. 48.
30. *The Political House*, pp. 56, 58.
31. Marsh, *Word Crimes*, p. 7. William Hone, *The Late John Wilkes's Catechism of a Political Member* (London: W. Hone, 1817); *The Political Litany* (London: W. Hone, 1817); and *The Sinecurist's Creed* (London: W. Hone, 1817). Marsh gives a full account of the trials.
32. Owen Chadwick, *The Victorian Church*, 2 vols. (London: Adam and Charles Black, 1966), vol. I, p. 46.
33. Marsh, *Word Crimes*, pp. 19–20.

34. *Political House*, in Rickword, *Radical Squibs*, p. 58.
35. *The Queen That Jack Found*, plate 6. Emphasis in original. One of the many outrages on the popular public consciousness during the Queen Caroline Affair of 1820 was the deletion of her name from the Book of Common Prayer.
36. See Chadwick, *Victorian Church*, vol. I, pp. 24–47 for a discussion of the Reform Act and the Church.
37. Robert Patten identifies the original for Hone and Cruikshank's 'Clerical Magistrate' as Charles Wickstead Ethelstone of the Collegiate Church, Manchester, 'one of George Cruikshank's frequent targets' (*George Cruikshank's Life*, vol. I, p. 162).
38. *Who Killed Cock Robin? A Satirical Tragedy* (London: John Cahuac, 1819).
39. Ibid., p. 3.
40. Ibid., p. 3. Emphases in original. The first verse of the original nursery rhyme reads as follows:

> Who killed Cook Robin?
> I, said the Sparrow,
> With my bow and arrow,
> I killed Cook Robin.

41. Ibid., p. 16.
42. Ibid., p. 9. Emphases in original.
43. Ibid., p. 6. Emphases in original.
44. *The Old Black Cock and his Dunghill Advisers in Jeopardy; or, The Palace That Jack Built* (London: Effingham Wilson, 1820).
45. Ibid., p. 17. Emphasis in original.
46. See V. A. C. Gatrell, *The Hanging Tree: Execution and the English People, 1770–1868* (Oxford: Oxford University Press, 1994). See also chapter 2. The Shakespeare motto accompanying figure 6 is taken from *The Tempest*.
47. Many other pamphlets written and published in response to Peterloo could also have been included in my analysis, were more space available. Hone and Cruikshank's *A Slap at Slop and the Bridge Street Gang* (London: William Hone, 1821) especially merits attention; it has been examined at length and with admirable clarity by Marcus Wood. See Wood, *Radical Satire*, pp. 205–13.
48. For a succinct account of the Queen Caroline Affair, see J. Stevenson, 'The Queen Caroline Affair', in J. Stevenson (ed.), *London in the Age of Reform* (Oxford: Oxford University Press, 1997), pp. 141–5. The Prince even seems to have gone through a Catholic marriage ceremony with one of his mistresses, Maria Fitzherbert, before he married Caroline. See James Munson, *Maria Fitzherbert, the Secret Wife of George IV* (London: Robinson, 2001).
49. Ibid., p. 334.
50. *On the Return of Queen Caroline to England* (Broadside, Cost 3d, Undated). This and several other texts referred to here can be found in a scrapbook in the British Library: *Satirical Songs and Miscellaneous Papers Connected With the Trial of Queen Caroline* (Large Scrapbook, Undated, BL shelfmark 1852.b.9). This is item 1 in the scrapbook. Emphasis in original.

51. *The Woes of Caroline* (London: James Catnach, 1820).
52. *The Magic Lantern; Or, Green Bag Plot Laid Open; A Poem, By a Wild Irishwoman, Author of 'A House That Caroline Built'* (London: S. W. Fores, 1820).
53. Ibid., p. 9.
54. Ibid., p. 15.
55. For a full account of Cobbett's role in the Queen Caroline Affair see George Spater, *William Cobbett: The Poor Man's Friend*, 2 vols. (Cambridge: Cambridge University Press, 1982), vol. I, pp. 398–408. See also Patten, *George Cruikshank' Life*, vol. I, p. 173, and W. H. Wickwar, *The Struggle for the Freedom of the Press, 1819–1822* (London: George Allen and Unwin, 1928).
56. See Patten, *George Cruikshank's Life*, vol. I, p. 173.
57. 'Letter From the Queen to the King', *Cobbett's Weekly Political Register*, 37 (19 August 1820), 313–25, 314.
58. Ibid., p. 319.
59. Column reprinted from the *New Times* (15 August 1820), in *Cobbett's Weekly Political Register* 37 (19 August 1820), 326–7.
60. See, for example, the shilling pamphlet *The Green Bag, 'a dainty dish to set before the King'. A ballad of the nineteenth century* (London: J. Robins and Co., 1820).
61. *Cobbett's Weekly Political Register* 36 (1 July 1820), p. 1,110.
62. Epstein, *Radical Expression*, p. 38.
63. Thomas Wooler, 'A QUEEN TO BE DISPOSED OF – A WIFE TO BE GIVEN AWAY', *Black Dwarf* 4:23 (Wednesday 14 June 1820), 797.
64. *Caroline and the Italian Ragamuffins!!*, in *Satirical Songs and Miscellaneous Papers Connected With the Trial of Queen Caroline* (large Scrapbook, n. d., British Library shelfmark 1852.b.9), item 30. 'Derry Down' is a nickname, invented by Hone, for Lord Castlereagh. Emphases in original.
65. Samuel Bamford, *God Save the Queen, A NEW SONG*, in *Satirical Songs and Miscellaneous Papers*, item 24, verse 5. Emphasis in original.
66. 'THE KING the Avowed Enemy of THE QUEEN. A New ROYAL GAME OF CHESS, played for half-crown stakes. Invented by Philoi-D'Or, With an Engraving, Designed and Executed by Mr J. R. Cruikshank* (London: T. Dolby, 30 Holywell Street, 1820), Price One Shilling.' Other such mock adverts include 'New Inventions! **The Majocchi Mouthpiece; Or,** NON MI RICORDO WHISTLE', in *Satirical Songs and Miscellaneous Papers*, item 39; and 'This Day is published, Price One Shilling, A SPY UPON SPIES; Or, The Milan Chambermaid! Developing Certain Particulars of the Mysterious Contents Of the Green Bag. BY ONE OF THE PRINCIPAL SPIES. Now publishing, in Parts, Price Six-pence', in ibid., item 23.
67. *THE KING the Avowed Enemy of THE QUEEN*, p. 2.
68. Marcus Wood has written extensively about mock adverts in the radical Regency press. See Wood, *Radical Satire*, passim.
69. Ibid., pp. 177. Wood remarks that forty-four editions were produced in the first four months after the pamphlet's release in 1820, and that two French editions were also published (p. 172).

70. William Hone, *The Queen's Matrimonial Ladder, A National Toy, With Fourteen Step Scenes; and Illustrations in Verse, With Eighteen Other Cuts* (London: Printed by and for William Hone, 1820), in Rickword, *Radical Squibs*, pp. 167–85.

71. Wood, *Radical Satire*, p. 172.

72. For an account of Cruikshank's role in the conception of *Oliver Twist* see Robert Patten, *George Cruikshank's Life, Times and Art*, vol. II: *1835–1878* (Cambridge: Lutterworth Press, 1996), pp. 36, 50, 51–3.

73. *Queen's Matrimonial Ladder*, in Rickword, *Radical Squibs*, p. 169.

74. Ibid., p. 177.

75. Ibid. Emphasis in original.

76. Patten, *George Cruikshank's Life*, vol. I, p. 438, n. 2, identifies George IV's three mistresses as Lady Hertford, Mrs Fitzherbert and Lady Jersey.

77. *Queen's Matrimonial Ladder*, in Rickword, *Radical Squibs*, p. 175.

78. Thomas Laqueur, 'The Queen Caroline Affair: Politics as Art in the Reign of George IV', *Journal of Modern History* 54 (1982), 417–66; McCalman, *Radical Underworld*, pp. 162, 176.

79. Clark, *Struggle for the Breeches*, p. 164.

80. It is an historiography also adopted by James Chandler in *England in 1819*.

CHAPTER 2: DICKENS AND NINETEENTH-CENTURY SHOW TRIALS

1. V. A. C. Gatrell comments that 'The crowd outside Newgate was bigger than any since the hangings of Holloway and Haggerton in 1808, it was said (forty-five thousand attended then)' (Gatrell, *The Hanging Tree*, p. 355).

2. Hackwood, *William Hone*, pp. 99–101.

3. Patten, *George Cruikshank's Life* vol. I, p. 124.

4. Gatrell, *Hanging Tree*, pp. 355–6.

5. Hackwood, *William Hone*, p. 101. Hone and Cruikshank's pamphlet was entitled *La Pie Voleuse. The Narrative of the Magpie; Or the Maid of the Palaiseau. Being the History of the Maid and the Magpie. Founded upon the Circumstances of an Unfortunate Female having been unjustly Sentenced to Death, on Strong Presumptive Evidence*, with a Preface, and Curious Anecdotes (London: Printed for William Hone, 1816). The pamphlet assuaged Hone's financial position, but was of course too late materially to assist Eliza Fenning.

6. See chapter 3 for an account of Dickens's popular theatrical borrowings in *Oliver Twist* and *The Pickwick Papers*. Hone's *La Pie Voleuse* was based on a French melodrama translated and adapted for the English stage by Pocock. See Patten, *George Cruikshank's Life*, vol. I, p. 125.

7. See for example John Fairburn, *The Case of Eliza Fenning, and Elizabeth Fenning's Own Narrative ... being a continuation of Fairburn's edition of the affecting case of Eliza Fenning* (1815); T. W. W[ansborough], *An Authentic Narrative of the Conduct of Eliza Fenning ... till her execution ... by the gentleman who attended her* (1815); *The Fullest Report Published on the Trial of*

Eliza Fenning . . . with . . . particulars . . . respecting . . . her execution, etc. (1815). Citations taken from Gatrell, *Hanging Tree*, p. 366, n. 46, no publication details given. Gatrell notes that the British Library copies of these and of Hone's pamphlet were destroyed in World War Two; I have been unable to locate any other extant copies.

8. Gatrell, *Hanging Tree*, p. 356.
9. Ibid., p. 363. Hunt's article is in the *Examiner*, 13 August 1815.
10. Letter to Walter Thornbury, 22 December 1866, in Pilgrim Letters, vol. XI, pp. 287–8. The essay on Fenning was published as 'Old Stories Re-Told', *All The Year Round* 18 (13 July 1867), 66.
11. Letter to W. H. Wills, 28 June 1867, in Pilgrim Letters, vol. XI, p. 384.
12. Ackroyd, *Dickens*, p. 127.
13. Ibid., pp. 123 and 135.
14. Letter to Henry Nethersole, 13 November [1834], in Pilgrim Letters, vol. I, p. 43.
15. Ackroyd, *Dickens*, pp. 311 and 776–7.
16. Ibid., pp. 118–19, 128, 148, 149.
17. For the theatricality of political trials see for example Julia Swindells, *Glorious Causes: The Grand Theatre of Political Change, 1789 to 1833* (Oxford: Oxford University Press, 2001).
18. Douglas Jerrold, *Black-Ey'd Susan* (1829), in George Rowell (ed.), *Nineteenth-Century Plays*, 2nd edn (Oxford: Oxford University Press, 1972), pp. 1–43; George Dibdin Pitt, *The String of Pearls (Sweeney Todd)* (1847), in Michael Kilgarriff (ed.), *The Golden Age of Melodrama* (London: Wolfe Publishing, 1974), pp. 243–62; Dion Boucicault, *The Colleen Bawn* (1860), in Rowell (ed.), Nineteenth Century Plays, pp. 175–231; Leopold Lewis, *The Bells* (1871), in ibid., pp. 469–502.
19. See for example Elizabeth Gaskell, *Mary Barton* (London: Chapman and Hall, 1848) and George Eliot, *Adam Bede* (London: Blackwood, 1859).
20. Gatrell, *Hanging Tree*, p. 169. On ballads and broadsides see also Leslie Sheppard, *The History of Street Literature* (Newton Abbot: David and Charles, 1973) and Robert Collison, *The Story of Street Literature* (London: Dent, 1973).
21. Dickens wrote two letters to *The Times* in 1849 deploring the behaviour of the crowd of spectators at the Mannings' execution. See Pilgrim Letters, vol. V, pp. 644–5, 651. Philip Collins documents Dickens's intense interest in the Mannings' case, in *Dickens and Crime* (1962; repr. Bloomington: Indiana University Press, 1968). Dickens followed the reporting of the Palmer trial at the Old Bailey in 1849 and wrote a long essay about it in *Household Words*, 14 June 1856. See 'The Demeanour of Murderers', *Household Words* 13 (14 June 1856), 505–7, in Michael Slater (ed.), *Dickens' Journalism*, vol. III: *'Gone Astray' and Other Papers From* Household Words, 1851–59 (London: J. M. Dent, 1998), pp. 377–83.
22. Charles Dickens, 'Lying Awake,' *Household Words* 6 (30 October 1852), 145–8, in Michael Slater, *Dickens' Journalism*, vol. III, pp. 88–95.

23. John Johnson Broadsides Collection, Bodleian Library, Oxford: 'Murders and Executions', Folder 1: 'Sentences of the Prisoners in Newcastle, Morpeth and Durham', February 1833; and 'A Calendar of the Prisoners In the Gaols of Durham, Newcastle, and Morpeth', 19 March 1836. Philip Horne has remarked that between 1801 and 1835, 103 death-sentences were passed on children under the age of fourteen for theft (none, though, were carried out). Philip Horne, Introduction, in *Oliver Twist*, ed. Philip Horne (1837–9; repr. London and New York: Penguin Books, 2003), p. xv.

24. See Epstein, *Radical Expression*, pp. 30–2.

25. See J. H. Stonehouse, *Catalogue of the Library of Charles Dickens from Gad's Hill [. . .]* (London: Piccadilly Fountain Press, 1935), pp. 113 and 7 for details of Dickens's ownership of the *State Trials* and of the *Annual Register* (1758–1860). Andrew Sanders has done important work in bringing to our attention the extent to which Dickens drew on the *Annual Register* in his novels. See Andrew Sanders, *The Companion to A Tale of Two Cities* (1998; repr. Robertsbridge Helm Information, 2002).

26. Epstein, *Radical Expression*, p. 32.

27. Ibid., p. 34.

28. For further details see Wood, *Radical Satire*, chapter 3. Other Regency trial parodies include: Thomas Wooler's 'High Treason: Examination of the Treasonable Potatoes', *Black Dwarf. A Weekly London Publication* 1:6 (15 February 1817), 59–62; his 'TRIAL EXTRAORDINARY'; and his 'The State Trials contrasted with the Manchester No Trials!' *Black Dwarf* 4:16 (26 April 1820), 541–66; William Hone's *Another Ministerial Defeat! The Trial of the Dog, for Biting the Noble Lord* (London: William Hone, 1817); and his *Non Mi Ricordo!* (London: William Hone, 1820), in Rickword, *Radical Squibs*, pp. 199–200. The first and the last of these will be examined later in the chapter.

29. [Thomas Wooler?], *A Verbatim Report of the Two Trials of Mr T. J. Wooler, Editor of the Black Dwarf, for Alledged* [sic] *Libels, Before Mr Justice Abbott, and a Special Jury, On Thursday, June 5, 1817. Taken in Short Hand by an Eminent Writer and Revised by T. J. Wooler* (London: T. J. Wooler, 1817), p. 96. This is a separately published pamphlet, no price indicated.

30. Ibid., p. 101.

31. On the history of disruptive laughter see Joseph M. Butwin, 'Seditious Laughter', *Radical History Review* 18 (1978), 17–34; Richard Hendrix, 'Popular Humor and "The Black Dwarf"', *Journal of British Studies* 16 (1976), 108–28; and Keith Thomas, 'The Place of Laughter in Tudor and Stuart England', *TLS* (21 January 1977), 77–81.

32. Mikhail Bakhtin, *Rabelais and His World*, trans. H. Iswolsky (Cambridge, Mass.: MIT Press, 1968), pp. 71–2.

33. Ibid., p. 92. Emphasis in original.

34. Kent and Ewen, *Regency Radical*, 'Introduction', p. 17.

35. Ibid.

36. Patten, *George Cruikshank's Life*, vol. I, pp. 130–1.

37. The three parodies were published in London by Hone himself in January and February of 1817.
38. Marsh, *Word Crimes*, p. 32.
39. William Hone, *The Three Trials of William Hone* (London: W. Hone, 1818), Second Trial, p. 4.
40. *The Third Trial of William Hone* (London: W. Hone, 1818), in Kent and Ewen, *Regency Radical*, p. 184.
41. Kent and Ewen, *Regency Radical*, p. 19.
42. Marsh, *Word Crimes*, p. 31.
43. Kent and Ewen, *Regency Radical*, p. 20.
44. Harriet Martineau, *The History of England During the Thirty Years' Peace 1816–1846*, 2 vols. (London: Charles Knight, 1850), vol. I, p. 44. Quoted in Ewen and Kent, *Regency Radical*, p. 10.
45. Thomas Wooler, Lead Article, *Black Dwarf* 1:50 (24 December, 1817), 1.
46. Epstein, *Radical Expression*, p. 32.
47. See Jan-Melissa Schramm, *Testimony and Advocacy in Victorian Law, Literature and Theology* (Cambridge and New York: Cambridge University Press, 2000), pp. 102 and 112 for the effects of the Prisoners' Counsel Act of 1836. Given that the novel would seem to be set in 1827, Dickens is here as elsewhere in his first foray into fiction guilty of anachronism.
48. John Bowen has written very illuminatingly, and more broadly, of the disruptively carnivalesque qualities of *The Pickwick Papers*. John Bowen, *Other Dickens* (Oxford: Oxford University Press, 2000), p. 79: '*Pickwick Papers* ... creates ... a fictional economy ... of impulse, excess, and misdirection. The novel is concerned to create, in a political culture that identifies festivity and celebration with Tory politics and the corruption of the democratic process, a very different festive culture. Many of the spaces of the novel, like the inn-yard in which Sam meets Pickwick for the first time, have the qualities of the marketplace or agora, where we find "a commingling of categories usually kept opposed: centre and periphery, inside and outside, stranger and local, commerce and festivity, high and low." There is a similarly transgressional mingling in the book's excessive and exorbitant plotting and characterization, its impure and distended fictional body, its generous and casual inclusiveness, its odd protuberances and strange holes.' Bowen quotes Peter Stallybrass and Allon White, *The Politics and Poetics of Transgression* (London: Methuen, 1986), p. 27.
49. Charles Dickens, *The Posthumous Papers of the Pickwick Club* ed. Mark Wormald (1836–7; repr. London and New York: Penguin Books, 2003), p. 447. Subsequent references will be included in parentheses in the main text.
50. Mikhail Bakhtin, *Problems of Dostoevsky's Poetics*, ed. and trans. Caryl Emerson (Minnesota: University of Minneapolis Press, 1984), p. 123.
51. Ginger Frost, in *Promises Broken: Courtship, Class and Gender in Victorian England* (Charlottesville and London: University of Virginia Press, 1995), notes that '[Bardell and Pickwick] went on to have an even bigger influence on legal writers

and practitioners [than on the general public]. Two legal volumes used Bardell v Pickwick as an example in their discussions of the law of hearsay. Barristers sometimes brought up the fictional case in the middle of real ones' (p. 2).

52. The British Library catalogue lists twenty-six editions in the first year of publication.

53. For full details of the Queen Caroline Affair see chapter 1.

54. William Hone, *Non Mi Ricordo!* (London: W. Hone, 1820). Emphases in original.

55. J. B. Buckstone, *Second Thoughts. A Comedy, in Two Acts* (London: William Strange, 1835).

56. 'Court of Common Plea. Norton v Melbourne', *Morning Chronicle* (23 June 1836), 2–5.

57. Ibid, p. 2, col. 2.

58. It is a critical orthodoxy that in *The Pickwick Papers* melodrama is confined to the interpolated tales and to the Fleet Prison scenes.

59. Wooler, 'High Treason', p. 60.

60. Dickens, *Oliver Twist*, p. 364. Emphasis in original. Subsequent references will be included in parentheses in the main text.

61. Charles Dickens, *Bleak House*, ed. Nicola Bradbury (1853; repr. London and New York: Penguin Books, 2003), p. 177. Subsequent references will be included in parentheses in the main text.

62. J. Ewing Ritchie, *The Night Side of London* (London: Tinsley Bros., 1858), p. 110. Ritchie's account of the general moral and cultural tenor of the Judge and Jury clubs has been repeated by Harold Scott, *The Early Doors: Origins of the Music Hall* (London: Nicholson and Watson, 1946) and Christopher Pulling, *They Were Singing* (London: George G. Harrap and Co., 1952). Judge and Jury clubs were established in London in the Garrick's Head in Bow Street by Renton Nicholson in 1841, and 'remained a feature of London night life until the seventies' (Pulling, *They Were Singing*, p. 173). My thanks to Janice Norwood for first alerting me to the likely connection between Judge and Jury clubs and the re-enactment of Nemo's inquest in the Sol's Arms.

63. Ritchie, *Night Side*, pp. 107–13.

64. Charles Dickens, *Great Expectations*, ed. David Trotter (1860; repr. London and New York: Penguin, 2003), pp. 165–6. Subsequent references will be included in parentheses in the main text.

65. Schramm, *Testimony and Advocacy*, pp. 115–16.

66. See, for example, Richard Maxwell, Introduction to *A Tale of Two Cities*, ed. Richard Maxwell (1859; repr. London and New York: Penguin Books, 2003), p. xiii.

67. Dickens, *A Tale of Two Cities*, p. 5. Subsequent references will be included in parentheses in the main text.

68. Gatrell, *The Hanging Tree*, p. 359.

69. I am indebted to Michael Gregory for my understanding of Dickens's manipulation of indirect and direct speech in the Old Bailey scene. See Michael Gregory, 'Old Bailey Speech in "A Tale of Two Cities"', *Review of English Literature* 6 (1965), 42–55.

70. For the original text of the trial see www.oldbaileyonline.org/html_units/ 1780s/t17810711-1.html Accessed 12 February 2005. For an account of the trial of Francis Henry De la Motte see Harvey Peter Sucksmith and Paul Davies, 'The Making of the Old Bailey Trial Scene in *A Tale of Two Cities*', *Dickensian* 100:1 (2004), 23–35.

71. Gregory, 'Old Bailey Speech', p. 47.

72. [Charles Dickens], 'A Detective Police Party', *Household Words* 1 (27 July and 10 August 1850), 409–14 and 457–60, in Michael Slater (ed.), *Dickens' Journalism*, vol. II: *'The Amusements of the People' and Other Papers, Reports, Essays and Reviews, 1834–51* (London: J. M. Dent, 1996), pp. 265–82.

73. Ackroyd, *Dickens*, pp. 499, 704.

74. Thanks to Andrew Sanders for pointing this out to me.

75. See for example a short item on 'Ernest Jones' in *The Red Republican*, 20 July 1850, p. 1, col. 3.

76. See Sanders, *The Companion to A Tale of Two Cities*, p. 155.

77. [Charles Dickens], 'Judicial Special Pleading', *The Examiner* (31 December 1848), in Slater, *Dickens' Journalism*, vol. II, pp. 137–42.

78. Marc Baer, *Theatre and Disorder in Late Georgian London* (Oxford: Clarendon Press, 1992), p. 260.

CHAPTER 3: DICKENS, POPULAR CULTURE AND POPULAR POLITICS
IN THE 1830S: *OLIVER TWIST*

1. W. M. Thackeray, 'Catherine', *Fraser's Magazine* 21 (February 1840), 211; in Wall (ed.) *Charles Dickens*, pp. 52–3. *Jack Sheppard*, by Harrison Ainsworth, was serialised in *Bentley's Miscellany* immediately after *Oliver Twist*.

2. Richard P. Fulkerson, '*Oliver Twist* in the Victorian Theatre', *The Dickensian* 70:3 (May 1974), 83–95, 84. Fulkerson's is a full and helpful outline of the novel's contemporary theatrical history.

3. Philip Horne, Introduction to *Oliver Twist*, p. xxxii.

4. [Thomas Peckett Prest], *Life and History of Oliver Twiss, Edited by 'Bos'* (London: Edward Lloyd, 1838–9); *Oliver Twiss, The Workhouse Boy, Edited by Poz* (London: James Pattie, 1838).

5. Gill, Introduction to *Oliver Twist*, p. vii. The novel was initially serialised in *Bentley's Miscellany* from February 1837 to April 1839.

6. Juliet John, 'Twisting the Newgate Tale: Popular Culture, Pleasure and the Politics of Genre', in her *Dickens's Villains: Melodrama, Character, Popular Culture* (Oxford and New York: Oxford University Press, 2001), pp. 122–40. See also Keith Hollingsworth, *The Newgate Novel, 1830–1847: Bulwer, Ainsworth, Dickens and Thackeray* (Detroit: Wayne State University Press, 1963).

7. William Hone, *The Power of Conscience Exemplified in the Genuine and Extraordinary Confession of Thomas Bedworth; Delivered to One of the Principal Officers of Newgate, the Night Before his Execution, on September 18,*

1815, for the Murder of Elizabeth Beesmore, in Drury Lane (London: William Hone, 1815). Other such commercially driven publications include his *Circumstantial Report of the Extraordinary Evidence and Proceedings Before the Coroner's Inquest, on the Body of Edward Vyse, who, on Tuesday Evening, March 7, 1815, was Shot Dead from the Parlour Windows of the House of the Hon. Frederick Robinson, M. P., in Old Burlington Street* (London: William Hone, 1815) and *The Extraordinary Trial of Capt. Geo. Harrower, at the Old Bailey, Feb. 17, 1816, on an Indictment for Marrying the Daughter of Paul Giblet, the Butcher, his Former Wife being Alive, a Lunatic in India* (London: W. Hone, 1816). Unfortunately I do not have circulation figures for *The Power of Conscience*.

8. Patten, *George Cruikshank's Life*, vol. I, p. 124. Unfortunately this frontispiece is missing from the British Library's copy of Hone's pamphlet. It would have been interesting to see Cruikshank's precursive illustration of the murder of Nancy.

9. Cruikshank's letter to *The Times* of 30 December 1871 claims that Oliver's character and story were his own idea.

10. Blanchard Jerrold, *Life of Gustave Doré*, vol. I (London: W. H. Allen, 1891), pp. 211–12; quoted in Patten, *George Cruikshank's Life*, vol. II, p. 36.

11. Henry James, *A Small Boy and Others* (New York: Charles Scribner's Sons, 1913), p. 120; quoted in Patten, *George Cruikshank's Life*, vol. II, p. 50.

12. Richard Ford, Review of *Oliver Twist*, *Quarterly Review* 64 (June 1839), 83–102, 101–2.

13. Hone, *Power of Conscience*, p. 9. Subsequent page references will be included in parentheses in the main text.

14. See, for example, the following, all from the 'Murders and Executions Broadsides' [Large Blue File], John Johnson Collection, Bodleian Library, Oxford: *Life, Trial, Sentence and Execution of Robert Davis, For the Murder of His Wife at Ball's Pond, Islington* (n.d); *An Account of the Cruel and Barbarous Murder of Mary Baker Supposed by Matthew Welch (with whom she lived in Adultery) in Drury Lane, London, early on Monday Morning, June 21, 1813; Trial, Conviction and Execution of Samuel Fallows, aged 24 years, On Friday, the 14th Day of April, 1823, At Chester, for the Wilful Murder of Betty Shawcross, his Sweetheart, near Stockport*; *The Trial of Corder, For the Murder of Maria Marten, at Polstead, Suffolk* [1828]; *Trial and Sentence of Thomas Drory For the Murder of Jael Denny at Doddinghurst* [c.1850]. The Maria Marten murder became firmly embedded in popular culture with many stage versions, usually known as *The Red Barn*.

15. Christopher Herbert, 'Rat Worship and Taboo in Mayhew's London', *Representations* 23 (Summer 1988), 1–24, 2. My thanks to Anne Schwan for bringing Herbert's work to my attention.

16. From Queen Victoria's Diary, 7 April 1839, in Philip Collins (ed.), *Dickens: The Critical Heritage* (London: Routledge and Kegan Paul, 1971), p. 44.

17. Quoted in Philip Collins (ed.), *Sikes and Nancy and Other Public Readings* (Oxford: Oxford University Press, 1983), p. 230.

18. Ibid., pp. 230–1.

19. The more familiar precedent is of course Bunyan's *Pilgrim's Progress*, of which Dickens owned a copy.

20. Ackroyd, *Dickens*, p. 228. One such is *Robert Blincoe's Memoir*, a tale of a workhouse orphan that Richard Carlile published in his newspaper *The Lion* in 1828. John Waller's assertion that Blincoe was 'the real Oliver Twist' is somewhat overstated, given that such orphan tales were in plentiful supply and it is unclear whether Dickens was familiar with it. See John Waller, *The Real Oliver Twist* (Cambridge: Icon Books, 2005).
    Certainly Dickens had, as Ackroyd comments, 'read autobiographies that emphasise the miseries and privations of childhood' (Ackroyd gives as an example Johnson's *Life of Richard Savage*), p. 228. See also Laura Peters, 'Perilous Adventures: Dickens and Popular Orphan Adventure Narratives', *Dickensian* 94:3 (1998), 172–83.

21. Pykett, *Charles Dickens*, p. 48.

22. I am indebted to Katherine Newey's essay, which first drew to my attention the fact that *The Climbing Boy* and *Oliver Twist* share the 'lost boy plot'; in perusing the play I have found a whole host of other remarkable similarities. See her 'Climbing Boys and Factory Girls: Popular Melodramas of Working Life', *Journal of Victorian Culture* 5:1 (2000), 28–44.

23. Richard Brinsley Peake, *The Climbing Boy; or, The Little Sweep* (1832; London: Dick's Standard Plays, No. 675, 1885), Act I, p. 6. All further references to this text will be included in parentheses in the main body of the text.

24. Newey, 'Climbing Boys', p. 39, p. 43 n. 54. [Charles Dickens], 'The First of May' (31 May 1836), in Michael Slater (ed.), *Dickens' Journalism*, vol. I: *Sketches By Boz And Other Early Papers, 1833–39* (London: J. M. Dent, 1994), pp. 168–75.

25. Newey, 'Climbing Boys', p. 39.

26. See Letter to Miss Austin, ?6 April 1833, in Pilgrim Letters, vol. I, p. 18, n. 3; Letter to Miss Fanny Kelly, 7 December 1845, in Pilgrim Letters, vol. IV, p. 448, n. 4; Letter to Thomas Beard, 1 January 1846, in ibid., p. 462, n. 3; Letter to R. B. Peake, 2 July 1847, in Pilgrim Letters, vol. V, p. 110; and Letter to W. C. Macready, 7 October 1847, in ibid., p. 171.

27. Ackroyd, *Dickens*, p. 230.

28. Ibid., p. 233.

29. Robert Seymour, *Humorous Sketches* (1834–6; London: repr. Henry G. Bohn, 1866), Scene 17 (np).

30. *Andrew Mullins – An Autobiography*, chapter 7 (np), in Seymour, *Humorous Sketches*.

31. My thanks to Paul Schlicke, whose essay, 'Bumble and the Poor Law Satire of *Oliver Twist*', *The Dickensian* 71:3 (1975), 149–56, first drew my attention to Seymour's Beadle; Paul's generosity with his research materials also put me on the track of several more of Bumble's antecedents.

32. As Marcus Wood remarks: 'Hone's pamphlets were still widely used as models for anti-government and anti-clerical satire in the revival of radical agitation

during the two years preceding the passage of the Great Reform Act.' See Marcus Wood, *Radical Satire and Print Culture, 1790–1822* (Oxford: Clarendon Press, 1994), p. 5. I would contend that the continuities persisted much further into the 1830s than this.

33. William Cobbett, *Cobbett's Legacy to Labourers* (London: 11 Bolt-Court, Fleet Street, 1835). See N. Edsall, *The Anti-Poor Law Movement, 1834–1844* (Manchester: Manchester University Press, 1971), p. 22, for the importance of Cobbett's role.

34. Guilland Sutherland, 'Cruikshank and London', in Ira Bruce Nadel and F. S. Schwarzbach (eds.), *Victorian Artists and the City: A Collection of Critical Essays* (Oxford: Pergamon Press, 1980), pp. 106–25, p. 107.

35. For a somewhat less expansive account of the melodramatic literature and culture of the anti-Poor Law movement than I am proposing in this chapter, see Hadley, *Melodramatic Tactics*.

36. See Lisa Cody Forman, 'The Politics of Illegitimacy in the Age of Reform: Women, Reproduction and Political Economy in England's Poor Law of 1834', *Journal of Women's History* 11:4 (Winter 2000), 131–56.

37. 'New Scheme for Maintaining the Poor', *Blackwood's Edinburgh Magazine* 43 (April 1838), 489–93; 490.

38. G. R. Wythen Baxter, *The Book of the Bastiles; or, The History of the Working of the New Poor-Law* (London: John Stephens, 1841), p. 125. Emphases in original. The variant spelling of 'Bastile' was widely adopted by anti-Poor Law protestors.

39. Ibid., pp. 115, 117, 118, 125. Emphases in original.

40. For fuller accounts of the political alliances within the anti-Poor Law movement see Clark, *Struggle for the Breeches*, pp. 179–96; Edsall, *Anti-Poor Law Movement*, especially pp. 167–86; Peter Mandler, *Aristocratic Government in the Age of Reform: Whigs and Liberals, 1830–1852* (Oxford: Oxford University Press, 1990), pp. 131–41; and M. E. Rose, 'The Anti-Poor Law Agitation,' in J. T. Ward (ed.), *Popular Movements c. 1830–1850* (London: Macmillan, 1970), pp. 78–94.

41. Bodleian Library, John Johnson Collection, 'Poor Law Box 3' (JJ), 'The New Poor Law Bill in Force' (Kent Street, Borough: Sharp, Printer, nd). Emphasis in original. Thanks to Louis James who has dated this for me as c. 1836. There is a second similar broadside in the same collection, similarly entitled 'The Poor Law Bill in Force'.

42. Josephine McDonagh, *Child Murder and British Culture 1720–1900* (Cambridge: Cambridge University Press, 2003), p. 117.

43. For an excellent recent account of modern adaptations of *Oliver Twist* see Juliet John, 'Fagin, The Holocaust and Mass Culture; or, *Oliver Twist* on Screen', *Dickens Quarterly* 22:4 (December 2005), 204–23. John's *Charles Dickens's Oliver Twist: A Sourcebook* (Abingdon and New York: Routledge 2006) includes reviews of modern screen versions.

44. James Mill, *Elements of Political Economy* (London: Baldwin, Craddock, and Joy, 1821), p. 2.

45. Beth Carney, 'Genres of Protest: Melodramatic and Satirical Responses to the New Poor Law of 1834', unpublished MA Coursework Essay, MA Victorian Studies, Birkbeck, University of London (2005), p. 13.

46. F. B. Head, 'English Charity', *Quarterly Review* 53 (1835), 473–539, 474, 476–7.

47. Ibid., pp. 478–9, 485.

48. Richard Ford, Review of *Oliver Twist*, *Quarterly Review* 64 (June 1839) 83–102, 94.

49. *The Times*, 21 August 1840, in Baxter, *Book of the Bastiles*, p. 116. Emphasis in original.

50. Thanks to Holly Furneaux for this suggestion.

51. Jeremy Bentham, *Book of Fallacies: From Unfinished Papers of Jeremy Bentham* (London: John and H. L. Hunt, 1824), pp. 392–3.

52. T. R. Malthus, *An Essay on the Principle of Population* (1798; repr. Harmondsworth: Penguin, 1970).

53. Ford, Review of *Oliver Twist*, p. 95.

54. The idea of 'alternative families' in Dickens was first suggested to me in Holly Furneaux's excellent PhD thesis. See Holly Furneaux, 'Homoeroticism in the Novels of Charles Dickens', unpublished PhD thesis, University of London (2005).

55. I would agree with John Bowen that Nancy is not a mother-figure in relation to Oliver. She is, rather, another of the lost children spawned, in Dickens's view, by the New Poor Law and the political economy that informed the legislation. See John Bowen, *Other Dickens* (Oxford: Oxford University Press, 2000), p. 103.

56. In 1840 Thackeray praised the workhouse scenes whilst attacking the 'Newgate' half of the novel: see his 'Catherine' in Wall (ed.), *Charles Dickens*, pp. 52–3. One hundred years later Humphry House reflected that 'We tend ... to think of the first part as a detached tract, preliminary to the novel that matters' (House, *The Dickens World*, p. 92). The most popular of the contemporary dramatic plagiarisms of the novel more or less ignored the workhouse scenes in favour of the lurid excitements of London's criminal underworld. See Fulkerson, '*Oliver Twist* in the Victorian Theatre'. Not all readers have treated the two parts of the novel discretely, though. K. J. Fielding, for example, also identifies a resonance between Fagin's philosophy of 'number one', which he elaborates in chapter 43 of the novel, and the individualistic vocabulary of early Victorian political economy: see K. J. Fielding, 'Benthamite Utilitarianism and *Oliver Twist*: A Novel of Ideas' *Dickens Quarterly* 4 (1987), 49–64.

57. Juliet John, *Dickens's Villains: Melodrama, Character, Popular Culture* (Oxford and New York: Oxford University Press, 2001), p. 9.

58. Louis James, *Fiction for the Working Man* (1963; repr. Harmondsworth: Penguin, 1974), p. 59.

59. Ackroyd, *Dickens*, p. 56.

60. Harriet Martineau, *A History of the Thirty Years' Peace 1816–1846*, 4 vols. (London: Bell and Sons, 1877–8), vol. III, pp. 102–3.

61. Josef L. Altholz, 'Oliver Twist's Workhouse', *The Dickensian* 97:2 (Summer 2001), 137–43, 138.
62. Ackroyd, *Dickens*, p. 231.
63. Brinsley Peake's *Climbing Boy* has a very similar structure, with the kindly, gentlemanly Mr Strawberry restoring justice at the close.

CHAPTER 4: CHRISTMAS IS CANCELLED: DICKENS AND DOUGLAS JERROLD WRITING IN THE 1840S

1. Letter to Douglas Jerrold [?9 or 10 November 1836], Pilgrim Letters, vol. I, pp. 192–3.
2. Douglas Jerrold, *Black-Ey'd Susan; or, 'All in the Downs.': A Nautical and Domestic Drama in Two Acts* (London: Thomas Hailes Lacy, [1829]), and *The Rent Day: A Domestic Drama in Two Acts* (London: Thomas Hailes Lacy, [1832]).
3. Theatre Review: '*Virginia* by John Oxenford and *Black-eyed Susan* by Douglas Jerrold at the Royal Marylebone Theatre', *The Examiner* (12 May 1849), in Slater (ed.), *Dickens' Journalism*, vol. II, pp. 156–9, p. 157. Slater lists nineteen theatre reviews in his complete listing of Dickens's known journalism. See Michael Slater and John Drew (eds.), *Dickens' Journalism*, vol. IV: '*The Uncommercial Traveller' and Other Papers, 1859–70* (London: J. M. Dent, 2000), pp. 436–46.
4. Michael Slater's excellent biography of Douglas Jerrold includes a chapter on the relationship between Jerrold, Dickens and Thackeray. See Michael Slater, *Douglas Jerrold 1803–1857* (London: Duckworth, 2002), chapter 10. Slater's is much the most comprehensive study to date. Others include Richard M. Kelly, *Douglas Jerrold* (New York: Twayne, 1972) and Blanchard Jerrold's much earlier *The Life and Remains of Douglas Jerrold* (London: W. Kent & Co., 1859).
5. The essay in question was 'Elizabeth and Victoria,' cited in Michael Slater, 'Carlyle and Jerrold into Dickens: A Study of *The Chimes*', *Nineteenth-Century Fiction* 24:4 (1970), 506–26, 523–4.
6. [Douglas Jerrold], *The Story of a Feather* (1843; repr. London: Bradbury, Evans, and Co., 1867). First serialized in *Punch* in 1843.
7. See Bruce A. White, 'Douglas Jerrold's "Q" Papers in *Punch*', *Victorian Periodicals Review* 15 (1982), 131–7 and, for a full account of Jerrold's role in *Punch* in the early 1840s Slater, *Jerrold*, chapter 7. More generally see Richard D. Altick, *Punch, The Lively Youth of a British Institution, 1841–1851* (Columbus: Ohio University Press, 1997), especially chapters 5 and 7.
8. [Douglas Jerrold], 'The "Milk" of Poor-Law "Kindness"', *Punch, or, The London Charivari*, 4 (1843), 46–7, 46. Emphasis in original.
9. Ibid, emphases in original. Sycorax is adoptive mother to the monstrous Caliban in Shakespeare's *The Tempest*.
10. Ibid.

11. John Napier, Esq., Magistrate, and Chairman of the Petworth Board of Guardians, before the Poor-Law Committee, March 1837, in Baxter, *Book of the Bastiles*, p. 127.

12. Slater, *Jerrold*, p. 37.

13. [Douglas Jerrold], 'The Corn Laws and Christianity', *Punch, or, The London Charivari* 1 (1841), 114.

14. [Douglas Jerrold], 'Wanted – Some Bishops!' *Punch, or, The London Charivari* 4 (1843), 226. Emphasis in original.

15. [Douglas Jerrold], 'An Archbishop on War', *Punch, or, The London Charivari* 5 (1843), 138.

16. [Douglas Jerrold], 'Letter XIV – To Mrs Hedgehog, of New York', *Douglas Jerrold's Shilling Magazine* 1:3 (January–June 1845), 540–2.

17. 'A. W.', 'The Winter Robin', *Douglas Jerrold's Shilling Magazine* 3:13 (January–June 1846), 29–30, 29.

18. Jerrold, Douglas, *The History of St Giles and St James* (1845–6, repr. Leipzig: Bernhardt Tauchnitz, 1852). It was originally published in *Douglas Jerrold's Shilling Magazine* between 1845 and 1846.

19. See chapter 1, p. 21 for my discussion of Hone's clerical magistrate.

20. Thomas Wooler, 'Affectation of Christianity by the "Higher Orders" ', *Black Dwarf. A Weekly London Publication* 3:4 (26 January 1819), 105–8, 105. Emphases in original.

21. William Cobbett, 'To the Reformers of Leeds, Preston, Botley' *Cobbett's Weekly Political Register*, 35:16 (21 December 1819), 484–503, 491. Emphases in original.

22. 'Anti-Malthusianism', *Northern Star*, 1 December 1838, p. 5. Quoted in McDonagh, *Child Murder*, p. 100.

23. Lucas, 'Past and Present'. *A Child's History of England* was serialized in *Household Words* between 25 January 1851 and 10 December 1853.

24. *Cobbett's Weekly Political Register*, 35:12 (4 October 1819), 383. Emphasis in original.

25. Slater, *Jerrold*, p. 168.

26. [Douglas Jerrold], 'A Royal Wife of – £3,000', *Punch, or, The London Charivari* 4 (1843), 256–7.

27. Ibid., pp. 256–7.

28. See chapter 1 for further details of Hone and Wooler's satirical assaults on the Prince Regent.

29. Slater, *Jerrold*, p. 37.

30. For an account of Dickens's editorship of the *Daily News* see John Drew, *Dickens the Journalist* (Basingstoke: Palgrave, 2003), chapter 5; David Roberts, 'Charles Dickens and the *Daily News*: Editorials and Editorial Writers', *Victorian Periodicals Review* 22:2 (1989), 51–63; and Ackroyd, *Dickens*, pp. 502–17.

31. Stonehouse (ed.), *Catalogue of the Library of Charles Dickens*, p. 106.

32. [Douglas Jerrold?], 'Slavery: The Only Remedy for the Miseries of the English Poor, By a Philanthropist', *Douglas Jerrold's Shilling Magazine*, 1:2 (January–June 1845), 116–19. Emphases in original.

33. Quoted in Slater (ed.), *Dickens' Journalism*, vol. II, p. 52.
34. Charles Dickens, 'Snoring for the Million,' *The Examiner* (24 December 1842), in Slater, *Dickens' Journalism*, vol. II, pp. 51–5, p. 53.
35. [Douglas Jerrold], 'The Beauties of the Police', *Pictorial Times* (29 April 1843), 102. Emphasis in original.
36. Ibid., emphasis in original.
37. John Forster, *Life of Charles Dickens*, 4 vols. (Leipzig: Bernhardt Tauchnitz, 1872–3), vol. III, p. 93.
38. Charles Dickens, 'A Christmas Dinner', in Slater (ed.), *Dickens' Journalism*, vol. I, pp. 216–20.
39. 'Lord Jeffrey on *A Christmas Carol* in a Letter to Dickens', in Collins (ed.), *Critical Heritage*, pp. 147–8, p. 147. Emphases in original. Lord Jeffrey had been deeply moved by the death of Little Nell in *The Old Curiosity Shop*.
40. [William Makepeace Thackeray], 'A Box of Novels,' *Fraser's Magazine* 29 (February 1844), 166–9, in Collins, *Critical Heritage*, pp. 148–50, p. 149. The 'Scotch philosopher' was one of Dickens's political mentors, Thomas Carlyle.
41. Collins (ed.), *Critical Heritage*, p. 144.
42. See Forster, *Life of Charles Dickens*, vol. III, pp. 87–8.
43. Quoted in Collins (ed.), *Critical Heritage*, p. 144. Subsequent Christmas Books were *The Chimes* (1844), *The Cricket on the Hearth* (1845), *The Battle of Life* (1846) and *The Haunted Man* (1848).
44. Letters to Southwood Smith, 6 and 10 March 1843, in Pilgrim Letters, vol. III, pp. 459–61. See also Ackroyd, *Dickens*, p. 415.
45. The Report also inspired Elizabeth Barrett Browning's 'The Cry of the Children' (1843) and sections of Disraeli's *Sybil* (1845). See Pilgrim Letters, vol. III, p. 459, n. 3.
46. Letter to Southwood Smith, 10 March 1843, Pilgrim Letters, vol. III, p. 461.
47. Schlicke, *Oxford Reader's Companion to Dickens*, p. 98.
48. Letter to John Forster, [21 February 1844], Pilgrim Letters, vol. IV, pp. 49–50, p. 50. Edward Richard Wright (1813–59) played Cratchit, with 'humorous indulgence' but 'occasional exaggeration' according to a review in the *Examiner* (Pilgrim Letters, vol. IV, p. 50, n. 3).
49. *Leader*, 4 July 1857, quoted in Collins (ed.), *Sikes and Nancy*, p. 2.
50. Charles Dickens, *A Christmas Carol*, in *The Christmas Books*, ed. Sally Ledger (1843–8; repr. London: J. M. Dent, 1999), p. 74. Subsequent references to will be included in parentheses in the main text.
51. [Jerrold], 'Beauties of the Police', p. 102.
52. Charles Dickens, *The Haunted Man*, in *The Christmas Books*.
53. Slater, *Jerrold*, pp. 149–50.
54. See ibid., p. 149 for further details.
55. Ibid.
56. Review of R. H. Horne's *A New Spirit of the Age*, *Westminster Review* 44:94 (June 1844), 374–7, in Collins (ed.), *Critical Heritage*, pp. 150–3, p. 151.
57. Letter to Forster (?mid-October 1844), Pilgrim Letters, vol. IV, p. 204.

58. Letter to Forster, 3 and [4] November 1844, Pilgrim Letters, vol. IV, p. 210.
59. Pilgrim Letters, vol. IV, p. 235, n. 6; Letter to Mrs Charles Dickens, 2 December 1844.
60. Robert Patten, *Charles Dickens and His Publishers* (Oxford: Clarendon Press, 1978), p. 161.
61. Review in the *Globe* (31 December 1844), quoted in Collins, *Critical Heritage*, p. 144.
62. Review in the *Union Magazine* (Febuary 1846), 234, quoted in Collins, *Critical Heritage*, p. 144–5.
63. 'A Christmas Garland,' *Northern Star* (28 December 1844), quoted in Collins, *Critical Heritage*, p. 158.
64. R. R. Madden (ed.), *The Literary Life and Correspondence of the Countess of Blessington*, 3 vols. (London: T. C. Newby, 1855), vol. II, p. 400.
65. Charles Dickens, *The Chimes*, in *The Christmas Books*, pp. 108–9. Subsequent references will be given in parentheses in the main text.
66. Review of R. H. Horne's *A New Spirit of the Age*, *Westminster Review* 44:94 (June 1844), 374–7, in Collins, *Critical Heritage*, pp. 150–3, pp. 152–3.
67. Letter to Douglas Jerrold, 23 January 1844, Pilgrim Letters, vol. IV, p. 28.
68. [Douglas Jerrold], 'Sir Peter Laurie on Human Life', *Punch, or, The London Charivari* 1 (1841), 14–15. Emphases in original.
69. [Douglas Jerrold], 'Peter the Great', *Punch, or, The London Charivari* 7 (1844), 157.
70. Slater (ed.), *Dickens' Journalism*, vol. II, p. 67. For a fuller account of the Mary Furley case see Michael Slater, 'Dickens's Tract for the Times', in Michael Slater (ed.), *Dickens 1970* (London: Chapman and Hall, 1970), pp. 99–123.
71. See [Douglas Jerrold], 'Atrocious Cruelty in Newgate', *Punch, or, The London Charivari*, 6 (1844), 187; and [Charles Dickens], 'Threatening Letter to Thomas Hood from an Ancient Gentleman By Favor of Charles Dickens', *Hood's Magazine and Comic Miscellany* (May 1844), in Slater, *Dickens' Journalism*, vol. II, pp. 67–73.
72. Unsigned Review of *The Chimes*, *The Times* (25 December 1844), p. 6.
73. [Jerrold], *Story of a Feather*, p. 39. Dickens read and enjoyed Jerrold's novel, writing to him in May 1844 that 'I am truly proud of your remembrance, and have put the "Story of a Feather" on a shelf (not an obscure one) where some other feathers are, which it shall help to show mankind which way the wind blows, long after *we* know where the wind comes from . . . nobody consulted it more regularly and earnestly than I did, as it came out in *Punch*' (Letter to Douglas Jerrold, [May 1844], Pilgrim Letters, vol. IV, p. 120).
74. Michael Slater speculates that Bowley could well have been based on Lord Brougham, whom Jerrold had attacked in *Punch* on 6 April 1844. Slater, 'Carlyle and Jerrold into Dickens', p. 524.
75. The three poems in question are 'The Fine Old English Gentleman', 'The Quack Doctor's Proclamation' and 'Subjects for Paintings (after Peter Pindar)', all of which have been reprinted in *The Works of Charles Dickens*, 40 vols. (London: Chapman and Hall, 1906–8), vol. XXXVI, pp. 467–73.

76. Drew, *Dickens the Journalist*, pp. 53–4.
77. Ibid., p. 55.
78. [Charles Dickens], 'The Fine Old English Gentleman' (1841), *The Works of Charles Dickens*, vol. XXXVI, pp. 468–9.
79. Drew, *Dickens the Journalist*, pp. 55–6.
80. [Charles Dickens], 'The Quack Doctor's Proclamation' (1841), *The Works of Charles Dickens*, vol. XXXVI, pp. 469–70, p. 470.
81. For a thoroughgoing assessment of Carlyle's influence on *The Chimes* in particular see Slater, 'Carlyle and Jerrold into Dickens'.
82. Ibid., pp. 523–4.
83. Letter to Douglas Jerrold, 3 May 1843, Pilgrim Letters, vol. III, p. 481.
84. Unsigned review of *The Chimes*, *Economist* (18 January 1845), 53–4, in Collins, *Critical Heritage*, pp. 164–7, p. 165.
85. Letter to John Forster, [13 August 1841], Pilgrim Letters, vol. II, p. 357.
86. Kathryn Chittick, *Dickens in the 1830s* (Cambridge: Cambridge University Press, 1990), p. x; Schlicke, *Oxford Reader's Companion to Dickens*, p. 33. Both quoted by John Bowen in his Introduction to *Barnaby Rudge* (London and New York: Penguin Books, 2003), p. xxxi.
87. Chittick, *Dickens in the 1830s*, p. xiii.
88. Ackroyd, *Dickens*, p. 327.
89. John Ruskin, Letter to W. H. Harrison, 6 June 1841, in Collins (ed.), *Critical Heritage*, pp. 100–1, p. 100; Henry Crabb Robinson, Extract from journal entry, 1 September 1841, in Collins (ed.), *Critical Heritage*, p. 102.
90. John Ruskin, Letter to Charles Eliot Norton, 19 June 1870, in Wall (ed.), *Charles Dickens*, p. 188.
91. Bowen, Introduction, p. xiv.
92. Ackroyd, *Dickens*, p. 345.
93. Bowen, Introduction, p. xiv.
94. Franco Moretti, *An Atlas of the European Novel* (London: Verso, 1999), p. 33.
95. John Bowen has written convincingly of *Barnaby Rudge* as a novel that stages a war between two ways of understanding human progress: 'History' – 'the struggle of classes' – and 'melodrama' – in which 'essential psychic conflicts of generations and families are played out' (Introduction, p. xviii).
96. Although mine is a more historicised reading, I would agree with Steven Marcus that in *Barnaby Rudge* Dickens 'contemplates [only] one kind of relation – that of fathers and sons'. Steven Marcus, *Dickens From Pickwick to Dombey* (London: Chatto and Windus, 1963), p. 184.
97. Ben Winyard, 'Paternalism, Perversion and the Past in *Barnaby Rudge*', unpublished MA coursework essay, MA Victorian Studies, Birkbeck College, University of London (2005), p. 9.
98. The most significant reading to date of John Chester in this context is in Robert Gilmour, *The Idea of the Gentleman in the Victorian Novel* (London: Allen and Unwin, 1981).
99. Earl of Chesterfield, *Lord Chesterfield's Letters*, ed. David Roberts (1774; repr. Oxford: Oxford University Press, 1992), p. x.

100. Schlicke, *Oxford Reader's Companion to Dickens*, p. 32. The eighteenth-century lord also provided Douglas Jerrold with satirical matter for 'Punch's Letters to His Son'. See for example 'Letter XI – On the Necessity of Hypocrisy', *Punch, or, The London Charivari* 3 (1842), 149.

101. Steven Connor's essay, in which he interprets the Maypole as 'a place of stagnation and oppressive stasis', supports my reading. See Steven Connor, 'Space, Place and the Body of Riot in *Barnaby Rudge*,' in Steven Connor (ed.), *Charles Dickens: Longman Critical Readers* (London: Longman, 1996), pp. 211–28, p. 218.

102. For Dickens's relationship to the Chartist movement see Noel Peyrouton, 'Dickens and the Chartists', *The Dickensian* 60 (1964), 78–88 and 152–61.

CHAPTER 5: POPULAR AND POLITICAL WRITING IN THE RADICAL PRESS: FROM DOUGLAS JERROLD TO ERNEST JONES, CHARTIST

1. James, *Fiction for the Working Man*, chapter 3; Haywood, *The Revolution in Popular Literature*, p. 139.

2. Chronology from the British Library's *Concise History of the British Newspaper in the Nineteenth Century*, on www.bl.uk/collections/brit19th.html, consulted 9 January 2006. For the development of the popular press in nineteenth-century Britain see James Curran and Jean Seaton, *Power Without Responsibility: The Press and Broadcasting in Britain* (London and New York: Routledge, 1997); Stuart Hall, 'Popular Culture and the State', in Tony Bennett, Colin Mercer and Jean Woollacott (eds.), *Popular Culture and Social Relations* (Milton Keynes, UK: Open University Press, 1986), pp. 22–49; James, *Fiction For the Working Man*, chapter 2; Kevin Gilmartin, *Print Politics: The Press and Radical Opposition in Early Nineteenth-Century England* (Cambridge and New York: Cambridge University Press, 1996); Raymond Williams, 'Radical and/or Respectable', in Richard Boston (ed.), *The Press We Deserve* (London: Routledge and Kegan Paul, 1970), pp. 14–26, and 'The Press and Popular Culture: An Historical Perspective', in George Boyce, James Curran and Pauline Wingate (eds.), *Newspaper History From the Seventeenth Century to the Present Day* (London: Constable, 1978), pp. 41–50.

   Ian Haywood's *Revolution in Popular Literature* and Martha Vicinus's *The Industrial Muse: A Study of Nineteenth-Century British Working-Class Literature* (London: Croom Helm, 1974), are the best general studies of radical and working-class literature of the period. Other accounts include: Altick, *The English Common Reader*; Phyllis Mary Ashraf, *Introduction to Working-Class Literature in Britain, Part Two: Prose* (East Berlin: Socialist Publications, 1979); Margaret Dalziel, *Popular Fiction 100 Years Ago* (London: Cohen and West, 1957); Christopher Harvie, *The Centre of Things: Political Fiction in Britain from Disraeli to the Present* (London: Unwin Hyman, 1991); Ian Haywood, *Working-Class Fiction: From Chartism to 'Trainspotting'* (Plymouth: Northcote House/British Council, 1997); James, *Fiction for the Working Man*; Gustav Klaus, *The Socialist Novel in Britain*

(Brighton: Harvester Press, 1982) and *The Literature of Labour: Two Hundred Years of Working-Class Writing* (Brighton: Harvester Press, 1985); and Victor E. Neuburg, *Literacy and Society* (Harmondsworth: Penguin, 1971).

3. Figures taken from Altick, *The English Common Reader*, p. 94.

4. *Daily News*, 21 January 1846, p. 1.

5. For further details see James, *Fiction for the Working Man*, chapter 3. For plagiarisms of *Oliver Twist* in particular see Holly Furneaux, ' "Worrying to Death": Reinterpreting Dickens's Critique of the New Poor Law in *Oliver Twist* and Contemporary Adaptations', *Dickensian* 101 (2005), 213–24.

6. Altick, *English Common Reader*, p. 290.

7. Thompson, *Making of the English Working Class* (1963; repr. Harmondsworth: Penguin, 1978), p. 805.

8. Williams, 'Radical and/or Respectable', p. 21.

9. Haywood, *The Revolution in Popular Literature*, pp. 145, 190.

10. Altick, *Punch*, p. 121.

11. Ibid., pp. 125–6.

12. Ibid., p. 186.

13. Pilgrim Letters, vol. IV, p. 643, n. 6.

14. Letter to Douglas Jerrold, 24 October 1846, Pilgrim Letters, vol. IV, p. 643.

15. To Mrs Brookfield, 13 July 1850, in *The Letters and Private Papers of W. M. Thackeray*, ed. G. N. Ray, 4 vols. (London: Oxford University Press, 1945–6), vol. II, pp. 80–1.

16. Slater, *Jerrold*, p. 183.

17. 'Douglas Jerrold's Shilling Magazine', *Athenaeum*, 14 December 1844, p. 1,160.

18. Slater, *Jerrold*, p. 195.

19. The 'Hedgehog' series was established in the first edition of the *Shilling Magazine*: [Douglas Jerrold], 'The Hedgehog Letters', *Douglas Jerrold's Shilling Magazine* 1:1 (January–June 1845), 72–7. Other campaigning political essays (they are numerous) include: 'The Social Position and the Character of the Bar', *Douglas Jerrold's Shilling Magazine* 2:12 (July–December 1845), 501–8; 'Temptations of the Poor', *Douglas Jerrold's Shilling Magazine* 1:5 (January–June 1845), 442–6; and J. L. M., 'My Temptations. By a Poor Man', *Douglas Jerrold's Shilling Magazine* 2:7 (January–June 1846), 55–6.

20. Pilgrim Letters, vol. IV, p. 643, n. 3.

21. Letter to Douglas Jerrold, 24 October 1846, Pilgrim Letters, vol. IV, p. 643.

22. Silverpen [Eliza Meteyard], 'The Poor Law in St Pancras Parish', *Douglas Jerrold's Weekly Newspaper* 11 (26 September 1846), 247.

23. 'Treatment of the Poor in Marylebone Workhouse,' *Douglas Jerrold's Weekly Newspaper* 12 (3 October 1846), 281.

24. 'The Poor Man's Church and its Rich Bishops,' *Douglas Jerrold's Weekly Newspaper* 47 (5 June 1847), 697.

25. 'The Riots in London and Glasgow', *Douglas Jerrold's Weekly Newspaper* 87 (11 March 1848), 338.

26. 'The Charter in and out of Newgate,' *Douglas Jerrold's Weekly Newspaper* 105 (15 July 1848), 912.

27. 'Eyewitness' [Thomas Cooper], *Douglas Jerrold's Weekly Newspaper* 2 (25 July 1846), 28–29, 28.
28. [Thomas Cooper], 'Eyewitness', *Douglas Jerrold's Weekly Newspaper* 6 (22 August 1846), 126.
29. *Douglas Jerrold's Weekly Newspaper*, 22 August 1846, 4 March 1848, 2 December 1848, 9 December 1848.
30. Williams, 'Radical and/or Respectable', p. 22.
31. Slater, *Jerrold*, p. 204.
32. Ibid., p. 250.
33. Ibid., p. 253.
34. See chapter 4 for a full account of these attacks.
35. Review of *The Chimes, Northern Star* (21 December 1844), 3. Emphases in original.
36. Brian Maidment, 'Magazines of Popular Progress and the Artisans', *Victorian Periodicals Review* 17:3 (1984), 83–94; Haywood, *The Revolution in Popular Literature*, p. 195.
37. Gustav Klaus has claimed that there were 'nearly a hundred' Chartist papers and journals. See his *Literature of Labour*, p. 48.
38. There is a growing body of literary criticism that concerns itself with Chartist literature. Much the best study of Chartist Poetry to date is Anne Janowitz's *Lyric and Labour in the Romantic Tradition* (Cambridge: Cambridge University Press, 1998). Studies of Chartist fiction include: Ashraf, *Introduction to Working-Class Literature in Britain, Part Two*; Steve Devereux, 'Chartism and Popular Fiction', in John Lucas (ed.), *Writing and Radicalism* (Harlow: Longman, 1996), pp. 128–46; Haywood, *Working-Class Fiction*, chapter 4; Ian Haywood, Editor's Introductions to *The Literature of Struggle* (Aldershot and Brookfield: Ashgate Publishing, 1996), *Chartist Fiction*, vol. I: *Thomas Doubleday, 'The Political Pilgrim's Progress'; Thomas Martin Wheeler, 'Sunshine and Shadow'* (Aldershot, UK, and Brookfield, USA: Ashgate Publishing, 1999), and vol. II: *Ernest Jones, 'Woman's Wrongs'* (Aldershot and Brookfield: Ashgate Publishing, 2001); Ian Haywood, *Revolution in Popular Literature*, chapters 6, 7 and 8; Klaus, *The Literature of Labour*, chapter 3; Y. V. Kovalev, Introduction to *An Anthology of Chartist Fiction* (Moscow: Foreign Languages Publishing House, 1956), trans. as 'The Literature of Chartism', *Victorian Studies* 2 (1958), 117–38; Jack B. Mitchell, 'Aesthetic Problems of the Development of the Proletarian-Revolutionary Novel in Nineteenth-Century Britain', in David Craig (ed.), *Marxists on Literature* (Harmondsworth: Penguin, 1975), pp. 245–66; Tim Randall, 'Towards a Cultural Democracy: Chartist Literature 1837–1860', unpublished PhD thesis, University of Sussex, 1994); Jutta Schwarzkopf, *Women in the Chartist Movement* (Basingstoke: Macmillan, 1991), chapter 2; Vicinus, *The Industrial Muse*, chapter 3; Martha Vicinus, 'Chartist Fiction and the Development of Class-Based Literature', in Klaus, *Socialist Novel in Britain*, pp. 7–25.
39. The distinction I am making here is not absolute: Gothicism, a close aesthetic neighbour to melodrama, was a populist offshoot of literary Romanticism;

and the struggle between moral opposites that characterises melodrama itself has Romantic antecedents. Broadly, though, these two categories offer a useful way of understanding the development of Chartist aesthetics at the mid-century.

40. Popular Chartist novels include Ernest Jones, *De Brassier: A Democratic Romance*, in Ernest Jones (ed.), *Notes to the People*, 2 vols. (London: J. Pavey, 1851–2), vol. I, passim, and *Woman's Wrongs: A Novel in Four Books*, in ibid., vol. II, passim. See also Ernest Jones, *The Maid of Warsaw; or, The Tyrant Czar: A Tale of the Last Polish Revolution* (London: George Pavey, 1854); Thomas Doubleday, *The Political Pilgrim's Progress*, serialized in *The Northern Liberator*, 19 January to 30 March 1839, repr. in Haywood (ed.), *Chartist Fiction*, pp. 17–63; G. W. M. Reynolds, *The Seamstress: or, The White Slave of England* (1850; repr. London: John Dicks, 1853); and Thomas Martin Wheeler, *Sunshine and Shadow: A Tale of the Nineteenth Century*, serialized in the *Northern Star* 31 March 1849 to 5 January 1850, repr. in Haywood (ed.), *Chartist Fiction*, pp. 72–200.

41. Joyce, *Visions of the People*, p. 47. See also p. 45: 'Above all, the evocative associations of the martyr are evident, combining forcefully with those of the gentleman.'

42. Ibid., p. 39.

43. See Miles Taylor, *Ernest Jones, Chartism and the Romance of Politics, 1819–1869* (Oxford and New York: Oxford University Press, 2003), passim.

44. Ian Haywood's fine account of Reynolds's traversing of the boundaries between popular and radical cultures can be found in chapter 7 of *The Revolution in Popular Literature*.

45. Autograph letter from John Pearcey to Ernest Jones, n.d., Seligman Collection, Box 5, Reel 3.

46. 'To the Subscribers for, and Readers of, the *People's Paper*', *People's Paper*, 8 May 1852.

47. Poster dated 25 February 1860, in Seligman Collection, Box 9, Reel 4.

48. Ernest Jones, *Notes to the People*, 2 vols. (London: J. Pavey, Holywell Street, 1851–2), vol. I, p. 20.

49. Ernest Jones, 'To the Chartists', *Notes to the People*, vol. II, p. 766.

50. 'Speech on Blackstone Edge', printed in the *Northern Star*, 8 August 1846; in John Saville (ed.), *Ernest Jones: Chartist. Selections from the Writings and Speeches of Ernest Jones*, (London: Lawrence and Wishart, 1952), pp. 88–90. Emphasis in original.

51. Letter to Charles Mackay, 9 August 1855: 'In prison I wrote (by stealth, on smuggled paper) "The New World", "The Painter of Florence", "Beldragon Church", and a number of minor pieces. The "Painter of Florence" is the poem now published under the name of "The Cost of Glory". Having no ink, I chiefly wrote WITH MY BLOOD' (Charles Mackay, *Forty Years' Recollections of Life, Literature and Public Affairs. From 1830 to 1870*, 2 vols. (London: Chapman and Hall, 1877), vol. II, p. 61, emphasis in original). There is of course a striking resonance here with Dickens's novel from 1859, *A Tale*

of Two Cities, in which Dr Manette, a prisoner in the Bastille, similarly writes with his own blood. See chapter 2 for further details.

52. Shepherd and Womack, *English Drama*, p. 201. Emphasis in original.

53. Thomas Cooper, 'Seth Thompson, the Stockinger', in *Wise Saws and Modern Instances* (1845), repr. in Haywood (ed.), *Literature of Struggle*, pp. 46–52.

54. Jones, *De Brassier*, p. 35 Subsequent page references will be provided in parentheses in the main body of the text.

55. Hadley, *Melodramatic Tactics*, p. 13.

56. Haywood, Introduction to *Woman's Wrongs*, p. xix. Earlier petitions had been made for the partial enfranchisement of women.

57. [Harriet Taylor], 'Enfranchisement of Women', *Westminster Review* 55 (1851), 289–311.

58. Mary Wollstonecraft, *The Wrongs of Woman, or Maria. A Fragment* (1798; repr. London: Oxford University Press, 1976); Charlotte Tonna, *The Wrongs of Woman* (London: Seeley and Burnside, 1844).

59. A number of tickets for Women's Suffrage meetings are in the Jones archives in the Seligman Collection, as is a copy of the Manchester Ladies College prospectus.

60. Anna Clark, *The Struggle for the Breeches*, pp. 220–1. Other studies which give an account of women's role in Chartism include Sally Alexander, 'Women, Class and Sexual Difference in the 1830s and 1840s: Some Reflections on the Writing of a Feminist History', *History Workshop Journal* 17 (1984), 125–49; Helen Rogers, *Women and the People* (Aldershot: Ashgate, 2000), chapter 3; Joan Wallach Scott, 'On Language, Gender and Working-Class History,' in her *Gender and the Politics of History* (New York: Columbia University Press, 1988), pp. 53–67; Schwarzkopf, *Women in the Chartist Movement*; Ruth L. Smith and Deborah M. Valenze, 'Mutuality and Marginality: Liberal Moral Theory and Working-Class Women in Nineteenth-Century England', *Signs* 13 (1988), 277–98; Barbara Taylor, *Eve and the New Jerusalem: Socialism and Feminism in Nineteenth-Century England* (London: Virago, 1983); Dorothy Thompson, 'Women and Nineteenth-Century Radical Politics: A Lost Dimension,' in Ann Oakley and Juliet Mitchell (eds.), *The Rights and Wrongs of Women* (Harmondsworth: Penguin, 1977) pp. 112–38, and *The Chartists: Popular Politics in the Industrial Revolution* (London: Temple Smith, 1984).

61. Walkowitz, *City of Dreadful Delight*, p. 87.

62. Vicinus, ' "Helpless and Unfriended" '; E. Ann Kaplan, 'The Political Unconscious in the Maternal Melodrama: Ellen Wood's *East Lynne*', in Derek Longhurst (ed.), *Gender, Genre and Narrative Pleasure* (Hemel Hempstead: Unwin Hyman, 1988), pp. 31–50, both cited in Walkowitz, *City of Dreadful Delight*, p. 87.

63. See chapter 7 for a full reading of *Bleak House*.

64. R. J. Richardson, 'The Rights of Woman' (1840), repr. in D. Thompson (ed.), *The Early Chartists* (London: Macmillan, 1971).

65. Thomas Frost, *The Secret*, serialized in the *National Instructor*, 25 May–19 October 1850; G. W. M. Reynolds, *The Mysteries of London*

(1845–55), abridged version of the first series reprinted by Trefor Thomas (ed.), *The Mysteries of London* (Keele: Keele University Press, 1996).

66. Satire spilled over into some of Jones's poetry, too, the most obvious example being his ironically titled 'The Royal Bounty', written in response to the news that 'the Queen, in consideration of the sufferings of her starving subjects, has been "graciously pleased" that the crumbs of bread from the Royal tables should be given to the Poor, instead of being thrown into the dust-bin': *Labourer* 1 (1847), 234. Thomas Doubleday's *The Political Pilgrim's Progress*, first published in the *Northern Star* between 17 January and 30 March 1839, is perhaps the most extended piece of satirical writing produced in the Chartist press.

67. See chapter 2 for an account of Sidney Carton's execution in *A Tale of Two Cities*. Dickens denies Fagin a 'staged' execution in *Oliver Twist*.

68. Jones, *Woman's Wrongs*, p. 612.

69. Ibid., pp. 611–12.

70. See Karl Marx, *Economic and Philosophical Manuscripts* (1844), and Karl Marx and Friedrich Engels, *The German Ideology* (1846), both repr. in David McLellan (ed.), *Karl Marx: Selected Writings* (New York: Oxford University Press, 2000), pp. 83–121 and 175–208.

71. Other mid-century stories about seamstresses include 'Ellen Lin, the Needlewoman', *Tait's Edinburgh Magazine* 17 (1850), 465–70; F. D., 'The Dressmaker's Apprentice; A Tale of Woman's Oppression', *Lloyd's Penny Weekly Miscellany* 3 (1844), 433–4; G. W. M. Reynolds, 'The Slaves of England. No. 1 – The Seamstress,' *Reynolds's Miscellany* n.s. 4 (23 March–20 July 1850) and n.s. 5 (27 July–10 August 1850); J. M. Rymer, *The White Slave. A Romance for the Nineteenth Century* (London: Office of *Lloyd's Weekly London Newspaper*, 1844); 'Silverpen' [Eliza Meteyard], 'Lucy Dean; The Noble Needlewoman,' *Eliza Cook's Journal* 2 (16 March–20 April 1850); Elizabeth Stone, *The Young Milliner* (London: Cunningham and Mortimer, 1843); Charlotte Tonna, 'Milliners and Dressmakers', in her *The Wrongs of Woman* (London: Dalton, 1843); and Camilla Toulmin, 'The Orphan Milliners: a Story of the West End', *Illustrated Magazine* 2 (1844), 279–85. My thanks to Ella Dzelzainis for providing me with all these references. Dzelzainis's excellent doctoral thesis contains detailed and important readings of these works of fiction as well as of Jones's 'Young Milliner'. See Ella Dzelzainis, 'Manufacturing Gender: Women, the Family and Political Economy in English Industrial Fiction, 1832–1855', unpublished PhD thesis, University of London, 2004. See also her 'Chartism and Gender Politics in Ernest Jones's "The Young Milliner"' in Beth Harris (ed.), *Famine and Fashion: Needlewomen in the Nineteenth Century* (Aldershot: Ashgate, 2005), pp. 87–97. Haywood's *Revolution in Popular Literature*, chapter 8, also discusses seamstress fiction.

72. Hadley, *Melodramatic Tactics*, p. 78.

73. Figures from James, *Fiction For the Working Man*, p. 45.

74. The Seligman Collection is a rich source of evidence for Jones's straitened circumstances in the early 1850s, numerous letters between husband and wife

discussing their impecuniousness. Jones also frequently had to borrow money from friends to keep his newspapers afloat.

75. Ian Haywood puts the circulation figure of *Notes to the People* 'in the low thousands', but I have been unable to verify his figure. See Ian Haywood, Editor's Introduction to *Woman's Wrongs*, by Ernest Jones (Aldershot, UK, and Vermont, USA: Ashgate Publishing), p. xvi.

76. Margot C. Finn, *After Chartism: Class and Nation in English Radical Politics, 1848–1874* (Cambridge: Cambridge University Press, 1993), p. 109.

77. Ibid., p. 110. Finn takes her figures from Charles Mitchell's *Newspaper Press Directory* of 1858, which itself based its figures on stamp tax returns.

78. One such can be found in the Seligman Collection, Box 10, Reel 5.

79. For a sympathetic account of the libel case see Saville, *Ernest Jones*, Appendix II. For an account antagonistic to Jones see Taylor, *Ernest Jones*, pp. 187–90.

80. Haywood, *The Revolution in Popular Literature*, chapter 7. Rohan McWillian, 'The Mysteries of George W. M. Reynolds: Radicalism and Melodrama in Victorian Britain,' in Malcolm Chase and Ian Dyck (eds.), *Living and Learning: Essays in Honour of J. F. C. Harrison* (Aldershot: Scolar Press, 1996). Anne Humpherys, 'G. W. M. Reynolds: Popular Literature and Popular Politics', *Victorian Periodicals Review* 16:3–4 (1983), 79–89, and 'Generic Strands and Urban Twists: the Victorian Mysteries Novel,' *Victorian Studies* 34:4 (1991), 455–72.

81. Slater, *Jerrold*, p. 1.

CHAPTER 6: *HOUSEHOLD WORDS*, POLITICS AND THE MASS MARKET IN THE 1850S

1. Letter to Miss Coutts, 12 April 1850, Pilgrim Letters, vol. VI, p. 83. Emphases in original. Ernest Jones, too, had partly entered the 1850s newspaper market in order to secure a regular income, writing to his wife that his *People's Paper* would be 'the provision for the future, the £10,000 a year' (Letter to Jane Jones, 4 April 1852, Seligman Collection, Box 5, Reel 3).

2. Haywood, *The Revolution in Popular Literature*, p. 170.

3. Avar Ellegård, 'The Readership of the Periodical Press in Mid-Victorian Britain', *Victorian Periodical Newsletter* 13 (1971), 3–22, 6.

4. [Charles Dickens], 'A Preliminary Word', *Household Words* 1 (30 March 1850), 1–2, in Slater (ed.), *Dickens' Journalism*, vol. II, pp. 175–9, p. 177.

5. Ibid., p. 178.

6. 'The Three Kingdoms', *Household Narrative of Current Events* (27 March–26 April 1851), 73–5, 73.

7. According to Miles Taylor, Jones 'masterminded the ten days of proceedings'. See Taylor, *Ernest Jones*, p. 144.

8. Jones, 'To the Chartists', p. 766.

9. Charles Dickens, *American Notes and Pictures From Italy*, ed. F. S. Schwarzbach and Leonee Ormond (1842 and 1846; repr. London: J. M. Dent, 1997), p. 97.

10. John Drew, *Dickens the Journalist* (Basingstoke: Palgrave, 2003), p. 67.
11. Letter to Lady Holland, 8 July 1842, Pilgrim Letters, vol. III, p. 262.
12. Drew, *Dickens the Journalist*, p. 74.
13. Letter to John Forster, [22 and 23 November 1846], Pilgrim Letters, vol. IV, p. 660.
14. Letter to William Bradbury, 28 July 1849, Pilgrim Letters, vol. V, pp. 582–3.
15. *Reynolds' Weekly Newpaper*, 8 June 1851, quoted in N. C. Peyrouton, 'Dickens and the Chartists II', *The Dickensian* 60 (1964), 152–61, 157.
16. Haywood, *The Revolution in Popular Literature*, pp. 220–1.
17. [Dickens], 'Preliminary Word', in Slater (ed.), *Dickens' Journalism*, vol. II, p. 177.
18. Slater (ed.), *Dickens' Journalism*, vol. II, p. 176.
19. Drew, *Dickens the Journalist*, pp. 114–15.
20. Letter to Henry Morley, 31 October 1852, Pilgrim Letters, vol. VI, pp. 790–1.
21. See Haywood, *The Revolution in Popular Literature*, chapter 7. McWilliam, 'The Mysteries of George W. M. Reynolds'. Humpherys, 'G. W. M. Reynolds', 79–89.
22. Drew, *Dickens the Journalist*, p. 115. [Charles Dickens and Henry Morley], 'Discovery of a Treasure Near Cheapside', *Household Words* 6 (13 November 1852), 193–7.
23. [Charles Dickens], 'The Amusements of the People. I', *Household Words* 1 (30 March 1850), 13–15, in Slater (ed.), *Dickens' Journalism*, vol. II, pp. 179–85, p. 181.
24. Ibid., p. 182.
25. [Charles Dickens], 'The Amusements of the People. II', *Household Words* 1 (13 April 1850), 57–60, in Slater (ed.), *Dickens' Journalism*, vol. II, pp. 193–201, p. 198. Emphases in original.
26. [Dickens], 'Amusements of the People. I', in Slater (ed.), *Dickens' Journalism*, vol. II, p. 180.
27. [Dickens], 'Amusements of the People. II', in Slater (ed.), *Dickens' Journalism*, vol. II, p. 196.
28. Ibid., p. 201.
29. Ibid., p. 200.
30. Lorna Huett, 'Among the Unknown Public; *Household Words*, *All The Year Round* and the Mass-Market Periodical in the Mid-Nineteenth Century', *Victorian Periodicals Review* 38:1 (2005), 61–82, 72.
31. Ibid., p. 78.
32. [Robert Chambers], 'Address to Reader', *Chambers's Edinburgh Journal* ns 1 (1844), 16.
33. Huett, 'Among the Unknown Public', p. 76.
34. Ibid., p. 78.
35. Graham Law, *Indexes to Fiction in the Illustrated London News (1842–1901) and The Graphic (1869–1901)* (St Lucia, Australia: University of Queensland Press, 2001), p. 3.
36. Joanne Shattock, 'Women's Work: Victorian Women Writers and the Press,' *Gaskell Society Journal* 14 (2000), 59–72, 70.

37. Letter to Mrs Gaskell, 30 January 1850, Pilgrim Letters, vol. VI, pp. 21–2. Emphasis in original.
38. Andrew Sanders, 'Serializing Gaskell: From *Household Words* to *The Cornhill*', *Gaskell Society Journal* 14 (2000), 45–58, 46.
39. Philip Collins, 'Angela Burdett Coutts', in Schlicke (ed.), *Oxford Reader's Companion to Dickens*, p. 123.
40. Letter to Miss Burdett Coutts, 4 February 1850, Pilgrim Letters, vol. VI, p. 28.
41. See chapter 4 for a full account of *The Chimes*.
42. Letter to Mrs Gaskell, 27 February 1850, Pilgrim Letters, vol. VI, p. 48. Emphasis in original.
43. Ibid.
44. Letter to Miss Burdett Coutts, 4 February 1850, Pilgrim Letters, vol. VI, p. 27.
45. [Charles Dickens], 'Home for Homeless Women,' *Household Words* 7 (23 April 1853), 169–75, in Slater (ed.), *Dickens' Journalism*, vol. III, pp. 127–41, pp. 136–7.
46. Ibid., p. 139.
47. See chapter 3 for a full discussion of Baxter's anti-Poor Law anthology.
48. [Dickens], 'Home for Homeless Women,' in Slater (ed.), *Dickens' Journalism*, vol. III, p. 137.
49. [Charles Dickens], 'A Sleep to Startle Us', *Household Words* 4 (13 March 1852), 577–80, in Slater (ed.), *Dickens' Journalism*, vol. III, pp. 49–57, pp. 52, 54.
50. Ibid., pp. 56–7. Jo makes his first appearance in the fourth number (June 1852) of *Bleak House*. See Kathleen Tillotson, '*Bleak House*: Another Look at Jo', in Colin Gibson (ed.), *Art and Society in the Victorian Novel: Essays on Dickens and his Contemporaries* (Basingstoke: Macmillan, 1989), pp. 16–28.
51. I am indebted to Ella Dzelzainis's reflections on the relationship between melodrama and Utilitarianism.
52. [Charles Dickens], 'A Child's Dream of a Star', *Household Words* 1 (6 April 1850), 25–26, in Slater, *Dickens' Journalism*, vol. II, pp. 185–8, pp. 186–7.
53. [Charles Dickens and Henry Morley], 'Drooping Buds', *Household Words* 5 (3 April 1852), 45–8, 45.
54. Ibid., p. 46.
55. Ibid.
56. This is where paupers infected with scabies – a mite infection – were treated.
57. [Charles Dickens], 'A Walk in the Workhouse', *Household Words* 1 (25 May 1850), 204–7, in Slater (ed.), *Dickens' Journalism*, vol. II, pp. 234–41, p. 236.
58. Ibid., pp. 236–7.
59. Letter to Jacob Bell, [12] May 1850, Pilgrim Letters, vol. VI, p. 99.
60. [Dickens], 'A Sleep to Startle Us', in Slater (ed.), *Dickens' Journalism*, vol. III, p. 57.
61. Quoted in Michael Slater, *An Intelligent Person's Guide to Dickens* (London: Duckworth, 1999), p. 68. Slater gives a well-rounded account of Dickens's attitude to progress and modernity in chapter 4 of his study. See also Percival Leigh's 'A Tale of the Good Old Times', *Household Words* 1 (27 April 1850),

103–6, a satirical attack on the barbarity of the centuries leading up to (and including) George III's reign.

62. Dickens, *American Notes and Pictures From Italy*, p. 461.

63. Letter to W. H. Wills, 22 August 1851, Pilgrim Letters, vol. VI, pp. 67–8. Emphasis in original. Dickens's proposal resulted in his satirical essay on the mode of bestowing titles in England, 'Proposals for Amusing Posterity', *Household Words* 6 (12 February 1853), 505–7.

64. [Dickens], 'Preliminary Word', in Slater (ed.), *Dickens' Journalism*, vol. II, p. 177.

65. Slater (ed.), *Dickens' Journalism*, vol. II, p. 305.

66. [Charles Dickens], 'To Working Men', *Household Words* 10 (7 October 1854), 169–70, in Slater (ed.), *Dickens' Journalism*, vol. III, pp. 225–9, p. 226.

67. [Charles Dickens], 'A Nightly Scene in London', *Household Words* 13 (26 January 1856), 25–7, in Slater, *Dickens' Journalism*, vol. III, pp. 346–50, p. 347.

68. [Charles Dickens], 'Railway Strikes', *Household Words* 2 (11 January 1851), 361–4, in Slater (ed.), *Dickens' Journalism*, vol. II, pp. 316–22, pp. 317–18.

69. Ackroyd, *Dickens*, p. 618.

70. Ibid., pp. 618, 666.

71. Deborah Wynne, 'Responses to the 1851 Exhibition in *Household Words*', *The Dickensian* 97:3 (2001), 228–34, 228.

72. [Charles Dickens and R. H. Horne], 'The Great Exhibition and the Little One', *Household Words* 3 (5 July 1851), 356–60, 357.

73. [W. H. Wills], 'The Private History of the Palace of Glass', *Household Words* 2 (18 January 1851), 385–91; [Charles Knight], 'Three May Days in London: The May Palace 1851', *Household Words* 3 (3 May 1851), 121–4. Lorna Huett has argued that even these are ambivalent and contain an element of satire. Lorna Huett, 'Commodity and Collectivity: *Cranford* in the Context of *Household Words*', *Gaskell Society Journal* 17 (2003), 34–49, 36. Paul Young has similarly argued that Charles Knight's short story 'A Christmas Pudding', whilst ostensibly celebrating a mid-century modernising account of international commerce, simultaneously undermines its narrative of capitalist progress. See Paul Young, 'Economy, Empire, Extermination: The Christmas Pudding, the Crystal Palace, and the Narrative of Capitalist Progress', *Literature and History* 14:1 (2005), 14–30.

74. [Henry Morley], 'What Is Not Clear about the Crystal Palace', *Household Words* 3 (19 July 1851), 400–2, 400–1.

75. [George Sala], 'The Foreign Invasion', *Household Words* 4 (11 October 1851), 60–4, 60.

76. Letter to Miss Burdett Coutts, 17 November 1851, Pilgrim Letters, vol. VI, p. 542.

77. Ackroyd, *Dickens*, p. 389.

78. [Henry Morley], 'The Manchester Strike', *Household Words* 13 (2 February 1856), 63–6, 63.

79. Drew, *Dickens the Journalist*, p. 123.

80. Edgar Johnson, *Charles Dickens: His Tragedy and Triumph* (1952; repr. Harmondsworth: Penguin, 1979), p. 365.
81. Drew, *Dickens the Journalist*, p. 124.
82. K. J. Fielding and Anne Smith, '*Hard Times* and the Factory Controversy: Dickens *vs.* Harriet Martineau', *Nineteenth-Century Fiction* 24:4 (1970), 404–27, 410.
83. [Henry Morley], 'Ground in the Mill', *Household Words* 9 (22 April 1854), 224–7, 224. The other essays, all by Morley, are: 'Fencing with Humanity', *Household Words* 11 (14 April 1855), 241–4; 'Death's Cyphering-Book', *Household Words* 11 (12 May 1855), 337–41; 'Deadly Shafts', *Household Words* 11 (23 June 1855), 494–5; and 'More Grist to the Mill', *Household Words* 11 (28 July 1855), 605–6.
84. [Harriet Martineau], *The Factory Controversy: A Warning Against Meddling Legislation* (Manchester: National Association of Factory Occupiers, 1855).
85. Fielding and Smith, '*Hard Times* and the Factory Controversy', p. 406. See also Peter W. J. Bartrip, '*Household Words* and the Factory Accident Controversy', *Dickensian* 75 (1979), 17–29, and Drew, *Dickens the Journalist*, pp. 123–8, for Dickens and Martineau's falling-out over factory legislation.
86. The following are all by Harriet Martineau: 'Flower Shows in a Birmingham Hot-House', *Household Words* 4 (18 October 1851), 82–5; 'The Magic Troughs at Birmingham', *Household Words* 4 (25 October 1851), 113–17; 'The Wonders of Nails and Screws', *Household Words* 4 (1 November 1851), 138–42; 'The Miller and His Men', *Household Words* 4 (24 January 1852), 415–20; 'An Account of Some Treatment of Gold and Gems', *Household Words* 4 (31 January 1852), 449–55; 'Rainbow Making', *Household Words* 4 (14 February 1852), 485–90; 'Needles', *Household Words* 4 (28 February 1852), 540–6; 'Time and the Hour', *Household Words* 4 (6 March 1852), 555–9; 'Guns and Pistols', *Household Words* 4 (13 March 1852), 580–5; 'Birmingham Glass Works', *Household Words* 5 (27 March 1852), 32–8; 'What There Is In a Button', *Household Words* 5 (17 April 1852), 106–12; and 'Tubal Cain', *Household Words* 5 (15 May 1852), 192–7. For her disavowal of the essays see *Harriet Martineau's Autobiography with Memorials by Maria Weston Chapman*, 2 vols. (London: Smith, Elder and Co., 1877), vol. 2, p. 419. Dickens wrote no articles himself that specifically address the Woman Question, but included in the journal a myriad of essays and fictional items about ordinary women's lives: those listed above by Martineau herself and many others. Martineau's comments seven years after Dickens's death to the effect that he refused to publish essays on women's employment opportunities are inaccurate. The explicitly anti-feminist 'Rights and Wrongs of Women', *Household Words* 9 (1 April 1854), 158–61, was written by a fellow professional female writer, Eliza Lynn.
87. Martineau, *The Factory Controversy*, p. 35.
88. Ibid., p. 44.
89. [Henry Morley and Charles Dickens], 'Our Wicked Mis-Statements', *Household Words* 13 (19 January 1856), 13–19, 13. Anne Lohrli attributes the

essay to Morley alone, following the *Household Words* Office Book entry. There is, though, ample biographical evidence of considerable input from Dickens. Anne Lohrli, *Household Words, A Weekly Journal 1850–1859, Conducted by Charles Dickens* (Toronto and Buffalo: Toronto University Press, 1973), p. 149.

90. [Morley and Dickens], 'Wicked Mis-Statements', p. 14.
91. Letter to W. H. Wills, 6 January 1856, Pilgrim Letters, vol. VIII, p. 10.
92. See note 1 above.
93. All figures are taken from John Drew, 'Household Words', in Schlicke, *Oxford Reader's Companion to Dickens*, pp. 281–6, p. 282.

CHAPTER 7: FLUNKEYISM AND TOADYISM IN THE AGE OF MACHINERY FROM *BLEAK HOUSE* TO *LITTLE DORRIT*

1. [Dickens], 'A Preliminary Word', in Slater (ed.), *Dickens' Journalism*, vol. II, pp. 175–9, p. 177.
2. See chapter 6 for a fuller account of Dickens's personal stance towards the Great Exhibition.
3. [Charles Dickens], 'A December Vision', *Household Words* 2 (14 December 1850), 265–7, in Slater (ed.), *Dickens' Journalism*, vol. II, pp. 305–9, 306.
4. Ibid., pp. 307–8.
5. Ibid., p. 307.
6. Dickens is also gesturing backwards to 'the baby savage' of *The Haunted Man*. See Dickens, *The Christmas Books*, p. 399.
7. [Dickens], 'A December Vision', in Slater (ed.), *Dickens' Journalism*, vol. II, p. 308.
8. Ibid., p. 308.
9. [Charles Dickens], 'The Last Words of the Old Year', *Household Words* 2 (4 January 1851), 337–60, in Slater (ed.), *Dickens' Journalism*, vol. II, pp. 310–15, p. 313.
10. Dickens, *Bleak House*, p. 734.
11. Robert Tracy, 'Lighthousekeeping: *Bleak House* and the Crystal Palace', *Dickens Studies Annual* 33 (2003), 25–53.
12. See ibid. See also Chris Vanden Bossche, 'Class Discourse and Popular Agency in *Bleak House*', *Victorian Studies* 47:1 (2004), 7–31, 8; and John Butt and Kathleen Tillotson, *Dickens at Work* (London: Methuen, 1957), pp. 180–2.
13. Bossche, 'Class Discourse', p. 8.
14. Sen, '*Bleak House* and *Little Dorrit*', 946.
15. I discuss the carnivalesque effect of the re-enactment of Nemo's Inquest in the Sol's Arms in some detail in chapter 2.
16. Dickens, *Bleak House*, pp. 189–90. Subsequent references will be included in parentheses in the main text.
17. Hone, *Three Trials of William Hone* (1818); 'From The First Trial', in Kent and Ewen (eds.), *Regency Radical*, p. 72.
18. Ibid., pp. 73–4.

19. 'Our Dear Brother' is chapter 11 of *Bleak House*.
20. 1 Corinthians 15:42.
21. For an excellent account of Dickens's negotiation of the concept of testimony see Schramm, *Testimony and Advocacy*. For *Bleak House* see especially pp. 104, 118–22.
22. Tracy, 'Lighthousekeeping', p. 45.
23. Philip Horne, Notes to *Oliver Twist*, p. 499, n. 2. See also Dickens's Letter to Thomas Haines in which he describes how he had been 'casting about for a magistrate whose harshness and insolence would render him a fit subject to be "shewn up"', and had a alighted upon the figure of 'Mr Laing of Hatton Garden'. (Letter to Thomas Haines, 3 June 1837, Pilgrim Letters, vol. I, p. 267).
24. Dickens, *The Christmas Books*, p. 476, n. 5.
25. See John Drew, 'Leigh Hunt', in Paul Schlicke (ed.), *Oxford Reader's Companion to Dickens* (Oxford and New York: Oxford University Press, 1999), p. 287; and Ackroyd, *Dickens*, p. 318.
26. See James Beresford Atlay, *The Victorian Chancellors*, 2 vols. (London: Smith, Elder, 1906–8), vol. I, pp. 144, n. 1.
27. John Forster, *Life of Charles Dickens*, 6 vols. (Leipzig: Bernhardt Tauchnitz, 1874), vol. 5, p. 42.
28. [Henry Fothergill Chorley], Review of *Bleak House*, *Athenaeum* (17 September 1853), 1087–8, extracted in Collins (ed.), *Critical Heritage*, pp. 276–9, p. 279.
29. Meisel, *Realizations*, p. 61.
30. John Stuart Mill, Letter to Harriet Taylor, 20 March 1854, in Collins (ed.), *Critical Heritage*, pp. 297–8, p. 298.
31. See Dickens's 'Sucking Pigs' essay in *Household Words* for an elaboration of the kind of satire against 'women with a mission' to which he subjects Mrs Jellyby. [Charles Dickens], 'Sucking Pigs', *Household Words* 4 (8 November 1851), 145–68 in Slater (ed.), *Dickens' Journalism*, vol. III, pp. 42–9.
32. See chapter 5 for an account of Jones's novel and its murderess.
33. [Dickens], 'A December Vision', in Slater, *Dickens' Journalism*, vol. II, p. 309.
34. [Chorley], Review of *Bleak House*, in Collins, *The Critical Heritage* p. 279.
35. Walter Bagehot, 'Charles Dickens', *National Review* (1858), extracted in Janice M. Allan, *Charles Dickens's Bleak House: A Source Book* (London and New York: Routledge, 2004), pp. 48–9, p. 49.
36. Letter to Mrs Richard Watson, 22 November 1852, Pilgrim Letters, vol. VI, p. 807. Sales figures taken from Schlicke, *Oxford Reader's Companion to Dickens*, p. 51.
37. H. Philip Bolton, *Dickens Dramatized* (London: Mansell, 1987), p. 349.
38. George Henry Lewes, open letter to the *Leader* (5 February 1853), 137–8, extracted in Collins, *The Critical Heritage*, pp. 274–5, p. 275. Lewes found Krook's spontaneous combustion implausible.
39. Letter to Mrs Richard Watson, 1 November 1854, Pilgrim Letters, vol. VII, p. 453.
40. Patten, *Dickens and His Publishers*, p. 244.

41. Ackroyd, *Dickens*, p. 46.
42. The modelling of the Lord Chancellor on Lord Lyndhurst places the action of the novel in 1827/8 when Dickens worked as a reporter in Lyndhurst's Court of Chancery; the fact that Mr Rouncewell senior is said to have died 'some time before the decease of the pretty fashion of pig-tails' (*Bleak House*, p. 106) suggests the novel is set in the 1820s or 1830s; the reference to the railroads that 'shall soon traverse all this country [Lincolnshire]' (p. 839) suggests the late 1830s. By contrast, Dickens's Preface clearly confirms the contemporaneity of the novel; the loss of a Tory seat to the Reformers in the novel itself suggests a post-Reform Act setting, as does the fact that Mr Rouncewell, the ironmaster, had been asked to stand for Parliament; the reference to the notorious Tooting Baby Farm (p. 156) that Dickens had reported on in the *Examiner* in 1848 locates the novel in the mid-century, as does the part played by the modern police force and a private detective in the novel.
43. [Dickens], 'The Amusements of the People. I', in Slater (ed.), *Dickens' Journalism*, vol. II, p. 180.
44. The following unsigned essays are all by Charles Knight: 'Illustrations of Cheapness: The Lucifer Match', *Household Words* 1 (13 April 1850), 54–7; 'Illustrations of Cheapness: A Globe', *Household Words* 1 (20 April 1850), 84–7; 'Illustrations of Cheapness: Eggs', *Household Words* 1 (11 May 1850), 158–61; 'Illustrations of Cheapness: Tea', *Household Words* 1 (8 June 1850), 253–6; 'Illustrations of Cheapness: The Steel Pen', *Household Words* 1 (7 September 1850), 553–5.
45. [Dickens], 'A Child's Dream of a Star', 25–6.
46. Lohrli, *Household Words*, p. 333.
47. Ackroyd, *Dickens*, p. 733. [Charles Knight], *Knight's Store of Knowledge For All Readers. Being a Collection of Treatises in Various Departments of Knowledge* (London: Knight, 1841).
48. Charles Dickens, *Hard Times* (1854; repr. London and New York, 2003), ed. Kate Flint, p. 12. Subsequent references will be included in parentheses in the main text.
49. See chapter 6 for a discussion of Dickens's essay on the Ragged Schools.
50. [Dickens], 'A Nightly Scene in London', in Slater (ed.), *Dickens' Journalism*, vol. III, p. 351.
51. Pilgrim Letters, vol. VII, p. 492, n. 3.
52. Letter to Charles Knight, 30 [December] 1854, Pilgrim Letters, vol. VII, p. 492.
53. [Dickens], 'A Nightly Scene', in Slater (ed.), *Dickens' Journalism*, vol. III, p. 351.
54. See chapter 6 for a full account of the dispute about factory legislation that was played out in the pages of *Household Words*. [Morley], 'Ground in the Mill'.
55. Dickens's account of the Preston strike, which anticipated the first instalment of *Hard Times* by six weeks, is more sympathetic than his fictional account of the strike in Coketown. Although he denied it, his trip to the Preston strike

probably at least partly explains his focus on industrial relations in *Hard Times*. [Charles Dickens], 'On Strike', *Household Words* 8 (11 February 1854), 553–9, in Slater (ed.), *Dickens' Journalism*, vol. III, pp. 196–210.

56. For an account of the shifts in Chartist writing between the concept of 'the People' and a more Marxist model of class conflict, see Jones, 'The Language of Chartism'.

57. [Richard Simpson], Review of *Hard Times* in *The Rambler* ns 2 (October 1854), 361–362, extracted in Collins (ed.), *Critical Heritage*, pp. 303–4, 303.

58. Patten, *Dickens and His Publishers*, p. 246.

59. Slater (ed.), *Dickens' Journalism*, vol. III, p. 225.

60. There were six changes of administration during the 1850s.

61. [Charles Dickens], 'Gone to the Dogs', *Household Words* 11 (10 March 1855), 121–124, in Slater, *Dickens' Journalism*, vol. 3, pp. 283–291, pp. 288–9.

62. Dickens, *Little Dorrit*, p. 923, n. 4, n. 5. Sadleir is generally acknowledged as the original for Merdle in *Little Dorrit*.

63. [Dickens], 'To Working Men', in Slater (ed.), *Dickens' Journalism*, vol. III.

64. Ibid., p. 226.

65. Ibid., p. 228.

66. Letter to Miss Burdett Coutts, 26 October 1854, Pilgrim Letters, vol. VII, p. 444.

67. [Charles Dickens], 'A Nightly Scene in London', in Slater (ed.), *Dickens' Journalism*, vol. III, p. 347.

68. Dickens, *Little Dorrit*, pp. 191–2. Subsequent references to this novel will be included in parentheses in the main text.

69. [Dickens], 'A Nightly Scene', in Slater (ed.), *Dickens' Journalism*, vol. III, p. 347.

70. 'The Thousand and One Humbugs', *Household Words* 11 (21 April 1855), 265–7, in Slater (ed.), *Dickens' Journalism*, vol. III, pp. 292–8, p. 295.

71. [Charles Dickens], 'Our Commission', *Household Words* 12 (11 August 1855), 25–7, in Slater (ed.), *Dickens' Journalism*, vol. III, pp. 318–24, p. 320.

72. [Charles Dickens], 'Cheap Patriotism', *Household Words* 11 (9 June 1855), 433–5, in Slater (ed.), *Dickens' Journalism*, vol. III, pp. 304–10, p. 308.

73. Letter to W. C Macready, 4 October 1855, Pilgrim Letters, vol. VII, pp. 715–16. Emphasis in original.

74. Dickens would have been influenced by Carlyle in his attack on inert government, and in particular by Carlyle's 'Donothingism' in *Past and Present* (1843), and by 'No-Government' and 'The New Downing Street' in *Latter Day Pamphlets* (1850).

75. Paternalistic relationships I associate with traditional, feudal society, patriarchal ones with modern commercial society. In this I am following August Bebel in *Women in the Past, Present and Future* (1885; repr. London: Zwan, 1988) and Friedrich Engels in *The Origin of the Family, Private Property and the State* (1884; London: Lawrence and Wishart, 1940).

76. Charles Dickens, *Dombey and Son*, ed. Andrew Sanders (1846–8; repr. London and New York: Penguin, 2002) p. 721.

77. See chapter 4, pp. 135–6 for my account of Dickens's attack on Lord Chesterfield through the figure of Sir John Chester in *Barnaby Rudge*.

78. 'Administrative Reform', Theatre Royal, Drury Lane, Wednesday, 27 June 1855, in *The Works of Charles Dickens*, vol. XXXVIII, pp. 413–21, p. 416.

79. 'Administrative Reform', p. 416. The reference to the 'bills that cramp and worry the people' would doubtless include the 1854 Sunday Beer Act, which had severely restricted Sunday opening hours for pubs and beer-houses. See Slater (ed.), *Dickens' Journalism*, vol. III, p. 310.

80. Trey Philpotts, 'The "Civil Service" and "Administrative Reform": The Blame Game in *Little Dorrit*', *Dickens Quarterly*, 17:1 (March 2000), 45–51, 48.

81. Dickens, *Little Dorrit*, p. 940, n. 5.

82. *The Times*, 16 May 1855, p. 9.

83. Philpotts, 'The Blame Game in *Little Dorrit*', p. 149. See also Claudia Klavner, 'Natural Values and Unnatural Agents: *Little Dorrit* and the Mid-Victorian Crisis in Agency', *Dickens Studies Annual* 28 (October 1999), 13–43, 21: 'emphasis on the breadth of Dickens's social critique can also obscure the fact that the moral illness that permeates the novel's societies is diagnosed by the narrator as precisely the failure of individual responsibility'.

84. [Dickens], 'To Working Men', in Slater (ed.), *Dickens' Journalism*, vol. III, p. 227.

85. I have found Margot Finn's work on debt and credit in the nineteenth-century English economy most helpful in formulating this part of my argument. See Margot Finn, *The Character of Credit: Personal Debt in English Culture, 1740–1914* (Cambridge and New York: Cambridge University Press, 2003).

86. Joel J. Brattin, 'The Failure of Plot in *Little Dorrit*', *Dickensian* 101 (2005), 111–15, 111.

87. Brooks, *Melodramatic Imagination*, p. 20.

88. Shaw, Foreword to *Great Expectations*, p. 52.

89. Ibid., p. 51.

90. [James Fitzjames Stephen], 'The License of Modern Novelists', *Edinburgh Review* 106 (July 1857), 124–56, in Collins (ed.), *Critical Heritage*, pp. 366–74, p. 368.

91. Ibid., pp. 369–70.

92. Ibid., p. 372.

93. [E. B. Hamley], 'Remonstrance with Dickens', *Blackwood's Magazine* 81 (April 1857), 490–503, in Collins (ed.), *Critical Heritage*, pp. 358–362, p. 360.

94. Figures taken from Schlicke, *Oxford Reader's Companion to Dickens*, p. 340.

95. Wall and Small, A Note on the Text, in Dickens, *Little Dorrit*, p. xxxiv.

Select Bibliography

ARCHIVES AND WEBSITES

Goldsmith's Library of Economic Literature, Senate House, University of London.
John Johnson Collection of Printed Ephemera, Bodleian Library, Oxford.
Seligman Collection, Butler Library, Columbia University.
Berg Collection, New York Public Library.
De la Motte trial: www.oldbaileyonline.org/html_units/1780s/t17810711-1.html.
British Library's *Concise History of the British Newspaper in the Nineteenth Century*: www.bl.uk/collections/brit19th.html.

PRIMARY SOURCES

A. W., 'The Winter Robin', *Douglas Jerrold's Shilling Magazine* 3:13 (January–June 1846), 29–30.
An Impartial Narrative of the Late Melancholy Occurrences in Manchester (Liverpool: Henry Fisher, 1819).
Bamford, Samuel, *Passages in the Life of a Radical* (1884; repr. Oxford: Oxford University Press, 1984).
Baxter, G. R. Wythen, *The Book of the Bastiles; or, The History of the Working of the New Poor-Law* (London: John Stephens, 1841).
[Beckett, Gilbert À], *Oliver Twiss, The Workhouse Boy, Edited by Poz* (London: James Pattie, 1838).
Bentham, Jeremy, *The Book of Fallacies: From Unfinished Papers of Jeremy Bentham* (London: John and H. L. Hunt, 1824).
Braton, Francis (ed.), *Three Accounts of Peterloo by Eyewitnesses: Bishop Stanley, Lord Hylton, and John Benjamin Smith* (Manchester: Manchester University Press, 1921).
[Chambers, Robert], 'Address to Reader', *Chambers's Edinburgh Journal* ns 1 (1844), 16.
Chesterfield, Philip Dormer Stanhope, Earl of, *Lord Chesterfield's Letters*, ed. David Roberts (1774; repr. Oxford: Oxford University Press, 1992).
Cobbett, William, 'To the Reformers of Leeds, Preston, and Botley,' *Cobbett's Weekly Political Register*, 35:16 (21 December 1819), 484–503.

[Cobbett, William] 'Cobbett's Evening Post', *Cobbett's Weekly Political Register* 35:19 (5 January 1820), 639–42.

Cobbett, William, *Cobbett's Legacy to Labourers* (London: 11 Bolt-Court, Fleet Street, 1835).

[Cooper, Thomas], 'Eyewitness', *Douglas Jerrold's Weekly Newspaper* 2 (25 July 1846), 28–9.

'Eyewitness', *Douglas Jerrold's Weekly Newspaper* 6 (22 August 1846), 126.

Cooper, Thomas, 'Seth Thompson, the Stockinger', in *Wise Saws and Modern Instances* (1845), repr. in Ian Haywood (ed.), *The Literature of Struggle* (Aldershot and Brookfield: Ashgate Publishing, 1996), pp. 46–52.

'Court of Common Plea. Norton v Melbourne', *Morning Chronicle* (23 June 1836), 2–5.

[Dickens, Charles], 'A Child's Dream of a Star', *Household Words* 1 (6 April 1850), 25–6, in Michael Slater (ed.), *Dickens' Journalism*, vol. II: *'The Amusements of the People' and Other Papers: Reports, Essays and Reviews, 1834–51* (London: J. M. Dent, 1996), pp. 185–8.

'A Child's History of England', *Household Words* 2–8 (25 January 1851–10 December 1853).

Dickens, Charles, 'A Christmas Dinner', in Michael Slater (ed.), *Dickens' Journalism*, vol. I: *Sketches By Boz and Other Early Papers, 1833–39* (London: J. M. Dent, 1994), pp. 216–20.

[Dickens, Charles], 'A December Vision', *Household Words* 2 (14 December 1850), 265–7, in Michael Slater (ed.), *Dickens' Journalism*, vol. II: *'The Amusements of the People' and Other Papers: Reports, Essays and Reviews, 1834–51* (London: J. M. Dent, 1996), pp. 305–9.

'A Detective Police Party', *Household Words* 1 (27 July and 10 August 1850), 409–14 and 457–60, in Michael Slater (ed.), *Dickens' Journalism*, vol. II: *'The Amusements of the People' and Other Papers: Reports, Essays and Reviews, 1834–51* (London: J. M. Dent, 1996), pp. 265–82.

'A Nightly Scene in London', *Household Words* 13 (26 January 1856), 25–7, in Michael Slater (ed.), *Dickens' Journalism*, vol. III: *'Gone Astray' and Other Papers From Household Words, 1851–59* (London: J. M. Dent, 1998), pp. 346–50.

'A Preliminary Word', *Household Words* 1 (30 March 1850), in Michael Slater (ed.), *Dickens' Journalism*, vol. II: *'The Amusements of the People' and Other Papers: Reports, Essays and Reviews, 1834–51* (London: J. M. Dent, 1996), pp. 175–9.

'A Sleep to Startle Us', *Household Words* (13 March 1852), 577–80 in Michael Slater (ed.), *Dickens' Journalism*, vol. III: *'Gone Astray' and Other Papers From Household Words, 1851–59 (London: J. M. Dent, 1998), pp. 49–57.*

Dickens, Charles, *A Tale of Two Cities*, ed. Richard Maxwell (1859; repr. London and New York: Penguin Books, 2003).

[Dickens, Charles], 'A Walk in the Workhouse', *Household Words* 1 (25 May 1850), 204–7, in Michael Slater (ed.), *Dickens' Journalism*, vol. II: *'The Amusements of the People' and Other Papers: Reports, Essays and Reviews, 1834–51* (London: J. M. Dent, 1996), pp. 234–41.

Dickens, Charles, 'Administrative Reform' (27 June 1855), in *The Works of Charles Dickens*, 40 vols. (London: Chapman and Hall, 1908), vol. XXXVIII, pp. 413–21.

American Notes and Pictures From Italy, ed. F. S. Schwarzbach and Leonee Ormond (1842 and 1846; repr. London: J. M. Dent, 1997).

Barnaby Rudge, ed. John Bowen (1841; repr. London and New York: Penguin Books, 2003).

Bleak House, ed. Nicola Bradbury (1852–3; repr. London and New York: Penguin Books, 2003).

[Charles Dickens], 'Cheap Patriotism', *Household Words* 11 (9 June 1855), 433–5, in Michael Slater (ed.), *Dickens' Journalism*, vol. III: *'Gone Astray' and Other Papers From Household Words, 1851–59* (London: J. M. Dent, 1998), pp. 304–10.

Dickens, Charles, *Dombey and Son*, ed. Andrew Sanders (1846–8; repr. London and New York: Penguin, 2002).

[Charles Dickens], 'Gone to the Dogs', *Household Words* 11 (10 March 1855), 121–4, in Michael Slater (ed.), *Dickens' Journalism*, vol. III: *'Gone Astray' and Other Papers From Household Words, 1851–59* (London: J. M. Dent, 1998), pp. 283–91.

Dickens, Charles, *Great Expectations*, ed. David Trotter (1860; repr. London and New York: Penguin, 2003).

Hard Times, ed. Kate Flint (1854; repr. London and New York: Penguin, 2003).

[Dickens, Charles], 'Home for Homeless Women', *Household Words* 7 (23 April 1853), 169–75, in Michael Slater (ed.), *Dickens' Journalism*, vol. III: *'Gone Astray' and Other Papers From Household Words, 1851–59* (London: J. M. Dent, 1998), pp. 127–41.

'Judicial Special Pleading', *The Examiner* (31 December 1848), in Michael Slater (ed.), *Dickens' Journalism*, vol. II: *'The Amusements of the People' and Other Papers: Reports, Essays and Reviews, 1834–51* (London: J. M. Dent, 1996), pp. 137–42.

Dickens, Charles, *Little Dorrit*, eds. Stephen Wall and Helen Small (1855–7; repr. London and New York: Penguin Books, 2003).

'Lying Awake', *Household Words* 6 (30 October 1852), 145–8, in Michael Slater (ed.), *Dickens' Journalism*, vol. III: *'Gone Astray' and Other Papers From Household Words, 1851–59* (London: J. M. Dent, 1998), pp. 88–95.

[Dickens, Charles], 'On Strike', *Household Words* 8 (11 February 1854), 553–9, in Michael Slater (ed.), *Dickens' Journalism*, vol. III: *'Gone Astray' and Other Papers From Household Words, 1851–59* (London: J. M. Dent, 1998), pp. 196–210.

Dickens, Charles, *Oliver Twist*, ed. Philip Horne (1837–39; repr. London and New York: Penguin Books, 2003).

[Dickens, Charles], 'Our Commission', *Household Words* 12 (11 August 1855), 25–7, in Michael Slater (ed.), *Dickens' Journalism*, vol. III: *'Gone Astray' and Other*

Papers From Household Words, 1851–59 (London: J. M. Dent, 1998), pp. 318–24.

'Proposals for Amusing Posterity', *Household Words* 6 (12 February 1853), 505–7.

'Railway Strikes', *Household Words* 2 (11 January 1851), 361–4, in Michael Slater (ed.), *Dickens' Journalism*, vol. II: *'The Amusements of the People' and Other Papers: Reports, Essays and Reviews, 1834–51* (London: J. M. Dent, 1996), pp. 316–22.

'Snoring for the Million' (1842), in Michael Slater (ed.), *Dickens' Journalism*, vol. II: *'The Amusements of the People' and Other Papers: Reports, Essays and Reviews, 1834–51* (London: J. M. Dent, 1996), pp. 51–5.

'Subjects for Paintings (after Peter Pindar)' (1841), repr. in Charles Dickens, *The Works of Charles Dickens*, 40 vols. (London: Chapman and Hall, 1906–8), vol. XXXVI, pp. 471–3.

'Sucking Pigs', *Household Words* 4 (8 November 1851), 145–68, in Michael Slater (ed.), *Dickens' Journalism*, vol. III: *'Gone Astray' and Other Papers From Household Words, 1851–59* (London: J. M. Dent, 1998), pp. 42–9.

'The Amusements of the People. I', *Household Words* 1 (30 March 1850), 13–15, in Michael Slater (ed.), *Dickens' Journalism*, vol. II: *'The Amusements of the People' and Other Papers: Reports, Essays and Reviews, 1834–51* (London: J. M. Dent, 1996), pp. 179–85.

'The Amusements of the People. II', *Household Words* 1 (13 April 1850), 57–60, in Michael Slater (ed.), *Dickens' Journalism*, vol. II: *'The Amusements of the People' and Other Papers: Reports, Essays and Reviews, 1834–51* (London: J. M. Dent, 1996), pp. 193–201.

Dickens, Charles, *The Christmas Books*, ed. Sally Ledger (1843–8; repr. London: J. M. Dent, 1999).

[Dickens, Charles], 'The Demeanour of Murderers', *Household Words* 13 (14 June 1856), 505–7, in Michael Slater (ed.), *Dickens' Journalism*, vol. III: *'Gone Astray' and Other Papers From* Household Words, *1851–59* (London: J. M. Dent, 1998), pp. 377–83.

'The Fine Old English Gentleman' (1841), repr. in Charles Dickens, *The Works of Charles Dickens*, 40 vols. (London: Chapman and Hall, 1906–8), vol. XXXVI, pp. 468–9.

'The First of May' (31 May 1836), in Michael Slater (ed.), *Dickens' Journalism*, vol. I: *Sketches By Boz and Other Early Papers, 1833–39* (London: J. M. Dent, 1994), pp. 168–75.

'The Last Words of the Old Year', *Household Words* 2 (4 January 1851), 337–60, in Michael Slater (ed.), *Dickens' Journalism*, vol. II: *'The Amusements of the People' and Other Papers: Reports, Essays and Reviews, 1834–51* (London: J. M. Dent, 1996), pp. 310–15.

Dickens, Charles, *The Letters of Charles Dickens*, vol. I: *1820–1839*, Pilgrim Edition, ed. Madeline House and Graham Storey (Oxford: Clarendon Press, 1965).

The Letters of Charles Dickens, vol. II: *1840–1841*, Pilgrim Edition, ed. Madeline House and Graham Storey and Kathleen Tillotson (Oxford: Clarendon Press, 1969).

The Letters of Charles Dickens, vol. III: *1842–1843*, Pilgrim Edition, ed. Madeline House, Graham Storey and Kathleen Tillotson (Oxford: Clarendon Press, 1974).

The Letters of Charles Dickens, vol. IV: *1844–1846*, Pilgrim Edition, ed. Kathleen Tillotson and Nina Burgis (Oxford: Clarendon Press, 1977).

The Letters of Charles Dickens, vol. V: *1847–1849*, Pilgrim Edition, ed. Graham Storey, K. J. Fielding and Anthony Laude (Oxford: Clarendon Press, 1981).

The Letters of Charles Dickens, vol. VI: *1850–1852*, Pilgrim Edition, ed. Graham Storey, Kathleen Tillotson and Nina Burgis (Oxford: Clarendon Press, 1988).

The Letters of Charles Dickens, vol. VIII: *1856–1858*, Pilgrim Edition, ed. Graham Storey and Kathleen Tillotson (Oxford: Clarendon Press, 1995).

The Letters of Charles Dickens, vol. XI: *1865–1867*, Pilgrim Edition, ed. Graham Storey, Margaret Brown and Kathleen Tillotson (Oxford: Clarendon Press, 1999).

The Posthumous Papers of the Pickwick Club, ed. Mark Wormald (1836–7; repr. London and New York: Penguin Books, 2003).

[Dickens, Charles], 'The Quack Doctor's Proclamation' (1841), repr. in Charles Dickens, *The Works of Charles Dickens*, 40 vols. (London: Chapman and Hall, 1906–8), vol. XXXVI, pp. 469–70.

'The Thousand and One Humbugs', *Household Words* 11 (21 April 1855), 265–7, in Michael Slater (ed.), *Dickens' Journalism*, vol. III: *'Gone Astray' and Other Papers From Household Words, 1851–59* (London: J. M. Dent, 1998), pp. 292–8.

Dickens, Charles, *The Works of Charles Dickens*, 40 vols. (London: Chapman and Hall, 1906–8).

[Dickens, Charles], 'Theatre Review: *Virginia* by John Oxenford and *Black-eyed Susan* by Douglas Jerrold at the Royal Marylebone Theatre', *The Examiner* (12 May 1849), in Michael Slater (ed.), *Dickens' Journalism*, vol. II: *'The Amusements of the People' and Other Papers: Reports, Essays and Reviews, 1834–51* (London: J. M. Dent, 1996), pp. 156–9.

'Threatening Letter to Thomas Hood from an Ancient Gentleman By Favor of Charles Dickens', *Hood's Magazine and Comic Miscellany* (May 1844), in Michael Slater (ed.), *Dickens' Journalism*, vol. II: *'The Amusements of the People' and Other Papers: Reports, Essays and Reviews, 1834–51* (London: J. M. Dent, 1996), pp. 67–73.

'To Working Men', *Household Words* 10 (7 October 1854), 169–70, in Michael Slater (ed.), *Dickens' Journalism*, vol. III: *'Gone Astray' and Other Papers From Household Words, 1851–59* (London: J. M. Dent, 1998), pp. 225–9.

[Dickens, Charles and Henry Morley], 'Discovery of a Treasure Near Cheapside', *Household Words* 6 (13 November 1852), 193–7.

'Drooping Buds', *Household Words* 5 (3 April 1852), 45–8.

[Dickens, Charles and R. H. Horne], 'The Great Exhibition and the Little One', *Household Words* 3 (5 July 1851), 356–60.

Disraeli, Benjamin, *Sybil; or, The Two Nations* (1845; repr. London: David Bryce, 1853).

Ernest Jones: Chartist. Selections From the Writings and Speeches of Ernest Jones, ed. John Saville (London: Lawrence and Wishart, 1952).

Head, F. B., 'English Charity', *Quarterly Review* 53 (1835), 473–539.

Hone, William, *Another Ministerial Defeat! The Trial of the Dog, for Biting the Noble Lord* (London: William Hone, 1817).

Non Mi Ricordo! (London: William Hone, 1820).

The Late John Wilkes's Catechism of a Political Member (London: W. Hone, 1817).

The Political House That Jack Built (London: William Hone, 1819), repr. in Edgell Rickword, *Radical Squibs and Loyalist Ripostes* (Bath: Adams and Dart, 1971), pp. 35–58.

The Political Litany (London: W. Hone, 1817).

The Political Showman – At Home! (London: W. Hone, 1821).

The Power of Conscience Exemplified in the Genuine and Extraordinary Confession of Thomas Bedworth; Delivered to One of the Principal Officers of Newgate, the Night Before his Execution, on September 18, 1815, for the Murder of Elizabeth Beesmore, in Drury Lane (London: William Hone, 1815).

The Queen's Matrimonial Ladder, A National Toy, With Fourteen Step Scenes; and Illustrations in Verse, With Eighteen Other Cuts (London: Printed by and for William Hone, 1820), in Edgell Rickword, *Radical Squibs and Loyalist Ripostes* (Bath: Adams and Dart, 1971), pp. 167–85.

[Hone, William?], *The Queen That Jack Found* (London: John Fairburn, 1820).

Hone, William, *The Sinecurist's Creed* (London: W. Hone, 1817).

The Third Trial of William Hone (London: W. Hone, 1818), repr. in David A. Kent and D. R. Ewen, *Regency Radical: Selected Writings of William Hone* (Detroit: Wayne State University Press, 2003), pp. 132–85.

The Whole Proceedings Before the Coroner's Inquest at Oldham, &c. on the Body of John Lees, who died of Sabre Wounds at Manchester, August the 16, 1819 (London: W. Hone, 1820).

The Three Trials of William Hone (London: W. Hone, 1818).

Hone, William and George Cruikshank, *A Slap at Slop and the Bridge Street Gang* (London: William Hone, 1821).

Jerrold, Blanchard, *Life of Gustave Doré*, vol. I (London: W. H. Allen, 1891).

The Life and Remains of Douglas Jerrold (London: W. Kent and Co., 1859).

[Jerrold, Douglas], 'A Royal Wife of – £3,000', *Punch, or the London Charivari* 4 (1843), 256–7.

'An Archbishop on War', *Punch, or the London Charivari* 5 (1843), 138.

'Atrocious Cruelty in Newgate', *Punch, or the London Charivari* 6 (1844), 187.

Jerrold, Douglas, *Black-Ey'd Susan; or, 'All in the Downs.': A Nautical and Domestic Drama in Two Acts* (London: Thomas Hailes Lacy, [1829]).

[Jerrold, Douglas], 'Letter VII – To John Squalid, Weaver, Stockton', *Douglas Jerrold's Shilling Magazine* 1:3 (January–June 1845), 264–6.

'Letter XIV – To Mrs Hedgehog of New York', *Douglas Jerrold's Shilling Magazine* 1:3 (January–June 1845), 540–2.

'Peter the Great', *Punch, or the London Charivari* 7 (1844), 157.

'Punch's Letters to His Son. Letter XI – On the Necessity of Hypocrisy', *Punch, or the London Charivari* 3 (1842), 149.

'Sir Peter Laurie on Human Life', *Punch, or the London Charivari* 1 (1841), 14–15.

[Jerrold, Douglas?], 'Slavery: The Only Remedy for the Miseries of the English Poor, By a Philanthropist', *Douglas Jerrold's Shilling Magazine* 1:2 (January–June 1845), 116–19.

Jerrold, Douglas, *The History of St Giles and St James* (1845–6), repr. (Leipzig: Bernhardt Tauchnitz, 1852).

[Jerrold, Douglas], 'The Beauties of the Police', *Pictorial Times* (29 April 1843), 102.

'The Corn Laws and Christianity', *Punch, or the London Charivari* 1 (1841), 114.

'The Hedgehog Letters', *Douglas Jerrold's Shilling Magazine* 1:1 (January–June 1845), 72–7.

'The "Milk" of Poor-Law "Kindness"', *Punch, or the London Charivari* 4 (1843), 46–7.

Jerrold Douglas, *The Rent Day: A Domestic Drama in Two Acts* (London: Thomas Hailes Lacy, [1832]).

[Jerrold, Douglas], *The Story of a Feather* (1843; repr. London: Bradbury, Evans, and Co., 1867).

Jerrold, Douglas, *The Writings of Douglas Jerrold*, 8 vols. (London: Bradbury and Evans, 1851–4).

[Jerrold, Douglas], 'Wanted – Some Bishops!' *Punch, or the London Charivari* 4 (1843), 226.

Jones, Ernest, *De Brassier: A Democratic Romance* (1851), in Ernest Jones, *Notes to the People*, 2 vols. (London: J. Pavey, Holywell Street, 1851–2), vol. I, passim.

Ernest Jones Chartist: Selections from the Writings and Speeches of Ernest Jones, ed. John Saville (London: Lawrence and Wishart, 1952).

Notes to the People, 2 vols. (London: J. Pavey, Holywell Street, 1851–2).

The Maid of Warsaw; or, The Tyrant Czar: A Tale of the Last Polish Revolution (London: George Pavey, 1854).

'To the Chartists', in Ernest Jones, *Notes to the People*, 2 vols. (London: J. Pavey, Holywell Street, 1851–2), vol. II, pp. 765–6.

Woman's Wrongs: A Novel in Four Books, in Ernest Jones, *Notes to the People*, 2 vols. (London: J. Pavey, Holywell Street, 1851–2), vol. II, passim.

[Knight, Charles], *Knight's Store of Knowledge For All Readers. Being a Collection of Treatises in Various Departments of Knowledge* (London: Knight, 1841).

'Three May Days in London: The May Palace 1851', *Household Words* 3 (3 May 1851), 121–4.

Leigh, Percival, 'A Tale of the Good Old Times', *Household Words* 1 (27 April 1850), 103–6.

'Letter from the Queen to the King', *Cobbett's Weekly Political Register*, 37:5 (19 August 1820), 313–25.

Mackay, Charles, *Forty Years' Recollections of Life, Literature and Public Affairs. From 1830 to 1870*, 2 vols. (London: Chapman and Hall, 1877).

Madden, R. R. (ed.), *The Literary Life and Correspondence of the Countess of Blessington*, 3 vols. (London: T. C. Newby, 1855).

Malthus, T. R., *An Essay on the Principle of Population* (1798; repr. Harmondsworth: Penguin, 1970).

Marchand, Leslie A. (ed.), *'Between Two Worlds': Byron's Letters and Journals* (London: John Murray, 1977).

Martineau, Harriet, *Harriet Martineau's Autobiography with Memorials by Maria Weston Chapman*, 3 vols. (London: Smith, Elder and Co., 1877).

[Martineau, Harriet], *The Factory Controversy: A Warning Against Meddling Legislation* (Manchester: National Association of Factory Occupiers, 1855).

Martineau, Harriet, *The History of England During the Thirty Years' Peace 1816–1846*, 2 vols. (London: Charles Knight, 1850).

A History of the Thirty Years' Peace 1816–1846, 4 vols. (London, Bell and Sons, 1877–8).

Illustrations of Political Economy (London: Charles Fox, 1834).

Mill, James, *Elements of Political Economy* (London: Baldwin, Craddock, and Joy, 1821).

[Morley, Henry], 'Ground in the Mill', *Household Words* 9 (22 April 1854), 224–7.

'The Manchester Strike', *Household Words* 13 (2 February 1856), 63–6.

'What Is Not Clear about the Crystal Palace', *Household Words* 3 (19 July 1851), 400–2.

[Morley, Henry and Charles Dickens], 'Our Wicked Mis-Statements', *Household Words* 13 (19 January 1856), 13–19.

'New Scheme for Maintaining the Poor', *Blackwood's Edinburgh Magazine* 43 (April 1838), 489–93.

Peake, Richard Brinsley, *The Climbing Boy; or, The Little Sweep* (1832; repr. London: Dick's Standard Plays, No. 675, 1885).

[Prest, Thomas Peckett], *Life and History of Oliver Twiss, Edited by 'Bos'* (London: Edward Lloyd, 1838–9).

Reynolds, G. W. M., *The Mysteries of London* (1845–55), abridged version of the first series reprinted by Trefor Thomas (ed.), *The Mysteries of London* (Keele: Keele University Press, 1996).

The Seamstress: or, The White Slave of England (1850; repr. London: John Dicks, 1853).

Ritchie, J. Ewing, *The Night Side of London* (London: Tinsley Bros., 1858).

[Sala, George], 'The Foreign Invasion', *Household Words* 4 (11 October 1851), 60–4.

Satirical Songs and Miscellaneous Papers Connected With the Trial of Queen Caroline (large scrapbook, n. d., British Library shelfmark 1852.b.9).

Seymour, Robert, 'Andrew Mullins – An Autobiography', in Robert Seymour, *Humorous Sketches* (1834–6; repr. London: Henry G. Bohn, 1866), chapter 7 [no pages].

Humorous Sketches (1834–6; repr. London: Henry G. Bohn, 1866).

Silverpen [Eliza Meteyard], 'The Poor Law in St Pancras Parish', *Douglas Jerrold's Weekly Newspaper* 11 (26 September 1846), 247.

Taylor, Harriet, 'Enfranchisement of Women', *Westminster Review* 55 (1851), 289–311.

'Temptations of the Poor', *Douglas Jerrold's Shilling Magazine* 1:5 (January–June 1845), 55–6.

Thackeray, William Makepeace, *The Letters and Private Papers of W. M. Thackeray*, ed. G. N. Ray, 4 vols. (London: Oxford University Press, 1945–6).

'The Charter in and out of Newgate', *Douglas Jerrold's Weekly Newspaper* 105 (15 July 1848), 912.

The Green Bag, 'a dainty dish to set before the King'. A ballad of the nineteenth century (London: J. Robins and Co., 1820).

The Magic Lantern; Or, Green Bag Plot Laid Open; A Poem, By a Wild Irishwoman, Author of 'A House That Caroline Built' (London: S. W. Fores, 1820).

'The New Poor Law Bill in Force' (Kent Street, Borough: Sharp, [1836?]), in Bodleian Library, University of Oxford: John Johnson Collection; Poor Law box 3 (JJ).

The Old Black Cock and his Dunghill Advisers in Jeopardy; or, The Palace That Jack Built (London: Effingham Wilson, 1820).

'The Poor Man's Church and its Rich Bishops', *Douglas Jerrold's Weekly Newspaper* 47 (5 June 1847), 697.

'The Riots in London and Glasgow', *Douglas Jerrold's Weekly Newspaper* 87 (11 March 1848), 338.

'The Social Position and the Character of the Bar', *Douglas Jerrold's Shilling Magazine* 2:12 (July–December 1845), 501–8.

'The Three Kingdoms', *Household Narrative of Current Events* (27 March–26 April 1851), 73–5.

Tonna, Charlotte, *The Wrongs of Woman* (London: Seeley and Burnside, 1844).

'Treatment of the Poor in Marylebone Workhouse', *Douglas Jerrold's Weekly Newspaper* 12 (3 October 1846), 281.

Trollope, Anthony, *The Warden* (London: Longman and Co., 1855).

Who Killed Cock Robin? A Satirical Tragedy (London: John Cahuac, 1819).

[Wills, W. H.], 'The Private History of the Palace of Glass', *Household Words* 2 (18 January 1851), 385–91.

[Wills, W. H., and Charles Dickens], 'Old Stories Re-Told', *All The Year Round* 18 (13 July 1867), 66.

Wollstonecraft, Mary, *The Wrongs of Woman, or Maria. A Fragment* (1798; repr. London: Oxford University Press, 1976).

Wooler, Thomas, 'A QUEEN TO BE DISPOSED OF – A WIFE TO BE GIVEN AWAY', *Black Dwarf. A Weekly London Publication* 4:23 (14 June 1820), 797.

[Wooler, Thomas?], *A Verbatim Report of the Two Trials of Mr T. J. Wooler, Editor of the Black Dwarf, for Alledged [sic] Libels, Before Mr Justice Abbott, and a Special Jury, On Thursday, June 5, 1817. Taken in Short Hand by an Eminent Writer and Revised by T. J. Wooler* (London: T. J. Wooler, 1817).

Wooler, Thomas, 'Affectation of Christianity by the "Higher Orders"', *Black Dwarf. A Weekly London Publication* 3:4 (26 January 1819), 105–8.

'High Treason: Examination of the Treasonable Potatoes', *Black Dwarf. A Weekly London Publication* 1:6 (15 February 1817), 59–62.

Lead Article, *Black Dwarf. A Weekly London Publication* 1:50 (24 December 1817).

'Manchester Tragedy – A Horrible Farce', *Black Dwarf. A Weekly London Publication* 3:35 (1 September 1819), 565.

'The State Trials contrasted with the Manchester No Trials!' *Black Dwarf. A Weekly London Publication* 4:16 (26 April 1820), 541–66.

[Wooler, Thomas], 'TRIAL EXTRAORDINARY: MR CANNING VERSUS THE RADICAL REFORMERS', *Black Dwarf. A Weekly London Publication* 4:15 (19 April 1820), 537–40.

SECONDARY SOURCES

Ackroyd, Peter, *Dickens* (1990; repr. London: Minerva, 1991).

Alexander, Sally, 'Women, Class and Sexual Difference in the 1830s and 1840s: Some Reflections on the Writing of a Feminist History', *History Workshop Journal* 17 (1984), 125–49.

Allan, Janice M., *Charles Dickens's Bleak House: A Source Book* (London and New York: Routledge, 2004).

Altholz, Josef L., 'Oliver Twist's Workhouse', *The Dickensian* 97:2 (Summer 2001), 137–43.

Altick, Richard D., *The English Common Reader: A Social History of the Mass Reading Public, 1800–1900* (1957; repr. Chicago and London: Chicago University Press, 1963).

Punch, The Lively Youth of a British Institution, 1841–1851 (Columbus: Ohio University Press, 1997).

Anderson, Patricia, *The Printed Image and the Transformation of Popular Culture* (Oxford: Oxford University Press, 1990).

Ashraf, Phyllis Mary, *Introduction to Working-Class Literature in Britain, Part Two: Prose* (East Berlin: Socialist Publications, 1979).

Atlay, James Beresford, *The Victorian Chancellors*, 2 vols. (London: Smith, Elder, 1906–8).

Baer, Marc, *Theatre and Disorder in Late Georgian London* (Oxford: Clarendon Press, 1992).

Bakhtin, Mikhail, *Rabelais and His World*, trans. H. Iswolsky (Cambridge, Mass.: MIT Press, 1968).

Problems of Dostoevsky's Poetics, ed. and trans. Caryl Emerson (Minnesota: University of Minneapolis Press, 1984).

Bartrip, Peter W. J., '*Household Words* and the Factory Accident Controversy', *The Dickensian* 75 (1979), 17–29.

Bebel, August, *Women in the Past, Present and Future* (1884; repr. London: Lawrence and Wishart, 1940).

Bolton, H. Philip, *Dickens Dramatized* (London: Mansell, 1987).

Booth, Michael R., *English Melodrama* (London: Herbert Jenkins, 1965).

Bossche, Chris Vanden, 'Class Discourse and Popular Agency in *Bleak House*', *Victorian Studies* 47:1 (2004), 7–31.

Bowden, Anne, 'William Hone's Political Journalism, 1815–1821', unpublished PhD thesis, University of Texas at Austin (1975).

Bowen, John, Introduction, in Charles Dickens, *Barnaby Rudge* (London and New York: Penguin Books, 2003).

 Other Dickens (Oxford: Oxford University Press, 2000).

Brattin, Joel J. 'The Failure of Plot in *Little Dorrit*', *Dickensian* 101 (2005), 111–15.

Briggs, Asa, *The Age of Improvement* (London: Longmans, Green, 1959).

Brooks, Peter, 'Melodrama, Body, Revolution', in J. Bratton, J. Cook and C. Lethal (eds.), *Melodrama: Stage, Picture, Screen* (London: British Film Institute, 1994), pp. 11–24.

 The Melodramatic Imagination: Balzac, Henry James, and the Mode of Excess (New Haven: Yale University Press, 1976).

Butt, John and Kathleen Tillotson, *Dickens at Work* (London: Methuen, 1957).

Butwin, Joseph M., 'Seditious Laughter', *Radical History Review* 18 (1978), 17–34.

Carney, Beth, 'Genres of Protest: Melodramatic and Satirical Responses to the New Poor Law of 1834', unpublished MA coursework essay, MA Victorian Studies, Birkbeck College, University of London (2005).

Chadwick, Owen, *The Victorian Church*, 2 vols. (London: Adam and Charles Black, 1966).

Chandler, James, *England in 1819: The Politics of Literary Culture and the Case of Romantic Historicism* (Chicago: Chicago University Press, 1998).

Chittick, Kathryn, *Dickens in the 1830s* (Cambridge: Cambridge University Press, 1990).

Clark, Anna, *The Struggle for the Breeches: Gender and the Making of the British Working Class* (London: Rivers Oram Press, 1995).

Collins, Philip, *Dickens and Crime* (1962; repr. Bloomington: Indiana University Press, 1968).

Collins, Philip (ed.), *Dickens: The Critical Heritage* (London: Routledge and Kegan Paul, 1971).

 Sikes and Nancy and Other Public Readings (Oxford: Oxford University Press, 1983).

Collison, Robert, *The Story of Street Literature* (London: Dent, 1973).

Connor, Steven, 'Space, Place and the Body of Riot in *Barnaby Rudge*', in Steven Connor (ed.), *Charles Dickens: Longman Critical Readers* (London: Longman, 1996), pp. 211–28.

Curror, James, and Jean Seaton, *Power Without Responsibility: The Press and Broadcasting in Britain* (London and New York: Routledge, 1997).

Dalziel, Margaret, *Popular Fiction 100 Years Ago* (London: Cohen and West, 1957).

Devereux, Steve, 'Chartism and Popular Fiction', in John Lucas (ed.), *Writing and Radicalism* (Harlow: Longman, 1996), pp. 128–46.

Drew, John, *Dickens the Journalist* (Basingstoke: Palgrave, 2003).

'Household Words', in Paul Schlicke (ed.), *Oxford Reader's Companion to Dickens* (Oxford and New York: Oxford University Press, 1999), pp. 281–6.

'Leigh Hunt', in Paul Schlicke (ed.), *Oxford Reader's Comparison to Dickens* (Oxford and New York: Oxford University Press, 1999), p. 287.

Dzelzainis, Ella, 'Chartism and Gender Politics in Ernest Jones's "The Young Milliner" ', in Beth Harris (ed.), *Famine and Fashion: Needlewomen in the Nineteenth Century* (Aldershot: Ashgate, 2005), pp. 87–97.

'Manufacturing Gender: Women, the Family and Political Economy in English Industrial Fiction, 1832–1855', unpublished PhD thesis, University of London (2004).

Edsall, N., *The Anti-Poor Law Movement, 1834–1844* (Manchester: Manchester University Press, 1971).

Ellegård, Avar, 'The Readership of the Periodical Press in Mid-Victorian Britain', *Victorian Periodical Newsletter* 13 (1971), 3–22.

Engels, Friedrich, *The Origin of the Family, Private Property and the State* (1884; Lawrence and Wishart, 1940).

Epstein, James, *Radical Expression: Political Language, Ritual and Symbol in England, 1790–1850* (New York: Oxford University Press, 1994).

Fielding, K. J., 'Benthamite Utilitarianism and *Oliver Twist*: A Novel of Ideas', *Dickens Quarterly* 4 (1987), 49–64.

Fielding, K. J. and Anne Smith, '*Hard Times* and the Factory Controversy: Dickens *vs.* Harriet Martineau', *Nineteenth-Century Fiction* 24:4 (1970), 404–27.

Finn, Margot C., *After Chartism: Class and Nation in English Radical Politics, 1848–1874* (Cambridge: Cambridge University Press, 1993).

The Character of Credit: Personal Debt in English Culture, 1740–1914 (Cambridge and New York: Cambridge University Press, 2003).

Forman, Lisa Cody, 'The Politics of Illegitimacy in the Age of Reform: Women, Reproduction and Political Economy in England's Poor Law of 1834', *Journal of Women's History* 11:4 (Winter 2000), 131–56.

Forster, John, *Life of Charles Dickens*, 4 vols. (Leipzig: Bernhardt Tauchnitz, 1872–3).

Frost, Ginger, *Promises Broken: Courtship, Class and Gender in Victorian England* (Charlottesville and London: University of Virginia Press, 1995).

Fulkerson, Richard P., '*Oliver Twist* in the Victorian Theatre', *The Dickensian* 70:3 (May 1974), 83–95.

Furneaux, Holly, 'Homoeroticism in the Novels of Charles Dickens', unpublished PhD thesis, University of London (2005).

'"Worrying to Death": Reinterpreting Dickens's Critique of the New Poor Law in *Oliver Twist* and Contemporary Adaptations', *Dickensian* 101 (2005), 213–24.

Gatrell, V. A. C., *The Hanging Tree: Execution and the English People, 1770–1868* (Oxford: Oxford University Press, 1994).

George, Dorothy, *Catalogue of Political and Personal Satires: Preserved in the Department of Prints and Drawings in the British Museum* (London: British Museum, 1935–54).

Gill, Stephen, Introduction to Charles Dickens, *Oliver Twist* (Oxford: Oxford University Press, 1999).

Gilmartin, Kevin, *Print Politics: The Press and Radical Opposition in Early Nineteenth-Century England* (Cambridge and New York: Cambridge University Press, 1996).

Gilmour, Robert, *The Idea of the Gentleman in the Victorian Novel* (London: Allen and Unwin, 1981).

Gregory, Michael, 'Old Bailey Speech in "A Tale of Two Cities" ', *Review of English Literature* 6 (1965), 42–55.

Hackwood, Frederick William, *William Hone: His Life and Times* (London: T. Fisher Unwin, 1912).

Hadley, Elaine, *Melodramatic Tactics: Theatricalized Dissent in the English Marketplace, 1800–1885* (Stanford: Stanford University Press, 1995).

Hall, Stuart, 'Popular Culture and the State', in Tony Bennett, Colin Mercer and Jean Woollacott (eds.), *Popular Culture and Social Relations* (Milton Keynes: Open University Press, 1986).

Harvie, Christopher, *The Centre of Things: Political Fiction in Britain From Disraeli to the Present Day* (London: Unwin Hyman, 1991).

Haywood, Ian (ed.), *Chartist Fiction*, vol. I: *Thomas Doubleday, 'The Political Pilgrim's Progress'; Thomas Martin Wheeler, 'Sunshine and Shadow'* (Aldershot and Brookfield: Ashgate Publishing, 1999).

Haywood Ian (ed.), *Chartist Fiction*, Vol. II: *Ernest Jones, 'Woman's Wrongs'* (Aldershot and Brookfield: Ashgate Publishing, 2001).

The Literature of Struggle (Aldershot and Brookfield: Ashgate Publishing, 1996).

Haywood, Ian, *The Revolution in Popular Literature: Print, Politics and the People* (Cambridge and New York: Cambridge University Press, 2004).

Working-Class Fiction: From Chartism to 'Trainspotting' (Plymouth: Northcote House/British Council, 1997).

Hendrix, Richard, 'Popular Humor and "The Black Dwarf" ', *Journal of British Studies* 16 (1976), 108–28.

Herbert, Christopher, 'Rat Worship and Taboo in Mayhew's London', *Representations* 23 (Summer 1988), 1–24.

Hollingsworth, Keith, *The Newgate Novel, 1830–1847: Bulwer, Ainsworth, Dickens and Thackeray* (Detroit: Wayne State University Press, 1963).

Horne, Philip, Introduction and Notes, in Charles Dickens, *Oliver Twist* (London and New York: Penguin Books, 2003).

House, Humphry, *The Dickens World* (London: Oxford University Press, 1941).

Huett, Lorna, 'Among the Unknown Public: *Household Words, All The Year Round* and the Mass-Market Periodical in the Mid-Nineteenth Century', *Victorian Periodicals Review* 38:1 (2005), 61–82.

'Commodity and Collectivity: *Cranford* in the Context of *Household Words*', *Gaskell Society Journal* 17 (2003), 34–49.

Humpherys, Anne, 'Generic Strands and Urban Twists: the Victorian Mysteries Novel', *Victorian Studies* 34:4 (1991), 455–72.

Humpherys, Anne, 'G. W. M. Reynolds: Popular Literature and Popular Politics', *Victorian Periodicals Review* 16:3–4 (1983), 79–89.

Islemann, H., 'Radicalism in the Melodrama of the Early Nineteenth Century', in M. Hay and A. Nikolopolon, *Melodrama: The Cultural Emergence of a Genre* (New York: St Martin's Press, 1996).

Jackson, T. A., *Charles Dickens: The Progress of a Radical* (1937; repr. New York: International Publishers, 1987).

James, Louis, *Fiction for the Working Man* (1963; repr. Harmondsworth: Penguin, 1974).

Janowitz, Anne, *Lyric and Labour in the Romantic Tradition* (Cambridge: Cambridge University Press, 1998).

John, Juliet, *Charles Dickens's Oliver Twist: A Sourcebook* (Abingdon and New York: Routledge, 2006).

   Dickens's Villains: Melodrama, Character, Popular Culture (Oxford and New York: Oxford University Press, 2001).

   'Fagin, The Holocaust and Mass Culture; or, *Oliver Twist on Screen*', *Dickens Quarterly* 22:4 (December 2005), 204–23.

Johnson, Edgar, *Charles Dickens: His Tragedy and Triumph* (1952; repr. Harmondsworth: Penguin, 1979).

Jones, Gareth Stedman, 'The Language of Chartism', in James Epstein and Dorothy Thompson (eds.), *The Chartist Experience: Studies in Working-Class Radicalism and Culture, 1830–1860* (London: Macmillan, 1982), pp. 3–58.

Joyce, Patrick, *Democratic Subjects: The Self and the Social in Nineteenth-Century England* (Cambridge: Cambridge University Press, 1994).

   Visions of the People: Industrial England and the Question of Class 1840–1914 (Cambridge: Cambridge University Press, 1991).

Kaplan, E. Ann, 'The Political Unconscious in the Maternal Melodrama: Ellen Wood's *East Lynne*', in Derek Longhurst (ed.), *Gender, Genre and Narrative Pleasure* (Hemel Hempstead: Unwin Hyman, 1988), pp. 31–50.

Kelly, Richard M., *Douglas Jerrold* (New York: Twayne, 1972).

Kent, David A. and D. R. Ewen (eds.), *Regency Radical: Selected Writings of William Hone* (Detroit: Wayne State University Press, 2003).

Kettle, Arnold, 'Dickens and the Popular Tradition', in David Craig (ed.), *Marxists on Literature: An Anthology* (1975; repr. Harmondsworth: Penguin, 1977), pp. 214–44.

Klaus, Gustav, *The Literature of Labour: Two Hundred Years of Working-Class Writing* (Brighton: Harvester Press, 1985).

   The Socialist Novel in Britain (Brighton: Harvester Press, 1982).

Klavner, Claudia, 'Natural Values and Unnatural Agents: *Little Dorrit* and the Mid-Victorian Crisis in Agency', *Dickens Studies Annual* 28 (October 1999), 13–43.

Kovalev, Introduction, in *An Anthology of Chartist Fiction* (Moscow: Foreign Languages Publishing House, 1956), trans. as 'The Literature of Chartism', *Victorian Studies* 2 (1958), 117–38.

Laqueur, Thomas, 'The Queen Caroline Affair: Politics as Art in the Reign of George IV', *Journal of Modern History* 54 (1982), 417–66.

Law, Graham, *Indexes to Fiction in the Illustrated London News (1842–1901) and the Graphic (1869–1901)* (St Lucia, Australia: University of Queensland Press, 2001).

Lawley, G. J., *Cruikshank Album*, (Berg Collection, New York Public Library).

Lohrli, Anne, *Household Words, A Weekly Journal 1850–1859, Conducted by Charles Dickens* (Toronto and Buffalo: Toronto University Press, 1973).

Lucas, John, 'Past and Present: *Bleak House* and *A Child's History of England*', in John Schad (ed.), *Dickens Refigured: Desires, Bodies and Other Histories* (Manchester and New York: Manchester University Press, 1996), pp. 136–56.

Maidment, Brian, 'Magazines of Popular Progress and the Artisans', *Victorian Periodicals Review* 17:3 (1984), 83–94.

Mandler, Peter, *Aristocratic Government in the Age of Reform: Whigs and Liberals, 1830–1852* (Oxford: Oxford University Press, 1990).

Manning, Sylvia, *Dickens as Satirist* (New Haven: Yale University Press, 1971).

Marcus, Steven, *Dickens From Pickwick to Dombey* (London: Chatto and Windus, 1963).

Marsh, Joss, *Word Crimes: Blasphemy, Culture and Literature in Nineteenth-Century England* (Chicago and London: University of Chicago Press, 1998).

Maxwell, Richard, 'Introduction', in Charles Dickens, *A Tale of Two Cities* (1859; repr. London and New York: Penguin Books, 2003).

McCalman, Iain, *Radical Underworld: Prophets, Revolutionaries, and Pornographers in London, 1795–1840* (Oxford: Clarendon Press, 1993).

McDonagh, Josephine, *Child Murder and British Culture 1720–1900* (Cambridge: Cambridge University Press, 2003).

McWilliam, Rohan, 'The Mysteries of George W. M. Reynolds: Radicalism and Melodrama in Victorian Britain', in Malcolm Chase and Ian Dyck (eds.), *Living and Learning: Essays in Honour of J. F. C. Harrison* (Aldershot: Scolar Press, 1996).

Meisel, Martin, *Realizations: Narrative, Pictorial and Theatrical Arts in Nineteenth-Century England* (Princeton: Princeton University Press, 1983).

Mitchell, Jack B., 'Aesthetic Problems of the Development of the Proletarian-Revolutionary Novel in Nineteenth-Century Britain', in David Craig (ed.), *Marxists on Literature* (Harmondsworth: Penguin, 1975), pp. 245–66.

Moretti, Franco, *An Atlas of the European Novel* (London: Verso, 1999).

Munson, James, *Maria Fitzherbert, the Secret Wife of George IV* (London: Robinson, 2001).

Neuburg, Victor E., *Literacy and Society* (Harmondsworth: Penguin, 1971).

Newey, Katherine, 'Climbing Boys and Factory Girls: Popular Melodramas of Working Life', *Journal of Victorian Culture* 5:1 (2000), 28–44.

Patten, Robert, *Charles Dickens and His Publishers* (Oxford: Clarendon Press, 1978).

    George Cruikshank's Life, Times and Art, vol. I: *1792–1835* (London: Lutterworth Press, 1992).

    George Cruikshank's Life, Times and Art, vol. II: *1835–1878* (Cambridge: Lutterworth Press 1996).

Peters, Laura, 'Perilous Adventures: Dickens and Popular Orphan Adventure Narratives', *The Dickensian* 94:3 (1998), 172–83.

Peyrouton, Noel C., 'Dickens and the Chartists I', *The Dickensian* 60 (1964), 78–88.

'Dickens and the Chartists II', *The Dickensian* 60 (1964), 152–61.

Philpotts, Trey, 'The "Civil Service" and "Administrative Reform": The Blame Game in *Little Dorrit*', *Dickens Quarterly*, 17:1 (March 2000), 45–51.

Pulling, Christopher, *They Were Singing* (London: George G. Harrap and Co., 1952).

Pykett, Lyn, *Charles Dickens* (Basingstoke: Palgrave, 2002).

Randall, Tim, 'Towards a Cultural Democracy: Chartist Literature 1837–1860', unpublished PhD thesis, University of Sussex (1994).

Rickword, Edgell, *Radical Squibs and Loyalist Ripostes* (Bath: Adams and Dart, 1971).

Roberts, David, 'Charles Dickens and the *Daily News*: Editorials and Editorial Writers', *Victorian Periodicals Review* 22:2 (1989), 51–63.

Rogers, Helen, *Women and the People* (Aldershot: Ashgate, 2000).

Rose, M. E., 'The Anti-Poor Law Agitation', in J. T. Ward (ed.), *Popular Movements c. 1830–1850* (London: Macmillan, 1970), pp. 78–94.

Sanders, Andrew, 'Serializing Gaskell: From *Household Words* to *The Cornhill*', *Gaskell Society Journal* 14 (2000), 45–58.

The Companion to A Tale of Two Cities (1998; repr. Robertsbridge: Helm Information, 2002).

Scott, Joan Wallach, 'On Language, Gender and Working-Class History,' in her *Gender and the Politics of History* (New York: Columbia University Press, 1988), pp. 53–67.

Schlicke, Paul, 'Bumble and the Poor Law Satire of *Oliver Twist*', *The Dickensian* 71:3 (1975), 149–56.

Schlicke, Paul (ed.), *Oxford Reader's Companion to Dickens* (Oxford and New York: Oxford University Press, 1999).

Schramm, Jan-Melissa, *Testimony and Advocacy in Victorian Law, Literature and Theology* (Cambridge and New York: Cambridge University Press, 2000).

Schwarzkopf, Jutta, *Women in the Chartist Movement* (Basingstoke: Macmillan, 1991).

Scott, Harold, *The Early Doors: Origins of the Music Hall* (London: Nicholson and Watson, 1946).

Sen, Sambudha, '*Bleak House* and *Little Dorrit*: The Radical Heritage', *English Literary History* 65 (1998), 945–70.

Shattock, Joanne, 'Women's Work: Victorian Women Writers and the Press', *Gaskell Society Journal* 14 (2000), 59–72.

Shaw, George Bernard, Foreword to *Great Expectations* (1937), in Dan H. Laurence and Martin Quinn (eds.), *Shaw on Dickens* (New York: Frederick Ongar Publishing, 1985).

Shepherd, Simon and Peter Womack, *English Drama: A Cultural History* (Oxford: Blackwell, 1996).

Sheppard, Leslie, *The History of Street Literature* (Newton Abbot: David and Charles, 1973).

Slater, Michael, *An Intelligent Person's Guide to Dickens* (London: Duckworth, 1999).

'Carlyle and Jerrold into Dickens: A Study of *The Chimes*', *Nineteenth-Century Fiction* 24:4 (1970), 506–26.

Slater, Michael (ed.), *Dickens' Journalism*, vol. I: *Sketches By Boz and Other Early Papers, 1833–39* (London: J. M. Dent, 1994).

Dickens' Journalism, vol. II: *'The Amusements of the People' and Other Papers: Reports, Essays and Reviews, 1834–51* (London: J. M. Dent, 1996).

Dickens' Journalism, vol. III: *'Gone Astray' and Other Papers From Household Words, 1851–59* (London: J. M. Dent, 1998).

Slater, Michael, 'Dickens's Tract for the Times', in Michael Slater (ed.), *Dickens 1970* (London: Chapman and Hall, 1970), pp. 99–123.

Douglas Jerrold 1803–1857 (London: Duckworth, 2002).

Slater, Michael and John Drew (eds.), *Dickens' Journalism*, vol. IV: *'The Uncommercial Traveller' and Other Papers, 1859–70* (London: J. M. Dent, 2000).

Smith, Ruth L., and Deborah M. Valenze, 'Mutuality and Marginality: Liberal Moral Theory and Working-Class Women in Nineteenth-Century England', *Signs* 13(1988), 277–98.

Spater, George, *William Cobbett: The Poor Man's Friend*, 2 vols. (Cambridge: Cambridge University Press, 1982).

Stevenson, J., 'The Queen Caroline Affair', in J. Stevenson (ed.), *London in the Age of Reform* (Oxford: Oxford University Press, 1997), pp. 141–5.

Stonehouse, J. H., *Catalogue of the Library of Charles Dickens from Gad's Hill [. . .]* (London: Piccadilly Fountain Press, 1935).

Sucksmith, Harvey Peter and Paul Davies, 'The Making of the Old Bailey Trial Scene in *A Tale of Two Cities*', *The Dickensian* 100:1 (2004), 23–35.

Sutherland, Guilland, 'Cruikshank and London', in Ira Bruce Nadel and F. S. Schwarzbach (eds.), *Victorian Artists and the City: A Collection of Critical Essays* (Oxford: Pergamon Press, 1980), pp. 106–25.

Swindells, Julia, *Glorious Causes: The Grand Theatre of Political Change, 1789 to 1833* (Oxford: Oxford University Press, 2001).

Taylor, Barbara, *Eve and the New Jerusalem: Socialism and Feminism in Nineteenth-Century England* (London: Virago, 1983).

Taylor, Miles, *Ernest Jones, Chartism and the Romance of Politics, 1819–1869* (Oxford and New York: Oxford University Press, 2003).

Thomas, Keith, 'The Place of Laughter in Tudor and Stuart England', *TLS* (21 January 1977), 77–81.

Thompson, D. (ed.), *The Early Chartists* (London: Macmillan, 1971).

Thompson, Dorothy, 'Women and Nineteenth-Century Radical Politics: A Lost Dimension,' in Ann Oakley and Juliet Mitchell (eds.), *The Rights and Wrongs of Women* (Harmondsworth: Penguin, 1977), pp. 112–38.

The Chartists: Popular Politics in the Industrial Revolution (London: Temple Smith, 1984).

Thompson, E. P., *The Making of the English Working Class* (1963; repr. Harmondsworth: Penguin, 1978).

Tillotson, Kathleen, '*Bleak House*: Another Look at Jo', in Colin Gibson (ed.), *Art and Society in the Victorian Novel: Essays on Dickens and his Contemporaries* (Basingstoke: Macmillan, 1989), pp. 16–28.

Tracy, Robert, 'Lighthousekeeping: *Bleak House* and the Crystal Palace', *Dickens Studies Annual* 33 (2003), 25–53.

Vicinus, Martha, '"Helpless and Unfriended": Nineteenth-Century Domestic Melodrama', *New Literary History* 13 (1981), 127–43.

   The Industrial Muse: A Study of Nineteenth-Century British Working-Class Literature (London: Croom Helm, 1974).

Walkowitz, Judith, *City of Dreadful Delight: Narratives of Sexual Danger in Late-Victorian London* (London: Virago Press, 1992).

Wall, Stephen (ed.), *Charles Dickens: A Critical Anthology* (Harmondsworth: Penguin Books, 1970).

Waller, John, *The Real Oliver Twist* (Cambridge: Icon Books, 2005).

White, Bruce A., 'Douglas Jerrold's, "Q" Papers in *Punch*', *Victorian Periodicals Review* 15 (1982), 131–7.

Wickwar, W. H., *The Struggle for the Freedom of the Press, 1819–1822* (London: George Allen and Urwin, 1928).

Williams, Raymond, 'Radical and/or Respectable', in Richard Boston (ed.), *The Press We Deserve* (London: Routledge and Kegan Paul, 1970), pp. 14–26.

   'The Press and Popular Culture: An Historical Perspective', in George Boyce, James Curran and Pauline Wingate (eds.), *Newspaper History From the Seventeenth Century to the Present Day* (London: Constable, 1978), pp. 41–50.

Wilson, Ben, *The Laughter of Triumph: William Hone and the Fight for the Free Press* (London: Faber and Faber, 2005).

Winyard, Ben, 'Paternalism, Perversion and the Past in *Barnaby Rudge*', unpublished MA coursework essay, MA Victorian Studies, Birkbeck College, University of London (2005).

Wood, Marcus, *Radical Satire and Print Culture, 1790–1822* (Oxford: Clarendon Press, 1994).

Wynne, Deborah, 'Responses to the 1851 Exhibition in *Household Words*', *The Dickensian* 97:3 (2001), 228–34.

Young, Paul, 'Economy, Empire, Extermination: The Christmas Pudding, the Crystal Palace, and the Narrative of Capitalist Progress', *Literature and History* 14:1 (2005), 14–30.

Index

CAMBRIDGE STUDIES IN NINETEENTH-CENTURY
LITERATURE AND CULTURE

General editor
Gillian Beer, *University of Cambridge*

Titles published